Personal Injury Litigation

Personal Injury Litigation

Seventh Edition

John Pritchard

Solicitor

and

Nicola Solomon

Solicitor

LONGMAN

ISBN 0 85121 8784

Seventh Edition 1992

Published by
Longman Law, Tax and Finance
Longman Group UK Ltd
21-27 Lambs Conduit Street
London WC1N 3NJ

Associated Offices
Australia, Hong Kong, Malaysia, Singapore, USA

A CIP catalogue record for this book is available from the British Library.

Printed and bound in Great Britain by
Mackays of Chatham

Contents

Preface ix
Table of Cases xi
Table of Statutes xii
Table of Statutory Instruments xiii
Abbreviations xv

Part I: A System of Working

1 Introduction 3
  1 General 3
  2 Personal injury: facts and figures 5
2 A Simple Accident Claim 6
3 A System of Working 9
  1 The diary 9
  2 Use of draft letters, precedents, etc 11
  3 A standardised filing system 13

Part II: The Straightforward Personal Injury Action

4 Investigating the Claim 17
  1 Taking instructions 17
  2 The client's accident questionnaires 18
  3 Investigating the circumstances of the accident 21
  4 Negotiating with the insurers 29
  5 Provisional damages 35
5 Special Damage and Interest 38
  1 Special Damage: Introduction 38
  2 Working out the specials 38
  3 Calculating the figures 44
  4 Interest 47
  5 High Court: special damage and interest 49
6 Commencing Proceedings 54
  1 Commencing proceedings 54
  2 Instructing Counsel to settle the claim 56
  3 Issuing proceedings in the County Court 59

4 Serving proceedings 62
5 Issuing the writ—High Court 63
6 Serving the writ 65
7 The acknowledgement of service 66
8 Form and layout of pleadings 67
9 Time 68
7 The Defence 69
1 Form of the Defence 70
2 Responding to the Defence 71
8 Payment in, and Interim Payment 77
1 The payment into court 77
2 The interim payment 82
9 Interlocutory Proceedings and Automatic Directions 87
1 Introductory 87
2 The application 87
3 The order 92
4 Appealing the order 94
5 Judgment with damages to be assessed 94
6 Automatic directions 95
10 Discovery of Documents and Amendment of Pleadings 98
1 Discovery of documents 98
2 The list of documents 99
3 When discovery is not complete 104
4 Specific Discovery from a third person 105
5 Close of pleadings 106
6 Amendment of pleadings 106
7 County court: amendment 107
8 Adding parties 108
9 High Court Discovery 109
10 High Court: Amendment 109
11 After Discovery 110
1 Introduction 110
2 Further and Better Particulars 111
3 Notice to Admit Facts 114
4 Notice to Admit Documents 114
5 Interrogatories 115
6 The proof of evidence 116
7 Exchanging witness statements 118
8 Medical reports 120
9 Engineer's report 123
10 Photographs and plans 125
11 Other agreed evidence 125
12 Split trial 126
13 Delay 126
14 Counsel's advice 127
12 Preparing for Trial 130

1 Interlocutory orders 131
2 Counsel's advice 131
3 Notice after one year's delay (High Court only) 132
4 Setting down for trial—County Court 132
5 Setting down for trial—High Court 133
6 Special damages 138
7 Medical Evidence 139
8 Photograph and plans 141
9 Continuing the negotiations 141
10 Structured settlements 142
11 Civil Evidence Act notices 143
12 The brief to counsel 145
13 Witness Summons (County Court) 149
14 Subpoenas (High Court) 149
15 Trial documents (County Court) 151
16 Trial documents (High Court) 151
17 Adjourning: settling 152
18 When the case is in the Warned List (High Court) 152
19 Thc trial 153
20 Judgment 156
21 Costs 156
22 Enforcement 157
13 Settling the Case 159
1 Settling before proceedings are commenced 159
2 Settlement after proceedings have begun 159
3 Is it better to obtain an order? 160
4 The alternative ways of ending the case 160
5 Drawing up the order 161
6 Provisional damages 162

Part III: Matters Requiring Special Care

14 Persons Under a Disability 167
1 Next friend 167
2 Settlement 168
3 Costs 171
4 Investment and paying-out of the settlement money 172
5 The order 174
6 Mental Health Act patients 174
15 Fatal Accidents 175
1 The two causes of action 175
2 The Law Reform claim 175
3 The Fatal Accidents claim 175
4 Taking instructions 176
5 Assessment of damages 177
6 Apportioning the settlement monies 181

16 Legal Aid Cases 183
1 The application 183
2 The certificate 184
3 Notifying the court and other parties 185
4 The duty to the Legal Aid Fund 187
5 Disbursements 188
6 Payment into court 191
7 Discharge or revocation of the certificate 191
8 Costs 192
9 Settling the case 194
17 The Limitation Period 195
1 When the three year period starts to run 195
2 The court's discretion to extend the three year period 197
3 Fatal cases 199
4 Procedure 199
5 Dismissal for want of prosecution 200
6 Dismissal for failure to fix a date 202
18 Medical Negligence Claims 203
1 Introduction 203
2 Taking instructions 204
3 Legal Aid 204
4 The letter of claim 205
5 Disclosure of the medical notes and records 206
6 Choosing the expert 207
7 Commencing proceedings 209
19 The Motor Insurers' Bureau 212
1 The uninsured defendant 222
2 The untraced motorist (the hit and run case) 223

Appendices

A Client's Accident Questionnaire 215
B Stock Letters 219
C Precedents 234
D Procedural Tables 261
E Actuarial Tables 284
F The Motor Insurers' Bureau Agreements 293
G Specimen Pleadings 314
H The Human Body: Bones and Muscles 348

Index 357

Preface

This is the seventh edition of Personal Injury Litigation. As before, the book summarises the practice and procedure involved in personal injury litigation. The aim is to emphasise the problems in a typical case, and to help the busy practitioner by collecting together materials that are needed to be an efficient and able litigator.

The text has been brought up to date as at 1 June 1992.

Since the last edition there have been many changes in personal injury laws as a result of the Civil Justice Review.

All personal injury cases worth under £50,000 now have to be started in the County Court and even cases for more than that amount are liable to be transferred. As a result the emphasis of this new edition has been changed to deal more comprehensively with County Court litigation. However, High Court litigation is also still covered in detail. At the time of writing the change in rules has still caused confusion and delays in many Courts and it is to be hoped that County Courts will be given more staff resources and training in the near future to deal with the serious cases that they are now asked to administer.

In view of the changes this edition is co-authored by Nicola Solomon who has extensive experience in High Court and County Court personal injury litigation.

The text of the Motor Insurers' Bureau Agreements and at the actuarial tables in Personal Injury in Fatal Accident Cases are reproduced with the permission of the controller of HMSO.

John Pritchard would like to continue to acknowledge his debt to the firm of W H Thompson (now Robin Thompson & Partners, and Brian Thompson & Partners) without whom the original edition of the book could not have been written and his colleagues at Powell Spencer and Partners, (in particular Greg Powell) for their help and assistance. Nicola Solomon thanks her colleagues and staff at Stephens Innocent. Many of the tactical hints in this volume derive from the experience and cunning of our colleagues in all these firms. However for errors that remain we are solely responsible.

JP and NS
June 1992

Table of Cases

Allen v Sir Alfred McAlpine and Sons Ltd [1968] 2 QB 229; [1968] 1 All ER 543; [1968] 2 WLR 366, CA 200

Bolam v Friern Hospital Management Committee [1957] 1 WLR 582; [1957] 2 All ER 118; 101 SJ 357 ....203, 224

Buck v English Electric [1977] 1 WLR 806; [1978] 1 All ER 271; [1977] ICR 629 ....197, 198

Davis v MoD (1985) *The Times*, 7 August, CA 196

Everett v Everett and Norfolk County Council (4 June 1991) 143

Grimsley v Grimsley and Meade (28 January 1991) 143

Gammell v Wilson [1982] AC 27; [1981] 2 WLR 248; [1981] 1 All ER 578, HL 180

Gurtner v Circuit [1968] 2 QB 587; [1968] 2 WLR 668; [1968] 1 All ER 328, CA 213

Hall v Wandsworth Health Authority (1985) 129 SJ 188; 82 LS Gaz 1329; *The Times*, 16 February 207

Harris v Empress Motors [1984] 1 WLR 212; [1983] 3 All ER 561; (1983) 127 SJ 647, CA 179

Hunter (George) & Son v Weir [1955] SLT (Sh Ct) 101; (1955) 71 Sh Ct Rep 343 203

Leadbitter v Hodge Finance [1982] 2 All ER 167 197

Lim Poh Choo v Camden and Islington Area Health Authority [1980] AC 174; [1979] 3 WLR 44; [1979] 2 All ER 910, HL 285

McCafferty v Metropolitan Police District Receiver [1977] 1 WLR 1073; [1977] 2 All ER 756; (1977) 121 SJ 678, CA 197

McIvor v Southern Health and Social Services Board [1978] 1 WLR 757; [1978] 2 All ER 625; (1978) 122 SJ 368, HL 106, 206

Melik & Co v Norwich Union Fire Insurance Society and Kemp [1980] 1 Lloyd's Rep 523 ....103, 104

Naylor v Preston Area Health Authority [1987] 1 WLR 958; [1987] 2 All ER 353; (1987) 131 SJ 596, CA 210

Practice Direction [1988] 2 All ER 102 237

Practice Direction [1992] 1 All ER 862 142

Quainoo v Brent and Harrow Area Health Authority [1982] NLJ 1100 180

Sidaway v Board of Governors of the Bethlem Royal Hospital and the Maudsley Hospital [1985] AC 871; [1985] 2 WLR 480; [1985] 1 All ER 643, HL 204

Smith v Manchester Corporation (1974) 17 KIR 1, CA 33

Waugh v British Railways Board [1980] AC 521; [1979] 3 WLR 150; [1979] 2 All ER 1169, HL 103, 210

Wright v British Railways Board [1983] 2 AC 773; [1983] 3 WLR 211; [1983] 2 All ER 698, HL 48

Table of Statutes

Access to Health Records Act 1990 . . . . .122, 206
Access to Medical Records Act 1990 . . 106
Access to Medical Reports Act 1988 . . 121
Carriage by Air Act 1961 195
Civil Evidence Act 1968 . . . . .73, 112, 118, 126, 138, 143, 145, 149
s 2 143
s 5 144
Civil Liability (Contribution) Act 1978 74,75
County Courts Act 1984—
s 40 . . . . .135, 260
s 52(1) 243
(2) 239
s 53 242
s 55 149
s 69 320
s 76 106
Companies Act 1985 62
Damages (Scotland) Act 1976—
s 1(4) 311
Factories Act 1961 100
s 14 72
s 28(2) 244
s 29 320
Fatal Accidents Act 1976 . . . . . .42, 79, 83, 179, 235, 255
s 2 (4) 255
Law Reform (Miscellaneous Provisions) Act 1934 . . . . .79, 175, 235, 255, 302
Legal Aid Act 1988 . . . . .162, 171, 237, 253, 259, 332
s 9(6) 254
Limitation Act 1980 . . . . .74, 177
s 11 . . . . .196, 197, 199
s 12 199
s 33 195–199
Mental Health Act 1983 . . . . .79, 167
Part VII 251
Road Traffic Act 1972 . . . . . .294, 297, 299
s 144 296
s 145(4) 298
(*b*) .298, 300
s 151 295
Pt VI 293, 296, 297, 299, 300, 301
Road Traffic Act 1988 . .212, 213, 297, 298
s 3 . . . . .23, 248
s 145 213
s 151 .61, 76, 213
s 152 213
s 153 76
Road Traffic (Consequential Provisions) Act 1988—
s 2(4) 297, 298
Supreme Court Act 1981—
s 32A 35
s 33(2) 239
s 34 106
(2) 242, 243
s 35A 235

Table of Statutory Instruments

Civil Legal Aid (General) Regulations 1989 (SI 1989 No 339)—
reg 82(2) 192
reg 83(2) 192
reg 105 192
Construction (Working Places) Regulations 1966 (SI 1966 No 94) 24
County Court Rules 1981 (SI 1981 No. 1687)—
Ord 5, r 11 177
Ord 6, r 1 .... 58, 59
(vi) 60
(5) 113
r 7 111
Ord 9 234
r 6 69
r 10 .... 126, 127
r 11 111
(3) 113
r 14 .... 71, 237, 238
Ord 11, r 1(8) 81
Ord 12, r 1 75
Ord 13, r 1(10) 94
r 3 127
r 7 124
(1) (g) 242
r 17 (g) 245
Ord 14 71
r 2 105
(5) 105
r 3 238
r 8 104
r 12 .... 82, 115, 247
Ord 15, r 1 107
r 2 107
Ord 17, r 11 .... 104, 132, 202, 210
(g) 99
(3) 118
(5) 122
(7) 241
(8) 132
(9) 127

County Court Rules 1981—*contd*
Ord 17, r 12 151
r 2 114
r 3 114
r 12(4)(a) 149
r 13 149
rr 14–24 144
r 28 97
Ord 22, r 6(a) 82
r 6A 36
High Court and County Courts Jurisdiction Order 1991 (SI 1991 No. 724)—
art 5 .... 235, 282
art 7 .... 133, 136
(5) 209
Legal Aid (General) Regulations 1980 (SI 1981 No. 1894) 60
reg 73(2) 188
reg 106 172
Motor Vehicles (Compulsory Insurance) Regulations 1987 (SI 1987 No. 2171) 294
Notification of Accidents and Dangerous Occurences Regulations 1980 241
Reporting of Injuries, Diseases and Dangerous Occurences Regulations 1985 (SI 1985 No. 2023) 102
Rules of the Supreme Court 1965 (SI 1965 No. 1776)—
Ord 3, r 6 256
Ord 6, r 8 236
Ord 12, r 8 66
Ord 13 66
r 2 67
Ord 14 .... 234, 237
Ord 15, r 7 177
Ord 16, r 1 75
Ord 18, r 1 113
r 2 69
r 12 111
(1A) 58, 59, 67
(6) 113

Rules of the Supreme Court 1965—*contd*
Ord 19, r 3 69
Ord 20 109
Ord 22, r 1(8) 81
Ord 24 109
r 2 .... 114, 241
(1) 241
r 7A 105, 241
(2) 242
r 8 135
Ord 25, r 1(3A) 202
r 6 121
r 8(3) 135
(5)(b) 210
Ord 26 115
Ord 27, r 5 114
Ord 28, r 2A(4) 95, 118
Ord 29, r 2 124
r 7A 124, 245
r 10 247
r 11 82
Ord 33, r 4A 126

Rules of the Supreme Court 1965—*contd*
Ord 34, r 10 283
Ord 37, rr 7, 8 36
r 9 .... 36, 82
r 10 .... 36, 37
Ord 38, r2 (a) 210
r 4 141
r 10 125
rr 20–30 144
rr 29–31 144
r 37 97
r 38 140
Ord 39, r 1 150
Ord 42, r 5 156
Ord 58, r 1 94
Ord 62 156
r 3 (12) 207
Ord 65, r 4 63
Ord 80, r 12 (6) 174
Social Security (Claims and Payments) Regulations 1979 (SI 1979 No. 628) . 241

Abbreviations

In addition to the conventional abbreviations, the following are used in this book:

DSS	Department of Social Security
DR	District Registry
MIB	Motor Insurers' Bureau
NI	National Insurance
RSC	Rules of the Supreme Court
CCR	County Court Rules
QBD	Queen's Bench Division
RCJ	Royal Courts of Justice

Part I

A System of Working

Chapter 1

Introduction

1 General

This guide is in four Parts.

Part I: This first introductory Part describes what is involved in the handling of a personal injury claim, and emphasises the need for an efficient system of working.

Part II: This follows the course of a typical personal injury claim (whether it be in the High Court or county court). The various procedural points that arise in practice are dealt with in this Part.

Part III: Here we deal with more complicated matters, fatal cases or cases where the plaintiff is under a disability, and also medical negligence claims. There is also a section dealing with limitation periods. A separate chapter summarises the points that must be borne in mind if a plaintiff is legally aided.

Part IV: This contains the Appendices which comprise the materials that enable the information in Parts II and III to be put to use. Although the procedural steps and devices are discussed in Parts II and III, the detailed procedural rules, precedents, drafts and stock letters are gathered together in the Appendices. By following this format, it is hoped that the main body of the text has remained easily understandable and that the essential simplicity of a personal injuries claim can be appreciated. The Appendices are set out below.

A Accident questionnaires for completion by the client
B Stock letters
C Precedents
D Procedural tables
E Actuarial tables
F The MIB agreements
G Specimen pleadings
H Diagrams of bones and muscles in the human body.

Throughout the text, the emphasis is on the plaintiff's case, rather than that of the defendant. This is because it is the plaintiff who takes the initiative at most stages of the action, and who is responsible for ensuring that it is prosecuted without undue delay. However, the defendant's steps in the action will largely be in response to those taken by the plaintiff and it is therefore hoped that the book will be found as useful to defendant's solicitors as to those for the plaintiff.

As a matter of convenience, the words 'plaintiff' and 'defendant' have been used throughout the text to refer also respectively to the plaintiff's solicitor and the defendant's solicitor, and the terms are only to be taken as referring to the clients, rather than to their solicitors, when the text makes it clear that this is intended.

The 1990 procedural changes and, in particular, the increase of county court jurisdiction in personal injury cases from £5,000 to £50,000 mean that the majority of cases will be brought in the county court. Therefore this book concentrates on the county court procedure although the High Court procedure is dealt with as it arises in each chapter. As a general rule, remember that the principles involved in the two courts do not differ so the plaintiff's tactics in the High Court will be similar to those in the county court, although it is true to say that the county court procedure will generally be less formal and that, at present, county courts are still less efficient than the High Court.

No great distinction is made in this book between road accident and workplace accident cases, for the principles applied in the two types of claims are usually identical. Where there are differences, these are referred to in the text. Generally, one can say that road accident claims ('runners') tend to be more straightforward than workplace claims. This is because the former will often be decided on the basis of applying a common-law principle to an agreed police report and plan, whereas the workplace case is more likely to require the consideration of expert engineering evidence as applied to statutory duties of care. Although the examples given in the text are usually based on road accident claims. they are just as applicable to workplace accident cases unless the contrary is stated. Medical negligence claims pose additional problems. An introduction on how to run a medical negligence claim is given in Chapter 18.

A book of this size cannot attempt to cover all the problems that could possibly arise in a personal injuries claim. The aim has been to provide a guide and summary containing the materials frequently used in personal injuries practice, but without quoting in-depth case references and authorities which can be found in more detailed publications. The County Court Rules and The Supreme Court Practice will provide a full guide for the practitioner who requires further advice and authority: and although the 'Green Book' and 'White Book' are formidable publications that the inexperienced litigator may find difficult to follow, they do provide the detailed authority that will be needed from time to time. The practitioner should also be equipped with detailed guides to the law of negligence and to the various statutory duties relating to accident claims, since this book assumes a knowledge of the relevant law.

The traditionally recommended books for personal injury practitioners are: Redgrave, Fife and Martchem's *Health and Safety at Work*; Kemp and Kemp, *The Quantum of Damages* and Bingham's *Motor Claims Cases.* As regards liability, many practitioners will prefer to have less detailed volumes available for easy access. Highly recommended is Tolley's *Health and Safety at Work Handbook.* This is relatively little known, hut provides all the authority that most solicitors are likely to need. On quantum, many solicitors find Munkman's *Damages and Personal Injury* to be more than sufficient: it is a little sketchy, but it does have useful summaries of 'going rates'. It is also useful to look at the monthly supplements to *Halsbury's Laws* for up-to-date figures and in July 1992 the Judicial Studies Board published *Guidelines for the Assessment of General Damages in Personal Injury Cases*, which has been sent to all judges and is likely to become a standard reference work.

The solicitor's aim must be efficient litigation, for not only will this be beneficial to the client in ensuring that the case is carefully prepared, it will also aid the practitioner by ensuring that the case is less time consuming than it might otherwise have been. The system of working described later in this Part is neither unique nor original. However, by combining the use of such a system with the drafts and precedents printed in the appendices, it will be possible to minimise the time spent on drafting and dictation.

2 Personal injury: facts and figures

The Civil Justice Review of 1988 contains various information on accidents and accident compensation. It stresses that accident victims seek compensation payments from various sources; about 1,800,000 new claimants obtain social security payments each year, 1,000,000 obtain occupational sick pay and 250,000 benefit from private insurance. About 340,000 people make tort claims each year of which nearly 300,000 are settled without the issue or proceedings. Only one per cent are disposed of by trial.

In 1986 court proceedings were started in about 51,000 personal injury cases, 24,000 in the High Court and 27,000 in the county court (at that time, of course, the jurisdiction of the county court was only £5,000). The number of completed personal injury trials in 1986 was 1,400 in the High Court and 3,500 in the county court. The great majority of these claims concerned injury suffered on the road or at work. The average time taken from the incident giving rising to the action to trial was over five years in the High Court and almost three years in the county court. The vast majority of awards were under £5,000.

Chapter 2

A Simple Accident Claim

Before describing (in Parts II and III) the details of a personal injuries action, it is necessary to summarise, very briefly, the sequence of events in a typical accident claim so that the more detailed discussion can be fitted into the overall framework of the action.

Having investigated the circumstances of the accident the solicitor will be able to form an initial opinion of the prospects of the defendant being liable to the plaintiff. If the matter is to proceed, a claim for damages will be made and correspondence will ensue with, in all probability, the defendant's insurers. If no negotiated settlement is achieved it will be necessary to commence proceedings.

A simple diagram of the steps in a county court action is shown opposite. A High Court action is broadly similar. It will be noted that few personal attendances at court are required (these are shown in circles on the diagram), since most steps take place through the post (in rectangular boxes on the diagram). It can also be seen that the action develops by a series of specified steps being taken within specified time periods, usually of 14 days.

The first step will be to issue the summons together with the Particulars of Claim, which is the formal pleading setting out the plaintiff's version of what happened, why the defendant is liable, and the extent of the claim. This will be accompanied by a medical report and statement of special damage. The solicitor or court then sends the proceedings to the defendant's solicitor together with the medical report and statement of special damage. The defendant should then serve a defence within 14 days.

Each side will then have an outline of the other's case. If the Defence attacks the plaintiff's case by making allegations of, for instance, contributory negligence, or counterclaiming for damages, it may be necessary for the plaintiff to serve a Reply and/or Defence to Counterclaim, within 14 days of the service of the Defence.

DIAGRAM OF STEPS TAKEN IN TYPICAL COUNTY COURT PERSONAL INJURY ACTION

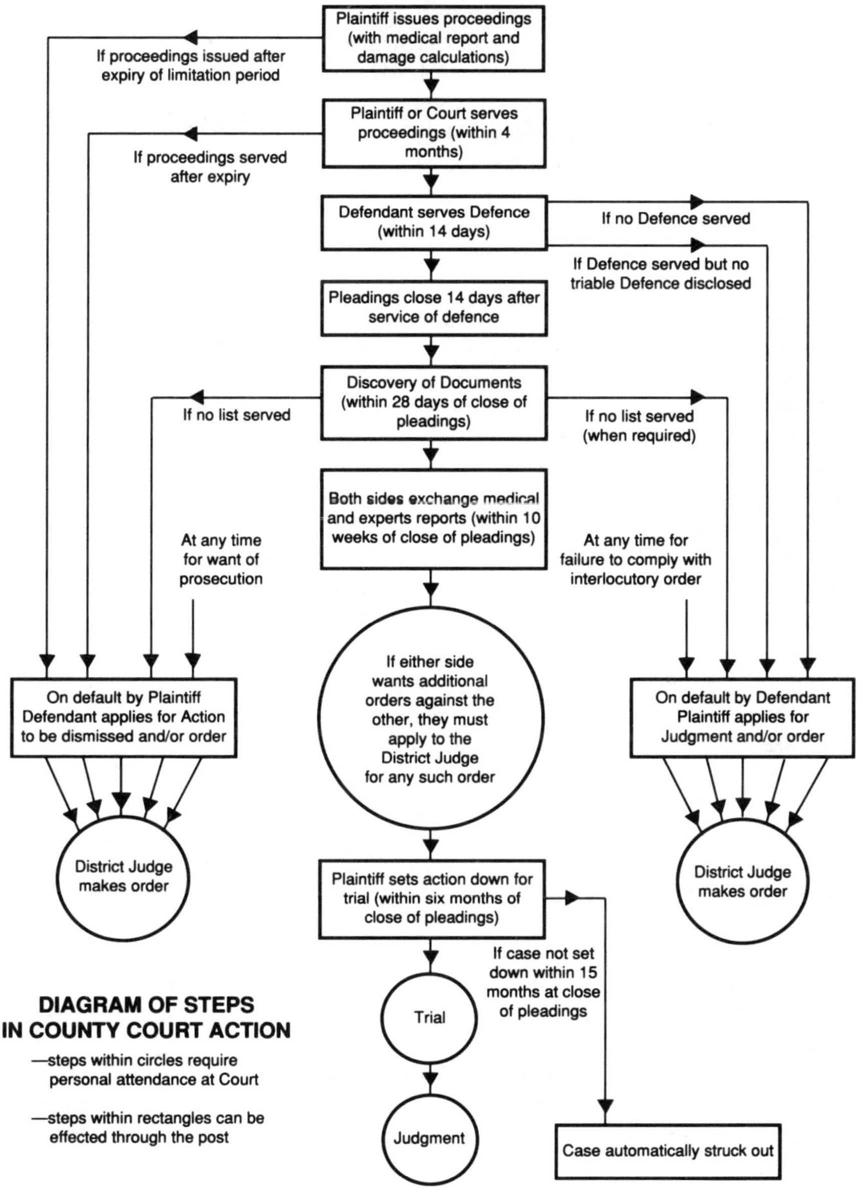

After the expiry of another 14 days the pleadings are deemed to be closed. The issues in dispute will now be apparent, but neither side will know how the other party intends to prove the case except in respect of the plaintiff's medical evidence. However, some of the documentary evidence is revealed because the plaintiff, and maybe the defendant as well, will have to serve a list of documents within 28 days of the close of pleadings. Not all documents have to be disclosed, just those that are relevant to the accident but which were not prepared as a result of the action (for example, the statement made by a witness which is included in the police report is disclosable, but a statement made by the same witness to the defendant's insurers would not be disclosable since it was made for the purposes of litigation).

At this stage it is usual to send the papers to counsel to advise on quantum and liability. Various interlocutory orders can be obtained by applying to the district judge: for instance, that the other side provide Further and Better Particulars of a pleading, interrogatories, that an interim payment be made to the plaintiff, and so on. If medical or other expert witnesses are to be called at the trial, then their reports will have to be disclosed to the other side unless an order is obtained from the court allowing witnesses to be called without their reports having been disclosed. The next step will be for the plaintiff to obtain a date for trial. Counsel will be briefed and the parties will attend court with their witnesses, for trial and judgment.

This may seem a very over-simplified description, but it is true to say that the great majority of personal injury actions (especially road accident claims) involve no steps beyond those set out above.

Many of the problems that arise in the course of litigation are self-made, such as a failure to press on with the action, a failure to diarise time periods, or a failure to prepare the case thoroughly. In order to avoid these pitfalls it is essential to organise a system of working, so that cases are diarised regularly for attention and the various time limits followed.

Chapter 3

A System of Working

The system of working described here is neither unique nor original. Like most things that work well, it is both simple and obvious, whilst requiring no real expense or effort to be put into operation.

It has three constituent parts:

(1) the diary—to note dates and time periods so as to ensure that the case does not 'fall asleep';

(2) use of draft letters, questionnaires, procedural tables and precedents (as set out in the appendices) to avoid repetitive dictation and typing;

(3) easily handled files—which provide information on the state of the case at a glance.

1 The diary

This is the one book that every litigation lawyer must have. The summary, in Chapter 2, of a simple accident action shows the importance of time periods in the development of the case. Failure to diarise these time periods can have disastrous consequences. For example, failure to issue proceedings within three years of the accident may well prevent the plaintiff from pursuing a claim against the defendant, and will probably give the client a professional negligence claim against you. Even the more mundane and seemingly less important time periods must be diarised and rigidly adhered to, for it is essential to any system of efficient litigation that files are not allowed to lie dormant. If the defendant does not adhere to the time limits laid down in the Rules, then the plaintiff should not hesitate to apply to the court for an order, and, when appropriate, judgment.

Strict adherence to time limits will reduce the amount of unnecessary correspondence which may not be recoverable on taxation, and will assist the client by ensuring that the case is heard before his or her memory, and those of the witnesses, fade.

Important dates to diarise: These are the most important of the time limits that should always be diarised—those in parentheses apply in High Court cases only:

- from date of accident —3 years' limitation period for plain-

	tiff to issue proceedings;
• on issuing proceedings	—4 months for service of proceedings on defendant; —7 days to notify insurers (or Motor Insurers' Bureau) in road accident claim that proceedings have been issued;
[• on serving writ	—14 days for defendant to file Acknowledgment of Service (including Notice of Intention to Defend) with the court;]
[• on filing Acknowledgment of Service	—14 days for plaintiff to serve Statement of Claim,]
• on service of county court proceedings or Statement of Claim	—14 days for defendant to serve Defence;
• on service of Defence	—14 days for plaintiff to serve Reply and/or Defence to Counterclaim (if necessary); —close of pleadings takes place 14 days after service of defence (or 14 days after service of Reply/Defence to Counterclaim, if served);
• at close of pleadings	—28 [14] days for automatic discovery of documents; —10 weeks for exchange of medical and other experts' reports that are to be used at the trial; —6 months to set the case down for trial (15 months before case is automatically struck out if not set down in the county court);
• on a payment into court	—21 days for acceptance by plaintiff after receipt of notice;
[• on issue of subpoena	—12 weeks for service on witness;]
• on judgment	—3 months for taxation of costs.

Remember: time now runs during the vacations.

It is usually advisable to make two entries in the diary: one for when the time period expires, and another some time before to act as a reminder. Many firms have computerised diary systems which will automatically note and remind you of these dates. No system is infallible so always keep a personal diary system too.

2 Use of draft letters, precedents, etc

Every accident claim will involve the writing of letters to persons such as doctors, witnesses and the DSS. Often these letters will be in essentially the same form for each case, differing only in the date of the accident and the name and address of the client. Accordingly there is great scope for the use of a system of draft letters whereby letters which frequently recur are not individually dictated, but instead the secretary is simply referred to the appropriate draft letter and told to type it out with the relevant particulars being inserted. Appendix B contains such draft letters, which cover most of the normal letters used in personal injury actions. For example, when commencing a road accident claim, the practitioner would use the standard accident questionnaire printed in Appendix A, and then instruct the secretary to send letters 2 and 4 (to investigate the circumstances of the accident), 12 and 13 (for medical evidence), 20 (for special damage details), and letter 23 (claiming damages from the defendant). Thus the time spent in the routine work of commencing a claim is kept to the minimum, and the use of these letters throughout the action ensures that the solicitor's energies are devoted to the important, decision-making aspects of the file, and not to the routine administration that is an inevitable part of any accident case.

The system can, of course, be taken further by putting the stock letters, and precedents, on to a word processing system. Alternatively, one could simply print or photocopy the draft letters, leaving blank spaces for the insertion of the particulars relevant to the individual case. Witness letters are an obvious example of how this can save a considerable amount of typing time.

As mentioned above, the client's initial instructions should be taken using a standard accident questionnaire. Specimen accident questionnaires for use in workplace cases and road cases, and a supplementary questionnaire for use in fatal accident claims, are printed in Appendix A. The use of these questionnaires ensures that full details of the accident are taken from the client and that all the details of the case are collected in this one, easily available, document. Not only will this be helpful to colleagues who may have to refer to the file, but it will also be a useful document to include in the papers sent to counsel when settling the Particulars of Claim.

In addition to the use of draft letters and accident questionnaires, it is necessary to have the more commonly used precedents easily to hand, so that, for example, the issuing of a notice of application or High Court summons becomes simple and straightforward, the secretary merely being referred to the appropriate precedent and told to insert it in the appropriate form. Appendix C contains the precedents to cover virtually every situation in a personal injury action. In addition, Appendix E contains 16 procedural tables that set out, step by step, the ways in which certain procedural matters are handled. For example, Procedural

Table 1 describes how an application or summons is issued and thus when issuing an application or summons the practitioner can refer staff to that procedural table, (and to the appropriate precedent to be inserted in the form of summons) and so avoid spending fee-earners' time on such a routine matter.

The use of pre-printed forms is clearly another way of saving money and time, and the practitioner should keep a stock of the more commonly used forms. There is, of course, no reason (subject to copyright questions) why the form cannot be typed out instead, although it may be more convenient to buy a pre-printed form and many of them are found in the Practice Forms section of the Green and White Books.

The following list of forms will be found sufficient for most purposes, and many personal injury practitioners will, in fact, find that they only need a few of these forms. The numbers quoted are the code-numbers of forms produced by the Solicitors' Law Stationery Society plc with the county court number quoted first and the High Court number (if different) in parentheses:

Name of Form	*Form No*
*Default Summons (Amount not Fixed)	N2
*Request for Default Summons (Amount not Fixed)	N201
*Writ (Central Office or District Registry)	[A1]
*Acknowledgment of Service	[E22PR]
Affidavit of Personal Service of Writ	[B36]
Affidavit of Postal Service of Writ	[B36B]
Affidavit of Service of Writ on Limited Company	[B36D]
Affidavit in Support of Substituted Service	[B35]
Order for Substituted Service of Writ	[H19]
Judgment in Default	N30 [D2]
*List of Documents	N265 [B9]
Affidavit verifying List of Documents	N265(1) [B8A]
Notice to Admit Facts	N281 [B53]
Summons for Directions	[S30]
Order on Summons for Directions (Central Office)	[H63]
Order on Summons for Directions (District Registry)	[H63A]
*Notice of Application	N244
Summons before Judge	[S1]
Order made by Judge	[H1]
*Summons before Master	[S1A]
*Order made by Master	[H2]
*Summons (District Registry)	[S1B]
*Order (District Registry)	[H2A]
Time Summons	[S2]
Notice of Application for Further Directions (Central Office)	[B58]

Notice of Application for Further Directions (District Registry)	[B58A]
*Notice of Appeal to Judge in Chambers	[B56]
*Notice of Payment into Court	1006 [B5]
*Acceptance of Payment into Court	1007
*Consent to be Infant's Next Friend	N235 [B29]
Affidavit on Infant Approval Summons	[B32]
Infant Approval Summons	[S20]
*Infant Approval Originating Summons	[S20B]
Order on Infant Settlement	699 [H20]
Request to Set Down for Trial	[B14C]
Notice of Setting Down for Trial	[B14B]
*Application to Fix Date of Trial	[B14D]
Certificate of Readiness for Trial	[B70A]
*Request for Witness	N286
*Notice to Produce Documents at Hearing	N284
*Subpoena: Praecipe for	[E20]
*Subpoena ad Testificandum	[G1]
*Subpoena Duces Tecum	[G2]
*Judgment after Trial without a Jury	[D11]
*Judgment in Pursuance of an Order	[D12]
*Legal Aid: Notice of Issue of Certificate	LA6
*Legal Aid: Notice of Amendment/Discharge/ Revocation	LA7

*essential for any personal injury practitioner.

3 A standardised filing system

Files are more than mere receptacles in which to keep the papers relating to a case. In a well-planned filing system the outside cover of the file will, alone, provide a summary of the progress made in that claim, eg the age of the case and whether it is legally aided.

Most firms will already have standardised filing systems, but there are one or two points that do need to be mentioned in this connection. Many people like to use at least two correspondence tags: one for party and party correspondence (a separate one for each defendant, if applicable), and one for solicitor/client/miscellaneous. Use different colour tags for each bundle. If the client is legally aided then have a separate tag for correspondence with the Legal Aid Board.

Each calendar year should have its own colour files. When opening a case it is suggested that the file be of the colour chosen for the year of the accident, and not the colour for the next year in which the instructions were taken. This enables the approximate age of the case to be easily seen and thus may provide warning of the impending expiry of a limitation period; at the least, it will enable the older (and, therefore, presumably more urgent) cases to be easily identified as needing attention.

On issuing proceedings it is advisable to open a second (documents) file, since the papers and copies will soon accumulate, and the presence of the second file will be a reminder that proceedings have been commenced. This second file might well be subdivided by paper or plastic folders into sections for pleadings, medical reports, legal aid, special damage papers, statements, police reports, discovery, summonses, counsel's advices, counsel's papers, copies, etc. It is vital to subdivide the papers in this way, otherwise, you will end up with a morass of unsorted papers, which will mean that you waste time whenever you come to the file. Many people like to keep documents in indexed ring binders or box files.

Devise a system for marking the outside cover of the file as the action progresses. One method is to add strips of coloured tape as certain steps are taken, so that a different colour strip would be added as the legal aid certificate was issued, the proceedings served, the close of pleadings (when the automatic Order for Directions is made), the case set down for trial, etc.

Important deadlines (eg for service of issued proceedings) should be written on the cover of the file and crossed out when the necessary action has been taken. These important deadlines should also, of course, be diarised. If there has been a payment into court, or an interim payment, then mark this clearly on the front of the file.

The keeping of full and accurate notes of the work done on a case will be of considerable assistance to the costs draftsperson when compiling the bill of costs, and to the taxing officer when looking through the papers on taxation. The file should therefore record all the work done on the case, and not merely the letters written. Thus, full attendance notes should be put in the file of all attendances with the client, witnesses, etc, and also of time spent in considering medical reports or working out special damage. This is important even if you also have a computerised time system as you will have to persuade a taxing officer not only that time was spent but that it was spent necessarily and properly.

Part II

The Straightforward Personal Injury Action

Chapter 4

Investigating the Claim

1 Taking instructions

When a client seeks advice in connection with an accident the first task is to take full instructions. This will enable you to form an initial view on liability, and to advise whether the claim is worth pursuing. If your firm operates the ALAS Scheme, then the first interview (giving a view on liability and costs) will be free.

At the initial interview, explain to the client, in understandable terms, that the onus is on the plaintiff to prove the defendant's breach of duty. Many people mistakenly think that they are entitled to damages either simply because they have suffered injury or loss, or alternatively, because they can show that the accident happened through no fault of their own.

If the client belongs to a trade union it may well be that the union offers free legal advice and assistance. Many trade unions only offer this service to a member whose accident arose at work, or on the way to or from work, although there are some unions that extend the service to cover all accidents. Accordingly, if the client is within such a scheme you should advise the client to apply to the union for assistance. The union will then instruct its own solicitors to act.

If the client is not within a trade union scheme, and is not particularly well-off, the next consideration will be whether the client is eligible for civil legal aid. The application form should be completed and sent to the legal aid office. The green form scheme can be used to cover the costs of completing the form and in discussing the claim with the client [see Chapter 16].

If the initial interview with the client is fixed in advance then write to the client confirming the time, and asking that the client prepare a written statement and sketch. This will concentrate the client's mind on the events that occurred and save time at the initial interview (use Stock Letter 1). This letter can also be used to set out such matters as your firm's charging rates and terms, advice about the legal aid statutory charge and, as is now compulsory, your complaints procedure.

2 The client's accident questionnaires

The initial interview will centre upon the completion of the appropriate accident questionnaire, which will provide the information needed to investigate and pursue the claim. It is useful to send the questionnaire to the client before the interview so that the client can complete the standard questions and will know what to expect of the initial interview. Three different accident questionnaires are printed in Appendix A, being for road, workplace or fatal accidents. These questionnaires are, on the whole, self-explanatory but there are a few points that may require clarification:

(a) The road accident questionnaire

'Details of accident'—make sure you understand exactly how the client alleges the accident happened. It is extremely useful to keep toy cars in your desk so the client can demonstrate at interview what happened. This will often show up any problems or inconsistencies in the client's case.

'Earnings'—exact wage details will be obtainable from the employers. The figure given by the client will provide an approximate check on the employer's figure and will enable special damage to be pleaded if there is delay in obtaining the exact figure. 'NI No and DSS Office'—for writing to obtain details of DSS benefits paid to the client, which will have to be repaid by the defendant under the Compensation Recovery Scheme.

'Previous Accidents and Injuries'—is there a pre-existing condition which might reduce the level of damages? If so, are there any past medical records or notes that should be obtained?

'Car Driver: Car Owner'—details of both are needed as the driver will often be the employee or agent of the owner, and the plaintiff's claim may be directed against both.

'Car Insurers'—write direct to the defendant's insurers if the defendant ignores the letter of claim, or if a letter to the defendant would be inappropriate (for example, in a fatal case).

'Client's Insurers'—if the client was driving at the time of the accident, the defendant's insurers will want to know if they have a sharing agreement with the plaintiff's insurers.

'Client's Cover and Excess'—even if client's cover is comprehensive there may well be uninsured losses to be claimed (for example, excess on the policy). If the cover is not comprehensive then the claim will include vehicular damage, towage, storage, travel, hire, loss of use, etc.

'Police Station'—ie the one which dealt with the accident, in order to obtain the police report which may provide all the information necessary to prove the case (see Stock Letter 4).

'Seat Belts Fitted and Worn'—it may be up to 25 per cent contributory negligence not to wear a seat belt, if fitted (unless irrelevant to the injury).

'Notice of Intended Prosecution'—if received is not conclusive that proceedings will be taken. If client has been warned to attend as a witness it is likely that the other side are being prosecuted. Police report will not be forwarded until prosecution proceedings have been completed.

'Pre-Accident Value'—client must obtain estimates of the cost of repairs and/or a signed statement from a reputable garage that the vehicle is beyond economical repair; if the latter, then also obtain a garage estimate of the vehicle's pre-accident value.

(b) The workplace accident questionnaire

The workplace accident section of the questionnaire is also largely self explanatory. The aim must be to elicit as much information as possible about the system of working, previous accidents or complaints, and the amount of experience and training the client had.

'Accident Book'—it is essential that the client report the accident to his employer as soon as it happens so that there can be no dispute about its occurrence. Does the client know whether there was a complaints book? If there was, are there any relevant entries that can be used to argue that the employer had been warned of the danger that led to the client's accident?

'Industrial Injuries Disablement Benefit'—a DSS benefit available to persons with a disability arising out of an industrial accident. Not only is this a valuable benefit, but in addition the papers received by a claimant who appeals against an award may contain valuable (free) medical opinions. This is especially useful in claims in which there is a dispute as to whether the plaintiff's condition arises from work; for example, dermatitis cases. Ensure that the client claims this benefit if there is any residual disability; note that the disablement need not be permanent (and that the applicant need not be incapable of work).

Bear in mind that the injury does not have to be especially serious for the client to be eligible for industrial injuries disablement benefit; all that is required is that there is continuing disability. A client who is in receipt of industrial injuries disablement benefit may become eligible for several other benefits—constant attendance allowance, exceptionally severe disablement allowance and reduced earnings allowance. Check that the client has applied for all available benefits.

(c) Supplementary questionnaire for use in fatal accident cases

Fatal accident cases will require additional information. See generally Chapter 15.

'Coroner's Court'—has the inquest been held? If not, it may be advantageous to attend on behalf of the dependants and so be able to question the proposed defendant and the witnesses (but note that legal aid will not be available). In any event it will be necessary to obtain a copy of the inquest depositions.

'Certificates'—birth, marriage and death certificates.

'Letters of Administration'—these, or a grant of probate, must be taken out.

'Receipts'—funeral, flowers, press notices, etc. The cost of unreasonably expensive headstones may not be allowed.

'Dependancy'—this may involve detailed calculation of the household's income and expenditure to work out the net financial loss to each dependant (or the family generally) arising out of the deceased's death. It is an artificial calculation and can cause distress. In particular, note amount of housekeeping, rent, community tax, heating, lighting and food bills. How much of this expenditure was attributable to the deceased? How much will dependants save by not having to feed and clothe the deceased? Who paid for annual holidays? How much did deceased spend on entertainment, cigarettes, and alcohol? (See Chapter 15, section 5.)

Multi-party cases Ask the client if anyone else was hurt in the accident, either directly or as a witness suffering nervous shock. If there are many plaintiffs, for example in a motorway pile up or drug case such as the Thalidomide disaster then you will need to contact witnesses and the Law Society to see if a steering committee has been set up to deal with the aspects of the case common to all parties ('the generic aspects'). The legal aid board may also bring its multi-party rules into play and insist that a nominated solicitor carries out the generic aspects. In any event you should contact other people involved to see if they are prepared to be witnesses or will be making claims which may strengthen your client's case.

Finally, ask the client to sign the accident questionnaire and in a non-legal aid case ensure that the client accepts responsibility for the legal costs and expenses. Make it clear that the defendant is unlikely to be ordered to pay all the costs of the case even if the client is successful and if, for example, the defendant goes out of business or is legally aided then costs may not be recoverable even in a successful case. Inform your client what costs are likely to be at each stage; in a simple road accident claim, the initial disbursements in obtaining police and medical reports should not exceed £200 but your costs may be much higher than this. You should consider asking your client to sign a contentious business letter and asking your client for money on account of costs and for disbursements.

Having taken instructions it will be necessary to open a file on the case and to diarise the expiry of the three-year limitation period running from the date of the accident.

If the case looks sound on liability, consider applying for legal aid straight away so that you will definitely be covered for the cost of the subsequent investigatory work. It is particularly important not to incur substantial expenditure (eg on a medical report) on behalf of a client who would be within the legal aid eligibility limits: such expenditure should await the granting of a legal aid certificate. (See Chapter 16).

Do not put off applying for legal aid because you think the case is a certain winner. What would happen if you incurred disbursements and did a substantial amount of work, only to find that the client then went to another solicitor?

3 Investigating the circumstances of the accident

Send off the initial stock letters. Write to witnesses (Stock Letter 2 if road accident; Stock Letter 3 if workplace accident), and remember that in workplace accident cases it is permissible to write to an allegedly negligent fellow employee before writing to the employers to claim damages. In a road accident case obtain the police report (Stock Letter 4) and consider whether the ambulance crew would be able to provide any useful additional information; if so, write to the ambulance service for a copy report stating the exact time and location of the accident. In a fatal case, write for the inquest depositions (Stock Letter 6). In a factory accident case write to HM Factory Inspector to ask whether the circumstances of the accident were investigated, and if so, request a copy of the report (use Stock Letter 7). Consider obtaining independent photographs of the accident site or the vehicles/machinery involved. (See Chapter 11, section 10.) It may well not be worth waiting for the results of your initial enquiries before making the claim for damages, for when it is clear that the client has a reasonably good case, one should not delay in sending off the initial letter of claim. The police report will not be forwarded if court proceedings are pending, but the police will, on request, identify the driver and insurers. At this stage, there is little to be gained by obtaining a medical report. The medical aspect will only relate to quantum and thus only arises for consideration when it has been decided to proceed with the claim for damages.

From whom should damages be claimed? In a road accident it will be necessary to claim from both driver and owner of the vehicle involved, if they are different people. Often the owner will be the negligent driver's employer. (Use Stock Letters 23 and 24.) If no reply is received then use Stock Letter 25 and write direct to the insurers, whose identity will be given in the police report.

In a workplace case, the letter of claim will be to the employer (Stock Letter 26) and also to the occupier of the premises, if this is not the employer. It should not be necessary to claim damages from a negligent fellow employee (although it might be necessary to sue such an employee if proceedings are commenced), and once in correspondence with the employer's insurers or solicitors ask them to confirm that a formal letter of claim to the negligent fellow employee will not be needed.

The initial letter of claim is brief and uninformative. Within a few weeks the defendant's insurers (or occasionally solicitors) will reply with a stock letter confirming their interest, and requesting details of the allegations of negligence, injuries received, losses, and expenses, and whether there is a continuing disability.

It is unlikely that you will have yet completed your enquiries, and accordingly it is advisable to reply in wide terms so as not to restrict possible future allegations. Alternatively, the position can be covered by writing 'at this stage it is alleged . . .'. You do not want to reveal your case but do not be obstructive; ensure that the other side have sufficient information to be able to investigate the claim.

If the defendant is the client's employer then request the insurers to provide the relevant wage details so that the loss of earnings can be calculated; they will apply to the Compensation Recovery Unit for a certificate of benefits paid and you will be sent a copy of the certificate. Also ask for copies of the entry in the accident book, and of any notification forms sent to the DSS (usually Form B176), or the Factory Inspectorate/Health and Safety Executive, together with other disclosable documents in their possession (see below for details of these documents).

Hopefully, replies will now have been received to the initial enquiries as to liability. Go through the witness letters carefully and put any contentious points to the client for comments.

Before considering the evidence in detail, consider whether criminal violence caused the injury. If so, and damages will exceed £1,000, a claim should be made against the Criminal Injuries Compensation Board; in this context 'criminal violence' can include arson, and skylarking by fellow employees. If the defendant is an uninsured motorist, or a hit-and-run driver, consider an MIB claim (see Chapter 19).

If the claim is small and the defendant is being prosecuted, consider applying to the court for a Criminal Compensation Order. However, in practice, criminal courts are reluctant to award compensation for personal injury. In any event, criminal compensation cannot be ordered as a result of a road accident.

(a) The road accident police report

If it is a road accident case there will usually be a police report. This can be a most helpful document which may save you considerable time and expense in investigating the circumstances of the accident. The format of the report will vary from constabulary to constabulary, but it will always contain the same basic information.

Check that the report makes it clear that the police did attend the scene of the accident and that the report is not based upon what the police were subsequently told. The name, age, address and insurers of the parties will be given together with details of the vehicles.

Check the statement of damage to vehicle, to see if the damage and point of impact are compatible with the client's and/or the defendant's version of the accident. Did the client mention any injuries at the time?

Study the plan. Usually, it will only be a sketch plan and not drawn to scale. If it marks the position of vehicles, note whether the vehicles were moved prior to the police arriving on the scene. Are there any skid marks? Was there any debris or wreckage which might indicate the position in the road where impact took place?

At the rear of the report will be all the statements, including those of witnesses. Check whether there is a statement from each witness: if any witness's statement is missing, or incomplete, write to that witness using Stock Letter 2. Read the statements carefully and compare the statement the client has given to you with the one given to the police. When was the statement taken? If taken shortly after the accident it may be regarded in a better light than if taken several days later.

There may also be a statement by the police vehicle examiner, which will record any defects found in the vehicle even if not directly responsible for the impact.

Finally, note whether proceedings were taken by the police. The most usual charge is under s 3 of the Road Traffic Act 1988 (ie careless driving, or driving without due care and attention). A conviction of the other driver will usually be proof of negligence and in practice will mean that the dispute with the other side will be as to the extent (if any) of the plaintiff's contributory negligence.

(b) The workplace accident engineer's report

As the plaintiff's solicitor, you may well need the expert advice of an engineer, ergonomist or other consultant if the accident involved the use of complicated machinery or if consideration has to be given as to the safety of a particular system of working. The advice of such an expert can either be:

(i) an opinion, in writing, given after considering the case papers (ie plaintiff's and witnesses' statements) and without the expert inspecting the *locus*. Such an opinion would probably cost over £150; *or*

(ii) a full report made after an inspection of the *locus*. This report would include photographs and a full discussion of the working conditions, and the operation of the machinery. The expert would consider how the system of working was unsafe. Such a report would probably cost in the region of £500.

As a general rule, an expert's report need not be obtained until proceedings are under way, and is usually received shortly before the papers are sent to counsel to advise. This is because you will probably know and understand the basic issues in question and merely require the expert to amplify and support the evidence. The disadvantage of not obtaining a report before the commencement of proceedings is that counsel is forced to settle the Particulars or Statement of Claim without the benefit of expert advice and, accordingly, the Particulars or Statement of Claim may not be as powerful as they might otherwise have been, and may later need to be amended. Frequently, the solicitor will let counsel decide whether a report is needed before action, (by stating in the instructions to counsel to settle the Particulars or Statement of Claim that counsel should telephone you if an expert's report is needed before the pleading can be properly settled) but the solicitor should always consider this carefully before sending down the instructions to save unnecessary costs. Alternatively, counsel may conclude allegations of negligence by giving notice that the allegations may be amended after the plaintiff has taken the advice of an engineer.

In complicated cases it will be essential to obtain expert advice before the Particulars or Statement of Claim are settled. If the claim could involve detailed breaches of statutes or regulations, then it is essential to have the expert's report before counsel settles the Particulars or Statement of Claim. This is particularly important in a workplace accident case, or a construction case (where there may well be breaches of the Construction (Working Places) Regulations 1966) or the new Regulations to be brought in under European Health and Safety legislation. Few solicitors are sufficiently experienced to be able to decide which of those Regulations have been broken, and expert evidence is essential. If a written opinion (without an inspection) will suffice then this can be obtained without undue problems. However, should a full report (requiring an inspection) be necessary then the proposed defendant's consent must be obtained before the expert and client can enter the premises; unfortunately, some insurance companies are obstructive on this point. The permission to inspect should not be granted subject to onerous conditions, such as the plaintiff being committed to sending the copy expert's report to the defendant.

Pre-action inspection: If consent is withheld (or unreasonable conditions are imposed) the proposed plaintiff can apply to the court for an order that the proposed defendant be obliged to allow facilities for inspection and the taking of photographs and even, if appropriate, of video films. To do this, you need to issue an Originating Application and swear an affidavit in support (for specimen see Precedent 8). Procedural Table 16 sets out the steps for issuing an Originating Application. Alternatively, you may decide to commence proceedings without further ado, and then issue an application in that action (see Precedent 9). This is an easier procedure since an affidavit is not essential, but it is clearly inappropriate if the inspection is a prerequisite to being able to decide whether the case is strong enough to issue. Solicitors should not hesitate to issue an Originating Application for pre-action inspection in cases where an inspection is vital in deciding whether to take the case further.

In legal aid cases ensure that the Legal Aid Board approves the expenditure before it is incurred.

If the accident involved a complicated piece of machinery it is advisable to obtain photographs of it, so that solicitors and counsel (and, eventually, the trial judge) are clear as to its appearance and mode of operation. Remember that the accident might lead to the machine being modified (eg erection of a fence or guard) so it is important to obtain photographs before that happens. If the plaintiff does not intend to arrange an engineer's inspection you should ask the defendant's solicitors to take photographs and submit them for the plaintiff's approval. If necessary a court order can be obtained to allow the plaintiff into the premises to take photographs (see Precedent 8). Consider obtaining an instruction manual for the machine from the manufacturer.

The Contentious Business Department of The Law Society will provide the names of experts who are prepared to provide reports and opinions in workplace cases, and also in road accident cases.

In a workplace accident case it may be possible to obtain a factual statement (including a description of any machine involved, and how it works) from the Factory Inspector. Prior to 1987, no fee was charged—now the minimum charge is about £60 (to be paid in advance). See Stock Letter 7.

The Health and Safety Executive publishes numerous booklets on industrial procedures and recommendations for good practice, which can sometimes be good evidence when arguing that there was an unsafe system of work. The Publications in Series List is available free from the Health and Safety Executive, Library, St Hugh's House, Stanley Precinct, Bootle, Merseyside, L20 3QY.

(c) Discovery of documents before commencement of proceedings

Just as an inspection of premises may be a prerequisite to being able to advise the client whether there is a case that is worth issuing, so may inspection of documents held by the proposed defendant be essential if the plaintiff is to know whether to proceed with an action. For example, the proposed defendant in a medical negligence case may hold case-notes and records which would enable the plaintiff's medical adviser to come to an initial view as to liability. Similarly, the proposed defendant may have records relating to the maintenance and repair of a vehicle involved in an accident.

The court has power to order the proposed defendant to hand over these documents to the plaintiff before proceedings have been commenced. As with an application for pre-action inspection of premises, the application for pre-action disclosure of documents is made by issuing an Originating Application. However, the court will need to be satisfied that:

(i) both parties are likely to be parties in subsequent personal injury proceedings; *and*

(ii) the respondent party has (or appears to be likely to have) in its possession, custody, or power, documents which would be relevant in those proceedings.

Note that if the court feels that discovery is not necessary at this stage, but can satisfactorily be postponed until due in the normal course of the action (see Chapter 10, section 1), it will not grant the order. In those circumstances the proposed defendant will recover the costs of the application, otherwise they are likely to be reserved.

The procedural requirements and precedents are printed in Precedent 7(1).

It may well be that the inconvenience of issuing the Originating Application can be avoided by merely threatening to do so and reminding the defendants that the court now has power to order discovery of documents prior to action. Indeed, some plaintiff's solicitors now take this further and write to the defendant's insurers in every case that 'as you will know the court can now order discovery of documents prior to the commencement of proceedings; I should be obliged if you will confirm that such an application will not be necessary, and that you will now forward copies of all your disclosable documents, in particular . . .'. Strictly, of course, the order would not be made unless the pre-action discovery were necessary, but this early disclosure of information can be most helpful to the plaintiff. Thus, when investigating an accident the solicitor should always consider whether you can obtain at this stage what you have traditionally had to wait until later for, namely inspection and discovery. In a suitable case, the two applications could be combined into one Originating Application seeking both orders.

Many plaintiff's solicitors write to the defendant's insurers or solicitors saying 'please forward copies of all your disclosable documents' as soon as the claim for damages has been acknowledged. Frequently, the documents will be disclosed even though there is no obligation on the defendant to do so at this stage!

For pre-action discovery of the medical notes in a medical negligence case see Chapter 18.

(d) Medical reports

Only obtain a medical report when liability has been investigated and when it is clear that the client's case is not hopeless. Also, it is preferable that the client's condition has stabilised before obtaining the report but it may be impossible to wait as medical evidence must now be served with proceedings. You must consider whether it is better to delay taking proceedings until the claim has stabilised—but always beware the three year limitation period. If necessary you can apply to the court for an order that the obligation to serve a medical report be delayed. If the injury is trivial then a general practitioner's report may suffice (use Stock Letters 10 and 11) but generally, a consultant's report will be needed, for the views of a GP will not carry sufficient weight. In a straightforward case, it may be sufficient to rely upon a report from the doctor who treated the plaintiff at hospital. Write to the hospital where the patient was treated (Stock Letters 12 and 13). But, if the case is more complicated, or if there is any suggestion of continuing disability, it is advisable to obtain an independent report (Stock Letter 14). This avoids the danger of the hospital doctor's report being influenced by the treatment given to the client.

You should also consider whether an additional report is needed from a different sort of specialist. For instance, the report of an orthopaedic consultant may well raise matters that should properly be referred to an ENT consultant, or psychiatrist. If in doubt, it is generally advisable to get an additional medical report. Many solicitors are reluctant to incur the expense of going to another doctor, but generally this is an unnecessary concern. It is true that the expenditure might have to be justified on taxation, but in most cases this will not be a problem. If in doubt as to whether the report is necessary, do not forget to obtain the client's authority to incur the disbursement (this is so for both private clients and legally aided clients; if legally aided, the expenditure may not be allowed on taxation and so will come within the statutory charge).

An additional report may be especially necessary for a plaintiff who complains of general nervousness or depression since the time of the accident. Vague complaints of this sort need to be backed up by specific medical evidence; it is usually advisable to obtain an initial report from the GP (giving general comments as to pre-existing condition, and the situation since the accident), and then go to a psychiatrist. The psychiatrist will of course, want full access to the GP's notes and records, and probably access to the hospital notes and records. You will probably have to get the client's signed consent (Stock Letter 19). Sometimes, the general nervousness and depression will lead to the plaintiff being unable to get a job; a feeling of 'I can't cope'. This can obviously have considerable effect on the valuation of the claim, since it will therefore be possible to claim a continuing, and future, loss of earnings. It is therefore more important than ever to get a psychiatrist's report justifying the plaintiff's attitude. A report from the Disablement Resettlement Officer will also be useful.

Do not forget there is no need to disclose all one's medical reports to the other side. So, if one obtains a report that is not favourable (eg if the psychiatrist says the the plaintiff is malingering), do not disclose it. It is only necessary to disclose reports that you intend to rely upon at trial.

The client will have to pay for these reports—usually about £25–£40 for a general practitioner's report and between £75 and £200 (and exceptionally up to £300 or more) for a consultant's report (in a legal aid case, obtain specific authority for fees which are unusually high). The client's losses and expenses in attending the examination will form part of the special damage to be included in the claim. Obviously there is no point in obtaining a report too early (for instance, if a broken leg is still in plaster).

On receipt of the report, read it carefully for any suggestions of 'compensationitis', 'functional overlay' or similar allegations of malingering. The report may conclude that the accident has exacerbated a pre-existing, but latent, condition (for example, arthritis that would have arisen of its own accord in the future) and thus reduce the level of damages that would otherwise be obtained. For a detailed explanation of medical terms, consult a medical dictionary (eg *Pears' Medical Encyclopaedia).* Diagrams of bones and muscles in the human body are reproduced in Appendix I at the end of this book.

Anything in the report which is likely to reduce the level of damages should be put to the client, unless it is clearly of a confidential nature, and would not have been included in the report if the doctor had anticipated that it would be revealed to the client.

The defendant's insurers (or solicitors) will ask for a copy of the medical report, but in all but the simplest cases, they are likely also to obtain their own report. The insurers should be offered facilities for a medical examination by the doctor of their choice, who should not previously have treated the client and it must be agreed that they will meet the client's losses and expenses in attending the examination. Use Stock Letter 15 to notify the client of the examination. In smaller cases it may be preferable to reply to the insurers that it 'would not be protecting my client's interests to disclose my medical report while liability is still in issue'. This is an invitation to the insurers to intimate that liability will not be in issue if in return the plaintiff's solicitor will forward the report. The insurers will avoid the expense of obtaining a report and in small cases that expense might be a substantial proportion of the claim's value. Obviously such a suggestion can only be made when there is little dispute as to liability.

Sometimes the insurers will offer to pay, if the plaintiff wishes to obtain a medical report from the GP or from the hospital doctor. In all but the most straightforward cases, this offer should be rejected. It is most foolish to agree to disclose a medical report before one knows what is in it. It is better to pay for one's own report, so that there is no obligation to disclose it (and if the report is adverse, one can simply go to a different doctor and hope that the second report will be more favourable).

It is often a good idea to tell a client to take photographs of any injuries before they have healed. These can give more meaning to a medical report and can serve as a useful reminder of the pain and suffering incurred. You can also suggest that your client keeps a diary of the severity and frequency of pain and limitations on activities caused by the injury. This will provide a vivid and useful record of the client's disability and the progress of recovery.

You may decide that the client does not have a case, and suggest that proceedings not be issued. If so, make sure you cover your professional position by formally advising as to the three year limitation period (should the client subsequently decide to sue). Use Stock Letter 8.

4 Negotiating with the insurers

(a) Conduct of negotiations

When both sides have completed their initial investigations it is possible that a representative of the defendant's insurers will attend the offices of the plaintiff's solicitors for an exploratory discussion. The correspondence between the parties will largely have been of an uninformative and stereotyped nature. Certainly, the insurers will not have admitted liability yet, although they might have written that 'liability will not be in issue' or that 'this is a case where we intend to make a payment', and it would be rare indeed for them to go back on such an implied admission of liability. Do not be surprised if all letters received from the insurers are headed 'without prejudice' despite the fact that these words are only necessary when suggesting values or inviting settlement.

At the meeting there will be an exchange of views on liability and the insurers will wish to know the approximate amounts involved. Both sides will try to learn the strengths and weaknesses of the other side's case so that further instructions can be taken. Accordingly, at this stage, it is unwise to reveal all the details of the client's case.

Most insurance representatives are good at their job. They will know the values of cases and may try to exploit an inexperienced opponent. Sometimes ridiculously low offers are put forward. If in doubt, discuss the case with colleagues and in cases of real difficulty send the papers to counsel to advise whether the offer should be accepted. As a general rule, it is safe to say that the first offer will not be the final offer.

Each individual has their own style of negotiating, which is developed with practice and experience. However, it should be remembered that the lawyer who has a reputation for being a 'tough negotiator' is likely to secure higher settlement offers than an easy-going colleague, although there will always be the exceptional negotiator who is able to use pure charm to secure high offers! By pressing on with, and immediately issuing, the cases that are strong on liability one will create an impression of being an uncompromising litigator, and this can be used to advantage when negotiating settlements in the weaker cases.

The insurers will be anxious to ensure that the commencement of proceedings is delayed in case the claim can be settled, and thus the extra expense and inconvenience of proceedings can be avoided. It is therefore essential that the insurers should be made aware of the client's willingness (indeed eagerness!) to become a plaintiff, and this can often be underlined by a solicitors' letter asking the insurers to nominate solicitors to accept service of proceedings.

Whilst no negotiator, however experienced, can make a weak case strong, there are general guidelines that may assist the inexperienced negotiator, while you develop a style of your own.

(i) Do not provide the insurers with too much detailed information unless they are clearly prepared to make a reasonable settlement, for otherwise they may use that detailed knowledge of the plaintiff's case to make a well-valued payment into court as soon as proceedings are issued. This is more difficult now that the rules demand disclosure of medical reports and special damages at a very early stage.

(ii) If the case is strong on liability, ask for an interim payment even before proceedings are commenced and suggest that if one is not forthcoming the case will be issued solely for the purpose of making an interim payment application to the master.

(iii) If at all possible issue in the High Court, particularly if there will be continuing loss of earnings (see Chapter 6 for county court limits). This will alert the insurer to the fact you have a substantial claim. Although High Court and county court practice are becoming more similar there are still tactical advantages to being a plaintiff in the High Court and, generally, costs awarded will also be higher.

(iv) In the negotiations before the commencement of proceedings, the insurers will seek to discover whether the client is willing and able to litigate. Thus, do not reveal the financial status of the client if outside the legal aid limits.

(v) If the case seems reasonable from the liability viewpoint do not delay but issue it as soon as possible (see below). Resist the temptation to postpone proceedings on the basis that if it 'is good on liability, it will settle'. This is most important; apart from giving an impression of aggressive confidence, interest will start running on the general damages as from the date of service (see Chapter 5, section 4).

(vi) Leave it to the insurers to put forward figures in settlement. When the defendant's representative attends the office of the plaintiff's solicitor s/he should be left to initiate the discussions, for it is not the plaintiff's role to make settlement proposals.

(vii) Frequently, the negotiations will revolve around the percentage of contributory negligence on the part of the plaintiff. It is sometimes helpful to compromise by accepting a higher percentage of contributory negligence but with the insurer's representative agreeing to the more generous valuation proposed by the plaintiff's solicitor. The result is that the client ends up with the same amount of money and the insurer's representative is able to report that they have negotiated a settlement with a high degree of contributory negligence.

(viii) Remind the other side that if the case goes to trial and judgment, they will have to pay interest on the damages; any settlement negotiated after the commencement of proceedings should reflect the interest due (see Chapter 5, section 4).

(ix) If an offer is made that is too good to be rejected but it is felt that the case is worth slightly more, do not reject the offer but write to the insurers that 'I cannot advise my client to accept' the offer, and so keep the offer open.

(x) Small increases in settlement offers can often be achieved by telephoning the insurers and explaining the problems raised by a 'difficult client' or counsel's opinion or alternatively, by agreeing to 'recommend the offer' to the client if it is increased slightly.

(xi) In an issued case the time for a plaintiff to negotiate with the defendant is when the other side is under pressure (for example, when the plaintiff has recently delivered a Request for Further and Better Particulars).

(xii) When accepting an offer always state that it is accepted 'subject to the payment of our costs'. This is especially important in unissued cases since the solicitor cannot tax costs and is thus powerless if the insurers should refuse to pay reasonable costs. If necessary, issue the case. See Stock Letter 9, for use when accepting offers. It is essential that the question of costs should not be postponed until after the claim has been settled.

The suggested profit cost figure will obviously depend on the size of the settlement and the work carried out before the settlement. If in doubt as to the rates to employ ask your local Law Society or a reliable costs draftsperson for the amounts likely to be allowed on a taxation in your area.

(xiii) Most important of all: prepare for the negotiations by going through the evidence thoroughly. Consider the weak points in the client's case and be able to answer them. In road accident claims the Highway Code will be found to contain many general statements that can be usefully adopted on behalf of the client's case. Do not forget to look up the relevant law, Bingham's *Motor Claims Cases* will be most helpful in road accident cases, while a study of the index to Redgrave's *Health and Safety at Work* will reveal whether there are any statutes or regulations that can be relied on in a workplace accident case.

(xiv) When reading the medical report(s) before meeting the insurers it is useful to make a short summary for use during the negotiations, so that the full extent of the injuries will not be overlooked.

(xv) Go through the various heads of damage listed below to ensure that all possible claims have been included. Apportioning a specific sum to each head of damages will often produce a considerably higher figure than the global sum that one might otherwise have assessed.

The most basic, and important piece of advice is not to reveal the weaknesses in your case at an early stage.

(b) Heads of damages

These can be pecuniary or non-pecuniary.

Pecuniary

(1) losses and expenses to date, including private medical expenses;

(2) estimated future losses and expenses;

(3) loss of earnings (or profits) to date, note that this can include the cost of services rendered by others to the plaintiff (eg the husband

who looks after his injured wife; the relative or friend who incurs expense whilst visiting the plaintiff in hospital). Such expenses are recoverable from the defendant to the extent that they are reasonable; so if the plaintiff needs someone in attendance it is only fair that the claim should include the cost of such professional assistance, even if, in fact, the expense is not incurred because a partner provides the attendance. If the plaintiff needs the service then the expense is recoverable, even if the work is done gratuitously by a friend or relative. Thus, in many cases, when the husband takes a few days off work to look after his injured wife, his loss of wages can form part of her claim against the defendant;

(4) estimated future loss of earnings (or profits), note that the multiplier to use for future losses and expenses should, in theory, be higher than that for future wage losses since the expenses will continue after retirement. In practice, this distinction will be lost in one overall multiplier. Explain to the client how the multiplier is assessed (for example a 35 year old male will not receive a multiplier of 30 but one of approximately 15, or less). Consult a book such as Kemp and Kemp when deciding on the size of the multiplier. The multiplier is worked out on the basis of age at the date of trial because, of course, actual loss of earnings will be calculated to the trial date, not at the time of the accident. Examples of multipliers awarded in recent fatal cases are given in Chapter 15, section 5. Pearson says that 'the present range of multipliers used by the courts, which has an effective maximum of 18, approximately corresponds to the assumption that a person who invests a sum of money in the UK will enjoy a rate of return on an investment of 4½ per cent per annum after the effects of tax and inflation have been taken into account. This assumption is not now realistic'. The Report then says that the multipliers are:

Period of years	Multiplier
5	5
10	8
15	11
20	13
25	15
30	16
35	17
40	18

These provide a useful guide for the personal injury practitioner. Refer to Appendix E for advice on (higher) actual multipliers although the use of actuarial multipliers is generally frowned on by the courts.

(5) loss of mobility in the labour market: loss of earning capacity, note that even though the client may have returned to a pre-accident occupation without a wage loss, any continuing disability may well put the client at a disadvantage on the open labour market where prospects

of employment may have diminished. This may even be true where a client has completely recovered but a new employer may be reluctant to employ them, feeling that the client may now have a predisposition to a similar injury, for example in occupational overuse injury (so-called 'RSI') cases. Even if the employers undertake to keep the client employed there is a disadvantage since the client dare not antagonise them, and will be unprotected if the firm should go bankrupt. This is called a disadvantage (or handicap) on the labour market, or a restriction on employment opportunities. Valuation is difficult, varying with the extent of the disability, the plaintiff's income, and the length of working life. In more serious cases awards can be up to £25,000. Most cases however are awarded less than £10,000. The case that clearly established that a plaintiff should be compensated for loss of mobility was *Smith* v *Manchester Corporation* (1974) 17 KIR 1. So, you may find such a payment referred to in correspondence as a *Smith* v *Manchester* or *Smith* payment. Always consider whether you can claim a *Smith* v *Manchester* award.

(6) Other pecuniary losses, such as value of free board and lodging, concessionary fares, use of a company car, loss of chance of enhancing reputation in one's profession etc;

Non-pecuniary

(7) pain, suffering and shock; if the plaintiff is unconscious and unaware of pain, it is held that there cannot be suffering and so no damages will be payable under this head;

(8) loss of the amenities of life (for instance, a deaf person can no longer hear the birds singing); an injured person may no longer be able to pursue previous hobbies and interests;

(9) bereavement or loss of expectation of life: see Chapter 15, section 2;

(10) inconvenience, discomfort, mental distress, and/or disappointment;

(11) loss of congenial appointment; this is a relatively new head of damage which can be claimed when a plaintiff can no longer carry out work that s/he particularly enjoyed even though neither earnings nor earning capacity are affected (for example a gardener forced to take up clerical work). Damages are usually in the region of £2,500–£4,500.

Frequently these heads of damages will overlap. However, they do provide a useful checklist for ensuring that full damages are being claimed.

Clearly, the most difficult items to value are pain, suffering, shock and loss of amenities of life. Discussions with colleagues may provide guidance, as may analysis of comparable examples quoted in Kemp and Kemp, *Current Law,* and the supplements to *Halsbury's Laws of England.* In July 1992 the Judicial Studies Board published '*Guidelines for the Assessment of General Damages in Personal Injury Cases*' which is likely to become a standard reference work for judges when considering awards, so you should also consider its suggestions. In more serious cases, take counsel's advice.

A starting point for such a valuation can be to decide what damages would be awarded for total incapacity of the part of the body in question, and then work down from there by deciding how the client's injury compares relatively, and what allowances should be made for that client as an individual; for example, sports and hobbies affected, age, occupation, sex and so on.

It is not difficult to decide the value of a serious case, for these are the cases that are reported. It is the less serious cases that present problems of valuation, as these are the cases that are not usually reported (although Kemp and Kemp does have some very useful reports of smaller cases), and where one is less justified in sending the papers to counsel. There can, of course, be so many variables. For example, if the client has an arm injury one can say that the loss or virtual loss of an arm is worth some £25,000–£35,000, and loss of use of an arm at least £10,000, but there are so many other possibilities, a bad fracture with arthritis may be worth £4,000, a stiff elbow £3,000, but each case has its own peculiar characteristics. Thus, is the arm used for working and writing? Does it affect hobbies? Is there an increasing risk of arthritis, or would arthritis have occurred anyway?

In the small cases, worth under £3,000, experienced practitioners can differ by 100 per cent in their estimated valuations and courts can vary even more. Some practitioners take a more mathematical approach by allowing £X for each week off work (or for which an industrial worker with the client's injury might have been off) and £2X for each week in hospital and ½X for every week the pain and suffering continued, and then add a percentage for the particular aspects of that case. The value of £X is, of course the difficulty, but many practitioners would put X at £150, while accepting that it might be too generous in the smaller cases.

(c) On settlement

When a case is settled, always:

(i) ensure that it is settled subject to payment of costs: see Chapter 4, section 3 (xii);

(ii) check that the costs of a legally-aided client are approved by the local office. Refer to Chapter 16 for how to do this;

(iii) consider whether the client is under 18; if so, the proposed settlement will probably have to be approved by the court. This applies whether the infant is the plaintiff or a dependant in a fatal accident claim; see Chapter 14, section 1;

(iv) (if proceedings have been commenced) consider whether the settlement should be recorded in an order of the court: see Chapter 13.

(d) Costs in cases settled for less than £1,000

Generally, the plaintiff who sues in the county court and limits the case to £1,000 will not recover any legal fees: this is the 'small claims' rule. Consequently, some insurance companies have adopted a policy of refusing to pay the plaintiff's legal costs in unissued cases if the claim is settled for £1,000 or less. The only way of retaliating against this practice is for the plaintiff's solicitor to issue the case and start proceedings, but you may be loath to do so in a small case where the main claim relates to loss of earnings or vehicular damage (ie in which the personal injury element is virtually non-existent). The claim (since no more than £1,000 is claimed) will be referred to arbitration which means no costs. But the plaintiff can then apply for the reference to arbitration to be rescinded because arbitration would be inappropriate 'having regard to the subject matter and the circumstances of the parties'. You may be able to convince the district judge that arbitration is unsuitable for a personal injury claim and so the no-costs rule will be avoided. Do not forget that a claim for vehicle repair costs will be treated as an unliquidated (not liquidated) claim. In practice, if you issue the case (even if the insurer has offered a damages-only settlement) you will get the plaint fee plus the fixed costs, so do not be bullied into accepting a no-costs settlement on the basis of the claim being worth no more than £1,000.

5 Provisional damages

Since 1985, the courts have been able to award provisional damages. The rules are complicated, but basically it must be shown that there is 'a *chance* that at some definite or indefinite time in the future the injured person . . . will develop some *serious* disease or suffer some *serious* deterioration in his physical or mental condition' (Supreme Court Act 1981, s 32A). The key points to note about this definition are:

- provisional damages can only be awarded in personal injury cases (but this includes disease cases);
- only *serious* cases are covered. Accordingly, it will only be a minority of cases that are suitable for provisional damages;
- there need only be a *chance* of deterioration (or disease developing); this is a relatively low burden of proof, especially since the plaintiff does not have to show that there is a probability of such a complication arising.

Potentially, the introduction of provisional damages could have transformed the handling of personal injury claims. In practice it has not done so. The courts were reluctant to lay down guidelines as to which cases are suitable, and the general view has been to reserve the use of provisional damages for the exceptional, complicated, case and to limit cases to those where there is a clear and severable risk of a different condition developing. So for example it was held that a person who had broken a joint, leading to a risk of future osteo-arthritis could not claim provisional damages as this risk was simply an aspect of the progression of the condition and not serious deterioration. Having said that, it would seem that many cases could still come within the definition set out above and such claims should always be considered.

Ord 37, rr 7–10 (as modified by CCR Ord 22 r 6a in county court cases) sets out further details. The main point to note is that a claim for provisional damages must be specifically pleaded. Thus, it is for the plaintiff to decide whether or not to include such a claim in the pleading; there is no way that the defendant can force a plaintiff to opt for provisional damages. Bear in mind that provisional damages only relate to specific risks, within specified time periods; the provisional damages rules do not cover general unforeseen risks in the future.

The order for provisional damages: There must be a court order for the provisional damages rules to apply. If the case goes to trial, then the judge's award of damages will recite the disability, and refer to the relevant documents. On the other hand, if the case is settled then it will be necessary for a consent order to be made (see Chapter 9, s 2). If the case is settled before the commencement of proceedings, then it will be necessary to start proceedings merely for recording the provisional damages award by way of a consent order (see Chapter 9, s 2). For the steps to be taken by the solicitors, and for the contents of the court file, see Procedural Table 19.

Applying for further damages: The provisional damages order will refer to the specific risks (of disease or deterioration) that are covered by the provisional damages order. In addition, it will set out a specified time period within which application can be made. Note, however, that the plaintiff can apply for that time period to be extended; and can apply more than once. On the other hand, the defendant cannot apply for the time period to be shortened.

If the plaintiff wants to apply for time to be extended, the application must be made within the stated period. If the plaintiff wishes to apply for further damages to be awarded, the procedure is:

- give three months' notice of this to the defendant (and the insurers, if known). The notice must be given within the period specified in the provisional damages order.
- within 21 days of expiry of the three month period of notice, the plaintiff must issue an application for direction of the future conduct of the action. At the application for direction of the future conduct of the action, the district judge will give directions for the conduct of the action (eg disclosure of medical reports, place and date of trial).

Interest: When further damages are awarded, then interest can be awarded on those further damages. But interest only runs from the date when the plaintiff gave notice to the defendant of intention to apply for further damages.

High Court: The procedure is very similar to the county court, see Ord 37 r 10.

In serious cases, the plaintiff's solicitor should always ask the doctors whether there is a chance that the plaintiff will develop a serious deterioration within a specified time period; if the doctor says that there is such a chance (and one suspects that most doctors would be reluctant to say that there was no chance) then the solicitor will have to consult with the client. It is suggested that the alternatives be put to the client. Either the client can opt to claim provisional damages, on the basis that the complications referred to in the doctor's report might develop. Alternatively, the client may decide that it would be preferable to have the case dealt with on a once-and-for-all basis with no possibility of coming back for a further claim of damages. Bear in mind that the normal (ie final) award of damages would usually include some compensation for the general risks and complications that could arise in the future; so, by opting for provisional damages there is a danger that the plaintiff may recover a lower figure. The options should be put to the client for a decision.

Generally, see Procedural Table 19.

Chapter 5

Special Damage and Interest

1 Special Damage: Introduction

Special damage strictly means the plaintiff's financial loss between the date of the accident and the date of trial. However, the term is frequently used to include also the plaintiff's projected future and continuing loss after the trial. The basic rule is that the plaintiff can only claim net loss, for example, a plaintiff will claim loss of earnings, net of income tax and national insurance, and also give full credit for income support and unemployment benefit received which will have to be repaid by the defendant to the Compensation Recovery Unit.

A plaintiff is now obliged to serve a statement of special damage with the Particulars or Statement of Claim. The statement must give full particulars of special damage including an estimate of future loss and a further statement must be served with any new medical report.

The aim should be to have as comprehensive and accurate a special damage calculation as possible and to ensure that this is updated before the trial and before any settlement. However, it has to be accepted that, in practice, it is often difficult to produce totally accurate figures. In most cases there is an element of guesswork, and some assumptions will have to be made. At this stage, one is not concerned with the last few pounds and pence of the calculation, but with an overall view of the likely level of special damage. Of course, later, if an offer of settlement or if a payment into court is made then there will clearly be a need to consider the figures very carefully with the client to decide what is realistically likely to be awarded at trial.

2 Working out the specials

The questionnaire: The first step is to take proper instructions from the client. At the initial interview the solicitor will have asked the client to keep a full note of all losses and expenses arising from the accident, and to forward the list (with all receipts) when requested (see Chapter 2, section 2). Now is the time for the solicitor to ask for that list, together with an estimate of likely future expenses, which should include telephone calls, stamps, medical expenses, travel to hospital, travel to the solicitor, and other similar expenses, as well as the more obvious losses such as wages. The solicitor can often save work by typing out a questionnaire for the client to complete. This should be subdivided into:

- wage losses,
- travel expenses,
- medical expenses (prescription fees and also private medical fees are recoverable),
- clothes,
- post,
- telephone,
- extra home help,
- special equipment necessary or purchased eg modified bath taps, automatic car.

This will help concentrate the client's mind and so reduce the chances of omitting particular items; it will also avoid any future dispute should the client later remember other expenses and blame you for not including them in the claim.

The use of a questionnaire will help ensure that all the special damage information is kept in one convenient place. Otherwise, it is easy to overlook individual items, if they are referred to in various letters from the client that have been received over a considerable period of time. So, try to get the client to complete the questionnaire, which can then be placed in a separate special damage sub-folder. It is helpful if the questionnaire also includes the following information:

- name and address of employers at time of accident;
- name and address of subsequent employers;
- name and address of pre-accident employers (if plaintiff had only been in employment for a few months at the time of the accident);
- did the client receive statutory sick pay?
- in addition, did the client receive extra sick pay (ie on top of the SSP) under a sick pay scheme? If so, does that extra sick pay have to be refunded to the employer? (see below)
- the client's national insurance number;
- the names of the various types of benefits received by the client since the accident (there is no need to know how much the client received);
- the addresses of any DSS offices from which the client claimed benefit;
- the address of any Job Centre from which the client claimed unemployment benefit;
- details of any Disablement Resettlement Officer who has assisted the client;
- if the plaintiff was self-employed:
  —name and address of accountant;

—name, address, and reference of tax office (with client's signed authority for Inland Revenue to supply solicitor with details of client's tax affairs);
—copy tax returns;

- does the client claim a married person's, or single person's, personal allowance for income tax?
- does the client make mortgage repayments that can be deducted when calculating income tax liability (see p 43)? If so, how much are the payments?

Wage losses: The main special damage item is likely to be the loss of wages whilst the client was off work. Wage details should be obtained from the employer (use Stock Letter 20), unless the employer is the defendant and you are in correspondence with its solicitor in which case ask them to forward figures. Check that the figures provided are adequate; the pre-accident average should be based on a period of at least six months, but check that the client did not have abnormally low earnings in that period (for example, if there was no overtime in that period due to a temporary illness or work shortage). Have there been any wage increases during the period since the start of the list? Is there now more overtime available? Has the plaintiff lost the chance of promotion, or missed a periodic bonus (for instance, at Christmas, or during holiday)? Has there been the loss of use of a company car? If so, how much is that worth? (In 1984, the going-rate for loss of a company car was put at £750-£1,000 pa. But in a 1986 case, £1,500 was the value of 7,000 private miles pa.) Generally, calculate the loss on AA cost per mile figures, but then be prepared to compromise!

All these questions will have to be put to the client.

If the client has changed jobs over the years and full wage details cannot be obtained from the various ex-employers, write to the local tax office for copies of the client's tax returns during those years. The tax office will also be able to provide the names and addresses of the previous employers if these are not known. If the tax office cannot provide the full information it may exceptionally be necessary to obtain an order of Specific Discovery against an ex-employer who will not supply the particulars requested (see p 105). Remember that the tax office will require the client's written authority before forwarding any of this information; use Stock Letter 22 to the client for consent, and write to the Inland Revenue using Stock Letter 21. Apart from knowing the client's earnings at the time of the accident, you will need to know the level of wages the client would have earned between the date of the accident and the date of return to work (assuming the client has returned to work). Ask the client to give an estimate of the likely loss of earnings over that period. Ask the employers for their estimate. If it is a large firm, they may be able to supply wage figures for a comparable employee (make sure the figures are gross, not net, because individual tax circumstances could distort the comparison), and that the employee in question is a true comparable (ie similar length of service; similar skills; similar amount of overtime, etc worked). Similar principles apply if the employer is the defendant in the action; ask the defendant's solicitors to obtain a letter from their client setting out the earnings the plaintiff would have received, or alternatively ask for earnings of a comparable employee. Remember to put the figures to the plaintiff to check.

It might also be worth considering obtaining comparable earnings from different employers in the same field and in complex cases you might consider obtaining an expert report. In any event, if it is necessary to get wage records from anyone who is not a party to the action (eg previous employer) then apply for specific discovery against that person. Refer to Precedent 7(5) for the steps to be taken. Do not simply rely upon being able to serve a subpoena or witness summons for production of the documents at the trial. It is important to have an estimate which is as accurate as possible in the schedule served with the claim because this may well form the basis of settlement negotiations. As a general rule, the plaintiff will have to bear the costs of specific discovery against a non-party; however, the plaintiff may eventually be able to recover them from the defendant, either by claiming them as special damage, or by claiming them as costs of the main action.

Problems can arise with a self-employed plaintiff who has not kept full (or accurate) accounting records. Considerable work may have to be done by accountants to produce presentable figures; the defendants will, of course, refuse to agree figures which are higher than those on the tax returns submitted by the plaintiff in previous years. Do remember that if the client's earnings had shown an upwards trend this should be reflected in the estimate of future loss.

Statutory sick pay: An employee who is off work is likely to receive statutory sick pay (SSP) for the first 28 weeks of absence in any three years. At the end of that time, the employee will no longer be entitled to SSP and so will have to claim DSS benefits (eg invalidity benefit; income support). The defendant will have to repay any SSP paid to the client under the Compensation Recovery Scheme (see below).

The Stock Letter to use when asking employers for details of wage losses (Stock Letter 20) asks for full details of SSP paid. In addition, it asks if there is a separate sick payment scheme. Often, employers (especially in the public service) will pay an employee full net basic wage whilst off sick, and this will be more than the SSP entitlement. However, this payment may, in theory, be made as a loan by the employers with the employee being under an obligation to refund the loan should damages be recovered for the accident from a third party. Thus, it is possible that the client may innocently state there was no wage loss, since full wages were received whilst off work. However, in these circumstances, the wage loss is the same as if the plaintiff had not received the sick loan, since there will be a duty to refund it. In such a case, the plaintiff's claim should include the usual special damage calculation, with the notional wage loss being claimed in full (ie net wage loss and SSP, but ignoring the extra sick pay loan). If the plaintiff's claim is only partially successful, the employer will usually accept that the plaintiff needs to find only a proportion of part of the sick pay loan; if the claim is settled by an *ex gratia* payment, the employer may not be entitled to any refund at all, since it may be arguable that no 'compensation' has been recovered. *State benefits:* In principle, the plaintiff can only claim net wage loss but before 1989 there were extremely complicated rules under which some state benefits were deducted in full when calculating the client's loss and some which were only deducted as to half or not at all. The Social Security Act 1989 s 22 aimed to rationalise the old law and arrange for repayment to the state of money paid to plaintiffs who later obtained damages. The new law only affects compensation (a) paid on or after 3 September 1990 and (b) in respect of (i) an accident or injury occurring on or after 1 January 1989 or (ii) a disease where the first claim for benefit was on or after 1 January 1989. The old law continues to apply to cases not caught by these dates and, in the unlikely event that you are dealing with such a claim (perhaps because the plaintiff is a child) you have to consider the complicated cases (or previous editions of this book!). The basic rule now is that the defendant has to deduct from any compensation an amount equal to all the benefits paid in respect of the injury or disease, whether or not the compensation has been reduced because of contributory negligence. The deduction is made only for amounts which have actually been paid in benefits up to the date of settlement, or for the first five years, whichever is sooner, and the compensator must pay over the amount deducted to the Compensation Recovery Unit of the DSS so that the full liability to pay compensation is met out of the compensator's own resources and the state funds are reimbursed. It is important to note that deductions are made from the compensation payment whatever the payment is stated to cover, including monies paid for special damages, general damages, loss of earnings or expenses or non-pecuniary loss or interest. However the rules do not affect small payments of £2,500 or less or Fatal Accident Act cases.

The defendant has the obligation on receipt of the compensation claim to notify the Compensation Recovery Unit (CRU) by completing the form CRU1. However it is sensible for the plaintiff's solicitor also to request the Certificate Form CRU1 in order to save time. The CRU will send a form CRU4 setting out all records to date and will contact the plaintiff's representative to confirm that the benefits were claimed and paid as a result of the injury. The certificate will be valid for eight weeks from the date of issue. These certificates are often wrong and should be checked extremely carefully with your client. If you have a query about them you should write immediately to the CRU.

When the case settles the defendant will apply to the CRU for a Certificate of Total Benefit. The defendant cannot make a compensation payment without that certificate. The certificate will specify the total of each relevant benefit paid up to the date immediately before the issue of a certificate and the rate of payment expected during the succeeding eight weeks and will be valid for eight weeks. The defendant will then deduct from any payments made to the plaintiff the amount to be paid to the Compensation Recovery Unit.

It is, therefore, extremely important when calculating your client's losses to calculate the full loss, disregarding any benefits that have been obtained since these benefits will be deducted from the amount paid to the client and repaid to the CRU in any event. As stated above, future state benefits will not be deducted and, when calculating future loss, you should strictly take into account the fact that the plaintiff might be entitled to state benefits. However, the payment of damages may take the client over the level of entitlement for income support so future losses may continue at the higher rate. For further details about the Compensation Recovery Scheme you should obtain the useful guides provided by the Compensation Recovery Unit whose address is Department of Social Security, Reyrolle Building, Hebburn, Tyne & Wear, NE31 1XB (Tel: 091 489 2266).

Private Health Insurance: Thc client does not have to give any credit for payments under a private health insurance scheme. Unlike state benefits it is considered that a client need not account for benefits obtained through their own foresight and such payments can be ignored by the solicitor preparing the schedule of special damage.

Income tax and NI: Obviously, full credit has to be given for income tax that would be deducted from the wages. This is because it is the net, not gross, wage loss that is claimed. It is for the plaintiff's solicitor to work out accurately the income tax and national insurance involved. It is not good enough to simply assume tax at 25 per cent and deduct it. Doing this fails to give the plaintiff any credit for his personal allowance and for other reliefs that might be available (eg on a mortgage of up to £30,000 the interest element is deductible for tax purposes). Conversely, a simple 25 per cent deduction does not give the defendant credit for the national insurance that has to be deducted. In practice, this can be a surprisingly large amount. It follows that in all but the most simple cases, it will be necessary for the plaintiff's solicitor to do an income tax and national insurance calculation. To do this, you will have to know the personal allowances available for each of the tax years (remember there is a larger allowance for a married person than for a single person), the tax rates, and the national insurance contribution rate. In addition, you will also need to know whether the plaintiff has a mortgage; if so, is it under £30,000, and how much are the interest payments? In practice, solicitors are not expected to obtain detailed information on this point, usually a defendant will not raise a query if the full monthly mortgage payment is claimed.

3 Calculating the figures

Before you can work out the special damage, you need to have checked all the items referred to above. In particular you will need:

- earnings details for the six months before the accident;
- wage rates applying since the date of the accident;
- details of any earnings received by the plaintiff since the accident (if there is a partial loss of wages);
- details of the date the client is likely to return to work (and at what salary, if there is likely to be continuing loss);
- details of DSS benefits or certificate from CRU;
- plaintiff's list of other expenditure;
- plaintiff's list of likely future expenses.

Calculate the special damage as follows:

1 Work out the net earnings prior to the date of the accident. Generally, this will be averaged over a six month period (but check that the figures are not abnormally low for some reason, see above).

2 Calculate the gross earnings that the plaintiff would have received during each of the tax years (or part year) since the date of the accident. This will be done using the figures supplied by the employer, or the gross earnings of a comparable employee. It is essential to calculate the gross figure for each tax year, so that income tax and NI can be properly worked out. If there was a wage-rate change during the year, then obviously that must be allowed for when working out the gross annual figure.

3 Now, work out the income tax. The table on p 52 sets out the necessary information. Take the gross earnings, and deduct:

—the single, or married person's allowance applying in that tax year;

—the full amount of mortgage interest (on loan of up to £30,000);

—any other allowances (eg spouse's earned income relief).

Having deducted those items, you will be left with the net taxable income for that year. Now, calculate the amount of tax that would have had to have been paid; the rate of tax is printed in the chart on p 52.

4 Work out the NI. National insurance contributions are based on the full (ie gross, not net) earnings. The percentage rate of contribution is set out, for the different tax years, on the table on p 52. So, simply multiply the gross wage figure for that tax year (ie as in 2 above) by the correct percentage figure.

5 You can now work out the net wage for that tax year. Deduct the amount of income tax (as in 3) and the amount of NI (as in 4) from the gross wage figure (ie as in 2). This will give you the net amount that the client would have earned in the pre-accident job.

6 Deduct any wages that the client did, in fact, receive during that tax year. For instance, it may be that the client was able to obtain less well-paid employment for all or part of the year. If so, full credit

will have to be given for the wages earned. Simply deduct the net amount received (ie net wages, net of tax and NI). You now have the net wage loss that can properly be claimed for that tax year.

7 You must now repeat this procedure for each successive tax year. Do not forget to allow for wage increases that the client would have received; similarly, do not forget to adjust the personal allowance rates, tax rates, and NI rates, in accordance with the figures in the table on p 52.

8 You will now have the plaintiff's net claimable wage loss from the date of the accident until the present time. It may in fact be convenient for you to project it through to the end of the current tax year. Now state separately the amount which the client has received from state benefits which must be repaid to the CRU.

9 Add on the client's other losses and expenses (eg expenses attending medical examinations, prescriptions, telephone calls, clothing, special equipment etc). See p 39.

10 Although not strictly necessary, it is advisable to work out the interest on the special damages. For how to calculate this, see p 48. Enter the amount of interest as a separate figure at the foot of the calculation.

11 You have now completed the special damage calculations to date. Since there may well be a considerable delay before the case goes to trial (when you will have to update the special damage again) it is helpful to keep your notes of how you worked out the figures. Also, do not forget to put the date of the calculation on the final set of figures.

12 Finally put in a figure for continuing loss ie the net annual loss of wages until the anticipated date of return or with a suitable multiplier if the client will not be able to return (see Chapter 4 section 4(b) guidance regarding an appropriate multiplier) together with an estimate of likely future expenses. You should give an allowance for continuing receipt of DSS benefits (since future benefits are not recouped by the CRU) but put in a reminder that income support may not be payable after settlement and so the continuing loss will be increased accordingly).

Having worked out the special damage you should send a copy to your client to check and ensure it is full and correct before sending it to counsel to draft in final form to accompany the particulars of claim.

Remind your client to let you know of all your new expenses as they arise and keep your special damage file up to date so that you can provide amended calculations whenever necessary (for example on serving further medical reports — which may necessitate a change to the estimate of future loss).

Actuaries and accountants: In most cases, the solicitor can do the special damage calculation. However, sometimes the figures become so complicated that specialist help is needed particularly if the client is or was self-employed. In practice, it is more likely to be with calculation of future pecuniary losses that such specialist evidence is required. If the accountant or actuary prepares a report (ie does more than simply the mathematical calculations), then the report will have to be disclosed if it is to be relied upon at trial. The position is the same as with medical reports except that expert accountant reports do not have to be served with the proceedings.

The defendant's solicitors may challenge the cost of using an accountant or actuary; they will probably say that the solicitor could have done the calculations. Even if there is a risk of this being said, it will often be worth the client's while to pay the extra money (in the knowledge that it will be a solicitor and client cost) in the hope that the extra expense will be covered by the increased amount of special damage. In any event, if the plaintiff is self-employed, or the director of a small company, it may well be the case that only an accountant can calculate the true level of lost earnings, and the likely level of future profits.

Sometimes, a plaintiff will have lost pension rights through early retirement brought on as a result of injuries. In such a case, the calculation of the loss in value of those pension rights can be extremely complicated. Sometimes the pension trustees will be able to provide approximate figures, but otherwise the advice of an actuary may be necessary. If an actuary is to be instructed, then send a copy of the pension scheme, trust deed, rules, and booklet; the date of commencement of pensionable service; details of pensionable salary; details of pension benefits awarded as a result of the accident or premature retirement; details of pension increases granted by the scheme; details of pension benefits to be taken into account in mitigation. Normally, you have to obtain this information from the employers or the pension trustees.

When preparing a report, the actuary will be faced with the problem of what assumptions should be made; in particular, the presumed annual rate of discount (ie the presumed rate of investment return that the plaintiff will be able to get from the capital sum invested). The courts adopt what is known as the Diplock approach, they assume 4–5 per cent per annum. In fact, this is totally unrealistic as has been conclusively proved by 'Actuarial tables with explanatory notes for use in personal injury and fatal accident cases' published by HMSO (and reproduced in Appendix E). This suggests that one takes the yield from index linked gilts with an end result of a more generous multiplier for the plaintiff. In practice, one probably has to go along with the Diplock approach, although one may try to split the difference between the two approaches.

It is normal to ask the actuary to prepare alternative calculations, on the two different bases. Be sure to provide the actuary with full instructions (ie full personal details of the plaintiff; special damage information; counsel's opinions).

Actuarial evidence without calling an actuary: In 1984, HMSO published 'Actuarial tables with explanatory notes for use in personal injury and fatal accident cases'. These tables are sets of multipliers for loss of earnings claims (depension age) for men and women according to their age at date of trial. They are reproduced in Appendix E. Different multipliers are given depending upon the rate of interest selected (tables cover $1\frac{1}{2}$–5 per cent). As one would expect, the use of such actuarial tables generally gives a higher multiplier than would usually be awarded by the courts. For instance, if one takes the multiplier for a loss of earnings claim to age 65 for a man aged 30 (on a typical $3\frac{1}{2}$ per cent Government Index Linked Stock) one gets a multiplier of 19.4. The traditional multiplier in such a case (based on precedents in the Law Reports) would probably be in the region of 16. So, there is a significant advantage to a plaintiff who can use these tables.

In practice, the defendant is likely to resist use of such tables. However, what the plaintiff can do is write to the defendant suggesting that the judge be allowed to use these tables without the assistance of an expert actuary witness, in an effort to reduce costs. It is unlikely that the defendant will agree, but the writing of such a letter may be sufficient to persuade the trial judge that the plaintiff should be allowed the costs of calling an actuary to give evidence because of the defendant's unreasonable conduct (it is advisable to specifically make this point to the defendant in the letter, and reserve the right to draw to the attention of the trial judge on the question of costs).

4 Interest

Claiming interest: A plaintiff is not automatically assumed to claim interest on damages. To avoid doubt on this score, the Particulars or Statement of Claim, and also the indorsement on the writ in High Court cases should specifically include a claim for interest. See the specimen pleadings in Appendix G, and the writ indorsements in Precedent 1, for the correct wording. In fact, the courts are now required to award interest 'unless the court is satisfied that there are special reasons to the contrary, and provided that judgment was for at least £200'. Thus, in the normal course of events, the plaintiff can expect interest.

The rates of interest: Different rates of interest apply for the different types of damages. One must differentiate between special damages (ie financial loss up to the date of trial and future loss), and general damages (ie compensation for pain, suffering and loss of amenities, etc).

- *General damages:* interest is at 2 per cent from the date of service of the proceedings. There are two points to note here. Firstly, the interest rate is fairly low (the theory is that the plaintiff benefits through inflation by having the date of trial postponed, and so does not need a high rate of interest). Secondly, interest only runs from the date of service of the proceedings: it does not run from the date of the accident, or the date of issue of the proceedings.
- *Special damages:* interest runs at half the court special account rate, from the date of the accident. Note that interest is only half rate, and that it runs from the date of the accident (not the date of issue, or of service of the proceedings). For how to work out

the figures, see below. Incidentally, there is authority for saying that the half-rate rule should be confined to cases in which special damage is incurred on a regular basis before trial (eg weekly wage loss). If the losses are irregular, or do not continue from the date of accident to the trial, then argue for more than half-rate interest.

- *Future loss:* future loss of earnings (ie from the date of the trial onwards) does not attract interest.
- *Fatal cases:* are treated in the same way. The pecuniary loss to date of trial is treated as special damage, whilst future pecuniary loss attracts no interest.

These guidelines were upheld by the House of Lords in *Wright* v *BRB* [1983] 2 AC 773. But the court did make it clear that in exceptional cases (in particular, when one party or the other had been guilty of gross delay) the court could increase or diminish the amount of interest, or alter the period for which it is allowed. So, the court has a discretion, which may be exercised in exceptional cases. Often, it seems to be exercised in favour of defendants!

Working out the interest: Interest on the general damages is easy to work out. Basically, take 2 per cent of the damages, as from the date the proceedings were served.

It is with special damages that the complications arise. Interest runs at half the court special account (formerly known as short term investment account) rate as from the date of the accident. Since the special account rate changes periodically, it can mean that it is an extremely complicated calculation. The rates of interest are set out in the following table. Fortunately, there are tables available that make the calculation of this interest a relatively straightforward matter. In particular, Mr R M Nelson-Jones (of Field Fisher and Waterhouse, London) has an annual article in The Gazette (usually in September) which contains a ready-reckoner table for calculating the interest. The table below appeared in his article in (1991) 34 LSG 17, and is reproduced with his kind permission.

The table sets out the total interest (on special account rate) that will have accrued if a case went to trial on 1 October 1991. For instance, if the accident had happened on 1 January 1983, the rate of interest would be 108.16 per cent (so the interest on the specials would be half of that). Similarly, for an accident on 1 October 1988, the special damage rate would be half of 39.97 per cent of the specials.

To stop the table going out of date, one adds on the daily rate of interest since 1 October 1991. Table 2 sets out the number of accumulated days that run in the six months following 1 October 1991. For instance, if a case was settled on 31 January 1992, there would be an extra 123 days' interest to be added on. On the assumption that the special account rate remains at 10.25 per cent, then the daily rate of interest will be 0.028 per cent (ie 10.25 per cent divided by 365). Thus, with 123 days' interest there would be an additional 3.44 per cent interest accruing since 1 October 1991. So, in the case of an accident that occurred on

1 September 1977, the total interest as at 1 January 1992 would be 174.96 per cent (ie the figure in the Table 1), plus 3.44 per cent (the interest between October and January 1992) giving a total interest of 178.40 per cent. Because interest on specials runs at half the normal rate, it follows that interest would be 89.20 per cent of the total specials.

It must be appreciated that interest can be sizeable if there is a significant special damage claim, especially if the case is old. This is why interest should always be set out at the foot of a special damage calculation. This will provide a useful reminder to the solicitor, and counsel, as to the interest that has accrued. This can be particularly valuable when considering the amount of payment into court.

5 High Court: special damage and interest

The rules on calculating special damages and interest are identical in the High and county courts.

Personal Injury Interest Calculation

Rates since 1976

From:	
1 October 1965	5%
1 September 1966	5.5%
1 March 1968	6
1 March 1969	6.5%
1 March 1970	7%
1 April 1971	7.5%
1 March 1973	8%
1 March 1974	9%
1 February 1977	10%
1 March 1979	12.5%
1 January 1980	15%
1 January 1981	12.5%
1 December 1981	15%
1 March 1982	14%
1 July 1982	13%
1 April 1983	12.5%
1 April 1984	12%
1 August 1986	11.5%
1 January 1987	12.25%
1 April 1987	11.75%
1 November 1987	11.25%
1 December 1987	11%
1 May 1988	9.5%
1 August 1988	11%

1 November 1988	12.25%
1 January 1989	13%
1 November 1989	14¼%
1 April 1991	12%
1 October 1991	10.25%

Table 1

	1975	**1976**	**1977**	**1978**	**1979**	**1980**
January	199.54	190.54	181.54	171.62	161.62	149.53
February	198.77	189.78	180.77	170.77	160.77	148.26
March	198.08	189.06	180.01	170.01	160.01	147.07
April	197.32	188.30	179.16	169.16	158.94	145.80
May	196.58	187.56	178.33	168.33	157.92	144.57
June	195.81	186.80	177.49	167.49	156.86	143.30
July	195.07	186.06	176.66	166.66	155.83	142.07
August	194.31	185.30	175.81	165.81	154.77	140.80
September	193.55	184.54	174.96	164.96	153.70	139.53
October	192.81	183.80	174.14	164.14	152.68	138.30
November	192.04	183.04	173.29	163.29	151.62	137.03
December	191.30	182.30	172.47	162.47	150.59	135.80

	1981	**1982**	**1983**	**1984**	**1985**	**1986**
January	134.53	121.81	108.16	95.53	83.41	71.41
February	133.46	120.54	107.05	94.47	82.39	70.39
March	132.51	119.39	106.06	93.48	81.47	69.47
April	131.44	118.20	104.95	92.43	80.45	68.45
May	130.42	117.05	103.92	91.44	79.46	67.46
June	129.36	115.86	102.86	90.43	78.44	66.44
July	128.33	114.71	101.83	89.44	77.46	65.46
August	127.27	113.61	100.77	88.43	76.44	64.44
September	126.20	112.50	99.71	87.41	75.42	63.46
October	125.18	111.43	98.68	86.43	74.43	62.52
November	124.12	110.33	97.62	85.41	73.41	61.54
December	123.09	109.26	96.59	84.43	72.43	60.60

	1987	**1988**	**1989**	**1990**	**1991**
January	59.61	47.85	36.99	23.78	9.53
February	58.58	46.92	35.88	22.57	8.32
March	57.64	46.04	34.89	21.48	7.23
April	56.60	45.11	33.78	20.27	6.02
May	55.63	44.20	32.72	19.10	5.03
June	54.63	44.20	31.61	17.88	4.01
July	53.67	42.62	30.54	16.71	3.02
August	52.67	41.81	29.44	15.50	2.01
September	51.67	40.87	28.33	14.29	0.99
October	50.71	39.97	27.27	13.12	
November	49.71	39.04	26.16	11.91	
December	48.78	38.03	24.99	10.74	

Table 2

31 October 1991	31
30 November 1991	61
31 December 1991	92
31 January 1992	123
29 February 1992	152
31 March 1992	183

Special damage: tax and NI rates

Tax Year	Personal allowances single person	married person	tax rate (basic)	NI rates Class 1		payable on earnings up to upper earnings limit of
1977/78	945	1,455	34%*	5.75%		£ 5,460
1978/79	985	1,535	33%*	6.50%		6,240
1979/80	1,165	1,815	30%	6.50%		7,020
1980/81	1,375	2,145	30%	6.75%		8,580
1981/82	1,375	2,145	30%	7.75%		10,400
1982/83	1,565	2,445	30%	8.75%		11,440
1983/84	1,785	2,795	30%	9.00%		12,220
1984/85	2,005	3,155	30%	9.00%		13,000
1985/86	2,205	3,455	30%	up to £35.50	0%	13,780
				£35.50–£55	5%	
				£50–£90	7%	
				£90–£265	9%	
1986/87	2,335	3,655	29%	£38–£60	5%	14,820
				£60–£95	7%	
				over £95	9%	
1987/88	2,425	3,795	27%	£39–£65	5%	15,340
				£65–£100	7%	
				over £100	9%	
1988/89	2,605	4,095	25%	£41–£70	5%	15,850
				£70–£105	7%	
				over £105	9%	
1989/90	2,789	4,379	25%	£43–£75	5%	16,900
				£75–£115	7%	
				over £115	9%	
1990/91	3,000	4,720	25%	up to £46	2%	18,200
				£46–£350	9%	
1991/92	3,290	5,010	25%	up to £52	2%	20,280
				£52–£390	9%	
1992/93	3,445	5,165	25%	up to £54	2%	21,060
				£54–£405	9%	

*reduced to 25% on first £750 of earnings

Specimen Special Damage Calculation
(Road accident in course of employment)

Calculation of pre-accident average wage

	£
Gross earnings 26 weeks prior to accident	8,650.00
Tax NI for 26 weeks prior to accident	1,948.00
Net earnings 26 weeks prior to accident	6,702.00
Net weekly average wage	257.76 pw

Calculation of wage loss

	£
Absent from work 92 — (insert any 14 weeks period in 1992) = 14 weeks	257.76 pw
Net loss while off work =	3,608.64

Other losses and expenses

	£
Expenses attending medical examination	9.75
Prescriptions, telephone calls, etc	12.40
Repairs to spectacles	24.00
Value of clothing	19.00
Husband's loss of earnings (2 days)	75.00
Vehicle—pre-accident value	1,450.00
—towage	25.00
—storage	100.00
—hire of alternative transport	56.00
TOTAL LOSSES AND EXPENSES	£1,771.15

	£
Gross special damage (£3,608.64 + £1,771.15)	5,379.59
Of which: repayable to Compensation Recovery Unit	

	£
Income support received	349.50
SSP received	476.00
	825.50

	£
Repayable to client	4,554.09

Interest on special damage to date [ ] days × [ ]% = [ ] continuing at [ ] per day

Future loss

Loss of earnings continuing	—	Nil
Purchase price of walking stick	—	£40

Chapter 6

Commencing Proceedings

1 Commencing proceedings

If a case is sound on liability, do not wait until negotiations with the insurers have broken down before you start proceedings. Generally, issue a case as soon as is practicable. This is so even if there is no dispute as to liability, and if you are merely waiting for the medical condition to stabilise. Press on, and issue the case, even if it is sound on liability, for:

(1) should negotiations eventually collapse, there will be less delay in taking the case to trial;

(2) pressure is increased on the defendants to offer a realistic sum;

(3) you could apply for an interim payment;

(4) your costs will be increased. Also, your costs position will be safeguarded, since you will be able to have the costs taxed, if you are unable to reach agreement with the other side. (You would not be able to have the costs taxed if proceedings were not commenced);

(5) interest on general damages (generally 2 per cent, see Chapter 5, section 4) only runs from the date the proceedings are served;

(6) perhaps most importantly, you will not have to worry about missing the three year limitation period. It is all too easy to put aside a case that is sound on liability, only to find that one has then missed the limitation period.

The basic rule should always be: if the case is sound on liability, press on with it although one must carry out detailed initial investigations before taking a claim since the 1990 rule changes demand that a medical report and statement of special damage be served with the proceedings.

In a legal aid case, check that the certificate covers the issue (and service) of proceedings.

In a private case, obtain the client's authority before issuing proceedings. Write to the client, putting on record the uncertainties and risks of litigation, and set out the possible financial liabilities. A further bill and request for money on account of costs will help bring this home.

(a) High Court or county court?

Most personal injury practitioners prefer to sue in the High Court. However any case which includes a claim for damages in respect of personal injuries must be commenced in the county court unless the claim is worth £50,000 or more. The £50,000 limit applies to the total aggregate value of the claim or claims so, for example, a claim by two plaintiffs who have general damages of £10,000 each, and special damages of 20,000 each (including future loss and the value of a car), could be started in the High Court. For circumstances in which cases can be transferred from the county court to the High Court see Chapter 12, section 5.

(b) Who to sue?

Make sure you are suing the right person. If the defendant is a limited company, it is usually advisable to do a company search. However, if you are in correspondence with the defendant's insurers, then it is often sufficient to simply ask them to confirm the correct name and address of the proposed defendant. Strictly speaking, that may not be good enough, but in practice it is inconceivable that they would be able to avoid liability through supplying the wrong information. If in doubt, do a search.

Ensure that the defendant is being sued in the correct name. This list covers the more common cases:

— *Sole trader:* sue in full name, or in trading name; for example, 'John Jones (trading as Jones Haulage)'.

— *Partnership:* sue in the name of the partnership or in the names of the individual partners. However, suing in the names of the partners, rather than in the name of the partnership, makes it more complicated to seize goods to enforce a judgment, although that is rarely necessary in personal injury cases. The proceedings need only be served on one partner, or on the person in charge of the firm's principal place of business.

— *Limited Company:* sue in the registered name of the company and serve the proceedings by sending them to the firm's registered office; see section 3 below. Note that many partnerships call themselves '& Co', without being registered as a company; a Companies House search will reveal the true position.

— *Government departments:* sue in the name of the department, and serve the writ on the solicitor to that department, or the Treasury Solicitor. The White Book (vol 2: para 6038) and the Green Book (under 'Crown Proceedings') both contain lists showing whether departments have their own solicitors or whether they rely on the Treasury Solicitor.

— *Local authority:* sue in the name of the local authority, and serve the writ on the solicitor to the authority or, if there is no solicitor, on the clerk to the local authority or the chairman.

— *State schools:* sue in the name of the education authority (usually the county council outside London).

— *Hospitals:* if the hospital is under the control of the local authority sue the local health authority. If it has contracted out sue the relevant hospital Trust. It is rarely necessary to sue the doctor responsible.

— *Police:* sue in the name of the chief constable, for example 'Sir XYZ (Chief Constable of the . . . Police Authority)'. In London, sue the Commissioner of Police in London. Serve the proceedings on the solicitor to the authority.

Vicarious liability: often, an accident will have been caused by the negligence of an employee who is acting in the course of employment. In such a case, the employer will be vicariously liable for the employee's negligence and so there will normally be no need to sue the negligent employee as well as the employer. But, if it should transpire that the employee was not acting in the course of employment at the time of the accident, then the employer will not be vicariously liable. So, it is usually advisable to issue the writ against both the employer (as first defendant) and the employee (as second defendant) but to take no actual steps against the employee. On the other hand, if the employer was to suggest (either in open correspondence, or in its defence) that the employee was not acting in the course of employment, then the action would be pursued, in the normal way, against the employee as well. In practice, it is a wise precaution to ask the employer's solicitors to confirm that they will not be disputing their client's vicarious liability should the employee be found to have been negligent; in that case, it should not be necessary to make the employee a defendant, and the action can be brought against the employer alone.

2 Instructing counsel to settle the claim

According to the White Book, 'the drafting of a proper pleading must . . . be a task fitted only for counsel'. In fact, the drafting of the Particulars or Statement of Claim is a technical process, and one that is best left to counsel (in any event, the low fees allowed to counsel make it a bargain from the costs point of view!). However, it is essential that the solicitor should appreciate the important function of the Particulars or Statement of Claim, if you are to be able to know what information counsel will require, and also if you are to be able to check counsel's draft properly.

The Particulars or Statement of Claim will summarise all the plaintiff's allegations, and the contentions to be made at trial, so that the defendant will be able to prepare a case in answer. It must be both comprehensive and accurate. In particular:

(1) The plaintiff's date of birth (or age) must be stated.

(2) Interest must be specifically claimed.

(3) Any conviction recorded against the defendant, and upon which the plaintiff intends to rely, must be specifically pleaded with the date and court particularised. If the defendant pleaded guilty then this should also be pleaded. This is especially important in road accident cases, for a conviction or guilty plea to a careless driving charge will often put the defendant in considerable difficulties.

(4) Any breach of statutory duty must be specifically pleaded. Refer to the relevant section of the statute.

(5) Medical complaints should be comprehensively pleaded, for this will give the judge an initial impression of the claim's value. Apart from the medical description of the injuries, include the ways in which they affect the plaintiff (eg embarrassment caused by facial scar; inability to pursue favourite hobbies and sports).

(6) There is no need to claim costs.

Since the Particulars or Statement of Claim will be the first document read by the judge, it is essential that it is accurate. Any errors may colour the judge's attitude to the plaintiff's credibility. In addition, the judge is more likely to be sympathetic to an allegation that has been made by the plaintiff from the start of his case, rather than one that has been inserted later as an amendment.

The 'Instructions to Counsel to settle the Particulars or Statement of Claim' should be typed out in the usual way. Many solicitors still prefer to use brief paper, although no barrister is likely to object if A4 is used instead. All relevant papers should be included, but do not send everything to counsel: save counsel's time by weeding out the unnecessary documents. The client's accident questionnaire, any useful letters from the client, the witness statements, police report, medical report(s), expert report and relevant party and party correspondence and your special damage calculations should all be forwarded to counsel, together with a copy of the proceedings, if they have already been issued. Include a copy of any legal aid certificate. Do not send the originals of important papers. The instructions themselves will not need to be lengthy, and it will rarely be necessary to discuss the details of the case since those should be clear from the papers.

Counsel's fee shall be on an agreed scale (currently up to £47 in the county court) although there is discretion to exceed these figures. Obviously, if the case is legally aided, then no fee is marked on the instructions; instead the words 'legal aid' are written on the backsheet.

The choice of counsel is important, as the strength of a pleading may well affect the outcome of the case and induce the defendant's solicitors to settle what is in fact a weak case. Ensure that counsel is experienced in personal injury work since the conduct of the case may well depend on counsel's advice. If colleagues cannot suggest a suitable name then consult the Law Reports and see which junior counsel, from which chambers, are reported.

When the draft Particulars of Claim is received from counsel, it should be checked, first, for inaccuracies, such as incorrect dates or motor vehicle registration numbers, and secondly, to ensure that all the necessary allegations (including statutory ones) have been made.

Medical reports: Ensure that your medical report substantiates all the personal injuries alleged in the Particulars of Claim. If it does not, check with counsel as to whether the allegation should be deleted or another medical report obtained (for instance a psychiatrist's report to support allegations of memory loss in addition to the orthopaedic report).

Special damage: If counsel has not done so, the particulars of special damage should be inserted (see Chapter 5), but they should be widely drafted. Any continuing loss of wages should be given, and losses and expenses should be summarised; it is better to include doubtful items at this stage as they can always be deleted later.

Do not expect counsel to send an advice or opinion with the draft Statement of Claim. It would be most unusual to do so, unless this was specifically requested by the instructing solicitor. If there is a particular point that counsel wants to mention it will usually be put in a covering note.

Once the plaintiff's solicitor has received counsel's draft Particulars or Statement of Claim, you should read it through carefully. Having done that, you should send it to the client for checking. While you should have all the information the client may well be reassured by seeing the document and if the case is complicated the client should be asked to check the detailed allegations.

The draft Particulars or Statement of Claim is then ready for typing on A4 paper. These days, typing on one side of the paper only (because of word processors) is acceptable. Otherwise, there should be no unnecessary blank sides, and the typing should be immaculate. If your software is compatible with counsel's you may be able to simply amend counsel's draft on your word processor. Out of respect for the court, make sure that it is neat, easy to read, and unmarked.

Medical report

A medical report, substantiating all the personal injuries alleged in the Particulars of Claim which the plaintiff proposes to adduce in evidence as part of the case at trial, must be filed with the Particulars of Claim when issuing the proceedings in the county court [Ord 6 r 1] and, in the High Court must be served with the Statement of Claim [RSC Ord 18 r 12(1) A]. It is therefore extremely important to ensure that the medical reports are full and complete. You may need a further medical report from an expert in another discipline. Although you are entitled later to serve updated medical reports, the reports filed with the Particulars have the status of a quasi-pleading and you will have to obtain leave of the court to amend them or to adduce further medical reports in respect of an injury not stated originally in the Particulars of Claim.

Statement of Special Damage

CCR Ord 6, r 1 states that, similarly, a Statement of Special Damages must be filed with the Particulars of Claim (or in the High Court served with the Statement of Claim [RSC Ord 18 r 12 (1) (A)] giving full particulars of the special damages claimed for expenses and losses already incurred and an estimate of any future expenses and losses (including loss of earnings and pension rights). See Chapter 5 for how to prepare the statement. If you are still awaiting further information at the time you wish to serve the Particulars of Claim you can put in such information as you have and state that 'further Particulars will be delivered after discovery'. However the rules do state that a full statement must be served at this stage and if you are not to be at risk of an aggressive defendant applying to strike out the matter for failure to serve a full Statement of Special Damage you should in these circumstances apply to the court for leave to serve the Statement later.

3 Issuing proceedings in the county court

In the county court you can prepare a Default Summons in form N1 and deliver it to the court with the requisite copies for the court to issue or you can issue a Request for Issue of Default Summons in form N201 for the court to issue the summons. There is really nothing to choose between the two methods and the information to put on the forms is very similar. Although it is probably slightly quicker to use the form N1 procedure most solicitors probably still use form N201. A completed copy of each form is shown in Appendix H. The forms are very simple. The only parts of them likely to cause problems are the following:

Question 4 — 'What the Claim is For': There is no need for a lengthy reply. All that is usually needed is the words 'Personal Injury'.

Question 5 — You do not now need to state where the claim arose because you may now start county court proceedings in any court. However if the defendant puts in a defence in a liquidated claim the case will automatically be transferred to the defendant's home court. In an unliquidated claim, such as most personal injury claims, the defendant can apply for a transfer to its home court but this may well be refused as courts take the view in personal injury actions that it is the plaintiff's solicitor who does all the work and the most convenient court will usually be that closest to that solicitor's office, although the matter might be transferred to another for trial. Some county courts have a habit of wrongly automatically transferring both liquidated and unliquidated claims on receiving a defence. If this happens you should immediately apply by letter for a transfer back.

Paragraph 7 — Solicitors' costs: Either write 'to be taxed' or put in the fixed costs on issuing a summons.

Arbitration Do not forget to delete the request for the case to be referred to arbitration (the last sentence of the form).

Address for service If the proceedings are to be served on solicitors then write a covering letter to this effect and add a note in the space on Section 6 on the form. Similarly, if you wish to have the summons returned to you for service make this absolutely clear by way of a covering letter.

The proceedings can then be issued. Refer to Procedural Table 18 for how to do this. In essence you will need to send to the court the following: Form N201, Particulars of Claim; medical report and a Schedule of Special Damage, court fee, notice of issue of legal aid certificate if appropriate.

If the medical report, Schedule of Special Damage or Particulars of Claim are not ready but you need to issue proceedings urgently, for instance because a limitation period is approaching, then make an application to the court for extra time in which to serve them.

Although there is no formal procedure in the court for what used to be called 'protective proceedings' (that is proceedings issued before service of the Particulars of Claim) some courts will consider informal arrangements whereby proceedings are issued but service is delayed pending the filing of the missing documents. You must ask your local court whether there are any such arrangements in force. If there are none you may have to make an application to the court under Ord 6 r 1(vi) asking for a further period of time in which to provide them or an order dispensing with the need for service.

If the case is urgent make sure that you take the documents to the court personally for issue as there are usually long delays in county court issue of proceedings. Obviously it is easier if you can delay issue of proceedings until such time as you have all the relevant documents.

Legal aid cases In legal aid cases there is another document that must be served. This is the Notice of Issue of Legal Aid Certificate. Failure to give notice will not invalidate service of the proceedings but it is a requirement of the Legal Aid Regulations that notice be given to the defendant that the plaintiff is legally aided. A failure to give notice could result in the plaintiff's solicitor being penalised as to costs. A specimen notice is printed in Appendix E. The notice should be completed with details of the plaintiff's certificate. Whilst the scope of the certificate must be stated, there is no need for limitations on it to be set out (unless the certificate relates to an appeal). Thus, the plaintiff need not disclose weaknesses (eg that the certificate is limited to the close of pleadings and then the taking of counsel's advice). In practice many plaintiff's solicitors overlook this and recite the limitations in the Notice.

Notifying the other side: There is no requirement that a defendant be told that proceedings have been issued but in road accident cases it is vital that the plaintiff notifies the other side that the proceedings have been issued within seven days whether in the High Court or the county court.

If the defendants are insured, the RTA 1988, s 151 requires that the defendant's insurers (or their solicitors) be notified within seven days. Use Stock Letter 28. In fact notice can be given before proceedings are commenced. So, in practice, the best course of action is to write to the insurers giving notice before the proceedings are issued. If the defendants are uninsured and the plaintiff's claim includes a personal injury element, then it is likely the MIB will meet any unpaid judgment. The 1988 MIB Agreement requires that they be notified of the issuing of the proceedings within seven days (see Chapter 19, section 1). Use Stock Letter 33. As with notification to insurers, notice can be given before the proceedings are issued. So once again, if in doubt give notice before the proceedings are issued.

This seven day notification requirement only applies to road accident cases. If notification is not given, the action can still proceed against the defendant. But the insurers of the MIB can then refuse to meet any judgment. In practice the MIB (and to a lesser extent, insurers) take a strict line. It is very easy to overlook the seven day period and it is a mistake that is commonly made. If this happens, and the MIB or insurers take the point, the only remedy is to issue new proceedings and then given them notice within the seven day period. Obviously this cannot be done if the three year limitation period has expired; if it has then a negligence claim against you is likely.

Renewing the proceedings: The proceedings are only valid for four months (six months if the defendant is outside the jurisdiction); they must be served within that time. But the plaintiff can apply *ex parte* for that period to be extended. This is called renewing the proceedings. See Precedent 2, for the steps to be taken.

The courts adopt a strict approach to applications for renewal. A good or sufficient reason must be shown, which, in practice, is limited to cases in which there are difficulties in serving the defendant. The mere fact that the plaintiff needs further time to collect evidence is not sufficient. In any event, if the court does renew the proceedings, bear in mind that this will have been done *ex parte,* without the defendant having been notified. That being so, the defendant is allowed to challenge the extension of the proceedings when served. It follows that it is always better to serve the proceedings within the four month period and not apply for an extension, unless there is no alternative.

4 Serving proceedings

A court will issue the proceedings and will send you a plaint note. They will normally serve the proceedings direct by post and will inform you of the date of service on the defendant. You should diary 14 days from the date of presumed service for service of the defence.

However the plaintiff's solicitor may request that the documents are returned for service, in which case they *must* be served within four months of issue (together of course with a copy of the medical report and the Schedule of Special Damage and any Legal Aid Notice of Issue of Certificate). The following rules apply regarding service in both the High Court and the county court:

(i) Service on an individual: service can be personal or by post.
(a) Personal service: the correct procedure is to approach the defendant personally, and serve or leave the proceedings with him/her.
(b) Postal service: the sealed proceedings are sent to the defendant's last known address by first class post (*not* second class, registered or recorded delivery). It must be first class post. The date of service will be deemed to be eight days after posting (ie seven days starting from the day after posting, inclusive of weekends and bank holidays). However, the defendant may be able to show that they did not receive the proceedings within that period, and, in particular, if the proceedings are returned undelivered by the post office then the service will not have taken place. As an alternative to posting, the proceedings can personally be placed through the defendant's letter box, in which case the same rules apply as if they were posted. Obviously, it is possible for disputes to arise as to service of proceedings delivered by post. It is therefore unwise to use the postal service when a limitation period is about to expire. In such cases, arrange for a process server to effect personal service, or try to get the defendant's insurers to agree to accept service (see below). In an MIB case remember to notify the MIB within seven days after service (see Chapter 19 and Appendix G).

(ii) Service on a limited company: service is by posting the sealed proceedings to the registered office of the company. Use Stock Letter 19. If first class post is used, then service is presumed to take effect on the second working day after posting; with second class mail, it is the fourth working day after posting (the Companies Act overrides the normal rules on postal service). Working days are Monday to Friday (excluding bank holidays). As an alternative, the proceedings can be left at the registered office.

(iii) Service on a firm (eg partnership): service is by personal service on any one partner, or by postal service (must be first class post) to the principal place of business. Service cannot be effected by putting the proceedings through the letter box.

(iv) Service on the defendant's solicitors: often the defendant's insurers will nominate solicitors to accept service on behalf of the defendant. This simplifies the procedure from everyone's point of view, so it is always worth while the plaintiff asking the insurers to nominate solicitors for acceptance of service. In this case, use Stock Letter 30 to serve the proceedings on the defendant's solicitor.

(v) Substituted service: If the plaintiff is having difficulties in serving the defendant, you can apply for the duration of the proceedings to be extended (see above). But a better alternative is to apply for substituted service on the defendant's insurers, or the MIB. These requirements are set out in CCR Ord 7 r 8 [High Court Ord 65 r 4]. This can be particularly useful in motoring cases. If a defendant gave a correct name and address, and then vanished, the MIB can be ordered to accept substituted service. On the other hand, if s/he gave a false name and address, then substituted service cannot be ordered.

Fax and document exchange: You cannot serve proceedings by either fax or DX (document exchange). However, it is possible to serve other papers by DX and if the other side put their DX number on the writ or Acknowledgment of Service then they are deemed to accept service of other documents in the proceedings by DX (service deemed on second business day). It should be noted that you cannot assume the other side will accept DX service merely because a DX number appears on their note paper. Other documents can be served by fax if a follow up copy is sent by post.

5 Issuing the writ—High Court

The High Court procedure is a little more complicated as the writ and Statement of Claim are usually served separately.

It is easy to issue a writ. All that is needed is a blank writ (ie Form Al, ordinary writ, unliquidated demand) together with a suitable writ indorsement (precedents are printed in Appendix C). A specimen completed writ is shown in Appendix F.

Complete the blank writ form as follows:

- insert the year;
- insert the plaintiff's full name;
- insert the defendant's full name. If there is more than one defendant, then list them, and describe them as first defendant, second defendant, etc;
- insert the defendant's name and address;
- at the foot of the first page, delete either Central Office, or District Registry (ie whichever one the writ is not going to be issued from);
- on the reverse side of the writ, type out the general indorsement. If you are using a writ form that is also valid for a liquidated claim then it is likely to have the words 'Statement of Claim' across

the top of the reverse side. Simply strike those words through, since you will be setting out a general indorsement, not a full Statement of Claim;

- add the indorsement to state that the claim is worth more than £50,000 and can therefore be started in the High Court (see below);
- at the foot of the reverse side is an indorsement stating that the cause of action arose within the jurisdiction of the District Registry. If that is not the case (and it certainly will not be if you are issuing in the RCJ) then delete that sentence;
- finally, the name and address of the solicitor issuing the writ has to be inserted, together with the address of the plaintiff.

The general indorsement: this goes on the reverse side of the writ, after the words 'the plaintiff's claim is for'. The indorsement is of a general nature, and gives a concise statement of the nature of the claim, and the remedy sought (ie damages and interest), so the defendant knows why he is being sued. It is not, for instance, sufficient to say the plaintiff's claim is for damages for personal injury'. It must be more specific than that.

Whilst it is counsel that settles the Statement of Claim, it is the solicitor who writes out the general indorsement. Alternatively, the solicitor can ask counsel to settle the indorsement, but it would be unusual to do this. In any event, counsel's fee for settling the writ indorsement would almost certainly not be allowed on taxation.

Refer to Precedent 1 for specimen writ indorsements covering all the common cases (ie road accidents; factory accidents; fatal cases; infant claims; medical negligence cases). Bear in mind that the plaintiff cannot introduce a fresh claim into the Statement of Claim, so it is important to ensure that the indorsement is widely drawn. That being so, it is best to follow the specimens given, which have been drafted as widely as possible. Note that interest is specifically claimed. The writ must also include an indorsement that the case may be started in the High Court because it is worth more than £50,000. Refer to Precedent 1 for this indorsement.

District Registry cases: on the foot of the reverse side of the writ is a statement to the effect that the cause of action arose within the particular District Registry. Obviously, if the claim did not arise within that DR, then that statement will have to be struck out. Certainly, it will have to be struck out in any RCJ case. If the indorsement remains intact, then the action will normally stay in that DR unless the defendant can show that the indorsement is incorrect. On the other hand, if the indorsement is struck out the action will stay in that DR unless the defendant completes the Acknowledgment of Service to the effect that it wants the action transferred to another DR (or to the CO). If the defendant requests this, then the action will be transferred unless the plaintiff notifies the DR of an objection within eight days of receiving the Acknowledgment of Service. (No form for this objection: apply by letter.) If this happens, an appointment will be fixed at the DR, and the parties will attend to argue as to which is the more suitable and convenient location. However, the defendant cannot ask for it to be transferred to another DR if the plaintiff has indorsed the writ (see above), or if the defendant resides, carries on business, or has its registered office, in that district.

If the defendant wants to have a CO case transferred to a DR, then a different procedure applies. There is no provision for such a request in the Acknowledgment of Service form, and instead the defendant should apply to the court by letter.

Remember that there is no need to have a case transferred to a different location just because it would be more convenient for the trial. The case can continue in the DR, but an order can later be obtained that the trial be at a more convenient location.

Issuing the writ: the writ is usually issued through the post. It can, however, be issued personally. Note that postal issuing of a writ is at the risk of the solicitor. Accordingly, do not use the post if the limitation period is about to expire; instead, arrange personal issuing of the writ. Steps to be taken for issuing a writ (either by post, or in person) are set out in Procedural Table 9. If the plaintiff is legally aided, do not forget to file a copy of the legal aid certificate, when issuing the writ.

The writ can be issued in London (RCJ) or in any DR; there is no requirement that the action must be in the locality where the defendant lives or the cause of action arose. As mentioned above, the writ should be issued in the court that is most convenient to the plaintiff's solicitor; if necessary, the actual trial of the case can be held elsewhere at a venue that is convenient to the parties and witnesses.

When the writ is issued: on receipt of the issued writ, diary it for four months. If it is not served within four months of the date of issue, then it will lose its validity. If that happened, fresh proceedings would have to be issued (but this could not be done if the three year limitation period had already expired). It is possible to apply for the four month period to be extended (see p 61 above).

Amendment A writ can be amended in any way, provided it has not been served. In addition, after service, it can be amended once provided the pleadings have not closed. Any other amendment needs the court's consent. See Chapter 10, section 6 for details.

6 Serving the writ

The issued writ (ie the original, which is kept by the plaintiff, and the sealed copy which will be served on the defendant) can now be served. Alternatively, it can be put to one side whilst the Statement of Claim is prepared, so that both documents can be served together. Generally, it is best to press on with the case and serve the writ as soon as it has been issued; in practice, it does not matter if the Statement of Claim is served late. In addition, interest on general damages (small though it may be: a mere 2 per cent) only runs from the date the writ is served (not issued), so delay in service should be avoided.

When the defendant is served with the writ, it will be served with the copy writ sealed by the court; the plaintiff retains the original writ (ie the copy with 'original' stamped in red capital letters in the left margin). In addition, the defendant will have to be given an Acknowledgment of Service form. A specimen is printed in Appendix G. All the plaintiff needs to do is complete the details of the action (ie division; action number; names of the parties) at the top of the front page. In addition, the name and address of the plaintiff's solicitor is put in the box at the top of page 2. The rest of the form is left blank, for completion by the defendant. The Acknowledgment of Service form does not have to be stamped by the court when the writ was being issued. The plaintiff's solicitor simply prepares it in the office and attaches it to the copy writ, when serving the writ. The rules on serving a writ are the same as those on serving proceedings in the county court, see section 4 above.

7 The Acknowledgment of Service

Whenever a defendant is served with a writ, it must be accompanied by a completed Acknowledgment of Service form (see above). The defendant then has 14 days in which to file the Acknowledgment of Service with the court. In default, the plaintiff can apply for judgment under Ord 13.

The Acknowledgment form includes a Notice of Intention to Defend. Thus, the defendant should complete the Acknowledgment of Service form, by stating in it an intention to defend the action. If it either fails to return the form, or fails to give Notice of Intention to Defend, then the plaintiff can apply for judgment under Ord 13.

All that is required of the defendant is to return the duplicate form to the court office; the court will then date stamp it, enter details in the cause book, and sent a stamped photocopy to the plaintiff. No copy is sent to the defendant. See Appendix G for a specimen Acknowledgment form.

By filing an Acknowledgment of Service, the defendant is not taken to accept any irregularities in the writ (eg if it was served out of time). In such a case, the defendant should return the Acknowledgment form in the usual way, and then issue a summons under Ord 12, r 8 for the writ (and/or service) to be set aside. This summons should be issued within 14 days (unless extra time is applied for, and granted). See above.

If the defendant does not file Acknowledgment of Service within 14 days (or if it files it, but fails to include the Notice of Intention to Defend) the plaintiff can apply for judgment. In practice, it is rare to do this if it is clear that the defendant does intend to defend. However, if the plaintiff does wish to enter judgment, you should wait a few days (to allow for postal delays) and then apply for judgment in default under Ord 13, r 2. The procedural requirements and precedents are set out in Precedent 3. Judgment will be given automatically, although at this stage it will be for interlocutory judgment with damages to be assessed; final judgment will be given once the damages have been assessed.

When the plaintiff receives the Acknowledgment of Service, you should read it carefully to check that notice of intention to defend has been given. Then, you should diary 14 days. That is the time, according to the rules, within which you should serve the Statement of Claim together with the medical report and Statement of Special Damages claim (Ord 18, r 12 1A). In practice, you may well have served the Statement of Claim with the writ, in which case you should diary 28 days from service for receipt of Defence.

Transfer to another DR: when the defendant completes the Acknowledgment form in a DR case, it should consider whether it wants the case transferred to a different DR (or, indeed, to the RCJ). See p 65 for the rules on this; the defendant completes paragraph 4 of the Acknowledgment form if it wants the case transferred.

8 Form and layout of pleadings

The layout of all pleadings is the same whether claim or defence, High Court or county court. The heading and statement of parties will be as on the writ or summons, and will, of course, include the action number. After the parties' names, the nature of the pleading is stated (eg Statement of Claim), and this will be followed by the pleading itself. The pleading will be set out in neat numbered paragraphs; there will be separate headings for breaches of statutory duty, particulars of personal injury, and particulars of special damage. In the case of a Particulars or Statement of Claim, it will finish with the phrase 'AND the Plaintiff claims DAMAGES' followed by the name of the counsel. Note that this is an unliquidated claim, and no figure is put on the general damages.

After counsel's name, type in 'SERVED this day of 19 by *(name and address of solicitor).* Solicitor for Plaintiff'. Refer to the specimen Particulars of Claim in Appendix G for how the document should look.

The backsheet will summarise the document, stating the court, action number, parties, nature of the pleading, name and address (plus reference and phone number) of the plaintiff's solicitor.

These rules apply for all pleadings. In addition, *any* pleading should include:

(1) year, letter, and number of action;
(2) title of action;
(3) the court and the division of the court;
(4) a description of the pleading;

(5) its date of service (if served by post, the date will be the next working day after posting);

(6) the name and address of the solicitor.

Further, the pleading must:

(7) contain the signature of solicitor (or counsel);

(8) be on A4 paper, with pages bound in green tape;

(9) be divided into numbered, consecutive paragraphs;

(10) show dates, sums and numbers in figures, not words;

(11) if a Particulars of Claim, state the date on which the proceedings were issued and the date of birth of the plaintiff (or his/her age). There should also be a claim for interest.

9 Time

A reminder of how time is calculated in the courts:

- If time runs out on a day on which the court office is closed, then time is extended to the next day on which the office is open (eg if time runs out on Sunday, then it is treated as running out on Monday). This applies in both the High Court and the county court.
- In computing a time period of seven days or less in the High Court, do not count Saturdays, Sundays, Bank Holidays, Christmas Day or Good Friday. For instance, a summons requiring two clear days' service, and which is due to be heard on Wednesday, must be served on or before the preceding Friday. In the county court, this rule only applies when computing a time period of three days or less (not seven days or less).

Chapter 7

The Defence

The defence must be served (that is, sent to the plaintiff's solicitors, and the court in a county court case) within 14 days of the Particulars of Claim being served, (or, in the High Court, within 14 days of the Statement of Claim being served, or within 28 days of the service of the writ, whichever is later (Ord 18, r 2)). This time period should be diarised.

Usually, the defence will not be served within the requisite time period. In fact, it will often be an impossibility for the defendant to do the necessary research, interviewing of witnesses, instructions to counsel, etc in such a short time. Plaintiff's solicitors are expected to grant at least two extensions of time; usually each extension is for a further 14 days. The plaintiff's solicitor should not allow too many extensions of time and the last extension should be stated to be 'final'. Thereafter the defendant will need to apply to the court for further time (use Precedent 5) should they want a further extension.

The defendant will probably welcome any delay in the progress of the action. Thus the plaintiff should not be reluctant to enforce the appropriate time periods throughout the case and require the defendant to issue a time application to gain further extensions and insist that they apply *ex parte* for a stay pending the hearing of the application if the time for defence will run out before the hearing date.

If no defence is filed within the appropriate time the plaintiff can apply for judgment in default with damages to be assessed (CCR Ord 9, r 6; RSC Ord 19, r 3). The procedural requirements and precedents are set out in Precedent 3. Judgment will be given automatically although at this stage it will be for interlocutory judgment with damages to be assessed. Final judgment will be given when the damages have been assessed.

In practice, however, if it is relatively clear that the defendant does intend to defend but has simply missed the time limit you would not normally enter judgment in default as a tactical move since the defendant can apply for judgment to be set aside and if some reasonable excuse can be found and if there is an arguable defence then it is almost certain that the application will succeed. Accordingly there is little point in the plaintiff seeking a default judgment when the previous correspondence shows that the defendant intends to defend as it only leads to delay. However the plaintiff will almost certainly be awarded all costs thrown away and entering judgment will show that the plaintiff intends to prosecute the case vigorously, so it might be worth considering if the defendant has failed to ask for an extension of time to serve the defence and you feel that it is not taking the claim seriously.

1 Form of the defence

In appearance, the defence will look much like the Particulars or Statement of Claim, in that it will be a typewritten document, set out in numbered paragraphs and complying with the pleading requirements set out in Chapter 6, section 9. See the specimen defence in Appendix G.

The defence may contain a simple denial of the claim, make admissions, contain allegations against the plaintiff, or raise points of law. Frequently, it will contain inconsistent defences pleaded in the alternative so as to give the defendant room to manoeuvre at trial. Thus, for example, the defence may commence by denying that the accident ever happened, but then in a later paragraph go on to allege that, if the accident did happen, it was the plaintiff's own fault (see specimen in Appendix G). It will often conclude with some such phrase as 'save as hereinbefore specifically admitted the defendant denies each and every allegation contained in the Statement of Claim as though the same were herein set out and traversed seriatim'; this is because in the High Court (though not in the county court) the defendant is deemed to admit anything in the Statement of Claim that is not specifically denied. Strictly, a blanket denial of all the plaintiff's allegations is not correct pleading, but in practice it will not be struck out.

Diary dates: when you receive the defence, you should diary:

(1) *14 days*—for the close of pleadings (after which date, a party can only amend a pleading or writ with the consent of the court);

(2) *42 days (28 days in the High Court)*—for discovery. Discovery should be completed 28 days after the close of pleadings, which generally means it should be completed 42 days after service of the defence (14 days less in the High Court);

(3) *12 weeks*—for exchange of experts' reports and defendant's medical report. The normal rule is that reports must be exchanged (if they are to be used at the trial) within ten weeks of the close of pleadings. In effect, this is likely to be 12 weeks from service of the defence. See Chapter 9, section 6;

(4) *28 weeks*—setting down for trial. The case is supposed to be set down for trial within six months of the close of pleadings. In practice, this rarely happens. See Chapter 12, section 4.

(5) *9 months*—from close of pleadings. A county court case will automatically be struck out if not set down by this date.

Unfortunately, few solicitors diary all these time periods. This is because there is no automatic sanction if they are not observed except for the automatic striking out in (5). In practice, the main requirement is to make sure the case does not now go to sleep. Even if all the above periods are not diarised, it is essential to diary it for (say) three months when the file can be reviewed generally.

2 Responding to the defence

The plaintiff should read the defence carefully; see what admissions are made (for example, time, place, parties to accident) and what are the real issues in dispute. It is often advisable to write to the client setting out the defence in the form of a questionnaire with space for comments.

Check that the defence does actually disclose a triable defence and that it is not just quantum that is in dispute. If that is so, then the plaintiff could apply, by summons, for interlocutory judgment with damages to be assessed under CCR Ord 9 r 14, or Ord 14. Use Precedent 4. For assessment of the damages use Procedural Table 7.

In theory, summary judgment could apply when the defendant does not admit liability, but his defence does not show a triable defence. In practice, however, it is usually difficult for the plaintiff to show that it is *impossible* for there to be a *bona fide* defence to the claim, and so Ord 9, r 14 is rarely applicable. Whether or not the defence admits liability, the plaintiff should consider applying for an interim payment. See Chapter 8, section 2.

The plaintiff's solicitor will also have to decide how to respond to the defence. It may well be that there are essential steps that you should now take, and also other steps, which whilst not essential, are advisable. So, you should check for:

(*a*) allegations of *contributory negligence* against the plaintiff (see below);
(*b*) allegations against a *third person* (see below);
(*c*) a *counterclaim* against the plaintiff (see below).

In any event, the defence may be unsatisfactorily pleaded, and thus allow the plaintiff to:

(*d*) request *Further and Better Particulars* of the defence (see Chapter 11, section 2);
(*e*) put questions to the defendant by way of written *interrogatories* (see Chapter 11, section 5);
(*f*) serve a *Notice to Admit Facts* on the defendant (see Chapter 11, section 3).

At this stage, the plaintiff must consider whether items (*a*) to (*c*) are raised; if so, you must deal with them immediately. In that case, the tactical matters (ie (*d*) to (*f*)) can be put aside for the moment. On the other hand, it may be that the defence raises none of these issues, in which case the next stage in the action will be discovery of documents (see Chapter 10, section 1).

(a) Contributory negligence

Frequently, a defendant will deny liability for the accident and conclude the defence by stating that 'the plaintiff's alleged accident was solely caused or alternatively contributed to by his/her own negligence in that s/he . . .', followed by a list of allegations setting out the various ways in which the plaintiff could have been to blame for the accident.

The defendant's objective is to obtain a percentage finding of contributory negligence against the plaintiff which will proportionately reduce the damages, or at least give the defendant something to argue about when negotiating a settlement with the plaintiff's solicitor. Any such allegation must be specifically pleaded otherwise it cannot be raised at trial (unlike, for example, a defence of inevitable accident) unless the trial judge gives leave to amend.

Remember, contributory negligence is not concerned with whether the plaintiff is partly responsible for the *cause* of the damage, but whether the plaintiff is partly responsible for the damage. For instance, failure to wear a seat belt can be contributory negligence if it contributed to the damage: even though it did not contribute to the *cause* of the damage. At the present time, up to 25 per cent seems to be the going rate for failure to wear a front seat belt, assuming that the defendant can show that the wearing of a seat belt would have avoided or reduced the plaintiff's injuries. If there is to be argument about the level of contributory negligence through failure to wear a seat belt, then remember that expert evidence will be necessary. Often this will be given by an expert medical witness, but an expert motor engineer might be more able to speak as to the injuries that would have been suffered had a seat belt been worn.

Contributory negligence can apply even where there is a strict duty created by statute. For example, in a case where the plaintiff alleges a breach of Factories Act 1961, s 14 (duty to fence machinery), the defendant might argue that the plaintiff 'failed to watch where s/he was putting his/her fingers, failed to keep the hand clear of the alleged moving part, was inattentive or otherwise exercised insufficient care for his/her own well-being'. (While this is presently a strict liability offence, after 1992 the duty to fence is likely to be subject to a reasonableness test under legislation to be brought in to comply with the European Use of Work Equipment Directive.)

Always put allegations of contributory negligence to the client. This is best done by incorporating the allegations (in easily understandable language) into a questionnaire for the client to complete. Type out the questionnaire, giving the client ample room in which to write answers. Put a space to sign and date the questionnaire, at the foot of each page (this could be useful if the client were to die before trial, and the document was to be put under the Civil Evidence Act). Having the client complete a questionnaire in this way will simplify the preparation of your instructions to counsel to advise, etc. It is also worth considering whether the allegations of contributory negligence should be put to any witnesses. If so, prepare similar questionnaires for them.

Do not forget to explain to the client how a finding of contributory negligence will reduce damages (if any).

Reply: there is no need to serve a pleading in response to the allegations of contributory negligence. This is because a plaintiff is assumed to deny allegations of contributory negligence. Only if the plaintiff wishes to raise fresh matters, or a point of law, will you need to serve a 'reply'. If you do serve a reply, then it should deny all the allegations. A reply will very rarely be necessary, but if one is served then the dates for close of pleadings becomes 14 days after its service (not 14 days after the service of the defence, as is usual). Do not serve a reply unless it is essential; if one is put in just for general denial of the contributory negligence allegations, it will not be allowed on taxation. In short, it is extremely unusual for a reply to be necessary in a personal injury claim.

Further and Better Particulars: allegations of contributory negligence are often made without justification, and are no more than a bargaining counter for the defendant in the negotiations. Weak allegations should be attacked by a request for Further and Better Particulars; if the allegations of contributory negligence can be exposed as being without foundation, the trial judge may possibly view the rest of the defence with scepticism. So, if contributory negligence is alleged, then consider sending the papers to counsel at an earlier date than one might otherwise have done, to ask whether a request for Further and Better Particulars of the defence should be made. See Chapter 11, section 2, for Further and Better Particulars. Exceptionally, interrogatories may be appropriate (see Chapter 11, section 5).

(b) Allegations against third persons

In the defence, the defendant may blame someone who is not a party to the proceedings. When this happens, the plaintiff's solicitor should immediately put any such suggestion to your client for comments and instructions. The solicitor then has to decide whether to sue that third party.

The alternatives open to the plaintiff are:

(1) *Ignore the allegation* and proceed to trial against the present defendant, on the assumption that should the trial evidence indicate some liability on the part of the third party, a fresh action can then be commenced against that third person. Do not forget that a plaintiff can opt to sue either or both of joint-tortfeasors. So if the present defendant were found only a few per cent liable, and the third party liable for the rest, the plaintiff could recover 100 per cent damages from the present defendant and leave it to the defendant to sue the third

person to try to recover that proportion of the damages (Civil Liability (Contribution) Act 1978). However, this is not a satisfactory course of action since the costs of the first action may well be lost and unnecessary delay incurred. More significantly, there is the risk of missing the three year limitation period. However, if the service of the defence is the first occasion on which the plaintiff has had grounds for considering that third person liable it may be possible to argue that the three years run from the date of the defence and not from the date of the accident (see Limitation Act 1980 and Chapter 17, section 1).

(2) *Sue the third person.* There are two ways of doing this:

(*a*) *issue separate proceedings* against the third person, so that there will then be two separate actions proceeding in respect of the one accident. The two actions can later be consolidated (see Precedent No 16) and then proceed together, as one action, to one trial;

(*b*) *join* the third person as an additional defendant in the present action. To do this the proceedings or High Court writ and Statement of Claim will both have to be amended and re-served on the present defendant. Amendment of pleadings is explained in Chapter 10, section 6.

In practice, it is usually option 2(*b*) (ie join the third person as a defendant in the action) that is followed. However, whichever option is adopted, it is vital that the expiry of the three year limitation period against the third person is diarised. It is important to do this, in case it should expire whilst the client's instructions are being taken (or whilst legal aid authority is being obtained).

If the third person allegation put forward by the defendant seems to be unfounded, the plaintiff's solicitor may well be reluctant to incur the delay and expense of suing this new defendant. However, the plaintiff's interests must be protected, for the evidence available to the defendant is not known and thus the allegation must be taken seriously. It may help to write to the defendant that, in the light of the defence, the plaintiff intends to protect the position by proceeding against the third person unless the defendant withdraws the allegations, and should the third person be held not liable it is the plaintiff's intention to ask that the costs of those proceedings be borne by the defendant in any event (that is, even if the plaintiff loses his case). This may encourage the defendant to drop an unfounded allegation.

Legal aid: if the plaintiff is legally aided, do not forget that it will be necessary to obtain authority before proceeding against the third party. In practice, if the plaintiff's solicitor writes a full letter of explanation to the local office marked 'urgent' you are likely to get a quick response. If the limitation period is about to expire, then point this out; and ask for an emergency decision.

Third Party Proceedings: the defendant can go further than just making such allegations in the defence, by actually commencing 'Third Party

Proceedings' against a third person (CCR Ord 12, r 1, RSC Ord 16, r 1).

Third party proceedings are a claim for an indemnity or contribution should the defendant be held liable to the plaintiff. To start such proceedings the defendant serves a Third Party Notice on the third person, who can then appear and file a defence to the defendant's claim for indemnity or contribution. A copy of the Third Party Notice will be sent to the plaintiff's solicitor, but note that it is the defendant not the plaintiff that is suing the third party, and the third party is not a party to the action *vis-à-vis* the plaintiff. If there is a possibility that the defendant will be held not liable, but that the third party may be liable, then the plaintiff should sue the third party (ie by amending to join that party as an additional defendant, or by issuing separate proceedings and then consolidating the two actions).

A defendant need not issue a Third Party Notice against a co-defendant. This is because the Civil Liability (Contribution) Act 1978 gives the courts a wide discretion to apportion liability and order contribution. Although the Third Party Notice is not needed, the defendant should make it clear to the co-defendant that it intends to rely on the 1978 Act: this can be done by a letter. A formal Third Party Notice would only be needed if it wanted (for instance) discovery, or leave to serve interrogatories against the co-defendant.

(c) Counterclaim

The defendant's pleading may be not merely a defence but a combined 'defence and counterclaim'. The latter part of this pleading will attack the plaintiff by setting up a fresh cause of action against the plaintiff. Thus in respect of this claim the defendant takes over the role of plaintiff, and the original plaintiff will have to act as a defendant by serving a 'defence to counterclaim' within 14 days, or otherwise run the risk of judgment in default of defence being obtained.

The object of allowing the defendant to introduce a claim against the plaintiff is to avoid multiplicity of proceedings: the claim can be of virtually any nature, and need not arise from the original cause of action. It will survive as a cause of action even if the main claim is settled.

In practice, the counterclaim will usually arise out of the same cause of action, and is frequently encountered in road accident cases. It causes little inconvenience to the defendant's solicitors to incorporate a counterclaim in the defence and it may well encourage the plaintiff to compromise. The effects of a counterclaim can be dramatic. For instance, take the case of a road accident claim where the defendant is basically to blame and suffered serious injury. The plaintiff's claim may be worth some £5,000 in personal injury and vehicular damage, whereas the defendant's would be worth, say, £30,000 on full liability. The plaintiff needs to be only 20 per cent to blame for the accident, for the plaintiff's damages to be less than the defendant's, the plaintiff will get £4,000 (ie 80 per cent of £5,000) and the defendant £6,000 (ie 20 per cent of £30,000).

Road accident cases: On receipt of a road accident counterclaim, the plaintiff should:

(1) *notify the insurers* immediately, otherwise they may be entitled to repudiate liability. They should already have been told of the accident and thus should be liable to indemnify the plaintiff in respect of costs and for any damages arising from the counterclaim. However, if the plaintiff is uninsured, then it is best to notify the other side (so they can claim against the MIB) and consider applying for legal aid. Do not forget that an insurance company may have repudiated liability, and yet be obliged to pay any damages, by virtue of their Road Traffic Act liability (RTA 1988, ss 151–153). In a typical case, the plaintiff's solicitors will simply notify the client's insurers of the counterclaim; the solicitor should set out the facts of the case, the prospects of success, and enclose copies of relevant papers (including the pleadings). You should also ask for confirmation that the insurers will indemnify the client, and enquire whether the insurers wish the plaintiff's solicitor also to act on their behalf in relation to the counterclaim. Some insurers are willing to do this; others insist that their own solicitors be instructed.

(2) *diary the 14 day period* for service of the defence to counterclaim. In practice, this is unlikely to be a sufficiently long time period. Accordingly, the plaintiff's solicitor should write to the defendant seeking extension of time, and stating that the client has every intention of disputing the claim. It is usually advisable to state what steps are being taken in response (ie instructions are being sought from the insurers, or an application for legal aid is being made). If a letter in those terms has been written, it is extremely unlikely that the defendant will apply for judgment in default (and if it did, it would almost certainly be set aside). However, if extensions of time are refused, the plaintiff will have to apply to the court for an extension (ie by time summons; see Precedent 4).

(3) *instruct counsel* to settle the defence to counterclaim. Normally this cannot be done until the insurers have agreed to instruct the firm, and indemnify the client (or, until legal aid is received). If counsel also settles a reply, then it should be included in the pleading so that there is just the one 'reply and defence to counterclaim'. Note that if a reply, or defence to counterclaim, is served then the pleadings close 14 days after its service, and not 14 days after service of the defence, which is the usual date. Diary the close of pleadings, and remember that the date for discovery to be completed is 14 days thereafter.

Chapter 8

Payment in, and Interim Payment

1 The payment into court

Despite the fact that liability is disputed, the defendant may pay money into court in satisfaction of the plaintiff's claim. If the plaintiff thinks the amount paid in is sufficient you can withdraw it within 21 days of notification, agree or tax your costs, and proceed no further with the action. If the plaintiff thinks the amount paid in is insufficient you can take the case to trial, but should the plaintiff not recover more from the judge (who will not know about the payment in) then the plaintiff will bear all the costs as from the date of payment in.

The payment in is thus a powerful weapon for the defendant since, even if the defendant is clearly liable, the defendant can put the plaintiff under considerable pressure as to costs by paying in at an early stage of the action. In fact, the defendant need not wait until service of the Defence. The defendant can pay in as soon as proceedings are served. In practice, this is extremely rare; however, when it does happen, it can have an extremely unsettling effect on the plaintiff! A payment in can even be made during the trial. Procedural Table 14 sets out the steps to be taken to effect a payment in, which can either be by post or by personal attendance at the court offices. (For the procedure in the High Court, see Procedural Table 12.) Note that the payment in form must specifically state if the sum paid in takes account of any counterclaim raised by the defendant or any interim payment that has been made to the plaintiff.

On receipt of a notice of payment in, the plaintiff should:

(1) Write to the defendant acknowledging receipt of notice; this must be done within three days (High Court only).

(2) Diary 21 days (from the date you received the notice) being the time for acceptance. If the payment in is accepted within that period the plaintiff can withdraw the money without further ado; unless one of the exceptions, below, applies (for example an infant plaintiff, or where there are several defendants). But after that time the plaintiff who wishes to accept will have to apply to the court for approval.

Because of this 21 day period for acceptance, a payment in will not be effective as to costs unless it is made at least 21 days before trial. Even then once the trial has started the judge may well exercise a discretion as to costs against the defendant.

(3) Consider whether the sum should be accepted by the client. Clearly, this will depend on the facts of the particular case, but if in doubt the papers should be sent to counsel to advise. Ensure that counsel has the full information needed for a valuation, such as up-to-date medical reports, special damage calculations, evidence as to liability: in short, you should send counsel the papers you would send if asking for advice in the normal way (see Chapter 12, section 13). If there have been previous payments in, be sure to enclose the earlier notices so that counsel is aware of the total sum in court. Although you should stress the urgency there may be a slight delay before counsel's advice is obtained. To minimise the risk of the defendant pressing on with the case (and so incurring costs that the plaintiff might eventually have to pay), it is advisable to write to the defendant, without prejudice, explaining that counsel's advice is being sought, and asking that the defendant's solicitor takes no further steps in the meantime and, if necessary, to extend the period in which the payment may be accepted.

(4) The next stage is to notify the client and advise whether the sum paid in should be accepted. Care should be taken when writing to the client, especially if you are advising rejection. The effect of the payment in should be explained, so that if the case should go on to trial, and the client then recovers no more than the amount paid in, there can be no complaint of not having been properly advised. However, it is not sufficient merely to explain the effects of the payment in; the client is entitled to advice from a solicitor and should be given a recommendation on whether or not to accept. If necessary, make an appointment for the client to come in and discuss it; be sure to write to the client after the meeting, repeating the warnings and advice. Stock Letters 34 and 35 can be used as the basis of the letter of recommendation advising the client to accept or reject.

If the plaintiff is legally aided, you may mistakenly think that a payment in will not be effective (ie on the basis that his costs are borne by the Legal Aid Fund). This is not so. If the plaintiff proceeds to trial, and recovers damages, but less than the payment in, then those damages can be used to pay the costs, and, of course, the statutory charge will apply. So, a legally aided plaintiff should be fully advised as to the risks of not accepting a payment in. One additional point to remember, in a legal aid case, is that some certificates specifically say that the local office is to be notified if any payment in is not accepted.

(a) Acceptance within 21 days

If the plaintiff decides to accept the payment in before the period for acceptance expires, you should notify the other side. In the county court send the court a copy of the notice of acceptance and they will arrange for payment out of the funds in court. In the High Court you will have to write to the Court Funds Office so that Her Majesty's Paymaster General will pay the money out. You can then have your costs taxed by the taxing officer without further order (if they cannot be agreed). The effect of accepting the payment in will be to stay the action.

The steps to be taken on accepting a payment in within the 21 day period are set out in Procedural Table 8(*a*). But, there are two occasions when this procedure will not apply, and when it will be necessary to apply to the court:

(1) *infant:* if the plaintiff is a minor (or a Mental Health Act patient), then the court must approve the acceptance and to make directions as to the way the money is to be applied. Thus, an application or a summons must be issued (see Chapter 14 and Precedent 21(*b*));

(2) *fatal:* in a fatal case, the payment in will not apportion the money between Law Reform Act or Fatal Accident Act claims, nor between the various dependants. Thus, an application will need to be issued for the court to make the apportionment. See Chapter 15.

If there was more than one defendant, then complications can arise.

Before filing the Notice of Acceptance, it is probably worth trying to agree costs with the defendant's solicitor. If costs cannot be agreed, then they will have to be taxed.

(b) Acceptance out of time

If the plaintiff should for some reason decide to accept the payment in after the 21 day period has expired, you will need to apply to the court for consent. Normally, this will be given without difficulty. But, occasionally, the defendant might object (eg if the plaintiff's medical condition has improved dramatically, or if the case is now much weaker on liability, in which case it might be unfair on the defendant if the plaintiff were able to accept the payment in). If the trial of the action has begun when the plaintiff decides to accept (for example, if the trial is not going as well as anticipated), the money can only be withdrawn with the consent of the judge and the defendant; even if that consent is forthcoming the plaintiff will, of course, be liable for the costs arising as from the date of payment in.

Generally, the defendant will consent to the money being accepted out of time. Normally, the parties will agree a form of order, and this will then be approved by the court as a consent order (in which case there will be no need for attendance at court). For the procedure to be followed, refer to Procedural Table 13(*b*). Precedent 32 sets out typical forms of order. The order should say who is to get any interest that has accrued on the money in court. Normally, this will go to the defendant, but it might be worth the plaintiff's solicitor seeing whether you can negotiate for the interest to go to your client. If so, that should be specifically stated in the order.

(c) Rejection of payment in There is no need to inform the other side if the payment in is not accepted. One simply does not file a Notice of Acceptance. If the money is not accepted, it will remain in court and will automatically be placed on a deposit account (the interest will be the defendant's). The case will then proceed to trial in the usual manner, and the payment in will not be mentioned to the judge nor in the pleadings. At the trial, when deciding whether the payment in has been beaten, one takes full account of any deductions for contributory negligence, and also full additions for interest.

If the plaintiff obtains judgment for more than the amount in court, then the judge will order the money to be paid out to the plaintiff (or to the plaintiff's solicitor, if the plaintiff is legally aided). Before this can happen, the solicitor will have to obtain the judgment, or, in the High Court, to lodge the Associates Certificate. In practice, this can cause delay, since these documents can take some time to be processed. But to avoid unnecessary delay, the plaintiff's solicitor should send the schedule to the court in advance, rather than await the documents. In addition, because of this delay, it is advisable that the judge's order provides that interest on the payment in (as from the date of judgment) should be paid to the plaintiff. Otherwise, it will go to the defendant.

More than one defendant: Complications can arise when one of several defendants pays money into court. If the plaintiff accepts the payment in, the action will automatically be stayed against that defendant. However, the actions against the other defendants will not have been stayed, and will remain in effect. Ideally, the plaintiff should file a Notice of Discontinuance (see Precedent 29) on the other defendants. But, if the plaintiff does this, those defendants will be able to apply for costs. To guard against this eventuality, the plaintiff should issue an application, asking for an order that the money be paid out to the plaintiff, and that the costs of the other defendants be paid by the defendant who has paid the money into court (and that the actions otherwise be stayed, etc). Hopefully, the court will make an order in these terms. If it does not, then the plaintiff is in difficulties. One suggestion might be to write a *Calderbank* letter to the other defendants (ie those who have not paid in, but who want their costs). This could state that the plaintiff was only refusing to accept the money paid into court because of the other defendants' attitude to costs; the letter should go on to say that the plaintiff is proceeding with the action purely to protect the costs position and that if those defendants should be found in any way to blame for the accident, the plaintiff will produce this letter to the court and invite the judge to make those defendants solely responsible for the costs. Whether such a tactic is effective is open to doubt; however, it can have the effect of concentrating the mind of the other defendants, and so encouraging them to negotiate a reasonable compromise solution.

Another suggested tactic might be to try including the other defendant's costs in the bill of costs to be paid by the defendant who paid into court.

Interest: Money paid into court is automatically put on deposit, once the 21 day period for acceptance has expired. When the money is paid out (ie at the end of the case) any interest will accrue to the defendant, unless the order specifically says otherwise (see above).

A payment in should take account of any interest that would have accrued on those damages (ie if there had been judgment). The High Court and county court rules do not specifically require the defendant to apportion a payment in between capital and interest; but the rules say that the payment in will be treated as including interest as if the date of payment in was the date of judgment (CCR Ord 11, r 1(8); RSC Ord 22, r 1(8)). If the case goes to trial, it may be difficult to work out whether the plaintiff has beaten the payment in. Often, it will be obvious. But, in a marginal case, the judge might have to work out how much of the payment in was interest. For instance, suppose there is a payment in of £20,000. The case goes to trial, and the plaintiff is awarded £19,000, plus £3,000 interest. Has the plaintiff beaten the payment in? The judge calculates that, at the date of payment in, interest amounted to £500. That being so, the value of the payment in is £19,500 (ie £20,000 less £500). On this basis, the plaintiff has not beaten the payment in (ie the plaintiff has recovered £19,000, and the payment in was for £19,500). In practice, of course, it can be difficult to calculate accurately the amount of interest in a payment in. This is because there are different rates of interest on general damages than for special damages. All one can do, is make an approximate guess. In practice, these rules are less trouble than one might expect.

Calderbank letter: A *Calderbank* letter is a letter which sets out a party's terms for settling the action (or making certain offers), in which that party reserves the right to bring the letter to the attention of the trial judge after judgment, on the question of costs. In effect, it is similar to a payment into court, except that there are no specific provisions for it in the rules. It was in the matrimonial field that *Calderbank* letters were first approved of (because there is no equivalent of the payment in) but they are now accepted to be of more general use and a defendant can protect its position by a *Calderbank* letter, as well as a judicious payment in. For instance, if one of the main issues in the action is the extent to which a pre-existing condition has been aggravated, then it might be possible to write a *Calderbank* letter conceding that the condition would have arisen after a stated number of years. If medical experts had not otherwise had to attend court, then it might be possible to persuade the trial judge to order that the medical costs should be paid by the plaintiff, even if the defendant loses the main action; providing of course, that the trial judge accepted the defendant's evidence as to when the condition would otherwise have occurred. Similarly, if there was an argument as to when an employer acquired 'knowledge' of a dangerous work practice then a *Calderbank* letter might be used if the defendant wants to concede a particular date.

Provisional damages: If the Statement of Claim includes a claim for provisional damages, then the defendant can make a written offer (by letter) which is akin to a payment in. The procedure is set out in RSC Ord 37, r 9, incorporated into CCR by Ord 22, r 6(*a*). This allows the defendant to offer (in writing) a specified sum of money in satisfaction of the plaintiff's claim, on the basis that the plaintiff's condition will not deteriorate (or the disease will not develop), and at the same time the defendant agrees to the making of an award of provisional damages in that sum. In effect, it is a *Calderbank* letter.

2 The interim payment

The interim payment is grossly under-used by plaintiff's solicitors. Few seem to appreciate that the rules are drawn in such a way as to make an interim payment more likely than not. Obviously, each case depends upon its facts, but it is always worth looking to see whether it is a case in which the plaintiff would be entitled to an interim payment.

Unfortunately, defendants (and their insurers) are reluctant to make interim payments. It is sometimes possible to persuade them to make an interim payment without the need for an application to the court, but, in practice, this will usually only happen when it is obvious that the plaintiff will recover large damages. But, the RSC and CCR are not so narrowly drawn. The basic requirement is that, if the case went to trial, the plaintiff would be likely to obtain judgment with substantial damages against any one of the defendants. So, all that is required is a likelihood of recovering 'substantial' damages.

The mere fact that there may be substantial contributory negligence by the plaintiff is irrelevant. As long as the end result (ie the damages after deducting contributory negligence) is a substantial award, then the plaintiff is entitled to an interim payment. Unfortunately, there is no definition of what is 'substantial', save that it must be over £500, but in practice this is rarely a difficulty. Perhaps £5,000 should be regarded as the minimum figure in practice.

Note also that the plaintiff need not show 'need'. In other words, the plaintiff does not have to show that the money is needed due to financial difficulty. Personal finances are, to a large extent, irrelevant.

The detailed requirements on interim payments are set out in CCR Ord 14, r 12, RSC Ord 29, r 11. For the application to succeed, the plaintiff will have to show that:

(1)
- liability has been admitted; or
- the plaintiff has already obtained interlocutory judgment (with damages to be assessed); or

- the plaintiff would recover substantial damages if the case went to trial.

and

(2)
- the defendant is insured; or
- is a public authority; or
- is a person of sufficient means to be able to make the payment.

In practice, of course, the vast majority of personal injury defendants are insured, and so it is merely a matter of you showing (on a balance of probabilities) that the plaintiff will recover 'substantial' damages. If there is more than one defendant, then you will have to show that the client is likely to get damages against that particular defendant (ie it is not good enough to say that one of several defendants will be liable).

Application is made to the district judge in the county court by notice of application or in the High Court to the master, by way of summons. The application must be supported by an affidavit which:

(1) sets out the special damage to date, so the court can see the level of the claim. It is best to do a special damage calculation, which can be included as an exhibit to the affidavit if it has not already been filed. In addition, all letters (eg DSS letters; employer's letters) relating to special damage should be included as an exhibit. Explain to the court how the special damage is calculated, by having a separate paragraph in the affidavit for each item of special damage.

(2) Exhibit the medical evidence. In practice, this means that you will simply attach the medical reports which were attached to the pleadings. However if you have a more up to date report this should also be exhibited.

(3) In a fatal case, the affidavit must state the names, ages and relationships to the deceased of the dependants, and how the claim is brought. See Chapter 15 for FAA cases.

(4) If (as is usual) the plaintiff's solicitor is swearing the affidavit, then you must ensure that the affidavit specifically states that you are authorised to make the affidavit on the plaintiff's behalf.

The overall guidance must be to make the affidavit detailed.

The application: Apply by way of application to the district judge in the county court or by summons to the master in the High Court. A specimen application, affidavit, and order for interim payment are given in Precedents 14 and 15. Ensure that the copy affidavit and copy application are served on the defendant at least ten clear days (weekends and holidays count as clear days) before the hearing. This is an important point to note, because the normal period for serving an application is only two days (excluding weekends and holidays). So, be sure to serve the affidavit well in advance and file the original in court. There is little guidance that can be given as to the likely amount of the interim payment. It is entirely at the court's discretion. Thus, it is not usual to ask for a specific sum in the application. In practice, courts tend to think in terms of giving two-thirds (or even perhaps, only half) of what they see as the eventual value of the claim. On other occasions, they will take the amount of provable special damage. In view of the sums involved, it is obviously wise for the solicitor to attend the application personally, rather than rely upon an inexperienced clerk. It is advisable for the solicitor to review the file generally before attending the application. This is because the district judge or master can treat the application as a summons for directions and may make any of the usual interlocutory orders and, in particular, may order an early trial. The wise solicitor will consider whether there are any interlocutory orders wanted; if so, you should give notice to the other side of your intention to raise these points. You should particularly consider the issue of a split trial or an early trial.

The court is entitled to order that interest be paid on the interim payment as well. Precedent 15 includes an application for interest. In practice, it may well be necessary to specifically ask the court to order interest, once it has stated the amount to be paid. It is likely to award interest if the amount of the interim payment is substantial, or if the trial is unlikely to come on for a long time. If interest is awarded, then the court should clearly state the rate of interest awarded, the period for which it is being awarded, etc. This is important in case the trial judge should eventually award interest on a different basis (eg at a different rate); if that happens the trial judge will want to be able to adjust the amount of interim payment so as to increase, or reduce, the interest due. Whether or not this is the case, the trial judge will still have to decide how the interim payment is to be deducted from the damages awarded (ie does it come off general damages, special damages, etc?). In view of the markedly different rates of interest awarded on the different types of damages, it can be very important to decide which head of damage the interim payment is apportioned to. It should be noted that the plaintiff should resist any suggestion by the defendant that an interim payment (whether voluntary or not) should cover special damages since this can reduce the interest paid at the time of the final award. For guidance, see Chapter 15, section 4.

If the application for the interim payment is unsuccessful, there is no reason why a further application cannot be made. The plaintiff can go back for repeated applications; and does not have to show, as used to be the case, that there has been a change of circumstances. Having said that, a plaintiff who makes repeated applications without good cause is likely to have to pay the defendant's costs of the unsuccessful applications.

Finally, note that a legally aided plaintiff can have an interim payment paid direct. The normal rule is, of course, that any money recovered in the litigation must go to the area office (who will hold on to it until the statutory charge, etc, is sorted out). Interim payments are a major exception to this: the money can be paid direct to the plaintiff and the solicitor need not account to the area office.

Payment in: If an interim payment is ordered, the defendant will want it paid out of any money that the defendant has already paid into court. So, the defendant should ask the master to order that the money be paid out of the sum already in court, and that the Notice of Payment be amended accordingly. If an interim payment is awarded before the defendant pays money into court, then the defendant will obviously want to ensure that any future payment in does take account of the interim payment already made. It is for the defendant to specifically state in the Notice of Payment In that £X has already been paid by way of interim payment, and this is being taken into account for the amount of the payment in. If the Notice of Payment In does not state this, then the further payment in will not be deemed to include the interim payment already paid out. In practice, the sensible defendant will automatically make a payment in as soon as an interim payment is awarded. The defendant may presumably pay a few pounds into court, and state that the money paid by way of interim payment is taken into account.

Disadvantages: Although interim payments are under-used, there are some practical problems which should be borne in mind:

(1) Many personal injury plaintiffs are of limited means. If the accident has been severe, it may well be that the plaintiff does not have a job and is living on income support. If that is the case, then an interim payment can back-fire. A person on income support who has capital of more than £8,000 will automatically cease to be eligible for benefit (between £3,000 and £8,000 there is a sliding-scale reduction in benefit, 1992 figures). This is a vital point to bear in mind. The risks are obvious; if the plaintiff's solicitor rushes out and gets an interim payment for the client, the client will be worse off! There is no point in getting an interim payment if the net effect will be to take the client off income support, or to seriously reduce the amount of benefit being received. Far better for the plaintiff to wait until trial for the award of damages. That way, the plaintiff will continue to receive income support in the period prior to trial. On the other hand, it might be wise for the plaintiff's solicitor to ask for an interim payment of an amount that will bring the plaintiff's capital up to £3,000 (but not a penny more!). That way, the client will get some money, but will not lose income support. In practice, the defendant may be only too ready to agree to a voluntary payment of this amount, when told that the alternative is an application before the master which may well result in a substantially higher interim payment.

(2) The main disadvantage of the application, from the solicitor's point of view, used to be that it involved the solicitor in extra work! In practice, there can be little doubt that this is why so few applications for interim payment were made. However, under the new rules a plaintiff will have done most of the necessary work when preparing the pleadings and one hopes that more applications will be made.

(3) In a legal aid case, the interim payment does not have to go to the Legal Aid Board, but can go to the plaintiff (see above). There is a risk, perhaps more theoretical than real, that the Legal Aid Board could then reassess the plaintiff's finances. If this happened, the plaintiff could perhaps lose legal aid, or be required to pay a hefty contribution! In practice, the Legal Aid Board do not adopt this argument (but, could it be because they are so rarely told that an interim payment has been made?).

Chapter 9

Interlocutory Proceedings and Automatic Directions

1 Introductory

The pleadings close 14 days from the service of the defence (or reply, or defence to counterclaim, if served, or the last date for service if not served in time). At that stage, both sides know what is being alleged, the approximate extent of the claim, and the issues in dispute.

The period between the close of pleadings and the trial of the action will be occupied in defining these issues more clearly, making preparations for the fair and efficient hearing of the trial, and disclosing some of the evidence to the other side.

The solicitor who is aware of the interlocutory orders that are available can use this stage of the action to build up the foundations of a client's case. Your opponent can be pinned down by being forced to clarify the defence or allegations, by being made to disclose some evidence.

The interlocutory orders mentioned in this, and later, chapters will not be suitable for every case. However, the solicitor must know which orders can be sought and how (and when) to apply for them. But, before considering the interlocutory stage in more detail, it is necessary to understand the mechanics of interlocutory proceedings, how to issue an application or summons, and how to draw up an order. That is explained in this chapter.

'The court' in interlocutory matters means either the master (in RCJ cases) or the district judge (in county court cases), and thence by way of appeal, the judge. In RCJ cases, a master is assigned to the action when the first summons is issued and he will, thereafter, hear all the interlocutory applications in that case.

2 The application

To get an order, it is necessary to:

(1) issue a notice of application (county court) or summons (High Court);

(2) decide whether the order can be applied for ex *parte*;

(3) consider whether the other side will consent to the order. If so, can the court's approval be dispensed with? Can the order be obtained through the post?

(4) have the order made. This will normally be by attending the hearing of the order in the district judge's chambers. But, some consent orders can be dealt with by post.

(5) draw up the order.

Each of these is dealt with in turn below.

Issuing the application: A summons or application can either be issued by post, or by personal attendance at the court office. In practice, it is more convenient to issue by post and this is what most solicitors do. The steps to be taken (both for post and personal attendance) are set out in Procedural Table 1.

A stock of blank notices of application (form N 244) and summons forms (Oyez S1A, RCJ, S1B, DR) should be kept in the office. Specimen notices of application and summons are printed in Appendix G. If preferred, they can be used as a precedent, and typed out on A4 paper. Three copies should be prepared. In the county court one will be retained by the court, one will be sent to you and the final copy will be served by the court on the applicant unless you request it to be returned for personal service. In the High Court the top copy will be stamped by the court when the summons is issued; it will then be returned to the applicant who will retain it; but then hand it to the master at the hearing. The other two copies (unstamped) will also be handed to the applicant who serves (posts) one copy to the other side, and keeps the other, for use at the hearing. Obviously, if there is more than one defendant then extra copies will be needed since each defendant will have to be served.

The blank form of Notice of Application or summons (as in Appendix G) is easy to complete. The only difficulty will lie with inserting the terms of the order that is being sought. Appendix C of this book sets out all the precedents needed to run a typical personal injury case. The appropriate wording should be inserted in the blank space on the summons form. Bear in mind that more than one order can be sought on a single summons, and such orders can be in the alternative if wished.

Follow the steps in Procedural Table 1 for issuing the Notice of Application. You must give the court an estimate of how long the hearing is likely to last. In the county court there is no fee and the notice will be served by the court as explained above. In the High Court there is a £10 fee to be paid and it is for the applicant (not the court) to serve the summons on all the other parties to the action. The top copy is not served (see above). A good copy (either a copy stamped by the court, or a good photocopy of the original) is served, usually by post, on each of the other parties.

The summons or Notice of Application must be served at least two clear days before the return date (see Chapter 6, section 10 for how time is calculated). In practice, it is advisable to give more than two days' clear notice, and courtesy demands that the other side be given as much warning as possible. The long delays in obtaining court dates in both the county court and the High Court mean that the date given will often be months rather than days away. From the practical point of view, an application by the other side for all adjournment is less likely to succeed if they have been given more than the minimum two days' notice.

There are, however, some cases when the other side need not be served with the copy summons. This is because, in a few cases, the applicant (usually the plaintiff) can apply *ex parte*.

Ex parte: In the following cases, the applicant can apply *ex parte* (ie he need not give notice, or serve a copy of the application, on the other side):

- to issue and serve proceedings out of the jurisdiction;
- to renew (ie extend the time for service) proceedings;
- for leave to give late Acknowledgment of Service (High Court only):
- for substituted service;
- to issue a third party notice;
- for personal representatives to take over the action of a deceased plaintiff;
- when seeking directions over a fund held for an infant.

In practical terms, it is applications by a plaintiff for substituted service or renewal of proceedings, and by a defendant for third party proceedings, that are the most common *ex parte* applications.

For the procedure on applying *ex parte* for an order, see Procedural Table 3.

Ex parte orders can be set aside. When the other party hears of the order, it can apply to the master for the original orders to be set aside. Note that this is not an appeal; it does not apply to the judge. Instead, it simply issues an application asking that the order, etc be set aside. There will then be a re-hearing. It is particularly important to note that such an application can be made in respect of an order that the time for serving proceedings be extended; in that case, if the application to set aside is successful, the plaintiff may well be out of time to serve the proceedings (see Chapter 6).

Consent orders: Sometimes, the other side will consent to the order being sought. Typically, this will be at the conclusion of the case, when the parties want a consent order which sets out the terms of settlement (eg agreed costs; money to be paid out of court to the plaintiff; interest on the money to go to the defendant, etc). In such instances, the order can be made by consent; which means that there is no need for an application or summons to be issued, and there is no need for the parties to attend. A different procedure therefore applies. This procedure is set out in Procedural Table 2.

A consent order can be made for any of the following:

- giving judgment with damages to be assessed;
- settlement of the case by dismissal, discontinuance, withdrawal, withdrawal of the record, stay, *Tomlin* Order, etc;
- setting aside of judgment in default;
- to have money paid out of court (ie when the 21 day period for acceptance has expired);
- an order relating to costs;
- for the proceedings to be transferred to the county court from the High Court;
- a time summons (eg for the defendant to have further time in which to serve its defence).

If the order does not come within this list, then no consent application is possible (eg interim payment; Further and Better Particulars; directions as to medical reports, infant approval, transfer from the county court to the High Court, etc). In these cases the consent of the court must be obtained. However, normally the court's consent is no more than a formality, and the application can be dealt with by a letter to the district judge in the county court or an application to the practice master in the High Court (which means that no prior appointment is needed), and the other side need not attend. Obviously, if the district judge or practice master takes exception to the terms of the order being sought, the matter should be adjourned to allow the attendance of both parties in the normal way. See Procedural Table 2. For Infant Approval Summonses, see Procedural Table 17.

Counsel: Most applications or summonses are conducted by solicitors, or their clerks. But, if the application or summons is particularly important, a party may well want to instruct counsel. It is important to decide in advance whether counsel is to be instructed, because this may result in the case being put in a different list. If the applicant wants counsel to attend, then you should make sure that this is clear to the court when issuing the application. To avoid any misunderstanding, it is best to tell the other side that counsel will be attending on the application. In the county court no differentiation is usually made in the time when cases with counsel are heard. In the High Court all cases with counsel are put in Counsel's List which is heard at noon. Naturally, whenever a party is served with a summons it should check that it is not listed for hearing at noon; if it is, then it will know that it is in Counsel's List.

In the High Court if the summons has not been put in Counsel's List (ie it is in the Ordinary List) but the other party, the party served with it, wants it to be in Counsel's List, then it should write to the other side straight away. It should ask the party who issued the summons to apply to the practice master to transfer the summons, by consent, to the noon list (or adjourn it for a special appointment). It is for the party who issued the summons to make the application to the practice master. If that party refuses to do so, then the party who wants it transferred should still appear at the hearing of the summons (in the Ordinary List) and make an application to the master for the case to be adjourned, and transferred to Counsel's List, etc and should also ask for the other side to pay the costs that have been unnecessarily incurred.

Counsel's List, at noon, is for the hearing of summonses that are not expected to last longer than 20 minutes. If a summons is likely to last for more than that time, then one should ask for a special appointment.

Special appointments: special appointments are normally given if a summons is likely to last for 20 minutes or more. If this is likely to be the case, then the party issuing the summons should apply for a special appointment (fill in the form, Precedent 6 in Appendix C). If the party served with the summons (ie the party who did not issue it) thinks that a special appointment is necessary, then it should ask the other side to apply to the practice master for the case to be taken out of the Ordinary Lists. If they refuse, then it should make application to the master at the normal hearing (ie as with counsel, above). Solicitors, and their clerks, can appear at special appointments; there is no need to be represented by counsel.

The hearing of the application—county court The person attending the application (normally a solicitor's clerk) should make themselves known to the court usher (outside the door). If the matter is by consent you should inform the clerk of this since you are then likely to be heard earlier. Cases are usually listed in batches timed every 15 minutes after 10 or 10.30 am, although some courts arrange half hourly batches. The pleadings and all the papers will already be for the district judge but it is sensible for the applicant to give a brief description of the nature of the claim and the order sought at the beginning. The district judge will listen to the arguments of the parties and consider what order should be made. The district judge will then make the order and the court office will draw it up and serve it on both parties. The order takes effect from the time it is made but as court offices are sometimes extremely slow in drawing up and sending orders it is sensible to make a note of the order that was made and write immediately to the other party setting out the terms of the order.

The hearing of the summons—High Court: Most summonses are in the Ordinary List (ie they are listed in batches, timed for half hourly intervals after 10.30 am). These are heard in Rooms 95 and 96. This assumes, of course, that the summons has not been put into Counsel's List, given a special appointment, or put in the Senior Master's List. (See above.) Most summonses are dealt with by solicitors' clerks. The first step is for the clerk to make himself known to the court clerk (outside the door). When both sides are present, the clerk will usher the parties in before the master. Before they are shown in, the applicants should give the sealed summons, and the pleadings, to the master's clerk. The clerk will, in turn, hand them to the master. However, since the master will have no idea what the action is about, the applicant should give the master a brief description of the nature of the claim, and the order sought. The master will then listen to the arguments of the parties, and then make the order, by endorsing it on the original, top copy, summons which is then handed back to the applicant. It is advisable for the applicant to make a note of what the master orders, since the handwritten orders can often be illegible!

Adjourning an application or summons: Once the application or summons has been issued, it can be adjourned. But, this can only be done with the written consent of the other side. Simply post the application or summons to the court, together with a copy of the other side's consent. On the other hand, if the summons or application has not been served then their consent will not be needed; simply endorse a certificate to that effect on the back of the summons or application.

Amending an application or summons: If an applicant issues an application or summons, and subsequently wishes to amend it, there is no need to re-issue. All you need do is simply notify the other side of your intention to amend, and then ask the district judge or master for leave at the hearing.

Other side not attending: If the other side do not attend, the master or district judge will probably make the order, if satisfied that the other side was served with it (eg by production of party and party correspondence in which they acknowledge receipt). Alternatively, the court may decide to adjourn the hearing either to a specific date, or generally (ie 'liberty to restore') in which case the applicant can restore it to the list on two clear days' notice to the other side.

3 The order

The order takes effect from the time it is made but obviously it is difficult to enforce without having the actual order stamped by the court.

County court: In the county court the order is drawn up by the court and the sealed order is then sent to all parties. There is often a delay of some weeks before receiving the order. As soon as you receive the order you should check it carefully to ensure that it accords with your handwritten note. If it does not you should immediately write to the court and the other party pointing out the error and asking them to amend it under the slip rule.

High Court: After the hearing of the summons it is for the applicant, not the court, to draw up the order and serve it. This is so even if the master did not make the order that the applicant wanted. Drawing up the order can be done by personal attendance at the court office, or through the post. In practice, of course, it is usually more convenient to have the order drawn up through the post. There are only two occasions when it is not necessary to draw up the master's order:

- a time summons (ie an order extending the time for service of pleadings, or for filing documents); and
- an order giving leave to amend a writ or pleading.

However, even in these cases, it is possible to draw up and serve the order if the applicant so desires.

In every other case the order must be drawn up by the applicant. The steps to be taken are set out in Procedural Tables 1 and 2. A supply of blank order forms should be kept in the office (Oyez form H2, or H2A for DR cases). A specimen order form is shown in Appendix H; if preferred, an order form can be typed out on A4 paper using that as a precedent.

The wording of the order:

'liberty to apply'	—may be added to allow the parties to come back to the court for matters arising in the working of the order to be dealt with;
'liberty to restore'	—if part (or all) of the application is not dealt with then the applicant can have the application restored to the list;
'no order'	—the court's decision cannot be reviewed, but the applicant can (*a*) appeal, or (*b*) issue a fresh application if there is new evidence or if the other side will consent to a review;
'costs reserved'	—the costs will be decided by the judge at the end of the trial;
'costs in the cause'	—costs will follow the final result of the case;
'plaintiff's (or defendant's) costs in the cause'	—if that party wins the action, it will get the costs of these proceedings, but if it loses then it does not have to pay the costs of the other side in these interlocutory proceedings;
'plaintiff's (or defendant's) costs (in any event)'	—that party will get the costs of the interlocutory application whatever the outcome of the action, however they cannot be taxed and paid until the end of the action;
'plaintiff's (or defendant's) costs forthwith'	—that party to get the costs of these interlocutory proceedings straight away, without having to await the outcome of the action;
'costs thrown away'	—this is used on a successful application to set aside an order. The applicant pays all the costs incurred in obtaining the order which has been set aside; there may be a separate order as to the costs of the application to set aside;

'costs of the day'	—used on a successful application for an adjournment, where the applicant is to pay the costs of the application to adjourn;
'legal aid taxation'	—this should be asked for whenever a client is legally aided whether or not you are successful in the application since it ensures that the costs will be recoverable from the Legal Aid Board even if it is not possible to recover them from the other party.

Finally, whenever an order is obtained against you, it is important to read it carefully. In particular watch out for an 'unless' order. This is an order that requires strict compliance, failing which the plaintiff's claim will be struck out (or the defendant's defence be struck out and judgment entered for the plaintiff). Such order should always receive top priority; if the solicitor fails to comply in time, and the client therefore loses the case, the solicitor may well face an action for professional negligence. It has to be said that the courts are generally reluctant to allow judgments, etc obtained under such orders to be set aside.

4 Appealing the order

County court: The district judge's order can be appealed to a judge in chambers Ord 13, r 1(10). Notice of appeal should be filed within five days. See Appendix C, Precedent 25 for form of notice and Procedural Table 4, Appendix D for the steps to be taken.

High Court: The master's order can be appealed to a judge in chambers (Ord 58, r 1). Notice of appeal should be filed within five days. The form of notice is printed in Precedent 25, Appendix C; alternatively, use the pre-printed Oyez Form No B56. The steps to be taken are set out in Procedural Table 4 in Appendix D. It is particularly important to note that if the hearing is estimated to last more than 30 minutes, then the parties should (by consent) ask for the case to be taken out of the Ordinary List. See above.

If the appeal is from a master's assessment of damages, or following the trial of the action by a master, then appeal is direct to the Court of Appeal, not to the judge in chambers.

Legal aid: In legal aid cases, do not forget to obtain the authority of the local office before incurring the costs of an appeal. A certificate does not normally cover an appeal.

5 Judgment with damages to be assessed

Sometimes, a plaintiff will get interlocutory judgment with damages to be assessed (eg if the defendant has failed to comply with an 'unless' order). When this happens, the plaintiff should then obtain an appointment before the district judge or master for the damages to be assessed. To do this, use Procedural Table 7.

6 Automatic directions

The normal rule in county court actions is that there should be a pre-trial review and in QBD actions a Summons for Directions. At this hearing, the court makes orders for the 'just, expeditious and economical' disposal of the case. But, personal injury cases are an exception to this rule: there is no pre-trial review or Summons for Directions.

Instead, there are what are called 'automatic directions'. Orders are deemed to have been made by the court, but without the need for either party to issue an application.

These automatic directions apply in all personal injury actions (except medical negligence cases). Often, these automatic directions will provide all the interlocutory orders that are needed. However, it should not be forgotten that they do no more than provide the bare outlines that are needed in every case. In practical terms, there are many other orders that can be sought, and indeed which should be sought. It is wrong to rely on the automatic directions as being sufficient. To that extent, the automatic directions are an encouragement to laziness on the part of solicitors. The efficient solicitor will always check what other orders could, and should, be obtained. For instance, you might decide that you need an order for amendment of pleadings. Further and Better Particulars, discovery by a defendant in a road accident case (who would not normally have to file a list of documents, see Chapter 10, section 2); different orders for experts' reports, trial in a different location, etc.

The automatic directions come into effect when the pleadings close. Normally, the pleadings close 14 days after service of the defence (or the date when it should have been served). If a reply, or defence to counterclaim is served, then the pleadings close 14 days after service of that document. The automatic directions are:

1 *discovery* within 28 days (14 days in the High Court), and inspection of documents within seven days after. See Chapter 10, section 1 for the rules on discovery;

2 *experts' evidence*. Within ten weeks of close of pleadings (ie three months after service of defence) the parties have to disclose the substance of the experts' evidence on which they intend to rely. In effect, they have to serve their written experts' reports on each other. If reports are not disclosed in this way, then they cannot be produced at trial (unless an order is obtained to the contrary). The automatic directions provide for exchange of reports, and both sides can call up to two medical experts, and one non-medical expert, at the trial. This assumes that those experts' reports have, of course, been disclosed to the other side.

3 *Exchange of witness statements*. From 16 November 1992 (18 November 1992 in the High Court) within 14 weeks of close of pleadings parties must serve written statements of the oral evidence on which they will seek to rely at trial (RSC Ord 28 r 2A(4)). Statements must be dated and signed and contain a statement by the witness, that the contents

are true to the best of the witness' knowledge or belief. They should be served simultaneously. A party cannot without leave of the court adduce evidence other than that which has been disclosed unless the court gives leave or unless new matters have arisen since the statement was served on the other party.

4 *setting down* within six months of close of pleading (see Chapter 12, section 4 for setting down);

5 *venue* A county court case will be heard at the nearest trial centre. An RCJ case will be heard in London; a DR case will be heard at the appropriate trial centre. But, it does not necessarily follow that a case started in the High Court will necessarily be heard in the High Court even if it is for over £50,000. Personal injury actions can be compulsorily transferred to the county court (when the case is set down for trial). See Chapter 12, section 5.

6 *trial* The case will be heard by a judge alone (ie no jury).

7 *photographs and plans* These, together with the contents of any police report, shall be receivable in evidence without the need for their makers to be called. They should be agreed if possible. See Chapter 11, section 9.

8 *estimated length* When the case is set down, the court must be told the estimated length of the trial.

If either, or both, of the parties want different directions to be made (eg case to be heard at a different location) then a notice of application or summons will have to be issued in the usual way. Refer to Procedural Table 1 for the procedure. If both parties are agreed on the form of order they want then a consent application can be issued; although the court's consent may still be necessary. See Procedural Table 2.

Experts' reports: medical and non-medical

Virtually every personal injury case will involve expert evidence: at the least, there will be a medical report setting out details of the plaintiff's injuries. It has always been customary for the parties to exchange reports, in the hope that they can be agreed, with the subsequent substantial saving in costs, through not having to call the experts to give evidence. The courts have now made this procedure virtually mandatory, both because of the requirement that the plaintiff's medical report be served with the Particulars or Statement of Claim and because the automatic directions provide that expert evidence (whether from a doctor; motor engineer; accountant, etc) cannot be called at the trial unless a written report of that evidence has been disclosed to the other side in advance. The rules are:

- experts' reports which are to be relied on at the trial should be disclosed to the other side within ten weeks of close of pleadings (ie three months of service of defence, etc). Reports that are obtained at a later date (eg shortly before setting down) should be disclosed as soon as they are available; *and*

- if the parties cannot agree each others' reports (or they cannot agree on one compromise report) then each can only produce two medical witnesses, and one non-medical witness to give evidence at the trial. These witnesses' reports must, of course, have already been disclosed to the other side.

Do not forget that the rules on disclosure of reports only apply to those reports on which a party intends to rely. If you do not wish to call the doctor or engineer to give evidence then there is no need to disclose the report, since you will not be relying upon it at trial. It follows that there is no need to disclose each and every report obtained. For instance, if the first doctor's report is adverse to the client it may well be worth trying another doctor who may adopt a more sympathetic approach, and thereafter that later report can be disclosed for use at the trial. The first report could simply be held back.

The rules were altered in 1987, so as to make mutual exchange of reports virtually compulsory. In the old days, it was possible for the parties to jointly agree on non-disclosure, and there were also instances when the court would not order disclosure. Now, the emphasis is different. RSC Order 38 r 37, which applies also in the county court by virtue of CCR Ord 20, r 28, says 'unless the Court considers that there are special reasons for not doing so, it shall direct that the substance of the evidence be disclosed in the form of a written report'. In other words, you have to disclose your experts' reports, unless you can show that there are 'special reasons'. All the indications are that the courts will construe the 'special reasons' exemption very narrowly.

This is particularly important as regards medical negligence claims. The courts have indicated that the old prejudice against disclosure of reports in medical negligence cases no longer applies. In essence, the fact that a case involves medical negligence allegations is not, of itself, a valid reason for the non-disclosure of reports.

Chapter 10

Discovery of Documents and Amendment of Pleadings

1 Discovery of documents

Discovery is when the parties send each other details of all the relevant documents they hold.

The county court rule is that discovery should take place within 28 days of the close of pleadings (14 days in the High Court) (and inspection of those documents within seven days thereafter). Since the pleadings normally close two weeks after service of the defence (see Chapter 9 section 1), it follows that discovery and inspection should normally be completed within two months of service of the defence.

Both sides must serve lists of documents, *unless*:

(1) *liability is admitted* in which case discovery is limited to the plaintiff disclosing documents relating to special damage. Since liability is admitted, the defendant will not normally have any relevant documents to disclose, and thus disclosure is limited to the plaintiff's special damages.

(2) *it is a road accident claim* in which case the same rule applies (ie discovery of plaintiff's special damage only). This is because most road accident claims do not involve documentary evidence (other than that which can be easily agreed, for instance, the police report). Thus, the defendant will not need to file a list.

These are the rules under the automatic directions (see Chapter 9, section 6). Thus, the plaintiff must always serve a list of documents (even if only limited to special damage documentation). On the other hand, the defendant need only serve a list if the action is a 'non-runner' in which liability is still an issue. However, the plaintiff can apply by application or summons to the court in appropriate cases, asking for discovery by the defendant (eg in a road accident case in which a latent defect is pleaded by the defendant, the plaintiff might want discovery of all maintenance records, etc relating to the vehicle).

Exchange of witness statements: to some extent the powers of the court to order disclosure of witness statements has undermined the traditional importance of discovery. Under the new provisions, the parties must exchange their witness statements; in effect, it is complete pre-trial discovery of all evidence as to fact.

For the High Court rules (which are very similar) see p 109.

2 The list of documents

Disclosure of documents is effected by serving a list of documents on the other side. The list will detail all the 'documents which are, or have been, in the party's possession custody or power' and which relate to any matter in question (CCR Ord 17, r 11(g)). The fact that a disclosed document may harm the party's case, and help an opponent, is irrelevant.

The list of documents must be in the prescribed form (Form N265). If an informal list (eg set out in a letter) is used, then the work done may not be recoverable on taxation.

A specimen list is shown in Appendix GC(10). There is usually no problem in completing the form:

- on the first page, delete plaintiff/defendant as necessary.
- in para (2) of the first page, one has to set out the reasons why privileged documents are not to be disclosed. Simply type in 'they are by their nature privileged from production'.
- in para (4) of the first page, one has to state the date when documents which are no longer in one's possession were last in possession. Usually, one can simply type in 'on the dates they were sent to their respective addressees in whose custody they now are'.
- on the second page, in Schedule 1, Part 1, material documents to be disclosed. In most personal injury cases the plaintiff will only need to disclose 'writ and pleadings in the action, correspondence common to all parties' and all the special damage documents, such as letters from employers, the DSS and the Inland Revenue. There may, of course, be other documents in particular cases.
- next, there is Schedule 1, Part 2, material documents that it is claimed are privileged from disclosure. Note that 'privilege' includes:
  —solicitor/client letters;
  —'without prejudice' documents;
  —documents prepared with a view to litigation;
  —legal aid application forms.

Usually, Schedule 1, Part 2 can be completed as follows:

- 'plaintiff's and witnesses' statements, engineer's report, and photographs, medical reports, instructions to counsel, counsel's advice and draft pleadings, [correspondence with the Legal Aid Board] notes, memoranda and other documents dealing solely with the preparation of the plaintiff's case'.
- Next, Schedule 2 has to be completed, (ie material documents which are no longer in the party's possession, custody or control). Usually, one can simply insert 'the originals of the copy documents set out

in the First Part of the First Schedule which were sent to their respective addressees on the dates shown on them'.

- Finally, it is necessary to complete the Notice to Inspect at the foot of the form: 'at the office of the solicitor of the above-named plaintiff upon an appointment being made' is suggested. In fact, personal inspection of documents only takes place when there is an exceptional quantity of paper to be gone through. In most cases, the solicitors simply ask each other to send photocopies of those documents that they wish to inspect (it is usual to charge a photocopying fee if more than a few documents are requested). Indeed, the rules now allow you to insist that the other side provide you with copies (rather than inspect) provided you agree to pay reasonable copying charges.
- When inserting the date of service, date it the next working day (unless the list is not being served by post, but is being served personally).

In a non-road accident case in which liability has not been admitted, the defendant's solicitor will also need to serve a list. Schedule 1, Part 2, and Schedule 2, of the form will usually be completed as in the plaintiff's list. It is therefore Schedule 1, Part 1 (ie material documents disclosed), that will interest the plaintiff. The plaintiff will want to make sure that the defendant has disclosed all documents, that is *any* material document relating to *any* matter in question between the parties. Thus, for example, evidence as to previous accidents that happened in similar circumstances; the maintenance records of an allegedly defective vehicle; the sick note records of a plaintiff who is alleged to be malingering; entries in the Suggestions Book and Complaints Book; forms completed for government departments; all of these, and more, may be disclosable. If the plaintiff thinks that the defendant has material documents that have not been disclosed, you should write asking for them; then, if they are not forthcoming, you should seek an order for disclosure of specific documents, and also require the defendant to swear an affidavit confirming that the list is complete (see below).

Some of the documents that a plaintiff should particularly look for are:

(i) entry in Accident Book. Note that an Accident Book (Form B1 510) must be kept at every factory (as defined by FA 1961), every mine and quarry, and, more importantly, at every workplace where there are ten or more people normally employed. Thus, most firms should have an Accident Book, and the book has to be kept for up to three years after the last entry in it. In practice, many employers are not aware of this obligation. It can be well worth mentioning this legal obligation to the defendant in correspondence, and threatening to report any breach. In addition, an employer who is notified of an accident (whether directly, or through an entry in the Accident Book) is required to take reasonable steps to investigate it. In addition, it must record any discrepancy between the details as given to it, and its own findings. Once again, few employers seem to be aware of this obligation. Note that these obligations arise irrespective of whether the Factory Inspectorate or Health and Safety Inspectorate have to be notified of the accident (see below);

(ii) entries in the Accident Book in respect of previous similar accidents;

(iii) relevant entries in the Complaints Book;

(iv) relevant minutes of a works safety committee or union or other inter-office memoranda or complaints;

(v) sick notes from general practitioner, reports from a company doctor which were not made in contemplation of a claim;

(vi) statement made by plaintiff to employer after accident;

(vii) statements made by an employee-witness to the employer after accident may be disclosable, if it was made as a matter of routine and not in anticipation of a damages claim;

(viii) any memorandum or notice issued before or after the accident which gives guidance on (or amends) the system of work and training records setting out training given to the employee and others in the use of the equipment involved in the accident;

(ix) receipts for the purchase of safety equipment if, for example, there is a dispute as to the availability of safety equipment;

(x) maintenance records of equipment, including vehicles, involved in accident, if there is a suggestion of a mechanical defect;

(xi) manufacturer's operating instructions for equipment involved in the accident reports or surveys (eg ergonomic reports) carried out on introduction or change of the equipment or systems blamed for the accident;

(xii) Form BI76. This has to be completed by the employer if the employee makes a claim for industrial injuries disablement benefits. A few years ago, virtually every industrial accident resulted in a Form BI76 being completed; that was because injury benefit could not be claimed unless the employer completed the form. But, injury benefit was abolished in 1983, and replaced with Statutory Sick Pay. Now, it is likely that an employer will only have to complete Form BI76 if the employee does claim industrial injuries disablement benefit. In practice, therefore, it is relatively rare for a BI76 to have to be completed. From the plaintiff's point of view, this is regrettable, because BI76 does require the employer to give a short version of how the accident happened;

(xiii) The Factory Inspectorate, or the Health and Safety Inspectorate, have to be notified of any accident causing death or major injury. Form F2508 is used. Note that 'major injury' means:
—fracture of skull, spine, or pelvis,
—fracture of any arm bone (unless in wrist or hand),
—fracture of any leg bone (unless in ankle or foot),

—amputation of hand or foot,
—loss of sight of an eye,
—any other injury resulting in admission as an in-patient for more than twenty-four hours (unless just admitted for observation).

Few employers (or their solicitors) seem to have heard of Form F2508 so it will often be necessary to ask specifically for the form. (The authority is the Reporting of Injuries, Diseases and Dangerous Occurrences Regulations 1985. 'RIDDOR') Finally, note that the 1985 Regulations require Form F2508 to be completed if the accident results in more than three consecutive days absence from work (excluding the day of the accident but including weekends etc).

The plaintiff's solicitor should check through Schedule 1, Part 1 of the defendant's list, looking for these items. If they are not there, then you should ask whether they are in existence. If you do not receive an unequivocal reply to the question, you should seek specific discovery and/or an *affidavit* verifying the list (see below).

It will be seen that most of these documents are not relevant to road accidents, and it is because defendants in road accidents rarely have disclosable documents that they are not automatically required to serve a list. The plaintiff, will, however, nearly always have special damage documents to disclose, and thus discovery by plaintiffs is made automatic even in road accident cases. It should not be forgotten that the court can always order a defendant to disclose documents. Thus, in a road accident case, or in an action in which liability has been admitted, the plaintiff's solicitor who thinks that the defendant has material documents should seek an Order for Specific Discovery (see below).

Incidentally, if the contents of a disclosed document are not clear (eg the handwriting is illegible, or it contains abbreviations) ask the defendant for an explanation. If necessary, obtain the information by serving Interrogatories.

Privilege: A defendant will frequently argue that a document is not disclosable since it is privileged as 'having been prepared for the purposes of litigation'. Often this is not a sustainable contention. If a plaintiff thinks that the defendant might have documents that would help, but which you presume the defendant is claiming privilege for, then the plaintiff should begin by looking in Schedule 1, Part 2 of the defendant's list. Often, Schedule 1, Part 2 will vaguely refer to 'other documents dealing solely with the preparation of the defendant's case'. If the plaintiff suspects that there may be disclosable documents, you should ask the defendant to specifically list all these other documents referred to in Schedule 1, Part 2, and in respect of which privilege is claimed. If the defendant refuses to do so, then the plaintiff should issue a summons, arguing that the defendant has failed to file a list of documents in accordance with the Rules and that judgment be entered in default. This may induce the defendant to list the privileged documents: in practice, the court will not give interlocutory judgment, but may well order the defendant to list the privileged documents.

Since the decision of the House of Lords in *Waugh* v *BRB* [1979] 2 All ER 1169, the scope of the argument that a document was prepared for the purposes of litigation has been considerably reduced. The test to be applied is: 'what was the dominant purpose of the author of the document?' If the dominant purpose (not necessarily the sole purpose) was in order to obtain legal advice, or aid the conduct of litigation, then it should be privileged. But, otherwise, it will not be privileged and so it will be disclosable. *Waugh* concerned an internal report on a railway accident; it had to be disclosed, despite the affidavit of the defendant's solicitor stating that one of its principal purposes was to enable him to advise BRB on its legal liability. In practice, therefore, if one can show that an internal inquiry is shown as a matter of routine (ie even when there can be no question of any legal liability) then the report should be disclosable. The same applies if the report is designed to prevent similar accidents occurring in the future, since then it cannot be said that litigation was its dominant purpose. Another useful case for plaintiffs to quote is *Melik* v *Norwich Union* [1980] 1 Lloyd's Rep 523. In this case, Woolf J held that an assessor's report to insurers was not privileged:

> It is quite clear ... that one purpose of the insurers in instructing the assessors must have been to have a report which could be used for the purpose of obtaining legal advice if that should prove necessary ... However ... it is not sufficient that a document should come into existence for a series of purposes, one of which is obtaining legal advice ... in this case the dominant purpose of the assessors making their report was to enable the insurers to ascertain the facts in order to come to a decision as to whether or not they should rely upon the clause of the policy in order to repudiate liability.

So, the assessor's report was not privileged. The moral is that plaintiff's solicitors should not be shy of asking for internal reports, provided it can be shown that these reports are prepared as a matter of routine, and that their dominant purpose is not for litigation. However, it has to be said that many courts take a much more restrictive approach than that outlined in the two cases referred to above. But, it is sometimes found that the quoting of these two cases to an inexperienced opponent will lead to the disclosure of useful papers!

Compulsory exchange of witness statements: Since 1987, it has been possible for the court to order an exchange of witness statements and since November 1992 it has been compulsory. The theory is that this does not affect the rules of privilege, but in practice it does cover all evidence of fact to be given at the trial. Accordingly, material that might previously have been exempt from disclosure as being privileged (eg the assessor's report in *Melik*), can now be accessed by the plaintiff if the defendant intends to rely on its contents. Witness statements should always be read carefully to see if they refer to any documents which did not appear in the list. If they do then you should immediately request discovery of such documents (and issue an application to obtain them, if necessary).

3 When discovery is not complete

The only occasions when a party is not automatically obliged to serve a list of documents are:

- the defendant in a road accident case;
- the defendant when liability has been admitted;
- when the defendant is the Crown;
- in third party proceedings.

Yet, even in these cases, the district judge can make an order for discovery (Ord 17, r 11). Further, a party who does not serve a list of documents within the prescribed time (whether discovery be automatic or by order) risks having its pleading struck out or the action dismissed.

One point to watch, however, is CCR Ord 14, r 8. This says that discovery will not be ordered if it is 'not necessary either for disposing fairly of the action or matter or for saving costs'. When there are only a few documents to be disclosed, a party will often list them in a letter and ask for the other side to dispense with the need for a formal list. In all but the most straightforward cases this practice should be avoided; the danger is that important documents may be overlooked or that the work done may not be allowed on taxation.

If no list is served: If the defendant is automatically obliged to give discovery (see above) and if the list has not been served within 14 days of the close of pleadings, the plaintiff should issue an application for the defence to be struck out and for judgment to be given to the plaintiff. For the steps to be taken, and the words to be used, see Precedent 7(2). The plaintiff should not hesitate to use this remedy, for it is virtually certain to result in the defendant serving a list without further delay. In practice, if the list is not served before the application is heard, the district judge is extremely unlikely to grant the plaintiff interlocutory judgment. In fact, the district judge will probably not even give an 'unless' order (ie that the list be served within 14 days, failing which judgment be entered, etc). Instead, the most likely outcome is that the district judge will simply give the defendant a period of time (usually 14 days) in which to serve the list. If the defendant does not comply with that time period, then the plaintiff would have to issue another application, asking for interlocutory judgment.

Affidavit verifying the list: If the list of documents is unsatisfactory, serve a notice requiring the other side to swear an affidavit verifying their list of documents. Use Precedent 7(3). Such a notice may well encourage a defendant to reconsider where certain documents are not, after all, disclosable. The affidavit (to be sworn by the party on whom the notice is served) is in Form N265(1), see Ord 14, r 2(5). Even if the notice does not result in the disclosure of any further documents, it will put the other side in a difficult and embarrassing position should they wish to produce new documents at the trial, something which should never happen, but unfortunately occasionally does. This is especially so with certain insurance companies who do not give full and proper instructions to their solicitors until the action is well under way.

If the other side do not serve an affidavit within 14 days of service of the notice, then apply to the court for an order that an affidavit be served within seven days (failing which, interlocutory judgment be entered for the plaintiff with damages to be assessed).

Specific discovery: If one suspects that the other side have documents they have not disclosed, then there is an alternative to asking them for an affidavit verifying their list. Instead, and this is usually a better procedure, one can seek an Order for Specific Discovery (Ord 14, r 2). This is a valuable procedure; solicitors should not hesitate to use it when they believe the other side have not disclosed all their documents. Precedent 7(4), gives a specimen application, affidavit, and order for usc in a workplacc accidcnt claim. It can easily be adapted for any other case. Note that an affidavit in support must be sworn, which states that the deponent's belief (ie the solicitor's belief) that the other party does have documents of the class sought (for instance, by referring to one's experience of similar cases when such documents were in existence; alternatively, referring to a statutory authority that obliges the defendant to have such documents, eg notification to Factory Inspectorate). The affidavit should also formally state the deponent's confirmation that the documents are relevant to matters in the action.

Specific discovery is an effective method of obtaining documents from an uncooperative opponent. The solicitor whose own list has already been served should not hesitate to employ it.

4 Specific discovery from a third person

It is possible to obtain an Order for Specific Discovery against a person who is not a party to the action RSC (Ord 24, r 7A applicable in county court proceedings by virtue of CCA 1984, s 76). Any party can apply to the district judge, by way of application, for an order that the third party disclose the specific documents requested. These must be documents that would be producible under a *Subpoena Duces Tecum* (see Chapter 13, section 13); an affidavit in support will have to be sworn. The procedural requirements, together with a specimen summons and order, are printed in Precedent 7(5).

This procedure is mainly used against hospitals that are reluctant to forward the plaintiff's medical notes and records to the plaintiff's advisers, unles ordered to do so by the court. If such a situation arises, the hospital should be advised that an order will be sought under Supreme Court

Act 1981, s 34 which is the statutory basis of third person discovery. In *McIvor* [1978] 1 WLR 757 it was held that the hospital cannot insist on the records just being sent to the plaintiff's own medical advisers; the plaintiff's lawyers may also examine them (see Chapter 18, section 5) although this is now clear from the Access to Medical Records Act 1990.

Pre-action discovery: Specific discovery from a third person should not be confused with discovery before the commencement of proceedings. It is possible to get discovery of documents before proceedings are commenced. For details, see p 25.

5 Close of pleadings

The pleadings close 14 days after the service of the defence (or 14 days after the service of any reply and/or defence to counterclaim). See Chapter 7, section 1. The date of the close of pleadings should be diarised, for its effects are twofold:

(1) As from the close of pleadings it is not possible to amend a pleading without applying, by application, to the district judge for leave to amend (see below).

(2) The automatic directions come into effect, in particular:
- (i) medical and expert evidence must be disclosed within 10 weeks (see Chapter 7, section 1);
- (ii) Discovery of documents should be completed within 28 days (see above);
- (iii) the case should be set down for trial within six months (see Chapter 12, section 4).

6 Amendment of pleadings

Since pleadings set out the allegations and contentions of the parties, they must be both accurate and up to date. If a pleading contains an error, or if the allegations and contentions have altered since it was settled, then it will be necessary to amend the pleading and to re-serve it on the other side.

Amendments can be made at any stage of the case, for the court will not allow the strict rules of pleading to defeat justice, unless the amendment will result in prejudice or an injury that cannot be compensated for by costs (see notes to Ord 15, r 1). Despite this, in practice, the courts are prepared to allow amendments at a late stage in the proceedings. It is not uncommon, for example, for a defendant to attend the trial court and to ask the judge for leave to amend the defence to include allegations of contributory negligence by the plaintiff; unfortunately, such applications are frequently successful, although the judge may well adjourn the hearing and order the defendant to pay the costs of the day. Similarly, it may be necessary to amend the particulars of injuries, or particulars of special damage, in the Statement of Claim if the plaintiff's condition has deteriorated, or to plead the outcome of a criminal proceeding relating to the accident which has been tried since the pleading was settled (see Chapter 6, section 5).

If an amendment is needed, it must be decided whether the district judge's leave is necessary.

7 County court: amendment

(1) *Amendment before service of Particulars of Claim:* If there is an error on the summons (eg too small a level of damages is claimed), then the plaintiff should file an amended request. At the same time, amended Particulars of Claim should also be lodged. This therefore allows the plaintiff to amend the nature of a claim.

(2) *Amendment before pre-trial review:* A party can amend the pleading, without the leave of the court, prior to the pre-trial review or close of pleadings in cases where the automatic directions apply. To do this, prepare the amended pleading, and serve a copy on the other side and file a copy with the court. See Chapter 9, section 6, for when the pleadings close. But, remember that a 'pleading' does not include Further and Better Particulars. The amendment(s) should be typed in red (or in black, and underlined in red); any amended words are not deleted, but are merely crossed out in red. The date of re-service of the pleading, and counsel's name, should also be inserted (once again in red, or underlined in red). Most importantly, across the top of the pleading one should also type (in red or underlined in red) 'Amended the . . . day of . . . 19 under Ord 15, r 2'. The pleading is then re-served in the usual way. The other side can then amend its defence (or reply and/ or defence to counterclaim) within 14 days, and without leave, if the amendments are consequent upon the new allegations or amendments made. It is of course important that all new allegations in a Particulars of Claim are denied by the defendant, otherwise it may be deemed to admit them. Note that any amendment can be made to any pleading, provided the pleadings have not closed (which will usually be 14 days after service of the defence). But, if the amendment relates to the addition or deletion of a party, or an altering of the cause of action, then it will also be necessary to obtain the court's leave. If the amendment is to add an additional plaintiff then the written consent of that plaintiff must be filed with the court. Precedents 13 and 14 set out the appropriate form of application and order. When the district judge has made the order, it may not be drawn up; this is one of the few occasions when an order does not have to be drawn up (see Chapter 8, section 2). However, the amended pleading must have the words 'Amended by order of the court ... dated ... the ... day of ... 199', typed in red across the top (or in black, underlined in red), and then be re-served.

(3) *After the pleadings have closed*, a pleading can only be amended with the consent of the other side, or with leave of the court. Once again, use Precedents 13 and 14.

Disallowing the amendment

We have seen that a pleading can often be amended without leave. However, even in these cases, it is possible for the other side to object. Within 14 days of re-service that party can apply by notice of application for the amendment to be disallowed. In practice, this happens rarely; the court would only be likely to make such an order if it would not have been 'just' to have allowed the amendment.

When considering whether to amend a pleading, remember that the court has the power to allow any amendment at any stage—however late—of any action. The costs of the application will usually be borne by the applicant, but it will generally be found that the court is ready to grant leave. An amendment will take effect as from the date of the original document it amends, and not from the date of the amendment.

Colouring the amendments

First amendments are in red. Subsequent amendments will be in green, with further amendments in violet, and then yellow.

8 Adding parties

Adding an extra plaintiff or defendant to the action is effected by amending the pleadings (as above). Precedent 14 sets out a typical application and order. Note that when the order allows an additional defendant to be added, the Particulars of Claim should not only bear the date of the amendment but have the words 'Amended pursuant to the order of the court dated the . . . day of . . .19' typed across the top in red.

As an alternative to amending the pleadings, an extra plaintiff or defendant can be introduced by the commencement of a separate action with its own pleadings. At a later stage, the two actions can be consolidated into one action, which will then proceed, as such, to one trial. Precedent 7 sets out a form of application and order for consolidation.

9 High Court Discovery

The rules are very similar to those rules in the county court except that discovery takes place 14 days after close of pleadings.

The List of Documents should be in form 26 Part II of the White Book (use Oyez form B9) and the relevant rules are under RSC Ord 24.

10 High Court: Amendment

The rules are found in RSC Ord 20 and are slightly more complex because often a writ will have to be amended as well as the relevant pleading. A writ can be amended in any way without consent if it has not been served and can be amended between service and close of pleadings without leave unless the amendment relates to the addition or omission of a party. After close of pleadings a writ can only be amended with leave of the court. Any pleading can be amended once only before the close of pleadings without need for leave and after the pleadings have closed it can only be amended with the consent of the other side or with the leave of the court.

As in the county court any defendant can subsequently object to such an amendment, to do this it issues a summons for the amendment to be disallowed.

The main difference from the county court procedure is that a copy of the amended pleadings must be served on the other side only and need not be filed with the court, although an amended writ must be filed with the court.

Chapter 11

After Discovery

1 Introduction

After discovery both sides should bring their files up to date and consider carefully the strengths and weaknesses of their respective cases. Only then will it be possible for the solicitors to consider properly what interlocutory orders should be sought, and what points should be raised when counsel is asked to advise.

This is a checklist of the main points to be considered after discovery;

(i) Are *Further and Better Particulars* needed of the other side's pleading?
(ii) Should *Further and Better Particulars* be provided of one's own pleadings (if requested)?
(iii) What *interrogatories* (if any) should be sought?
(iv) Would a *Notice to Admit Facts* be useful?
(v) Is *discovery* complete? If so, how do the documents disclosed affect the case, and should they be put to the client?
(vi) Update full *proofs* for the client and all witnesses in preparation for exchange of witness statements. Are any other witnesses needed?
(vii) Is the *medical evidence* satisfactory? Which further report(s) should be considered for exchange with the other side?
(viii) Is there any other *expert evidence* that might assist?
(ix) Are *photographs* and *a plan* needed?
(x) What *evidence (if any) can be agreed* with the other side (eg a police report)?
(xi) What *other interlocutory orders* should be sought?
(xii) Have the *automatic directions* been complied with?
(xiii) Does a *Notice of Intention to Proceed* have to be served (ie if no step taken for twelve months)? [High Court only]
(xiv) Has the *special damage schedule* been brought up to date?
(xv) Does the *legal aid certificate* need to be extended? (Often, certificates are limited 'to all steps up to and including Discovery').

This checklist will also serve as a checklist of points to be considered when preparing the instructions to counsel to advise, but the points raised should not be delayed until that time. For example, it may well be that the instructions to counsel cannot be prepared until one or more of these matters has been resolved. For instance, if the solicitor decides that Further and Better Particulars of allegations of contributory negligence are needed, then you may send instructions to counsel to settle the request, issue an application and seek the order; and not ask counsel to advise until the Particulars have been received.

Thus, the solicitor must resist the temptation, once the pleadings have closed, of sending all the papers off and asking counsel to advise 'generally'. You must consider in your own mind the very matters on which you will be asking counsel to advise, and only after taking any necessary preliminary action will you dictate the instructions to counsel to advise.

The following paragraphs deal in more detail with points raised in the checklist. All of these points should be considered in every case: obviously, not all will be applicable, but some must be. In any event, do not forget to make a clear note in the file of the time spent considering all these various matters, so that this time can be included in your bill of costs.

2 Further and Better Particulars

The procedure is identical in the county court and High Court.

Any pleading must contain a summary of the material facts on which a party intends to rely (but not the evidence needed to prove those facts). Thus, it is open to the other parties to argue that the pleading (be it Particulars or Statement of Claim, defence, counterclaim, defence to counterclaim, etc) is insufficiently pleaded, and that therefore Further and Better Particulars of the pleading should be provided (CCR Ord 6, r 7 and Ord 9, r 11; RSC Ord 18, r 12).

In theory, if the pleading has been properly settled by counsel there should be no need for Further and Better Particulars since they will only be ordered to clarify facts and allegations already pleaded. However, in practice, counsel will want to draft the pleading in such a way that it preserves some scope for manoeuvre, and does not pin the client down too narrowly. Thus, counsel will have two irreconcilable objectives, and it is usual to retain the scope for manoeuvre and leave it to the other side to seek an order for Further and Better Particulars.

Knowing when to seek Further and Better Particulars is largely a matter of experience, although helpful guides are printed in some of the textbooks on pleading. A simple example is when a road accident Particulars of Claim states that the plaintiff 'will rely on the relevant provisions of the Highway Code'; the defendant would then seek an order for Further and Better Particulars, asking which particular provisions of the Highway Code will be relied on by the plaintiff. Similarly, in workplace accident cases it is common for the defendant to plead contributory negligence claiming that the plaintiff 'knew or should have known' of the particular danger; in such a case the plaintiff should request Further and Better Particulars of the defence, asking for all facts and circumstances relied upon as giving the plaintiff this knowledge. This can be taken a stage further, for if the Further and Better Particulars of the defence were still not specific enough, the plaintiff could seek an order for Further and Better Particulars of the defence.

A specimen request, in a road accident case, for Further and Better Particulars of the defence, together with the Further and Better Particulars of the defence, will be found in the set of pleadings printed in Appendix G.

Answering the Request: When the defence is served, the plaintiff frequently receives a Request for Further and Better Particulars of the Particulars of Claim. It is best to put this request to the client in the form of an easily understood questionnaire. Set out each of the points, in turn, with sufficient room for the client to be able to insert answers. At the foot of each page of the questionnaire, write 'signed ... dated ...'. This could simplify matters if the client subsequently died, and the answers had to be put in under the Civil Evidence Act. By setting out the answers in a questionnaire, it will enable counsel to have the client's full instructions in a convenient format, and it will simplify counsel's task of considering how, and whether, Further and Better Particulars should be supplied.

The service of a Request for Further and Better Particulars does not have any immediate effect. In particular, it does not count as a 'pleading', and so it does not extend the date for close of pleadings. In addition, it is only when the court orders that the Further and Better Particulars be provided, that a party need do so. If the court's order is ignored then (as with any time limit laid down in an order) the other side can apply for judgment (or for the action to be struck out, if applicable).

Often, a plaintiff or defendant will have no objection to providing Further and Better Particulars requested, and in that case there will be no need to obtain an order.

Obtain counsel's approval before agreeing to provide Further and Better Particulars, and always instruct counsel to settle them if counsel settled the original pleading. Counsel's draft should be checked against the client's completed questionnaire, and then typed out in the same form as a pleading (see Chapter 6, section 6, and the specimen Further and Better Particulars in Appendix G). The layout of the document will be the same whether the Particulars are given voluntarily or pursuant to an order. In either case, the Particulars should begin by reciting the request or order that led to the Particulars being given.

The typed document should then be served by post on the other parties to the action, not just the party who made the request.

Sometimes, it will be felt that a request for Further and Better Particulars is no more than a fishing expedition. If so, then refuse to provide the Particulars, and leave it to the other side to seek an order.

Making a Request: Similarly, a request for Further and Better Particulars should be typed out as a pleading and in the same form as the specimen in Appendix G. The request should be sent to the other side together with a covering letter asking for the Further and Better Particulars to be supplied. This must be done even when it is clear that the other side will not provide the Particulars without an order being made; unless the request is first made by letter, the court may well refuse to make an order (CCR Ord 9, r 11(3) and RCJ Ord 18, r 12(6)). The cost of the letter will be recoverable on taxation.

If the request is not met then it will be necessary to go before the court and obtain an order. Precedent 1 gives the usual form of summons and order; see also the specimen summons and order printed in the specimen pleadings in Appendix G.

If counsel feels that the Further and Better Particulars are important then it may well be advisable to instruct counsel to attend on the hearing to argue the point before the court. (Do not forget to put a High Court summons in Counsel's List.)

In conclusion, always consider in every case whether Further and Better Particulars should be sought. They are useful in pinning down defendants on the extent of the defence, and this is particularly so with allegations of contributory negligence which are often pleaded as a matter of routine and with little or no justification. When they are pleaded in vague terms it is often the case that the defendant has no real evidence as to what happened, and a request for Further and Better Particulars of the defence will expose the weakness of the allegation.

Particulars of special damage: Although a detailed schedule of special damage should be served with the Particulars or Statement of Claim sometimes only brief particulars are given. An aggressive defendant may well attack this, as being an inadequate pleading. Strictly speaking, the defendant's proper response is to request Further and Better Particulars of the Claim, asking the plaintiff to particularise the special damage claim. However, it has to be said that some defendants short-circuit the procedure, and instead simply issue a summons for an order that the plaintiff's claim be struck out, on the basis that the plaintiff has not served a proper Particulars or Statement of Claim (ie in breach of CCR Ord 6, r 1(5) or RSC Ord 18, r 1). Unfortunately, it is not unknown for a court to allow such an application, and make an 'unless' order against the plaintiff. If that happens, the plaintiff will have to make sure that the Particulars of Special Damage that you subsequently serve are detailed, otherwise, you might face an application for the Statement of Claim to be struck out, for your failure to comply with the 'unless' order!

3 Notice to Admit Facts

The defence will sometimes admit certain facts about the claim, such as the date, time, place, and identity of the parties, and vehicles involved and so on (for instance, see specimen defence in Appendix G). Subsequent correspondence or negotiation might result in further facts being admitted, and these would generally be recorded in open letters.

However, it is more likely that the defendant will not wish to make the plaintiff's task any easier, and so few admissions are likely to be made. Thus, the plaintiff will have to call witnesses at the trial just to prove those facts. To avoid this, the plaintiff should serve a Notice to Admit Facts on the other side; unless the facts referred to within the Notice are admitted within seven days, the cost of proving them will normally fall on the other side, whatever the outcome of the case (CCR Ord 20, r 2; RSC Ord 24, r 2). If the defendant is being obstructive, the service of a Notice to Admit Facts may well encourage it to be less uncompromising.

A Notice to Admit Facts could be used, for example, in a road accident case when the defendant has put in a general denial of the facts of the case, including such basics as the date of the accident, and thus the plaintiff would feel obliged to call the police officer who attended to confirm that the accident occurred on the date alleged. The Notice to Admit Facts makes it likely that these costs will be borne by the other side, although the trial judge still has a discretion.

A Notice to Admit Facts can be served by either a plaintiff or a defendant, but it cannot be served more than 21 days after the case has been set down for trial. Use in the county court Form N 281 or in the High Court Oyez Form B53 or type out the Notice using Precedent 10. The admission is in Form N 282.

In practice, the Notice to Admit Facts is rarely used by plaintiff's solicitors. It is difficult to know why this should be so, for it can be a convenient and easy way of bringing pressure to bear on the defendant, whilst, at the same time, forcing it to give some thought to the strength of its evidence. Indeed, the fact that it is used so rarely means that the defendant will be surprised to receive a Notice, and may well be impressed with the knowledge of the plaintiff's solicitor and the vigour with which you are pursuing the case!

4 Notice to Admit Documents

There is a similar procedure available for documents. Any party can serve a notice on the other side requiring them to admit the authenticity of documents specified therein (CCR Ord 20, r 3; RSC Ord 27, r 5). As with a Notice to Admit Facts, it can be served by either a plaintiff or a defendant, but it cannot be served more than 21 days after the case has been set down for trial. Use in the county court Form N 283 or in the High Court Oyez Form B12.

The other side can reply by serving a Notice of Non-Admission within 21 days and thus be put on risk as to costs; unless such a notice is served they are deemed to admit the documents. There is no need to serve a Notice to Admit in respect of documents that are in the other party's list, since a party is deemed to admit the authenticity of documents that it discloses.

This procedure is useful for avoiding the expenses of calling witnesses to prove formally such items as garage bills, hire receipts, and so on. Similarly, it can be used for photographs, plans and other non-controversial documentation. As with the Notice to Admit Facts, it is used relatively little in practice, it should be used more.

Documents referred to in pleadings: If the other side refer to a document in a pleading or affidavit, they will normally provide a copy. If they fail to do so, the remedy is to put in a formal Notice to Produce a Document.

5 Interrogatories

Interrogatories are questions put to the other side, in an effort to discover more of the facts of their case, but not their evidence.

Interrogatories can only be put with the court's consent. An order must always be obtained. Interrogatories are a complicated topic, and one that the inexperienced litigator may well wish to leave in counsel's hands. The notes to Ord 26 in the White Book lay down the guidelines as to when Interrogatories will be allowed in both the High Court and the county court (where they are incorporated through CCR Ord 14, r 12), and these are, in essence, if they are necessary for fairly disposing of the case or for saving costs. In practice, though, courts have been very wary of interrogatories and apply the rules strictly. Interrogatories are not to be used as a form of 'fishing expedition', nor to question the other side's veracity, and the mere fact that the same question would be allowable in cross-examination will not suffice. Similarly, they will not be allowed for obtaining admissions if a particular witness will have to attend court anyway; thus, they are unlikely to be allowed if (for example) they ask the position of the defendant's car, or when the driver first noticed the plaintiff's car. Such facts should, in any case, be disclosed when witness statements are exchanged. It is in professional negligence cases (particularly medical negligence claims) that interrogatories can be particularly useful. In such cases, the plaintiff's expert is often in some difficulties since the plaintiff does not know the accurate sequence of factual events. If that is so, then interrogatories may supply the factual information which will enable the expert to strengthen a report.

When the point in issue relates to a straightforward factual matter (eg 'Is it true that immediately after the accident you said to the plaintiff, "I'm sorry, it was my fault"?') it may be worth putting it to the other side by means of a Notice to Admit Facts (see above). The other side will probably ignore the Notice, but they might occasionally be induced to give an answer. If so, that answer might prove useful during the cross-examination at trial.

Interrogatories should usually be settled by counsel in view of the exactness of wording required in pinning down the other side in their answers, and in reassuring the court that it is not a 'fishing expedition'. They should be simple direct questions, based on the Particulars or Statement of Claim. The style and layout of the interrogatories is as in any other pleading (see Appendix G).

Unlike Further and Better Particulars, the RSC state that interrogatories cannot be served or answered without the leave of the court, so even if the other side should agree with them, it is essential that an order be formally made allowing them to be served. Apply by application; Precedent 12 shows the form of summons or application and order to be used.

When served with interrogatories, it is important to obtain the client's full instructions. This is best done, as with Further and Better Particulars, by setting out the questions in a questionnaire. This will be of great assistance to counsel when settling the 'Answers to Interrogatories'.

6 The proof of evidence

Ideally, one should prepare a full type-written proof for the client and all witnesses. Do not rely on photocopies of letters, but type out a proof that is clear, orderly and unambiguous. Counsel will need this when advising and it will form the basis of witness statements to be exchanged.

If a proof was taken from the client before the papers were sent to counsel to settle the claim, then that proof may well need bringing up to date. If the changes in the proof were only minor then it is easier to do a supplementary proof to attach to the first one, although one, fully comprehensive proof will still have to be prepared when the case goes to trial or witness statements are exchanged.

In fact, it must be accepted that solicitors often do not bother to update or prepare full proofs at this stage. In a straightforward case, it may well be felt that it is sufficient to supply counsel with a copy of the plaintiff's original statement, together with photocopies of recent letters, etc. The same applies to witness statements. There is some justification for this practice: by sending the copy letters to counsel (rather than the solicitor adapting them and incorporating them into a proof) there is no danger of the solicitor putting words into a client's mouth. It is all too easy to slightly alter the emphasis of what a client said, and so distort the version of events. Obviously, if the case is complex, or if the client's letters are muddled and unclear, then it is essential to type out a full proof but in all cases it will help you to pinpoint areas where more information is needed and to concentrate your mind on the questions in issue.

Everyone develops their own individual style of proof-taking and it is something that becomes easier with practice. Since counsel will rely on the proofs of evidence it is essential that they should be detailed and clear with the contents set out in a logical sequence. Counsel should not have to hunt around for the facts, and in a lengthy proof it is helpful to insert sub-headings (such as the accident, previous accidents, allegations of contributory negligence, work history, etc).

Some solicitors still type out proofs on brief paper, so counsel has room to add notes; however, these days, it is also common for proofs to be on A4 paper, double spaced which makes them easier to file and convenient to use as witness statements.

Begin the proof with:
'[NAME ...] WILL SAY AS FOLLOWS' and in the first paragraph state the client's (or witness's) full name, address, occupation, date of birth (and marital status and number of dependants if relevant).

When acting for a plaintiff the second paragraph should be a short summary of the date of the accident, what happened, who was responsible, and what effect it had on the plaintiff. This will enable counsel to form a quick initial impression of the case before reading the full facts, so that counsel will have the relevant considerations in mind while reading the proof. The proof should then record, in full detail, the circumstances of the accident in chronological order. In a workplace accident case it may be necessary to precede this with a description of the process being carried out, the machines being used, and the hierarchy of command in the workplace. Describe the weather and the lighting (if relevant). How experienced was the plaintiff, and how much instruction had the plaintiff received in that particular task? Had the plaintiff previously made complaints that the equipment or system of work was unsafe? Set out briefly why the defendants are to blame and then deal with any points raised by the defence; be careful not to develop the evidence beyond that actually given by the client (or witness), and wherever possible use the words and phraseology given in the client's/witnesses' letters or previous statements. Go on to deal with all allegations of contributory negligence and incorporate the plaintiff's own words from the completed questionnaire sent on receipt of the allegations. Go through the rest of the pleadings, giving the plaintiff's comments on any Further and Better Particulars and interrogatories. Include only a brief description of the injuries received since counsel will have a copy of the medical report to refer to, but do set out in full the sort of information that will not be included in the report, such as how the injuries affect the plaintiff's social life, hobbies, sports, marital relations, and ability to carry out everyday tasks such as dressing in the morning. Clients often relish telling you in great detail the effect which the accident has had on their sex life—you only need to give a summary of this to counsel!

Next, set out a precis of the special damage position. Clearly, this is no place for a detailed special damage calculation which will already have been prepared and served. However you will need to show the reason behind every item of special damage claimed and how the client is to prove it, for example if you claimed the cost of a car with power steering explain why the client is prevented by injuries from driving an ordinary car. It is also important to set out the full employment details, including the amount of any continuing wage loss, and the prospect of the plaintiff finding employment. Often, it will be necessary to set out the plaintiff's employment history for a few years prior to the accident (ie so that counsel can see whether the client had a steady work record, and thus would have been likely to have continued employment had the accident not happened). This can be done by asking the client to provide a full curriculum vitae. In any event, if there has been a payment into court, then the employment (and social) information should be as detailed as possible, so counsel can give it proper consideration when advising on acceptance.

Put the words 'signed' and 'dated' at the foot of each page of the proof. This will enable it to be put in under the Civil Evidence Act, if its maker should die before trial (see Chapter 13, section 11).

Send the proof to the client (or witness), asking them to read it carefully, make any alterations or additions that may be necessary and sign and date each page. If it is a witness's statement that is being prepared, then give the witness a stamped addressed envelope (one should do everything one can to keep witnesses happy!).

It is vital to make a note on the file of the time spent in drafting, and dictating, the proof; otherwise the costs draftsman will be unlikely to include the time in the bill. In practice, it is not always necessary to see witnesses, since many accidents can be accurately described in a letter or telephone call. But, if the facts are complicated, or the witness is a poor correspondent, then do not hesitate to arrange a personal interview. Never be ashamed to admit that you do not understand a description of events. It is extremely helpful to keep a set of toy cars in your office drawer so a witness can show you exactly how an accident happened.

7 Exchanging witness statements

From November 1992 parties are obliged to exchange witness statements of all the oral evidence on which they will seek to rely at trial within ten weeks of close of pleadings, and if they fail to do so they are not entitled to adduce such evidence without the leave of the court (RSC Ord 38, r 2A(4); CCR Ord 17, r 11(3)). If you object to producing witness statements then you will have to apply to the court for an order that statements need not be exchanged. However the general approach of the court will be strongly in favour of mutual disclosure of witness statements, whilst the court will take into account any objections raised, it is very much a case of their being a presumption in favour of exchange.

It is possible for the court to order different rules as to exchange depending upon differences of fact or with different witnesses. Thus, the order made by the court can be general (ie applying to all witnesses as to fact), or specific (ie specifying the issues of fact, or the witnesses) to whom it applies and you can therefore apply for a variation in the automatic directions; for example that one witness statement will not be served until you have seen the defendant's statement. Again, this is only likely to be granted in exceptional circumstances.

You obviously only have to disclose witness statements that are to be used at the trial. Accordingly, if you obtain an unfavourable statement from a witness you are not necessarily obliged to disclose it; you can simply decide not to call that witness.

Written statements that are eligible for disclosure should only contain facts. They must not contain anything inadmissible, and nor must they contain hearsay (or statements of information or belief). In particular, there can be no statements of opinion. In general terms, a written statement that is put in should not seek to anticipate the evidence of another witness (eg from the other side), or to contradict it, or otherwise to deal with it. The idea is not that the written statement should answer questions that could be put in cross examination.

Follow the general guidelines (above) for the style and layout of a witness statement that is to be exchanged. In particular, check that the statement contains the witness's name, residence, occupation; in addition, if the witness is one of the parties (or an employee of one of the parties), then this should be stated. Generally, try and adopt a chronological sequence in the statement. Use double space typing, on one side of the paper only; preferably get the statement signed and witnessed.

The general principle is that the advance disclosure of witness statements does not replace the giving of oral evidence at the trial. For instance, if you do not call a witness at the trial, then no other party can put in that witness evidence in trial (although the judge does have a discretion on this). Conversely, if you do call the witness then that witness cannot give evidence that is different (or additional) to that in the disclosed statement (unless the additional evidence relates to new matters that have arisen in the course of the trial, or unless you can get the consent of the other side or the judge).

When typing out witness statements, bear in mind the provisions of this rule. Any matters of opinion etc (ie inadmissible evidence that cannot be included in the disclosed statement) should perhaps be put in a second, supplementary, statement which will be shown to counsel. Thus, always consider whether a witness's statement should be split into two separate statements—one (dealing with fact only) for exchange, and the other (dealing with opinion) that is not to be exchanged. Counsel may wish to draft the witness statements which are to be exchanged so do not be offended if your draft is amended.

8 Medical reports

The plaintiff will already have obtained at least one medical report. This should have been obtained before proceedings were commenced and served with the proceedings.

One's own report: Go through the medical report, and decide whether it will be good enough for counsel to use when advising. If a payment into court has been made, it may be necessary to obtain a further report, but, normally, there will be no need for a second report at this stage. This is because medical evidence relates primarily to quantum, not liability, which is the main issue before counsel at this stage. As a general rule, there is no need to obtain a further medical report until shortly before the trial, or until the defendant has put forward a reasonable offer in settlement. However, if an excessively long time has elapsed since obtaining the first report or if you are aware of significant changes in the plaintiff's condition, then do not be reluctant to update it. Do not forget to check whether the defence raises any medical questions, on which a further medical report is needed. General comments on when medical reports are needed and what they should contain are set in Chapter 4, section 3(b).

Do not forget there is no need to disclose all one's medical reports to the other side. So, if one obtains a report that is not favourable (eg if the psychiatrist says that the plaintiff is malingering), do not disclose it. It is only necessary to disclose reports that you intend to rely upon at trial.

If you do end up with several reports, then remember that the automatic directions only give you authority to call two doctors at the trial. If you want to call three or more doctors, then you will have to get the other side to consent, or alternatively issue an application.

If you intend to rely solely on the report served with the claim then you need not exchange a further report under the automatic directions. However if at any time you do disclose a further report it must be accompanied by a further statement of special damage. In the county court only both of these must be filed with the court as well as served on the other side.

Finally, ensure that the particulars of injuries pleaded in the Statement or Particulars of Claim are sufficiently full and up to date. If any new complaints have arisen since the Statement or Particulars of Claim, then consider amending. Generally, the defendant will simply accept a letter from the plaintiff's solicitor summarising the proposed amendment, in which case there will be no need for an order and the amendment can be made at trial (if thought necessary).

Allowing the other side to examine the plaintiff: The defendant must be allowed to examine the plaintiff. If the plaintiff refuses facilities (or lays down unreasonable conditions) then the defendant's remedy is to apply for the proceedings to be stayed. In practice, this rarely happens.

The general principle is that a plaintiff cannot object to examination by a particular doctor (eg because that doctor is well-known as a 'defendant's doctor'). A more specific objection is needed. In practice, this is extremely difficult to sustain. Similarly, the plaintiff cannot normally insist upon having another person or the plaintiff's own doctor present when the defendant's examination is carried out. The courts have suggested there might be exceptions to this (eg a particularly nervous plaintiff; a brain damaged plaintiff; if the defendant's doctor is known to be particularly fierce in cross-examining), but such exceptions are rare. On the other hand, if the defendant's doctor wants to carry out tests on the plaintiff, then the plaintiff may be able to object. In effect, there is a difference between an ordinary medical examination and one involving experiments or diagnostic procedures (eg patch-testing for dermatitis; exploratory operation; administering drug or anaesthetics; or even the use of hypodermic syringe). Against this, there is authority for taking a more robust approach, and saying that the plaintiff cannot object even if the examination involves a real (but minimal) risk, provided the defendant is prepared to compensate for that risk. The notes in the White Book (Ord 25, r 6) discuss the conflicting authorities.

Instead of asking for facilities for medical examination, the defendant may simply rely on the plaintiff's report.

The plaintiff's solicitor cannot insist on being given a copy of the defendant's report unless the defendant intends to rely on it. If this is made a pre-condition of submitting to an examination by the defendant then the defendant can apply for the action to be stayed. However, if the defendant is the plaintiff's employer then the plaintiff *can* demand a copy of the report *prior* to it being sent to the defendant under the provisions of the Access to Medical Reports Act 1988.

When writing to the defendants confirming they may have facilities for examination, do not forget to state that this will be on the basis that they reimburse the plaintiff for all losses and expenses arising out of the examination; it is also advisable to ask that the doctor makes the appointment directly with the plaintiff (otherwise, you may have the inconvenience and unnecessary work of having the appointment made through you).

Disclosing the medical notes and records: The defendant's doctors may well want access to the plaintiff's medical notes and records. They may want access to the hospital notes and records (ie following the accident), but sometimes they will go further, and ask for the pre-accident GP's notes and records. From the plaintiff's point of view, there is little to be gained by giving consent. Disclosure of such notes and records can, generally, only work against the plaintiff, in that there is always the chance that the defendant will be able to find some entry in the records that might enable it to argue that there is a pre-existing condition, etc. So, generally, try not to agree. However, it must be accepted that the courts will nearly always allow access to such medical notes and records, provided the defendant can show some reason for wanting them. As regards the post-accident records an order will nearly always be made. As regards the pre-accident records, an order will be made if there is some justification (usually, a letter from the defendant's doctor in vague general terms seems to be accepted). So, at the end of the day, the plaintiff will probably have little choice but to agree to the disclosure of the notes and records. In practical terms, the best response when asked for these records is to ignore the request!

When authorising the release of the notes and records, the client's signed consent will be necessary. Use Stock Letter 18; that precedent attempts to narrow down the scope of disclosure by confining it to a specific doctor nominated by the defendants, and stating that the records are not to be shown to the defendant's solicitors, etc.

If the hospital (or GP) refuses to release the notes, then third person discovery may be necessary (see Chapter 10, section 4). However this is now unlikely since the Access to Health Records Act 1990 gives patients a right to have copies of all medical records.

The automatic directions: Remember that the automatic directions made on the close of pleadings say that if medical evidence is to be given at trial:

- the doctor's report must have been disclosed to the other side within 10 weeks of close of pleadings;
- if the report(s) are not agreed, each side can only produce two medical witnesses at trial;
- if the reports are not to be disclosed, or if more than two witnesses are needed at the trial, then an application will have to be issued.

The automatic directions are quite clear: medical reports have to be disclosed to the other side (unless there are 'special reasons', which will be rare). Thus, the solicitor should consider:

(*a*) Which report(s) should be relied upon and thus be available for disclosure to the other side?

(*b*) Are there 'special reasons' why the court may decide that reports should not have to be exchanged?

(*c*) If the other side are to supply a copy of their report do not forget to ask for a copy of any covering letter from the doctor.

Exchanging and agreeing reports: You will have already sent at least one report to the defendant. You should now send any other report you wish to disclose and demand disclosure of the defendant's reports. Defendants often disclose medical evidence at an extremely late stage and it is difficult to prevent this although CCR Ord 17, r 11(5) makes it clear that if disclosure is to be made by more than one party then it should be mutual exchange, medical for medical and non-medical for non-medical, within the time provided by the rules. One way to encourage compliance is to tell the defendant that, having disclosed the plaintiff's report, you intend immediately to set the case down for trial ten weeks from the close of pleadings (ie the end of the time period for disclosure in the automatic directions). You should then go on to state that it will then be too late for the defendant to disclose any report with a view to its maker appearing at trial since such report will not have been disclosed in accordance with the automatic directions. Unfortunately, however, the defendant who fails to disclose in time simply has to apply to the court for an order that it may serve its report late and such applications will usually be granted. You will, though, have the advantage that the court is likely to give a strict timetable for the service of the report and give the plaintiff the costs of the application. Once you have received the defendant's report you should send it to your own medical expert to see if any parts can be agreed and whether you need an updated or amended report in the light of any allegations made by the defendant's doctor.

For the need to update the medical reports before trial, and to lodge them with the court before trial, see Chapter 12, section 8.

Meetings of experts: the court can order that both sides' experts get together (on a without prejudice basis) to see what parts of their evidence they can agree, and which parts they cannot agree. Accordingly, consider this as a possibility once exchange has taken place. This procedure is not within the automatic directions; accordingly, if the other side will not consent to your suggestion, then you will have to issue an application.

9 Engineer's report

In a workplace accident case it is usual to have an engineer's report to illustrate the workings of the machinery and to explain how the accident occurred, how it could have been avoided, and why the defendant was to blame. If the complaint is about poor systems of work then an ergonomist's report may be required. Referring back to Chapter 5, section 3(*b*), it will be seen that either a written opinion (without an inspection of the *locus*), or a full report (involving an inspection) could be obtained. The engineer's report or opinion should be to hand well before the papers are sent to counsel to advise.

It is surprising how many plaintiffs' solicitors will rush to obtain medical reports but will fight shy of obtaining an engineer's report. Since liability is more basic than quantum, they should be more concerned to have a helpful engineer's report than a medical report. It is not only the highly technical cases that benefit from having an engineer's report, for any case that involves consideration of good working practices will be strengthened if such evidence is given by an expert witness rather than by the plaintiff's workmates. Similarly, in road accident cases an engineer may be able to give evidence as to how the collision occurred. In a legal aid case obtain the authoritry of the Legal Aid Board before commissioning a report.

Remember that the automatic directions made on the close of pleading (see Chapter 9, section 6) require that if engineering evidence is to be given at the trial:

- the engineer's report must be disclosed to the other side within 10 weeks of close of pleadings;
- if the report(s) are not agreed, each side can only produce one non-medical expert witness at the trial;
- if report(s) are not to be disclosed or if more than one witness is needed at the trial, an application will have to be issued: see Chapter 9, section 6 for details.

Inspection: If an inspection is necessary, obtain the prior consent of the defendant. It will be recalled that prior to commencement of proceedings it is possible to obtain an Order for Inspection by issuing an Originating Application or Summons; when proceedings have been commenced, an order can be obtained by issuing an Application or Summons in the action. When making such an application, an affidavit in support is not essential, although in more difficult cases, or when the need for the inspection is not apparent from the pleadings, it is advisable to swear an affidavit setting out why the inspection (and photographs or video) are needed. Precedent 9(1) gives a specimen summons and order. Further details can be found in the notes to Ord 29, r 2 in the White Book which is incorporated into CCR by Ord 13, r 7.

If the premises or goods to be inspected are not the defendant's, but belong to someone who is not a party to the action, it will be necessary to obtain that person's consent. If consent is withheld, apply for an order by issuing an application or summons supported by an affidavit, and serve copies on the parties and the non-party. See Precedent 9(2); further details will be found in RSC Ord 29, r 7A.

When consent has been given (or a court order obtained) ask the engineer to arrange a convenient time with the plaintiff and defendant: the plaintiff should, if possible, attend the inspection and it will be noted that the summonses in Precedent 10(1) and (2) authorise the expert's attendance. There is no need for the plaintiff's solicitor to attend the inspection.

A meeting of the experts: the court can order that experts get together, to see which parts of their reports they agree (or do not agree). This possibility was introduced in 1987, and it is likely to become increasingly common. From the court's point of view, it clarifies the issues, and makes the trial more straightforward. From the experts' point of view, they can arrange a convenient meeting to see whether they can thrash out their differences in the privacy of their own rooms—rather than having to wait around in court, and then be cross examined. Not surprisingly, many experts (whether engineers or doctors) prefer this procedure. Accordingly, always consider whether it is advisable for the experts to get together for a without prejudice meeting. If so, and the other side will not agree, then you will have to issue a summons. For more on this see Chapter 12, section 8.

10 Photographs and plans

Now is the time to consider whether photographs and plans should be prepared for exchange and, if possible, agreement with the other side. Remember that the automatic directions allow photos, a sketch plan, and the contents of a police report, to be given in evidence without the court's prior consent (see Chapter 9, section 6). Obviously, the parties should try to agree these items.

Photos. In serious cases the police will often have taken photographs, and will provide copies on request. Otherwise, consider instructing a professional photographer. In view of the amount this is likely to cost, it is often advisable to notify the other side that one intends to have photographs taken, and ask them to confirm that they agree that this is advisable. This should protect the position on taxation. On the other hand, in a straightforward case, it may be possible to get the client to take a few photographs, but courts do not like this as perspective on non-professional photographs can be very misleading. Obviously, if possible, photographs should be taken at a much earlier stage before conditions change or the vehicles involved are scrapped.

Plan: Most road accident cases benefit from having a sketch plan to assist the court and witnesses. Consider whether the sketch plan at the back of the police report will suffice. It is important to remember in 'collision cases' (which will, of course, include most road accident claims) that one must obtain the court's authority before incurring the cost of having a plan, other than a sketch plan, drawn up, for otherwise the taxing officer may not allow the surveyor's fee if the other side did not agree to a plan being prepared (RSC Ord 38, r 10). However, the taxing officer does have a discretion and can allow the cost if you can establish that it was reasonable to prepare the plan for use at the trial. Since the fee is likely to be at least £125, it is essential in a road accident case to get the other side to agree beforehand that a plan should be obtained (or alternatively issue an application to get the court's consent). In legal aid cases you should also obtain prior authority from the Legal Aid Board.

11 Other agreed evidence

Is there any other evidence that could be agreed with the other side in an effort to reduce costs? For example, the police report will contain much independent evidence which neither side disputes, and even if it is not possible to agree the whole report (including the statements attached) it may well be possible to agree the officer's report on the circumstances, weather conditions, place of accident, and so forth. Similarly, employer's letters as to earnings should be agreed with the other side. If the other side do not agree with them, then either serve a Notice to Admit Documents (see Chapter 11, section 4), or serve a Civil Evidence Act Notice (see Chapter 12, section 11).

In view of the fact that exchange of witness statements is becoming the norm, one should always consider carefully whether evidence can be agreed in advance. If so, then this will avoid the delay and expense of calling witnesses to formally prove agreed facts.

12 Split trial

Normally liability and quantum are both determined at one trial, but it may be more convenient to try a preliminary point first, and then have the main trial after that preliminary point has been resolved. The obvious example is with a case that is straightforward on liability, but complicated from a quantum point of view (eg if the medical evidence is complex, and the prognosis is unclear). In such a case, it is sensible to have a split trial, with liability being established first, and then a subsequent hearing for quantum.

Solicitors should not be reluctant to ask for a split trial. There is no need to show that the case is in any way unusual or difficult. All that has to be shown is that it would be just and convenient to have a split trial, which, indeed, would be so in many cases. Defendants should remember that they too can apply for a split trial; it is not the sole prerogative of the plaintiff. This can be especially useful in a case which the defendant thinks weak on liability, but which is likely to involve much expensive medical evidence.

Refer to Precedent 18 for the steps to be taken when asking for a split trial. Note that RSC Ord 33, r 4A allows the defendant faced with a split trial to make a percentage admission of liability by letter (rather like a payment into court). If the defendant is not held to be more liable than as admitted in the letter, then the plaintiff will face a costs penalty (ie as with the payment in).

Provisional damages: The courts can now make an interim award of damages, following trial. This allows the plaintiff to come back at a later date, when the medical condition has stabilised. This is therefore an alternative to a split trial. See Chapter 15, section 5.

Speedy trial. Consider also whether there should be a speedy trial. In very simple cases, the court may make an order for a speedy trial by directing that an application be made to the clerk of the lists to fix a date for the hearing, usually within one week. Application has to be made by application or summons (see Procedural Table 1). Usually the parties are in agreement as to the need for a speedy trial and so a consent application can be issued (see Procedural Table 2).

13 Delay

County court cases There are various stages at which the county court will automatically strike out cases if there has been delay: under Ord 9,

r 10 if a Default Summons is served but there is no admission, defence or counterclaim and yet judgment has not been entered the action will be struck out. This is designed to cover the event where the parties reach agreement but do not inform the court. Under Ord 13, r 3 if the hearing of any action or matter has been adjourned generally and within 12 months of the day on which the order was made adjourning the action or matter generally no party has applied to have the date fixed, then the court officer will give notice to all parties and unless any party applies within 14 days after receipt of the notice to have a date fixed for the hearing or have the hearing again adjourned the action or matter will be struck out. However, the most likely rule to affect you and the one that must be very carefully diarised is Ord 17, r 11(9) introduced in October 1990 which states that after 15 months from the close of pleadings the action will automatically be struck out if no request has been made for a hearing date. You should watch this very carefully since all too often there can be a long delay, for example, if you are negotiating or waiting for your client's injuries to stabilise. You should always make an application for an extension in good time as you should not assume that the action, once struck out, would easily be reinstated, particularly if the limitation period has expired.
High Court cases: Although a case will not automatically be struck out for failure to set down, if a case has gone to sleep, it may be that more than one year has elapsed since the last proceedings in the action. If so, a month's notice must be given to the other side before any further step is taken. This means that if a year has elapsed since the last pleading was served, or the last order made, then notice must be given. Mere correspondence (and exchange of medical reports) does not count. The form of notice is set out in Precedent 24.

In practice, it is particularly important to remember this point when setting down for trial. All too often, there has been a delay of more than one year by the time the case is set down.

14 Counsel's advice

Dictating the instructions to advise: Only after the solicitor has brought the file up to date, and considered all the points mentioned in this chapter, can you properly dictate the instructions to counsel to advise. Many solicitors ignore the need to consider the papers in such detail, and, upon completion of discovery, simply to send off the papers to counsel on the assumption that counsel will then advise and tell them what needs to be done. This practice must be avoided for otherwise counsel will receive incomplete instructions and be denied the advice and opinion of an instructing solicitor. Moreover, the solicitor will find that such a thorough review of the case at this half-way stage will usefully clarify the issues in your own mind, and draw attention to those parts of the file that need to be strengthened.

It is unlikely that counsel will have previously considered quantum or liability except in particularly difficult cases, for an advice or opinion is not given when the claim is settled unless specifically requested, or unless there are particular points that counsel wishes to bring to the instructing solicitor's attention. Thus the papers to be sent to counsel on being asked to advise must be full and detailed.

As with instructions to settle a pleading, sort out which papers counsel needs and list the enclosures at the start of the instructions. Send copies, not originals, of documents and ensure that a copy of any legal aid certificate (and notice of amendment) is included. The instructions will not usually be lengthy, but should draw counsel's attention to any specific points that require consideration. The instructing solicitor should not be reluctant to give counsel the benefit of opinion, for counsel will value the advice of a fellow professional.

Check for any limitation on the legal aid certificate. Often the certificate will be limited to close of pleadings, discovery, and the taking of counsel's advice. If so, specifically point out to counsel that written advice is needed for legal aid purposes.

The low brief fee allowed for instructions to advise on quantum and liability makes this a 'best buy' for solicitors, so do not be reluctant to use counsel's services and send the papers back for a further opinion in a complicated case. Remember that a solicitor who acts on counsel's instructions will usually have a good defence to a professional negligence claim; besides which, clients are always pleased to be told that 'counsel advises' and it is often helpful to have an outside view of a case.

On receipt of counsel's advice: Go through the advice carefully. If it is unclear or ambiguous, telephone counsel to clarify the position; make an attendance note of the phone conversation.

It is helpful to photocopy the advice and place a copy on the inside front cover of the file; mark all paragraphs that require action to be taken and tick them when the action has been completed. This will provide a quick guide as to the progress of the case prior to setting down for trial.

Type out any Further and Better Particulars settled by counsel. Any request for Further and Better Particulars should be sent off by letter before an application is issued; and while this is not obligatory with interrogatories, it is only courtesy to serve them well before the hearing of the application.

Are there any points that now need to be taken up with the client? Should the client be sent a copy of the advice? Generally, send the advice to the client but ensure that you explain it fully in a covering letter. Certainly, in a difficult case it may help to quote extracts from an advice or opinion in an effort to condition the client to compromising the claim. The client may also, of course, be able to answer some of the problems that cause concern to counsel.

Finally, consider whether the case is worth what you originally thought it was. If it is worth more, should it be transferred to the High Court for trial? If it is worth less and is in RCJ, should it be transferred to the county court?

Legal aid: If your client has a limited certificate, send a copy of the advice to the local office and ask them to extend the certificate.

Chapter 12

Preparing for Trial

The next stage is for the parties to start preparing for the trial. Once the interlocutory orders have been complied with, the case will be set down, and eventually the parties will attend court for the trial and judgment.

This is a checklist of the main steps to be taken when preparing for trial:

(1) Check that all *orders* have been complied with.
(2) Ensure that *counsel's advice* has been carried out.
(3) Consider whether the papers should go back to counsel for *further advice*.
(4) Check that any limitation on the plaintiff's *legal aid* certificate has been removed.
(5) [High Court only] Has there been *a year's delay* since the last proceeding in the action? If so, give one month's notice to the other side.
(6) *Set down* the case for trial and notify the other side.
(7) [High Court only] Consider whether a *fixture* is needed.
(8) [High Court only] File *Certificate of Readiness* if trial is to take place out of London.
(9) Consider whether the case should be transferred between the High Court and county court.
(10) Bring *special damage* and *medical* evidence up to date; have they (and *any plans and photographs)* been agreed with the other side?
(11) Would it be helpful for there to be a without prejudice meeting of the doctors (or other expert witnesses)?
(12) *Lodge the special damage* calculation, and agreed medical reports, with the court.
(13) Prepare and deliver the *brief* to counsel.
(14) *Notify client,* witnesses, and experts of date of trial.
(15) Issue and serve *subpoenas.*

These matters are considered below.

1 Interlocutory orders

Check that any order made by the court has been fully complied with.

If the other side do not comply with the terms of an order, issue an application for judgment in default; Precedent 7(2) for use when seeking judgment in default of discovery can be adapted as necessary. Issue the application in the usual way (Procedural Table 1), and, if the application is successful, enter judgment in accordance with Procedural Table 4.

2 Counsel's advice

Go back to counsel's advice. If you marked those paragraphs that needed action to be taken, then check that they have all been ticked off as having been attended to.

Consider whether it is necessary to go back to counsel again. For instance, the court may have refused to make an order that counsel thought essential; (if so, should there be an appeal to the judge), or the medical reports disclosed by the other side may seriously question the previous valuation of the case.

If in doubt, go back to counsel and send off 'Further Instructions to Counsel to Advise'. At this stage, the instructions should raise specific questions and not be a general discussion of the case. If counsel is asked to advise as to quantum then specifically say so in the instructions. Would counsel like a conference with the plaintiff before drafting the advice? Should a leader be brought in?

There can often be a considerable delay between the time when counsel advises in the interlocutory stage, and the time when the papers are sent prior to trial. If you are worried that counsel has not seen the papers for some time, then do not hesitate to send the papers again. If you need a justification, you can always say that the client is anxious to meet counsel in conference!

If the client raises the question of using a leader, then discuss this with the counsel you have already instructed. Only in extremely complicated cases will a leader be justified. In any event, it is vital to give the client advance warning of the likely (high) level of fees that a QC would charge. Get the client's specific authority to incur this level of expenditure (asking for money on account will probably bring this home). If a client is legally aided, it will be necessary to get the local office's approval. This will only be given in most exceptional cases. In addition, the legally aided client should be asked to authorise the expenditure; after all, the bringing in of a QC may be disallowed on taxation, in which case the statutory charge may mean that the client bears the cost through a deduction from damages. This is a point which is easily overlooked; always obtain the client's authority before incurring major expenditure of this sort.

3 Notice after one year's delay [High Court only]

In the High Court the other side will have to be given one month's notice, if no proceeding has been taken in the case for a year. In practice, it frequently happens that there is a year's gap between there being any orders and the case being set down. So, prior to setting down, the plaintiff should check whether one month's notice has to be given to the other side. If so, use Precedent 24.

There is no equivalent rule in the county court, so there is no need to give one month's Notice of Intention to Proceed if it is a county court case in which no step has been taken for a year, but beware the automatic striking out provisions (see below).

4 Setting down for trial—county court

It is the plaintiff's duty to set the case down for trial. The automatic directions require that the case be set down for trial within six months of the close of pleadings (remember that pleadings normally close two weeks after service of the defence: see Chapter 9, section 6). However, this time limit is usually no more than wishful thinking! It is extremely rare for personal injury actions to proceed so quickly. More often than not, cases are set down out of time. The procedure for setting down or fixing a date for trial is very different in the High Court and county courts.

Automatic striking out: In the county court the automatic directions (CCR Ord 17, r 11) now provide that the case will automatically be struck out if the plaintiff does not apply to fix a date for hearing within 15 months of close of pleadings. Obviously it is essential not to miss this time limit since cases are unlikely to be reinstated easily, particularly if the primary limitation period has expired in which case you are likely to find yourself facing a negligence action.

Which court? Unless otherwise ordered the case will be heard in the court (or in the nearest trial centre) where the action is proceeding. The appropriate trial centre for each county court is set out in the County Court Directory which forms an appendix to the Green Book.

However if a party wants the action to be tried elsewhere then an application must be made (which can be by consent if the other party agrees).

Fixing a Date: To fix a date for trial the plaintiff simply writes to the clerk of the court with a note which should, if possible, be agreed by all parties giving an estimate of the length of the trial and the number of the witnesses to be called (Ord 17, r 11(8)). The clerk of the court will then fix a hearing date without reference to the parties. It is therefore extremely important that you ask all witnesses and counsel for dates inconvenient to them and inform the court of these dates when applying for a trial date. It is courteous also to ask the other side if there are any dates which they wish to avoid.

The court will fix a date and will give all parties not less than 21 days notice (but usually considerably more!) of the date fixed.
Transfer to the High Court: A party can apply to transfer to the High Court for trial. In practice this is only likely to be granted if it is now clear that the case is worth well over £50,000 or if it is between £25,000 – £50,000 and is complex in fact or law or raises questions of general public importance (Art 7 of the High Court and County Courts' Jurisdiction Order 1990). Such cases would include fatal cases, medical negligence cases where the questions of fact are likely to be complex or 'disaster' or other cases of public interest. The application can be made at any time by notice of application in the normal way. If you have a case which has to be started in the county court because it is worth under £50,000 it is well worth considering a transfer to the High court at a very early stage if it comes into one of the above categories.
Adjournments etc: It is important that the parties notify the court if there is a change in the estimated length of the trial. For instance if the defendant decides to admit liability, then this will clearly affect the length of the trial and the court should be told. Any application to adjourn will normally have to be made to the judge and may well result in a costs order being made against the party requesting the adjournment.

5 Setting down for trial—High Court

Again the plaintiff must set the case down for trial within six months of the close of pleadings.
Consent to set down: Strictly speaking, it is necessary to get consent if the case is to be set down out of time (ie more than six months after the close of pleadings). The consent would have to be obtained from the defendant (eg an open letter), or failing that, from the court (by way of summons). In practice, it is rare for a plaintiff to ask for leave to set down out of time. Certainly, it is a point that is only rarely taken by a defendant. This is probably due to the fact that in all QBD actions in which there is Summons for Directions, there is no need to apply for consent to set down out of time; however, because personal injuries have automatic directions (not a Summons for Directions) this automatic exemption does not apply. It has been suggested that this was an oversight when the rules were drafted, and certainly many practitioners do not appreciate that, strictly speaking, there is still a need to obtain permission to set a case down out of time. In practice, most plaintiff's solicitors prefer to ignore the requirement to obtain consent to set down out of time; they simply go ahead and do it. Do not forget to give one month's notice before setting down if no step has been taken in the action for a year (see above).
Which court? The automatic directions say that the case should be heard in the court (or in the nearest trial centre) where the action is proceeding.

In other words, actions in the Central Office (ie London) will be heard at the RCJ, and DR actions will be tried in the nearest trial centre. These are:

Midland and Oxford Circuit:	Birmingham, Lincoln, Nottingham, Stafford
North Eastern Circuit:	Leeds, Newcastle, Sheffield, Teesside
Northern Circuit:	Carlisle, Liverpool, Manchester, Preston
South Eastern Circuit:	Greater London (ie RCJ), Norwich, Lewes
Wales and Chester Circuit	Caernarvon, Cardiff, Chester/ Mold, Swansea
Western Circuit:	Bodmin, Bristol, Exeter, Winchester

For a full list of DRs, with their appropriate trial centres, see White Book, Vol 2, para 1055.

These trial venues are not compulsory. If the parties both agree, then another venue can be chosen without the need for an order. Simply lodge the consent of both parties when setting down. On the other hand, if one party wants the action to be tried elsewhere, and the other does not, then a summons will have to be issued, asking for the venue to be changed.

Similarly, the automatic directions assume that the case is of Category B complexity. There are three categories:

Category A:	cases of great substance, or great difficulty, or of public importance.
Category B:	cases of substance or difficulty.
Category C:	other cases.

So, if it is felt that the case is Category A, a summons will have to be issued. The benefit of having the case in Category A is that a more experienced judge will hear it.

Procedure on setting down: The case is set down by sending two bundles of copy pleadings (plus £30 fee) to the court where the case is to be tried.

In practice, the court can be extremely fussy about the correct presentation of the bundles of documents (ie the order in which the papers are bundled; their appearance; and the other procedural requirements). Carefully follow the steps set out in Procedural Table 9. This sets out the full requirements when setting down. Particular points to note are that the various documents are bound in a specified order; not in chronological order. Also, the last document in the bundle must be a Statement of Parties (ie full details of the solicitors, with their references, etc). A statement of value is also needed to certify that the case is still worth more than £50,000. If medical reports have been agreed they should also be lodged. Also, there must be an indorsement on the bundle, stating that the automatic directions (ie Ord 24, r 8) have been complied with, and giving an estimated length of trial. Refer to Procedural Table 9.

One point to remember is that the court can, when the case is set down, decide that it should be transferred to the county court. It is often wise to anticipate this difficulty by adding an extra paragraph to the letter sent to the court when setting down; in that paragraph express concern at the prospect of it being transferred to the county court, and give reasons why the case should not be transferred. (See below.)

Notifying the other side: The other side must be notified within 24 hours of the case being set down. Use Stock Letter 43.

Compulsory transfer to the county court: A High Court case can be compulsorily transferred to the county court (CCA 1984, s 40). If no statement of value is lodged on setting down then the case will automatically be transferred to the county court. However even if you certify that the case is worth more than £50,000 the case can still be transferred against the wishes of the parties.

The parties are supposed to consider such a transfer before the case is set down for trial. If they are both in agreement, then a consent order can be made. On the other hand, if only one of the parties wants transfer to take place, then a summons will have to be issued by that party, asking for directions as to the mode of trial (under Ord 25, r 8(3)).

In practice, it will usually be the case that both the plaintiff and the defendant want the action to remain in the High Court. Although there might be a cost saving in transferring the case to the county court, most practitioners prefer to have cases tried before an experienced High Court judge, rather than a county court judge who may have limited experience of personal injury actions. Also, the plaintiff will probably feel that a county court judge will not be used to awarding large damages, and this may result in the plaintiff getting lower damages than would otherwise have been the case. Accordingly, it is unlikely that either the plaintiff or the defendant will want the case to be compulsorily transferred to the county court.

To overcome this problem, each personal injury action which is set down under the automatic directions is scrutinised by a master. He will look at the pleadings and decide whether it might be suitable for compulsory transfer to the county court. In effect, the master will be looking for the straightforward cases. Generally, cases worth up to £75,000 to £150,000 may be regarded as suitable for transfer, if the master feels they are not complicated enough to warrant the attention of a High Court judge. If the master feels that the case is suitable for transfer, then a court summons will be issued and sent to the parties shortly after the case has been set down.

It should be easy to tell whether the summons has been issued by the court (ie through the master's intervention), or by the other side. If it was at the master's initiative, it will have 'court summons' in the top left hand corner, and will be on a printed form. Alternatively, if it was the other side who made the application, then the wording of the summons will say 'For an order on the application of the defendant . . .'.

When a court summons is received, the parties should confer. It may well be that they are both vehemently opposed to transfer to the county court. It has to be accepted that the High Court has seen compulsory transfer as a way of quickly clearing the lengthy backlog of cases waiting to be heard. Thus, many practitioners feel that cases are being transferred to the county court when they should be remaining in the High Court. Unfortunately, the mere fact that both parties oppose transfer will not be a sufficient reason to prevent transfer. Something more specific will be needed. In short, the parties will have to do what they can to persuade the master that the case is more complicated than it looks or if it falls into the criteria set out in the High Court and County Courts Jurisdiction Order 1990 (see under county court, above).

If, at the hearing of the summons, the master confirms that the case is to be transferred to the county court, then the High Court will forward all the papers to the county court (see Precedent 33 for the steps to be taken). The setting down fee will be returned to the plaintiff.

Non-compulsory transfer to county court: Compulsory transfer of a case to the county court should not be confused with the more traditional transfer. Typically, this will happen when a plaintiff begins a case in the High Court, and then decides (eg because the medical evidence is not as strong as it originally seemed) that the case is worth less, and so should be transferred to the county court. To do this, the plaintiff issues a summons. For the procedure, see below section 20. If the plaintiff knew that the case is worth less than £50,000 but fails to transfer it down, the courts may penalise the solicitor personally in costs.

The listing of the case: Once the case has been set down in the High Court, it will be placed in the list of cases for trial. The procedure in the RCJ is slightly different from that in the DR.

All personal injury cases are heard by a judge only; so they go in the 'Non-Jury Listing'. Initially, the action will be put in the General List, in which case it will simply wait its turn for trial in the usual way. But, there are two other possibilities;

- It can be transferred to the *Short Cause List,* if the estimated time of hearing is no more than four hours. It will be remembered that an estimate of the length of hearing has to be written on the copy pleadings when the case is set down for trial (see above).
- Alternatively, an application can be made for a *Fixture.*

In theory, an action could appear in the Warned List (ie likely to be heard in the next week or so) as little as a month after the case has been set down. In practice, of course, the backlog of cases makes this extremely unlikely.

In most personal injury cases the parties prefer to apply for a fixture. This avoids the uncertainty of a case being in the General or Short Cause Lists, since there is then no way of knowing exactly when it will be heard: obviously, the date of trial will depend upon the progress of the other cases in the list. To avoid the danger of doctors, witnesses and barristers being unavailable, it is preferable to apply for a fixture. This may delay the date of trial, but it avoids uncertainty.

The basic rule is that an application for a fixture should be made within four weeks of the case being set down. If it is not made within four weeks, then consent has to be obtained from the other side (ask them for a letter). In practice, both sides will probably want a fixture, so the obtaining of consent is likely to be a formality. If the other side refuse consent, then it is necessary to make an application to the judge in charge of the Non-Jury List. Such applications are rare.

The application for a fixture is made on Oyez Form B14D. This form has to be completed by both parties (it includes details of numbers of witnesses, names and addresses of counsel, etc). Normally, the plaintiff completes it and sends it to the clerk of the lists. An appointment will be fixed, and the form returned to the plaintiffs, who will then forward it to the defendant for completion. The solicitors should then:

- instruct counsel's clerk, to attend the hearing (as the clerk will have counsel's diary and know dates when he is not available),
- check with expert witnesses (and, perhaps, with other witnesses) if there are any particular dates to be avoided.

Not all solicitors send a representative to the hearing. In practice, it is more likely to be a discussion between counsel's clerks, to ensure that an inconvenient date is not chosen. It is extremely unlikely that the clerk of the lists will not agree to a fixture. In practice, the clerk is likely to fix a date; it could well be a year or 18 months hence (in London).

Alternatively, the clerk of the lists may refuse to give it a fixture. Instead, the clerk can leave it in the General List, but mark it 'not before . . .'; or he can leave it in the General List and mark it to keep its place in the List (ie 'KP'); or the clerk can simply order that it remains in the General List. If either side is unhappy with the decision, an appeal can be made to the judge (within seven days).

It is important to realize that once a fixed date has been given, then that date can only be altered, or vacated, with the consent of the judge in charge of the lists.

Adjournments, etc: It is important that the parties notify the court if there is a change in the estimated length of the trial. For instance, if the defendant decides to admit liability, then this will clearly affect the length of the trial, and the court should be told.

If the case is not a fixture, it is relatively easy to get an adjournment. A consent application is made to the clerk of the lists and it will normally be approved without any difficulty. On the other hand, if the case is in the Warned List, then the judge's permission will be needed (and the courts do seem to be tightening up on granting leave). If it is not a consent application, then it will be necessary to apply to the judge.

If the case is a fixture, then an application to adjourn, etc must be made to a judge.

6 Special damages

Check that the special damage calculation is up-to-date. Should you be writing for up-to-date figures (eg to Compensation Recovery Unit, employers, Inland Revenue)? If so, send off the appropriate letters immediately. Make a note to do the special damage calculation once you have replies to all those letters.

Ensure that the other side has been sent a copy of the updated special damage calculations, and the supporting documents. Will they agree the calculations? Usually defendants will delay agreement until the last moment and then try to agree to a compromise (ie lower) figure. Try to avoid this by writing to them sometime before trial giving a date by which they should agree the calculation, failing which subpoenas will be issued and served on the people needed to prove the figure, and stating that the plaintiff will ask that those costs be the defendant's in any event. Threatening the service of a Notice to Admit Facts or Documents may also encourage an agreement, as may a Civil Evidence Act notice (see Chapter 12, section 11).

If the special damage calculation is correct, do not compromise on it; if necessary, call the DSS officials and employers' wages clerk to prove the figures formally, and ensure that the plaintiff formally proves out-of-pocket losses and expenses when giving evidence.

Although the plaintiff's future continuing loss of wages (ie after trial) is not strictly a special damage item, it is usual for the plaintiff's solicitor to calculate such a figure on the basis of past earnings, likely wage increases, promotion prospects, and so on and the rules state that the figures should appear in the schedule of special damage. Send the calculation to the other side for agreement but be more prepared to compromise than with the special damage calculation, since the figure must, at best, be only a guess. Obviously, if the supporting evidence is strong (for instance, trade union official, or Department of Employment rehabilitation officer) do not compromise but try to convince the judge that the calculation is fair and reasonable.

Continuing loss will often depend upon the attitude of the plaintiff in seeking out work and being prepared to 'have a go' at a new job. The defendants may well suggest that the plaintiff is not putting sufficient effort into job-hunting activities, or even that the plaintiff has 'compensationitis' and 'will make a good recovery upon receipt of the settlement monies'. Be prepared to refute these suggestions at trial, even if the defendants have only hinted at them previously, by calling medical evidence (whether it be in an agreed report or by oral evidence of the doctor) and the evidence of social workers, rehabilitation officer, or new employer, to show that (as is often the case) the allegations of malingering are totally unfounded. It is often advisable to write to the other side informing them that these people will be called unless the continuing loss figure is agreed beforehand.

If the plaintiff is receiving income support or family credit benefit, do not forget that this will end once the plaintiff gets damages (assuming the plaintiff's capital will then exceed £8,000: between £3,000 and £8,000 there is a sliding scale reduction). So, when working out the future loss be sure to exclude income support (see Chapter 5).

The Schedule of Special Damage: The plaintiff must update the Schedule of Special Damage, for use by the trial judge (see Chapter 5). Full particulars of special damage must be set out, including any claim for loss of earnings; loss of future earning capacity; medical or other expenses due to disability; loss of pension rights. Thc Schcdulc should be set out in the form and style of any other pleading (see Appendix G).

7 Medical evidence

Is this up to date? Presumably, reports will have been exchanged by now (see Chapter 11, section 8), but ask the other side to exchange any further reports they have received. Try to avoid delay in exchange; the more the other side are allowed to delay, the less time there will be in which to consider their medical evidence (and, if necessary, go back to one's doctor for comments).

If the other side's medical evidence is in agreement with one's own, suggest that the better of the reports goes in as agreed evidence. Failing that, agree them both, or agree them subject to certain paragraphs being deleted. There will then be no need to call the doctors to give evidence, and a considerable sum of costs can be saved.

Check that 'agreed' reports really do agree! It is not uncommon to find that agreed reports do contain differences of opinion. For instance, if one doctor estimates that a pre-existing condition would have disabled the plaintiff within five years, there is no agreement if the other doctor gives a period of seven years. The doctors, will have to be called if the reports cannot be agreed.

If you are thinking of agreeing a report, the safest course of action is to send the other side's report to your own doctor, and get confirmation that it is agreed. If the doctor does not agree then you will at least have a letter from your doctor highlighting the areas of difference, which may well simplify counsel's task at the hearing.

If the disagreement between the doctors relates to the possibility of the plaintiff suffering a deterioration in condition (or developing a disease) then the case might be suitable for provisional damages. For instance, if it is unclear whether accident-induced arthritis will cause the plaintiff to give up work in, say, five years' time or 15 years' time, then the answer may be to opt for provisional damages. If so, it might well be possible to agree the rest of the report (ie everything except the prognosis as to arthritis).

Do not forget to update the report before trial. If the case is a fixture, it is sensible to diary the case approximately eight months before the fixed date; at that time, write to the doctor requesting an up-to-date medical. This should ensure that your medical report is no more than six months old at the date of trial. As a general guide, one can say that a report should never be more than 12 months old, preferably not more than six months old.

A without prejudice meeting of the experts: Consider whether it would be helpful for the doctors to meet, to see if they can resolve their differences. Since 1987, RSC Ord 38 r 38, which is also incorporated into CCR, allows the court to order that there be a meeting 'without prejudice' of such experts within such periods before or after the disclosure of their reports as the court may specify, for the purpose of identifying those parts of their evidence which are in issue. Where such a meeting takes place the experts may prepare a joint statement indicating those parts of their evidence on which they are, and those which they are not, in agreement.

So, if the evidence is complex—and the doctors are far apart—consider issuing a summons for the court to order a meeting of experts under RSC Ord 38 r 38. Remember that this does not just apply to doctors' reports, it can also be ordered in respect of, for example, engineers' reports.

Lodging agreed reports: If medical reports are agreed, then they must be lodged with the court. It is for the plaintiff to do this. But, if the reports are not agreed, then they do not have to be lodged with the court. However it will be helpful for all parties if you prepare a bundle of reports (whether agreed or not) for use at the trial.

The plaintiff's solicitor should prepare the bundle. Place all the agreed reports in order, as one bundle, and number each of the pages. Then, prepare a front sheet which is an index. Set this out as though it were a pleading (ie names of parties; action number, etc, see p 67) and set out an index to the bundle. This should set out the page numbers; the name and speciality of the doctor; the date of the report; and the party for whom the report was prepared. This is best done by having columns headed date, name of expert, speciality, date of report, prepared for. Do not forget to take spare copies (for the other side, yourself, and your counsel). Make sure that the numbering of all the copies is identical to the numbering on the copy to be lodged with the court!

If there is other expert evidence (eg engineers' reports) that has been agreed, then this should also be included in the bundle or put in a separate bundle.

8 Photographs and plans

Ensure that photographs and plans have been sent to the other side for agreement. While in the county court there is no particular time limit for this in the High Court no photograph or plan will be admissible in evidence unless it has been sent to the other side for their agreement at least ten days before the date of the trial, or unless the judge gives leave at the trial (Ord 38, r4).

If the other side will not agree the photographs and/or plan, it is advisable to subpoena their makers to prove them formally. Notify the other side and inform them that the judge will be asked to order that the other side bear these costs in any event; consider serving a Notice to Admit Documents (see Chapter 11, section 4).

9 Continuing the negotiations

When pressing ahead with the preparations for trial you should not overlook the possibility of negotiating a settlement to the action, for there is no point (apart from an increased bill of costs!) in pressing on to trial when an action can be settled for its full value. However, many defendants feel that if a plaintiff is to receive compensation before the time of trial and avoid the uncertainties of trial it should be paid for by a lower damages figure. Whilst there is obviously an element of truth in that, the reverse is also true, namely that the defendants are also avoiding the uncertainties of trial (and possibly higher damages) and the costs of the trial, so do not be tempted to under-settle a case. If the case is good, press on to trial unless a reasonable settlement is offered. Do not forget that the defendant's solicitor will often be tied down by the instructions of the insurance company. Many insurance companies relish 'horse-trading negotiations' and with such companies it is often helpful to ask for considerably more than the case is worth, on the assumption that they will then offer much less, and it may be possible to settle the case for its true value with the insurers feeling they have managed to negotiate a low settlement.

Many insurance companies give very poor initial instructions to their solicitors and thus the defendant's solicitor may be 'in the dark' for the early part of the action. However, by the time of setting down, the solicitor should be fully instructed and have an idea of the value of the case. Do not be reluctant to telephone the other side (a suitable pretext can usually be found) to see if they are prepared to settle now and avoid the costs of trial. Factors that could help induce a settlement at this stage are:

(1) the suggestion that leaders might be necessary;

(2) in a legal aid case, a reminder to the defendants that even if they succeed they are unlikely to recover costs from the plaintiff in excess of the legal aid contribution, and that, accordingly, whether they win or lose, the action is going to cost the defendants a considerable sum of money, some of which might be saved by settling now. Obviously, if there has been a payment into court, this argument will lose some of its force (see Chapter 8);

(3) a statement that the brief to counsel has not yet been delivered, but will be in a certain number of days' time. Once the brief is delivered counsel is entitled to the brief fee, even if the case settles, and so by settling now (rather than at the door of the court, for example) the defendants can avoid that fee. In fact, it is now generally accepted that counsel should renegotiate the fee in those circumstances, and cannot insist on the full amount on the brief. However, it is an argument that may impress an inexperienced opponent!

Customarily, any negotiations in person always take place at the office of the plaintiff's solicitor. As in all negotiations, do not disclose the weakness of your client's case. Beware the defendant's solicitor who comes for a discussion, extracts a figure that the plaintiff's solicitor would regard as a fair compromise, and then goes away to pay a lesser sum into court. It is sometimes worth trying to reach an understanding that the discussion will not be used for that purpose, and that the defendant's solicitor will only be seen at this late stage if the defendant agrees not to make a payment into court after the discussion.

Any offer in settlement must be put to the client for instructions, but advise the client fully as to the adequacy (or otherwise) of the offer and the costs consequences of acceptance and refusal.

10 Structured settlements

Structured settlements are still rare. In essence, a structured settlement allows money to be invested in an annuity fund; the income from the annuity is then treated as tax-free by the revenue. For instance, in one of the first structured settlement cases, the case was settled for a total of £410,000. Of that, £110,000 was paid out as a lump sum to the plaintiff; the remaining £300,000 was invested in an annuity (producing £25,500 per annum, index linked, and tax-free).

As it stands, structured settlements are so rare that there are no clearly defined guidelines on the procedure to be adopted. In essence, it is a matter of consulting with the insurance industry to see what sums may be available on an annuity basis, given the likely settlement figures. Certainly, the approval of the Inland Revenue is crucial, since the whole structure of the settlement depends upon payments being tax-free. A recent Practice Direction [1992] 1 AER 862 sets out the procedure in settlements of claims in the High Court to deal with the administrative difficulty caused by the short period over which life offices keep open offers of annuities at a given price.

The case referred to above was discussed in (1989) *Gazette* 26 July, 3. Also relevant is a letter from the plaintiff's solicitor in (1989) *Gazette*, 6 September, 9. There, the judge suggested guidelines that could be followed when seeking court approval. Firstly, one would need a detailed counsel's opinion assessing the value of the claim and its constituent elements on a conventional basis, together with the appropriate lump-sum for settlement. Careful consideration of life expectancy (based on the medical opinions) should be included. Next, one would need a report by accountants or other financial experts as to the fiscal and investment advantages of a structured settlement (in particular, as regards as to the life expectancy, and likely future costs of care). There would also have to be evidence that there are available sufficient funds outside the structured settlement to meet any foreseeable capital needs of the plaintiff. In addition, one would want a draft of the agreement to have been submitted to the Inland Revenue and approved in principle by them; also, of course, Court of Protection approval might also be needed. Useful recent cases regarding structured settlements include *Grimsley* v *Grimsley and Meade* (28 January 1991) and *Everett* v *Everett and Norfolk County Council* (4 June 1991).

There is little doubt that structured settlements will become increasingly popular, and firm guidelines and procedures will soon emerge. In the meantime, in cases of substantial value, it is always worth considering whether a structured settlement approach might produce a better settlement for the plaintiff.

11 Civil Evidence Act notices

Is there any witness who cannot attend court, but whose evidence could be given in writing? If so, there are several possibilities:

- a special examiner can take the evidence of a witness who is unable to attend the trial (for example) because of illness.
- a written record of the witness's evidence may also be admissible by:
  —leave of the court (under the general discretion of the judge given at trial)
  —agreement between the parties
  —service of a notice under the Civil Evidence Act.

In practice, it is service of a Civil Evidence Act notice that is usually used to allow written evidence to be given. The CEA deals with two broad categories of evidence. Firstly, there is hearsay evidence (ie opinion, etc) of someone which has been recorded in a document, such as a proof or statement. That proof or statement can be put in as evidence (CEA 1968, s 2). In addition, the Act deals with official records and notes (ie records and notes kept by a person who is under a duty to keep such notes, for instance, a clerk who keeps hospital records, DSS benefit records, wage details, etc). These are dealt with by CEA 1968, s 5.

Usually, a CEA notice (CCR Ord 20, r 15 or RSC Ord 38, r 21) is only served when a witness is abroad, dead, ill, untraced, or if the witness cannot be expected to recall the accuracy of the statement (CCR Ord 20, r 16 incorporating RSC Ord 38, r 25). Obviously, if it is official records and notes that are being put in evidence, then it cannot normally be expected that the witness will recall the accuracy of the records (since, presumably the witness deals with hundreds, if not thousands, of such records each year). With hearsay evidence, or a statement or proof, the justification of serving a CEA notice is likely to be that the witness is abroad, dead, ill, or untraced.

The other side must be sent a copy of the evidence, and be notified of the intention to put the evidence in without calling the witness at the trial. This notice cannot normally be given more than 14 days before the day fixed for trial in the county court, or in the High Court the much more stringent requirement of 21 days after setting down. The other side can object by serving a counter-notice, within seven days in the county court or 21 days in the High Court. If no counter-notice is served then the evidence is admissible without the witness being called to attend trial. But, if a counter-notice is served, then the evidence will not be admissible unless the witness attends court, or unless the judge exercises discretion to allow it. Alternatively, the applicant can issue an application, with a view to persuading the court that there is sufficient reason why the witness cannot attend. In addition, the other side can, within seven days in the county court or 21 days in the High Court, serve a notice of intention to call evidence affecting the credibility of the maker of the statement, and also evidence of inconsistent statements (CCR Ord 20, rr 21 and 22 and RSC Ord 38, rr 30 and 31).

The procedural rules on CEA evidence are found in CCR Ord 20, rr 14–24 and RSC Ord 38, rr 20-30. These are summarised in Precedent 26, which includes a specimen notice and application.

In fact, the court can override these time limits if it wants to. Under CCR Ord 20, r 24 and RSC Ord 38, r 29 hearsay statements can be admitted at trial, even though the other rules have not been complied with. As always, the test is one of fairness; so, if the parties have deliberately withheld the hearsay evidence until the last moment they might be penalised in costs (or, exceptionally, refused leave to use the evidence).

The main disadvantage of putting evidence in under the CEA is that the evidence is disclosed to the other side before the trial but this disadvantage will largely disappear in light of the increased practice of exchanging witness statement before trial. Against that, there is the advantage that it cannot be destroyed by cross-examination. When it is formally necessary to prove records, it is advisable to serve a CEA notice if the other side will not agree the records; if the other side unreasonably serve a counter-notice insisting that the maker attend court, it may be that the judge will penalise them as to costs. CEA notices are especially useful for forcing the other side to agree uncontroversial evidence (eg trade union information as to the rates of pay currently being paid in a particular industry; letter from Department of Employment as to attendance of the plaintiff at a Job Rehabilitation Centre, etc). With such evidence it is usually sufficient to state in the notice that 'maker cannot reasonably be expected to have any recollection of matters relevant to the accuracy or otherwise of the statement'. An alternative way of forcing the other side to agree evidence is to serve a Notice to Admit Documents. This will often have the desired effect. See Chapter 11, section 4.

Evidence given in previous court proceedings: If the subject matter of the action has already been discussed in a court (for example, in a road accident case there may have been a magistrates' court prosecution at which full statements were made), serve a CEA notice (in the same way as if dealing with a statement or record). But, in this case, the other side cannot serve a counter-notice objecting to the evidence going in. Their only remedy is to apply to the court by way of application. The form of notice and application is similar to those used for statements and records under the CEA.

Do not forget to consider amending the claim to record any conviction (and a guilty plea). In addition, obtain a memorandum of conviction from the court and ask the defendant to admit the conviction.

12 The brief to counsel

Do not leave counsel's brief until the last moment. It is often tempting to do so in the hope that the case will settle before the work is done, but it is unfair to both counsel and the client to dictate the brief hurriedly at the last moment. Besides which, the preparation and dictation of the brief will be rewarded on taxation.

In a private case, telephone counsel's clerk to agree a brief fee. The amount of the brief fee will obviously vary with the complexity of the case, and the experience of the individual barrister. As a rough guide, one can say that the brief fee for a straightforward road accident case will be at least £500. Legal aid briefs do not, of course, bear a fee.

It is important that the preparation of the brief receive undivided attention and concentration; the instructing solicitor will know the case in far more detail than counsel, and it is essential that the solicitor's full views be communicated to counsel. Even if counsel knows the case well and has had several conferences with the client, it is still essential to do a full brief. There can be no way of guaranteeing that a particular counsel will not be part-heard on the day of trial, in which case the brief will go to another barrister who may know nothing about the case.

Do not treat counsel as omnipotent and omniscient. Counsel will be only too pleased to read the opinion of a professional colleague and to receive a full and detailed brief. It is surprising how many solicitors will have a file open for several years and put a considerable amount of work into the case, only to waste it all by not dictating a full brief to counsel. The brief to counsel is the culmination of all the labours that have gone into the file; it must be given the attention and time it deserves.

Since the brief may in exceptional circumstances be returned and sent to another barrister on the eve of trial, ensure that the brief is easy to follow and well laid out. It may help to sub-divide the brief into headings, so that counsel can easily find a way around the papers.

Additionally, remember that the brief will be examined on taxation and will be a major influence on the taxing officer's assessment of the case's complexity. A thin brief of little substance is likely to colour the taxing officer's attitude, as are statements in the brief such as 'this is a straightforward road accident case presenting no problems': every case has its problems.

Dictating the brief: When dictating the brief to counsel it may be helpful to approach it as follows:

(1) List enclosures. Always include writ or summons and pleadings (not the High Court Acknowledgment of Service), orders, party and party correspondence, lists of documents and documents disclosed, counsel's advices, legal aid documents, medical reports, engineers' reports, notice of payment in statements and proofs, etc. Do not enclose unnecessary papers, such as summonses. Make the list of enclosures comprehensive; refer to each individual item by name and date. This will make it easier for your secretary to collate the papers, and it will enable counsel to easily check that nothing has been omitted.

If there are lots of enclosures, then it is best to sub-divide the papers; have different bundles for medical evidence, special damage, etc. If the court bundle has already been prepared then this should be sent which will save duplication of work and avoid confusing counsel.

The plaintiff's proof, and those of witnesses, should be brought up to date. If you have typed out proofs, there is no need to include letters from witnesses, but do keep them in the file. If you are re-typing statements of witnesses whose evidence has already been exchanged with the other side, then consider whether you are making amendments that have to be disclosed to the other side. Your witnesses will be constrained to giving evidence on matters of fact that have previously been covered in their disclosed statements (assuming that witness statements were exchanged). Accordingly, your witnesses cannot deal with other matters at trial (unless they arise in the course of the trial, or unless consent is obtained). If in doubt, therefore, serve a copy of the amended statement on the other side.

(2) Start the brief by telling counsel some short details about the case and the plaintiff. State why the action is being brought against the defendant, and give the plaintiff's age, occupation and marital status and dependants (if relevant). An introductory paragraph of this sort will enable counsel to know what the action is about before reading the detailed instructions, and thus he can have the relevant questions and issues in mind.

(3) Give a summary of the client's version of what happened. Counsel will have the plaintiff's proof, so there is no need to go into full detail. Stress major allegations and clarify any points that may not be clear.

(4) Go through the pleadings. Summarise the allegations pleaded by counsel in the claim and set out the defendant's admissions and denials. Do not forget to deal with Further and Better Particulars. Draw counsel's attention to any allegations of contributory negligence and to the plaintiff's (and witnesses', if applicable) comments on these allegations.

(5) Deal with interrogatories and Notice to Admit Facts.

(6) Next, tell counsel what evidence is available to prove the case. List the witnesses who will be at court; outline the essential features of the witnesses' evidence and how it helps the client's case. Do not set out the witnesses' evidence in full, but refer counsel to the proof.

Similarly, tell counsel what any expert witness (for instance, an engineer) will say: refer to the strong and weak parts of the report and mention the points that you think counsel might usefully pursue when cross examining the other side's expert. What evidence has been agreed? (For example, police report, photos, plans.) List the witness statements that have been disclosed and deal with the contents of the other side's witness statements. If you have recently updated any statements, then make sure that counsel has a copy of the latest version and also the earlier (disclosed) version, to allow comparison between the two. Should you be disclosing a copy of the updated statement if there are any significant changes in what is being said?

(7) Discovery. Mention the documents disclosed and what relevance they have.

(8) So far, the brief has concentrated on factual matters, that is the hard evidence needed to prove the case. Now it is necessary to discuss how counsel can go about winning the case and to suggest which parts of the defendant's case are weak and should be attacked. Tell counsel if there are doubts as to the reliability of some of the client's witnesses, or if it is thought that the plaintiff will be easily confused during cross examination. How much (if any) contributory negligence should the client be prepared to concede? Refer back to counsel's advice and the action taken since then.

(9) Deal with the relevant law. Many briefs ignore the law and assume that counsel will come to court equipped to deal with any point that

arises. Often this is correct, but do not necessarily assume it! Do not be reluctant to tell counsel what the law is, or how you interpret the recent cases.

(10) Go through the medical evidence. Have reports been agreed? Will any doctor be attending court?

(11) Set out the special damage position. Tell counsel whether the calculation enclosed has been agreed. If not, list the people who will be called to prove it and how the calculation is worked out. Usually counsel will have a copy of the special damage calculation as served on the defendant. Do not forget to explain how you worked out the details of your calculation.

Explain any doubtful parts of the calculation and how much could reasonably be agreed as a compromise.

Refer to the calculation even if an all-in figure has been agreed with the other side, for the judge may want to know how the figure is made up. Set out your calculations of interest.

(12) What is the case worth? If you have views on this, then tell counsel.

At the same time, tell counsel what offers have been made in correspondence, or payments made into court.

(13) Does counsel want a conference, other than at the door of the court? As a general rule, it is worth having a conference. Apart from ensuring that the barrister prepares the case properly, it will reassure the client. After all, it is not encouraging to arrive at court on the day of the trial, and to meet one's barrister for the first time only a few minutes before the case begins.

(14) In the concluding paragraph remind counsel of any special order that should be sought from the judge. Set out the dates of the accident and service for the purposes of calculating interest. Are there any costs that were awarded at interlocutory hearings that can be claimed even if the case is lost? Tell counsel what time to attend court; ensure that there will be ample time to meet the client and expert witnesses, especially if there is a possibility of 'brief-swopping' which will result in a substitute counsel being used.

Ideally, the brief should be delivered to counsel some two or three weeks before trial. Keep a copy of everything that has been sent to counsel, as these may be needed for last-minute negotiations with the other side.

Notify everybody. Write to the client (Stock Letter 37), the witnesses (Stock Letter 38), doctors (Stock Letter 40) and experts (Stock Letter 41) notifying them of the trial date. If there is a road accident counterclaim, write to the client's insurers who are financing that part of the action and bring them up to date on the position and prospects. Check that counsel's clerk is watching the lists and has received the brief. Is the original estimate of the length of trial still correct? If not, notify the clerk of the lists.

13 Witness Summons (county court)

In the county court there is no need to formally summons doctors or experts who have agreed to attend but all other witnesses should be sent a Witness Summons, either to give oral evidence or to produce documents. The form is set out as N20 and N20(1) in the county court forms and application is made on Form N286 to the court either by post or personally. The summons may not be issued less than seven days before the date on which attendance is required (CCR Ord 20 r 12(4)(*a*)). There must be a separate summons for each witness but this can be issued without the name of the witness being inserted.

To call a witness outside the jurisdiction of the court but within the UK (ie Scotland or Northern Ireland) it is necessary to apply *ex parte* to a master of the QBD by summons for a subpoena (County Courts Act 1984, s 55). For the procedure see 14 below. The court cannot order the attendance of a witness outside the UK and in these circumstances you should use a Civil Evidence Act notice (see 11).

Service The Witness Summons must be served at least four days before the hearing. Service should be done personally. Ensure that you enclose enough conduct money to enable the witness to get to and from the court. It can also be served by post by a officer of the court if the solicitor gives a certificate for postal service. However a witness will not fined for failing to appear at the return day unless the court is satisfied that the Witness Summons came to the witness's knowledge in sufficient time and with sufficient conduct money. You should therefore never arrange to serve a Witness Summons by post unless the witness has agreed such service and will acknowledge receipt. A witness who has been served with a Witness Summons must attend court or face imprisonment and an action for damages caused by non-attendance. A witness who believes attendance is unnecessary can apply to the court if there is an irregularity or if attendance will be oppressive or an abuse of the process of the court. If a witness is unable to attend (eg because of serious illness) then consider applying for an adjournment of the trial. Alternatively consider applying to the district judge for an order under CCR Ord 20 r 13 that an examiner be appointed to take the witness's sworn evidence.

14 Subpoenas (High Court)

In the High Court the procedure is slightly different: there is normally no need to subpoena doctors or experts who have agreed to attend, but all other witnesses should be subpoenaed. There are two types of subpoena:

- *subpoena ad testificandum,* for a witness who is to give oral evidence,
- *subpoena duces tecum,* which orders a person to produce documents at the trial (for example, one might be served on a hospital registrar to produce case notes).

Amazingly, it is not possible to issue a writ of subpoena through the post; thus, personal attendance at the action department of the court (either the court where the action has been proceeding or the court where the trial is taking place) is necessary. They will need a completed *praecipe* (Oyez Form E20; also printed in White Book as Form 28 in Appendix A; also obtainable in Inland Revenue Office, RCJ, rooms 2 and 6). Complete the writ of subpoena (Oyez Form G5 for *subpoena ad testificandum,* and Oyez Form G6 for *subpoena duces tecum),* hand it to the court officer and the subpoena will be stamped and returned for personal service. The *praecipe* is stamped and retained by the court.

In the case of the *subpoena duces tecum* there must be a separate subpoena for each witness, but it is not necessary to specify the documents at the time of issue; these can be inserted later by the solicitor. In the case of the *subpoena ad restificandum* this can also be issued without the names of the witnesses being inserted; a note is made in the margin of the number of persons that can be served, and their names can be inserted subsequently. Once they have been inserted, they cannot then be crossed out. However, it should be remembered that a subpoena should be served personally and it may be more convenient for the process server if there is only one name on each form of subpoena.

Precedent 28 suggests suitable wording for several subpoenas.

To issue a subpoena on a person outside the jurisdiction of the court (eg Scotland or Northern Ireland) it is necessary to apply ex *parte* to the master (see Procedural Table 3). The court cannot order the attendance of a witness who is outside the UK.

Service: The subpoena must be served within 12 weeks of issue, and it must be served at least four days before the hearing. It is most important to diary these time limits. In particular, it is all too easy to issue a subpoena, only to find that the trial is postponed, which may mean that the subpoena will no longer be valid. So, when issuing a subpoena, diary the three months' period for its expiry, and also diary the date by which it must be served.

Service of the subpoena must be in person (it cannot be by post, unless the witness is prepared to accept postal service). Be sure to enclose sufficient conduct money to enable the witness to get to the court and to cover subsistence during the trial. Once served with the subpoena, the witness must attend court or face imprisonment and an action for damages in respect of non-attendance. A witness who thinks attendance is unnecessary can apply to the master if there is an irregularity, or if attendance would be oppressive or an abuse of the process of the court.

If a witness is unable to attend court (eg because of a serious illness) then consider applying for an adjournment of the trial. Alternatively, consider applying to the master for an order that an examiner be appointed to take the witness's sworn evidence. Usually, the examination will be recorded by a shorthand transcript (generally, see Ord 39, r 1).

15 Trial documents (county court)

The rules regarding trial documents are set out in CCR Ord 17, r 12. At least 14 days before the hearing the defendant should inform the plaintiff of the documents which it wishes to have included in a trial bundle. However it is more normal for the plaintiff to produce the first index and send it to the defendant with a request to be informed of any other documents which the defendant requires within 14 days of trial.

At least seven days before the day fixed for the hearing the plaintiff must file with the court one copy of the paginated and indexed bundle comprising the documents on which either party intends to rely or which either party wishes to have before the court, together with two copies each of any Request for Particulars and particulars given and Answers to Interrogatories (it is usually more convenient to provide two bundles of all the pleadings and relevant orders properly indexed and including those documents), two copies of all witness statements which have been exchanged and experts' reports which have been disclosed together with an indication of whether the contents of such documents are agreed. (It is usual to set these out with an index showing page numbers, name and speciality of expert, date of report, party for whom it was prepared and whether it is agreed) and two copies of all requisite legal aid documents.

It is sensible to put all documents in separate bundles eg pleadings, legal aid documents, documents, plans and photographs, witness statements and expert reports. Each bundle should be indexed and bear the case heading. It should be headed with a description of its contents and it should bear an index page setting out each document and its pagination. Ensure that the pagination is the same in every document and that all pages are included. Judges find nothing more irritating than confusion over court bundles. Ensure there are sufficient copies for the court, counsel, you, the other party and a spare copy for witnesses. You can charge the other party photocopying costs for preparation of their bundle.

16 Trial documents (High Court)

Ensure that there are sufficient numbers of all necessary documents; in particular have sufficient copies of reports, plans, witness statements, photographs, and special damage calculations. Are there enough copies for both solicitors and both counsel, the judge, and the witness? Ensure that any copies are clear; if they are not, the court may require the solicitor responsible to provide an explanation and you might also be penalised on costs. If there are bundles of documents, and the pages are numbered, check that the pagination on each is identical.

If any medical (or other experts') reports have been agreed the plaintiff must lodge an indexed bundle with the court (see this chapter, section 8).

17 Adjourning: settling

Often, the parties start serious negotiations shortly before the trial. As a result, they may want an adjournment, or they may have been able to work out acceptable terms of settlement.

For the procedure on taking a case out of the list, see this chapter section 4.

For how to formalise or record a settlement, see Chapter 13.

18 When the case is in the Warned List (High Court)

In the county court you will have been given a fixed date for trial and in the High Court you will normally have obtained a fixed date because of the need for expert witnesses (see section 6.) However if you have not applied for a fixture the case will be warned.

When the case appears in the lists as warned for the next day, telephone the client and his witnesses telling them when and where to attend. Also telephone the expert witnesses and doctors. Telephone counsel's clerk to check that counsel is available. Be reluctant to accept another barrister at this late stage, point out that the brief was sent down a considerable time ago, and that counsel knows the case intimately. Do not accept a substitute barrister unless there is absolutely no alternative. Consider telling the clerk that you will not use those chambers in future. Remember that the client will probably be appalled to find that the counsel who had previously dealt with the case, and settled the pleadings, has now dropped out. If there is no choice but to find another barrister try to find another barrister that you know and have seen in action or comes with the recommendation of colleagues, insist that counsel's clerk telephones around for you and that the replacement counsel has experience of personal injury work. Insist that counsel speaks to the substitute about the case. Arrange an early conference and consider whether the brief fee needs amending. Consider telephoning the substitute barrister to have a general word about the case, even before the substitute has looked through the papers.

If the original counsel is part-heard for only a short period, it may be worth telephoning the clerk of the lists to see whether the case can be put back for an hour or two.

19 The trial

General conduct: Ensure that everyone, including counsel, is at court well before the case is likely to start. This will enable counsel to discuss the case fully with his solicitor, the expert witnesses, and the client.

Be prepared for a settlement offer to be made at this stage. Frequently, the defendant's solicitor will come to court to be advised by counsel that they should settle on a compromise basis. The plaintiff's solicitor should therefore have decided beforehand what is the lowest figure that the client should be advised to accept. Do not be pushed into a hasty settlement at the door of the court. Remember that counsel's brief fee, witnesses' and experts' costs have all been incurred and that a settlement at this stage will not save the day's costs. The client will by now be prepared to have the matter heard in court and may be deeply suspicious of any last-minute settlement negotiated at the door of the court.

Marshal the witnesses together. Introduce counsel to the client. Remind the witnesses that they will not be able to refer to their proofs when giving evidence; tell them to stand up straight in the witness box, hands out of pockets, and to speak in a deliberate, loud voice to the judge (not counsel), and call both counsel and judge 'sir' (or 'madam' if appropriate!) Reassure them against answering questions that they do not fully understand: if in doubt they should ask for the question to be repeated, or simply state that they do not understand the question. Answers should be short and to the point, especially during cross-examination; gratuitous comments and asides should be avoided. If the judge is taking a note of the evidence, the witness should pause frequently so that the judge can note down all that is said. Warn witnesses of the dangers of cross-examination; the other side's counsel will question their veracity and try to get them to lose their temper or become confused. Explain the layout of the court and who is who.

Once in court the instructing solicitor will sit behind counsel (unless there is a leader in which case the leader will sit in front) and be available to answer counsel's queries, take notes, and provide copy documents as and when they are required.

The solicitor should, so far as is possible, take a verbatim note of the evidence given. This is especially important when counsel is speaking and so unable to note down exactly what a witness says. Note the time when the case starts, who is present, the time when a witness gives evidence, adjournments, and so on.

Whilst doing all this, it is very easy to forget about the client. Make sure you explain what is happening at every stage and give the client a copy of any document referred to so that the client can follow the evidence and make comments.

The case is opened by the plaintiff's counsel who then calls the plaintiff's witnesses, who are examined, cross-examined, and then re-examined. At the close of the plaintiff's case the defendant's counsel may submit that there is no case to answer, or state that the defendant does not intend to call any witnesses (if so, the plaintiff's counsel addresses the court, and the defendant then has the last word). But, more usually, the defendant's counsel will open the case for the defence and then call the defendant's witnesses, make a closing speech, and then the plaintiff's counsel has the last word. Finally, the judge will sum up, give judgment and deal with costs.

When a witness has completed giving evidence, find out if the witness wishes to leave: if so, instruct counsel to ask the judge if the witness may be released. Thank the witness and ask the witness to send a note of net losses and expenses in attending court. Explain that any conduct money the witness has already received will be set off against this loss, and that an employer's certificate should be sent if the sum claimed is sizeable.

Judgment: Take a full note of the judgment. After it has been given, counsel should ask the judge for any particular orders that may be necessary. In particular:

(1) *Payment out of money in court.* Only after judgment should the trial judge be told of any sum in court. The money in court can only be paid out by order of the court, so the judge must be requested to formally order payment out to the successful party or, if the plaintiff's damages are less than the sum in court, to order that the judgment sum be paid to the plaintiff, and the balance to the defendant. If the damages awarded by the judge are close to the amount paid into the court, it may be necessary to work out the interest element in the payment in (see Chapter 5, section 4 for how this is done). In addition, if the plaintiff beats the payment in, then counsel should ask for an order that the interest arising from the date of trial (not from the date of payment in) be paid to the plaintiff. Otherwise the interest will go to the defendant (see Chapter 5, section 4).

(2) *Costs.* Normally these will follow the event, unless there has been a payment in which the plaintiff has not beaten, in which case the plaintiff will pay the costs as from the date of payment in. Remember that the interest is added to the damages when deciding whether the payment in has been beaten. The solicitor should go through the file checking to see whether there were any orders as to costs made by the court in interlocutory proceedings, when costs were to be other than 'in the cause'. If any costs were 'reserved', then the judge should now be asked to make an order in respect of them. All too often, solicitors fail to get these additional costs paid.

(3) *Payment of money into court.* This will be necessary if the successful plaintiff is an infant, or if the action is a fatal accident claim and one of the dependants is an infant.

(4) *Interest.* A plaintiff who recovers more than £200 will be entitled

to interest. See Chapter 5, section 4 for the rules on interest, and how the calculations are made.

A complication can arise if there has been an interim payment. If the interim payment was specifically stated to be for a particular head of damages (eg it was clearly for an item of special damages) then there is no difficulty; the interim payment will be deducted from the final award of that category of special damage. Thus, the plaintiff will not get interest from the date of interim payment in respect of that sum. Usually, however, the court does not state that an interim payment is attributable to a specific head of damages, and nor is it apportioned between the respective heads of damages. In this case, the trial judge will have to decide how the interim payment is to be deducted. Generally, it will be deducted on a *pro rata* basis between the various heads of damages. However, the judge may be persuaded to deduct it from one head of damage only. Obviously, the plaintiff should argue that it comes solely out of general damages, and the defendant will want it to be taken solely out of special damages (respectively minimising/maximising the amount of interest that will be lost).

(5) *Stay of execution.* Any party may request a stay of execution for a specific period, whilst an appeal is considered. When considering whether an appeal is necessary, a transcript of the evidence or judgment may be necessary. In the county court apply to the clerk of the court on Form EX 107 (available from the court). In the High Court use Oyez Form B81. Remember that the costs may not be recoverable. Note that notice of appeal to the Court of Appeal must be served within six weeks of the order or judgment. Leave to appeal is necessary in relation to a consent order or judgment, costs, or the interlocutory order of a judge in chambers. In legal aid cases specific authority must be obtained for any appeal proceedings.

Once judgment has been given, and its effect explained to the client, any exhibits should be collected from the judge's clerk and kept in a safe place in case of an appeal. Ensure that a full attendance note is attached to the file setting out the time spent in court and in travelling, the status of the person attending court, travel expenses, etc.

The associate's certificate: In the county court all orders are drawn up by the clerk and sent to the solicitors for the parties. In the High Court, after the judgment, the judge's associate will draw up a certificate setting out:

(i) the time occupied by the trial;
(ii) the judgment;
(iii) costs;
(iv) any order made by the judge permitting the receipt in evidence of plans, photographs, and models not previously made available to the other side (see p 125).

In DR cases the certificate should be collected from the associate immediately after the hearing, together with the copy bundle of pleadings that was lodged with the court when the case was set down. At the RCJ, the certificate and pleadings are sent to the solicitor entitled to draw up judgment, and not collected in person.

Provisional damages: If the judge awarded provisional damages, then the judgment will have been worded, 'The judge awarded to the plaintiff by way of immediate damages . . . (set out generals and specials) . . . upon the assumption that the plaintiff would not at a future date as a result of the act or omission giving rise to the cause of action develop the following disease, namely, . . . *or* suffer deterioration in his physical or mental condition of the following type . . . And the judge further ordered that if the plaintiff at a future date (within years) did so develop such disease *or* did so suffer such deterioration s/he should be entitled to apply for further damages'. In addition, the judge will say what documents are to be kept by the court to help on any future assessment of damages. These documents ('the case file') will normally be made up of copies of the associate's certificate (High Court only); the judgment; the pleadings; transcript of oral judgment; all medical reports put before the court; transcript of the plaintiff's own evidence as to physical condition and of the medical evidence as the judge thinks may be necessary. A list of the documents will be attached to the associate's certificate (High Court only) and the judgment.

The plaintiff's solicitor will need to tell his client what the effect of the award of provisional damages is. You should give written notice to the client of the limitation period for going back to court. Generally, see Chapter 4, section 5, and Procedural Table 19.

20 Judgment

A form of judgment will be needed before costs can be taxed or money drawn out of court. In the county court this will be prepared by the court and served on all parties.

In the High Court the plaintiff's solicitor is responsible for drawing up the judgment, irrespective of who won the case. The procedural steps to be taken on drawing up judgment are set out in Procedural Table 8 (see Ord 42, r 5).

21 Costs

The taxation of costs is inconvenient and time-consuming. Accordingly, always try to negotiate a compromise figure with the other side.

There is no room in a book of this sort to deal adequately with costs. Reference should be made to the White Book (Ord 62 in particular), but it may be helpful to remember that costs can be awarded on either the standard or indemnity basis. In most cases the standard basis will apply.

If it is not possible to agree costs on the basis of an initial schedule drawn up by the solicitor, the drawing up of a bill of costs is usually best left to a professional costs draftsperson; they advertise their services in the legal journals, and generally charge seven per cent of costs if the bill is taxed or six per cent if it is not taxed. Most solicitors find it more profitable to employ a costs draftsperson rather than spend time preparing the bill of costs. Not only are taxed costs often low, but the costs draftsperson's fee also has to be budgeted for.

Before sending the file to the costs draftsperson, ensure that it is neat and tidy. The full value of dictating comprehensive attendance notes and records of work done can now be appreciated, for they will give considerable assistance to the draftsperson when preparing the bill and also to the taxing officer when considering the bill as drawn.

The case should be diaried for three months from the date of judgment, for the application for the taxation and bill of costs should be filed within that time. Also in the High Court a Notice of Intention to Proceed (p 132) will be needed if there is more than a year's delay between judgment and applying for taxation. Interest runs on costs at the judgment rate (currently 15 per cent) from the date of judgment, not the date the costs are taxed. Because of the delays in the taxation process this interest can often be considerable and you should not forget to ask for it when costs are either taxed or agreed.

On receipt of the bill from the costs draftsperson, make a further attempt to agree costs with the other side; remember that they will be equally reluctant to be inconvenienced by a taxation. It is always best to try to agree a costs figure. This is equally desirable if the case is settled before trial, or even if it is settled before action. It is impossible to give definite figures as to what are reasonable costs, for it depends upon the complexity and value of the case, one's relationship with the other side, the stage reached in the action, and so on. However, there is no doubt that many solicitors greatly undervalue their negotiated costs.

Where there are two or more defendants the plaintiff will sometimes win against one defendant, but lose against the other defendant. In such cases, the order for costs is usually a Bullock Order (ie the successful defendant recovers his costs from the plaintiff who, in turn, recovers those costs, plus own costs, from the unsuccessful defendant). If the plaintiff is legally aided, or unlikely to be able to pay the successful defendant's costs, the order will probably be a Sanderson Order (ie the successful defendant recovers his costs direct from the unsuccessful defendant who also pays the plaintiff's costs).

22 Enforcement

Usually the defendant will be an insurance company and there will be no difficulty in obtaining payment of damages and costs awarded. However if you do not have to take enforcement proceedings refer to the detailed procedures set out in the Green Book and White Book and note that any judgment over £5,000 in the county court must be transferred to the High Court for enforcement.

Chapter 13

Settling the Case

1 Settling before proceedings are commenced

The vast majority of personal injury claims are settled through negotiation, and without the plaintiff commencing proceedings. When this happens, there is normally no need for court approval to be obtained; only if the plaintiff is an infant (or other person under a disability) must the court be involved.

Accordingly, the settlement will simply be referred to in the correspondence between the parties. The insurance company might ask the claimant to sign a form of receipt, confirming that the settlement is in full and final satisfaction of all claims arising from the accident. Some insurers do; others do not. In any event, such a document is not necessary. If the claimant's solicitor agrees to settle the claim on a client's behalf, and then accepts the cheque, there is little doubt that such a settlement would be binding on the claimant. If the claim had been under-settled, then the client's claim would be against the negligent solicitor, rather than against the insurers.

Obviously, if the claimant does not have legal advice, then it might be possible to have an under-settlement set aside.

Infant cases: If the claimant is an infant, then the settlement must normally be approved by the court. It will therefore be necessary to issue an originating application solely for this purpose. See Chapter 14, section 2(*a*) for more on this. Similar principles apply for any other person under a disability (eg mental patient).

2 Settlement after proceedings have begun

Here, we are dealing with the situation in which the plaintiff has begun proceedings, and then reached agreement with the other side. This may be through negotiation, or by the plaintiff deciding to accept the payment into court. Either way, it is now agreed that the case should go no further. The procedural requirements will depend upon how far the case has got:

(1) *if the case has not been set down*, then the court need not be notified. The parties can simply close their files, and that will be the end of the matter. In the county court if the plaintiff does not apply to fix a date for trial within 15 months of close of pleadings the case will automatically be struck out. However, if it is a legal aid case or if money has been paid into court, and the plaintiff is out of time for accepting it, then an order will be necessary (see below). In any event, even if money is not being paid out of court, many solicitors prefer to formally close the case by lodging a joint request that the record be withdrawn (use Precedent 31) (and an order for legal aid taxation be made (if appropriate)).

(2) *if the case has been set down for trial*, then, once again, the parties do not need a formal court order (unless money is being paid out, etc). However they are obliged to inform the clerk of the lists, and they must apply for the record to be withdrawn (see below).

3 Is it better to obtain an order?

While there is often no formal need for an order recording the settlement (unless the plaintiff is an infant; money in court being accepted out of time, etc) the parties can have an order drawn up if they wish, and this will of course be done by way of a consent application. But, is it advisable to have an order? The obvious argument in favour is that it ensures certainty and finality. Everyone knows where they stand. The court will have been notified and the plaintiff may feel happier with a formal order. In addition, if costs have not been agreed, then it will allow for taxation of costs (although costs usually are agreed when a negotiated settlement is reached).

Whether to draw a formal order is ultimately a matter for the solicitor to decide. If in doubt draw an order.

4 The alternative ways of ending the case

There are four procedural devices that can be used to end the litigation:

(i) *Notice of Discontinuance:* In the county court use Form N279 or Procedural Table 916. In the High Court use Oyez Form B19, or Precedent 29. But, if more than 14 days have elapsed since service of the defence, the plaintiff will have to obtain the master's consent. In practice, of course, this will not cause any difficulty; a straightforward consent order can be obtained (see Procedural Table 2 for the steps to take). Note that if an action is discontinued the defendant is automatically entitled to its costs from the plaintiff. Ensure therefore that the notice of discontinuance is signed by both parties and states that there will be no order for costs.

(ii) *Dismissal:* the defendant can obtain an order for dismissal of the action.
(iii) *Judgment:* the plaintiff can enter judgment.
(iv) *Stay:* the court can order a stay of proceedings.

It is the last of these four procedures, the stay of proceedings, that is normally used when recording a settlement. A stay is, in effect, a freezing of the action, and the freezing can be permanent or temporary, depending on the wording of the order. If the action is simply stayed, then it will be frozen permanently, and the parties will be unable to go back to the court if there is some dispute as to the carrying out of the agreed terms of settlement. Thus, for example, if the defendant refused to pay the plaintiff's costs, the plaintiff's remedy would be to start a fresh action for the costs rather than re-apply to the master for a further order against the defendant.

Accordingly, the stay sought on the order should be temporary rather than permanent unless all matters as to costs and damages have been agreed, finalised, and carried out. The usual order is for a permanent stay, except as to any problems arising in the working of the settlement. For instance, if there is a dispute as to the costs of the action then the parties will be able to go back to the court. This is called a 'Tomlin Order' and should normally be used when recording a settlement.

5 Drawing up the order

Since the parties will be in agreement as to the terms of the settlement, it will be possible to have a consent application or summons (ie so no attendance in court is necessary). This assumes, of course, that the plaintiff is not an infant (or other person under a disability). For the steps to be taken, refer to Procedural Table 2.

Also, refer to Precedent 31. This sets out various alternative forms of order that can be sought, and the steps to be taken. Follow those steps carefully. It will be seen that a typical order deals with the following points:

- usually, it is the plaintiff who types out the draft order and sends it to the defendant. The defendant then endorses consent in the margin of the draft order. Because it is by consent, the parties do not usually bother to issue an application or summons.
- the order will refer to the action being stayed, and state how much the plaintiff is accepting in full and final settlement.
- if any interim payments have been made, then it will be stated that full credit is to be given for those (give a total figure; also refer to each individually, by date and amount).
- if there is money in court, then it will be ordered that that money be paid out to the plaintiff's solicitors.
- if there is any more money to be paid to the plaintiff (eg in addition to the payment in) then the order will say it must be paid to the

plaintiff's solicitors within, say, 14 days.

- it is usual to state that interest accruing on the money in court be paid out to the defendant's solicitors. Strictly speaking, this is not essential, but it is advisable to include it.
- next, the order will deal with costs. If these have been agreed, then the figures should be set out (ie total figure, apportioned between disbursements, profit cost, and VAT). If the costs have not been agreed, then the order will record that the defendant has to pay standard basis costs, to be taxed in default of agreement.
- if the plaintiff is legally aided, then there should be an additional clause allowing the plaintiff's costs to be taxed pursuant to the provisions of the Legal Aid Act 1988.
- finally, the order will confirm that the defendant, provided that it pays the various amounts referred to, is discharged from all further liability. The order will also say that there be liberty to apply (ie the parties can go back to the court) if there are any problems in enforcing the terms of the order.

The plaintiff posts the consent order (ie the draft order with the defendant's consent written on it) to the court. When the sealed order is returned, the plaintiff should then send a copy to the defendant; the defendant will then forward any money (ie damages and costs) that has yet to be paid.

Money in court: There are further complications if there is money in court. Refer to Procedural Table 13, for the steps to be taken. In brief, the plaintiff has to send the order, together with two copies of Payment Out Schedule (ie Form P3) and a request form. In a legal aid case the request form is Form 11; if it is not legal aid, then use Form 10.

6 Provisional damages

If the settlement involves provisional damages, then the parties have no choice but to obtain an order from the court. Normally, this is done by simply issuing an application or summons, for a consent order.

In most respects, the wording of the summons will be similar to that in an ordinary consent order (see above). But, in addition, it has to contain full details of the provisional award. Thus, it must specify the disease or deterioration which it has been assumed will not occur, and which will entitle the plaintiff to come back for further damages if it should arise in the future. Basically, one can adapt the wording that should be used by the judge when giving judgment in a provisional damages case (set out in Chapter 12, section 18). However, in all but the most straightforward cases it may be felt that it is advisable to have counsel draft the relevant part of the summons. Until such time as the clear practice, and set of precedents, emerges, the plaintiff's solicitor may prefer to entrust this work to counsel. In addition, the summons should set out the documents that will comprise the case file (usually, copy order, pleadings, agreed statement of facts, agreed medical reports). Refer to Procedural Table 19.

When the consent order is made, it is for the plaintiff's solicitor to prepare the case file, and forward it to the court.

If proceedings have not been commenced in the action, then clearly it is not possible to issue a consent summons to formalise the provisional damages. In that case, it is suggested that the best procedure is to issue an originating application or summons (ie commence an action) solely for the purposes of obtaining an order relating to the provisional damages. Adapt Precedent 16, as necessary; the order can be by consent (unless the plaintiff is an infant or patient). Do not forget to make it a term of the settlement that the defendant pays the costs arising from the originating summons; it is usually best to try to agree a specific figure in advance.

Part III

Matters Requiring Special Care

Chapter 14

Persons under a Disability

If the plaintiff is a minor then he or she will be regarded as being under a disability. As such:

- the minor cannot sue in his or her own name. Accordingly, s/he has to sue through the name of an adult (the 'next friend');
- the court must approve any settlement of the minor's claims. This is to ensure that the minor is not being taken advantage of, and that the claim is being settled for a proper sum;
- the minor's solicitor must have costs approved by the court. Once again, this is to protect the minor from exploitation (by a solicitor who might otherwise overcharge).

Similar principles apply to Mental Health Act patients.

1 Next friend

Since the minor cannot sue in his or her own name, a willing adult must be named as the 'next friend' and assume responsibility for the costs of the action. Usually, the next friend will be a parent, although any other adult friend is competent to act. The solicitor should write to the next friend, pointing out the potential liabilities, and explaining that the next friend's role is to act as an officer of the court in conducting the minor's litigation. The mere presence of the next friend gives the defendant some security as to costs. Thus, the next friend assumes responsibility for the costs of the action, although there is a right of indemnity against the minor. Because of this costs liability, the next friend should not be treated as a mere cipher by the minor's solicitor; instructions and advice should be sought as though the next friend were a plaintiff.

When the solicitor writes to the next friend, you should ask the next friend to confirm the date of birth (so there is no doubt the next friend is over 18), and also that there is no conflict of interest with the minor (for instance, as would be the case if the minor had been injured whilst a passenger in a car driven by the negligent next friend).

The next friend will also have to sign a Consent Form, agreeing to act as next friend. In the county court this form must be witnessed by a solicitor. In the High Court the solicitor signs a separate certificate (see below). This will have to be lodged with the court when the proceedings are issued (see below). A precedent Consent is printed at 19(1) High Court, 19(3) county court.

Issuing the proceedings: The county court summons or High Court writ should be prepared in the usual way (see Chapter 5, section 2). The only difference will be that the name of the plaintiff in the title will appear as:

'ABC, a Minor, by CDE . . . (*state relationship*) and Next Friend'.

This will also appear as the heading on all pleadings.

In the High Court when issuing the writ, the next friend's Consent Form must be lodged, together with a certificate from the solicitor, confirming that there is no conflict between the next friend and the minor plaintiff. The Solicitor's Certificate is printed as Precedent 19(2), it can either be prepared as a separate document or endorsed on the writ.

When the minor reaches age 18: When the minor becomes of full age (ie 18 years) then s/he should take over, and adopt, the proceedings. This is done by a Notice of Adoption being filed with the court. In addition, a copy must be served on all the parties to the action. Thereafter, the title of the action will read:

'ABC (late a minor but now of full age)'.

The action will then proceed in the usual manner, as though the plaintiff had never been a minor. In particular, it will no longer be necessary for any settlement to be approved by the court.

A Notice of Adoption is printed as Precedent 20.

2 Settlement

Any minor settlement must be approved by the court. The court will want to approve the amount being paid in settlement of the claim, the amount being paid in respect of solicitor's costs, and also give directions as to how the money is to be utilised.

The procedure will depend upon whether proceedings have already begun. If they have, then it will be a matter of issuing a summons (or a Notice of Application, if county court proceedings). If proceedings have not yet begun, then it will be necessary to commence proceedings, by Originating Application or Originating Summons in the High Court.

(a) Minor settlement: when the case has not been issued

Most personal injury claims are settled without recourse to the issuing of a writ or county court summons. Minor claims are no exception to this generalisation. However, when the plaintiff is a minor then the solicitor must bring the claim before the court so that the court can approve the terms of settlement. This should be done, however small the amount involved.

In practice, if the sums involved are trivial (eg under £500) it is not uncommon for the insurers to pay the settlement monies direct to the minor's parents, and to accept their discharge as a receipt; alternatively, the insurers may call the offer an *ex gratia* payment. However, this practice is not to be recommended, and should be avoided.

From the next friend's point of view, it is better if the claim is approved by the court; that ensures that the minor plaintiff cannot later sue for under-settling the case. The defendant will also be better protected if the court approves the settlement; the minor will be bound by the terms of settlement, and will be unable to reopen the case at a later date. So, the minor's solicitor should resist any suggestion of an informal settlement, and instead should insist that an Infant Approval Originating Application be issued. This is especially so if there is the slightest possibility of a future deterioration in the minor's medical condition (eg a risk of epilepsy because of concussion).

So, the minor's solicitor should insist that the court approve the settlement. Do not forget to ask for the costs arising on the Originating Application to be paid by the defendant (try to agree a fixed sum to cover the cost of the Application and the work arising).

In county court cases the commencement of proceedings for an Infant Approval is by way of Originating Application or normal summons. In the High Court it is by way of an Originating Summons, not a writ. Refer to Procedural Table 17, for the steps to be taken on issuing an Infant Approval Originating Application. The Originating Application can either be typed out using the specimen application printed in Appendix G as a precedent, or a pre-printed form can be used (Oyez Form No S20B).

For a suggested wording of orders that might be sought on the summons (ie as to payment out of next friend's costs; investment of money; agreement of costs, etc) see Precedent 21(*a*).

Once the Originating Application or Summons has been issued, it should be served in the same way as any proceedings (see Chapter 16, section 3). The defendant does not have to file a defence or High Court Acknowledgment of Service, although it will be expected to attend before the court on the return date stated in the Originating Application or Summons.

Note that the application or summons should not state the proposed settlement figures but it should contain a brief statement of the action together with a request for approval of the settlement or compromise. This is because the court will not want to know the figures until it has had an opportunity of hearing the full facts of the case, and making up its own mind.

It is not usually necessary to have counsel attend an Infant Approval Application. The minor's solicitor should tell the court how the accident was caused, why it is alleged that liability attaches to the defendant, and the extent to which (if at all) the defendant admits liability. The solicitor should also explain how the defendant could be shown to be liable. Any police report should be produced, together with witness statements, counsel's advice on liability, and of course the medical evidence. In short, the plaintiff's solicitor should provide the court with a brief résumé of the case. The defendants will then have an opportunity of addressing the court. In practice, they are unlikely to have much to add to what the plaintiff's solicitor has said. When the court has considered the facts of the case, and been informed of the amount of the offer, it will give its decision. Usually, it will approve the summons as drawn, and agree the settlement figures. However, it may decide to adjourn the hearing so that the medical condition can have a further chance of stabilising, or may suggest an alternative settlement figure. The court will only approve the settlement figure if it is 'reasonable', taking into account such factors as the risks of litigation, the desire of the parties to settle, the lack of evidence, etc. Thus, the court will be prepared to approve a low *ex gratia* payment in a hopeless case. There is no need for there to be an affidavit. Some courts insist that the next friend approve the settlement so it is usually advisable to get the approval in writing beforehand so it can be shown to the court. The court may also want to known how much interest the plaintiff would have got, so it is advisable to calculate the interest separately in case this point is raised.

Exceptionally, the court may ask to see the infant, and adjourn the hearing accordingly (although this would be most unusual, except in cases involving deformity, or injuries such as facial scars, or if the injuries are particularly serious). Having approved the settlement figures, the court will then consider whether it should approve the solicitor's costs (see below), and will also make directions for the investment or utilisation of the money (see below).

If, for some reason, the court does not approve the settlement then it does have power to order that the Originating Application or Summons be treated as a summons or a writ respectively. In practice, this rarely happens, and the court will normally direct that separate proceedings be commenced in the usual way.

(b) Infant Approval: if the case has already been issued

If an issued case is being settled, then the proposed terms of settlement must go before the court for approval (and for approval of the costs, and so the court can give directions as to the handling of the money).

In the county court this is by way of notice of application and in a High Court case, the plaintiff should issue a summons in the usual way; in practice, of course, this will be a Consent Application, so Procedural Table 2 should be used. Precedent Infant Approval Summons, and Orders, are printed as Precedent 21(*b*). Note that a special appointment must be obtained for the hearing of the application; refer to Precedent 6 for the form that has to be completed.

The hearing of the application will be similar to the hearing of an Infant Approval Originating Application (ie in an unissued case). In particular, it is important to make sure that the settlement figures are not set out in the form of summons, so the court can make up its own mind as to a proper valuation of the case. See above.

If the court does not approve the proposed settlement, it may decide to treat the hearing of the summons as a pre-trial review or Summons for Directions, and make such orders as the court thinks fit for the 'just, economical and expeditious disposal' of the case. It is therefore advisable for the parties to consider beforehand what orders they should seek in case the terms of settlement are not approved.

Accepting a payment into court: If a minor plaintiff wants to accept money paid into court, an application or summons will still have to be issued. The minor cannot simply withdraw the money from court. The usual procedure applies: issue an application or summons, asking for the proposed terms of settlement (including payment out of the money in court) to be approved. Specimen orders are set out in Precedents 21(*b*) and 31. There is no need to serve the usual notice of acceptance of payment in on the other side, because the application or summons will have to be issued to accept the money.

3 Costs

In the same way that the settlement figures must be approved by the court, so too must the costs.

The typical Infant Approval Application or Summons will state that the defendant pays the plaintiff's costs, to be taxed if not agreed, on the standard basis.

What of the costs between the minor plaintiff and own solicitor? It may well be (and often is the case) that the minor's solicitor will accept the costs being paid by the defendant in full and final settlement. In other words, the plaintiff's solicitor will waive the excess that could be recovered. If so, that will be recorded in the order. However, if the plaintiff's solicitor is not prepared to accept the amount of costs being paid by the defendant, then the solicitor will have to have the costs taxed. The position will depend upon whether the infant is a private client, or legally aided:

- in a legal aid case, the order will simply be that the plaintiff's solicitor's costs be taxed pursuant to the Legal Aid Act 1988;
- in a private case, the plaintiff's solicitor can insist on an order that the costs be paid on an indemnity basis, to be taxed, and that the difference between those costs and the taxed, standard basis costs be paid out to the solicitor from the infant's damages. Note that this is an inconvenient arrangement from the solicitor's point of view. This is because the standard basis costs must also be taxed, because they form part of the solicitor's remuneration. The solicitor

cannot simply have the excess (ie the amount above the costs paid by the defendant) taxed. Not surprisingly, the defendant may take exception to this, if it has already offered a reasonable sum in respect of costs. Bear in mind, that in those circumstances the plaintiff may find it difficult to justify the defendant having to pay the full taxing fee, in which case the plaintiff will bear it. Add to that the fact that a costs draftsperson's fee will probably have to be paid, and the plaintiff's solicitor may well conclude that it is not worth pursuing the excess indemnity costs. In practical terms, this is why many solicitors simply agree to accept the costs as paid by the defendant, and waive their entitlement to any excess.

Until relatively recently, the minor's plaintiff's costs had to be taxed; there was no way that the parties could simply agree their costs, and have that agreement rubber-stamped by the court. That is no longer the position. The parties can agree their costs (ie as between plaintiff and defendant, but not between minor plaintiff and own solicitor) and have those costs approved by the court. In practice, that is what plaintiffs' solicitors will usually attempt to do. The usual procedure is to state in the Infant Approval Summons the amount agreed as costs so that the court can consider the level of costs, and then agree that taxation can be dispensed with. The plaintiff's solicitor will also be expected to waive any additional costs (ie 'the plaintiff's solicitor waiving all further costs').

In a legal aid case, there is a further complication. Under reg 106 (see Chapter 16, section 8(1)) of the 1989 Regs), the Legal Aid Board must assess costs that are agreed without taxation. In practice, this is likely to be a formality, but the plaintiff's solicitor should write to the Legal Aid Board setting out the position and confirming that the solicitor does waive any entitlement to additional costs.

Refer to the specimen orders in Precedent 21, for typical costs orders on an Infant Approval.

4 Investment and paying-out of the settlement money

The court will have to order what is to happen to the settlement money.

Often, the order will provide for relatively small sums to be paid out to the next friend to cover expenses (eg loss of wages when attending solicitor's offices for appointments, etc). Normally, that money can be paid out direct to the next friend, without difficulty.

It is as regards the rest of the settlement money that the difficulties are likely to arise. The courts take a cautious attitude. Clearly, if the sums are large, then they will have to be invested. But, many solicitors and parents feel that it is not unreasonable to hand modest sums (eg £2,000 or so) to parents, so they can administer the money for the child's benefit. However, this is not the attitude taken by the courts. Only if the sums are trivial (eg £150 or so) is the court likely to agree that the money can be paid to the parent or guardian. Even then, the court may prefer that the solicitor buy National Savings Certificates for the child. On the other hand, if the child is a teenager, then sums up to (for instance) £1,000 could be put into the National Savings Bank, to await the attainment of majority. The parents could hold the bank book for the child. If larger sums are involved, then it will be necessary to invest the money. Until relatively recently, the usual procedure was to transfer the money to the minor's local county court, and let it be administered from there. These days money in the High Court is likely to remain there, although not necessarily in London. A typical order will be along the lines of 'The defendant within ... days do pay the sum of £x into the Court Funds Office to be invested and accumulated in short term investment account for the benefit of the minor ... pending further order, and that all further proceedings relating to the investment and application of the said fund be transferred to the ... District Registry'. Applications for some of the money to be released should be made to the court holding the money (most will accept a letter of application, but check the local procedure).

If the minor settlement arises under a fatal accidents claim, then it may be possible to apportion the monies between the spouse and/or several children. See Chapter 15, section 6.

Applications for sums to be paid out: The parents may well want some of the money to be paid out, at a later date, to cover expenditure on the child. This application is made (as indeed is any application for variation of investments) by letter from the next friend to the chief clerk in the county court or the Master's Secretary Office in the RCJ. Applications are normally dealt with by correspondence, although a personal interview with the court will be arranged if it seems to be necessary. If the child is a teenager, then the court may accept an application (by letter) from the minor personally.

The court will be on the look-out for conflicts of interest between the parents and the child. The basic approach will be to say that the minor's interests are paramount. It should be borne in mind that parents cannot normally use the money for the maintenance of the minor. Generally, damages awarded to a minor cover pain, injury, and future disability, not everyday maintenance expenses (although, obviously, there would be the exceptional case if the child needed special treatment, etc). Thus, the normal rule is that a parent should not be able to save money and use the child's money, simply because the child has recovered damages. The general rule is that payments for running expenses, and maintenance of the child, if allowable, should come out of income, not capital. If there is real difficulty with the next friend, the court may decide to ask the court welfare officer to help; in extreme cases, the Official Solicitor may be substituted as the next friend. Certainly, if application is made to use the damages so as to buy a house or flat (for instance, specially adapted for the disabled infant) then the Official

Solicitor will almost certainly be involved to vet the desirability of the purchase.

5 The order

Once the court has made the order, it will have to be drawn up in the usual way ie by the court itself in the county court or by the applicant's solicitor in the High Court. It should be drawn up promptly, and in any case within seven days. However, the defendant should not await receipt of the order before paying any money into court.

Refer to Precedent 21 for specimen orders in typical Infant Approval cases.

6 Mental Health Act patients

A plaintiff who has a mental disorder within the meaning of the Mental Health Act 1983, which makes the plaintiff incapable of managing and administering property and affairs, is regarded as a 'patient'.

As a patient, the plaintiff will be under a disability. Therefore, similar considerations apply as with a minor. In particular:

(i) the plaintiff must sue via a next friend. The heading of the action will be 'ABC by CDE next friend'. There is no mention of the fact that the plaintiff is a patient.

(ii) if a plaintiff becomes a patient after the action has been commenced, then the solicitor should immediately apply for a next friend to be added to the proceedings.

(iii) if the action is brought with the sanction of the Court of Protection, then no compromise can be made without that court's approval. The damages will also have to be paid to the Court of Protection. Depending upon the amount involved, it may well be the case that the damages have to be administered by the Court of Protection, not the High Court. See the notes in the White Book to Ord 80/12/6.

Chapter 15

Fatal Accidents

1 The two causes of action

There are two different causes of action that arise on a death. The first is on behalf of the estate of the deceased (the Law Reform claim), and the other is on behalf of the dependants (the Fatal Accidents claim). The two are distinct: the former is on behalf of the estate, the latter on behalf of the dependants.

2 The Law Reform claim

This claim is brought on behalf of the deceased, under the Law Reform (Miscellaneous Provisions) Act 1934. It will cover:

(i) financial loss incurred by the deceased prior to death (eg lost wages, and expenses whilst in hospital);

(ii) compensation for the pain and suffering arising prior to the death. Obviously, if death was instantaneous then there would be no compensation under this head;

(iii) funeral expenses (if paid by the estate).

3 The Fatal Accidents claim

This gives the relatives of the deceased a separate claim for the losses they have suffered. This has three heads:

(i) 'bereavement' (£7,500) for certain dependants;

(ii) the dependancy claim for the financial losses suffered by the relatives;

(iii) the funeral expenses (if paid by the dependants).

Bereavement: The fixed sum for bereavement is £7,500 for deaths occuring after 1 April 1991, £3,500 before. But, the bereavement payment can only be claimed by:

- the spouse, or
- the parents, if the deceased was unmarried and under 18.

If the deceased was over 18, and not married, then no bereavement payment can be made. Note in particular that parents cannot claim bereavement, and nor can a common law spouse (or an ex-spouse).

Who is a dependant? A dependancy claim can only be brought by certain categories of relatives. In fact, the definition is fairly wide. It can include parents, grandparents, children, spouses, ex-spouses, etc. In addition, it can include a common law spouse but he or she must have been living with the deceased for at least two years before the accident (it is therefore a stricter test than under the Family Provision legislation). Also, any person treated as a parent, or a child of the family, can claim to be a dependant, as can grandparents, step-parents, foster parents, etc. In practice, there are relatively few dependants who cannot bring a Fatal Accidents claim (except a friend or partner of the same sex, a platonic friend of a different sex or a recent co-habitee).

4 Taking instructions

When taking instructions in a fatal claim, use the appropriate road or workplace questionnaire, printed in Appendix A, and in addition use the supplementary questionnaire printed in section 3. Be sure to obtain the birth and marriage certificates of the dependants, and the birth, marriage and death certificates of the deceased. Arrange for personal representatives to be appointed so that they can bring the claim; however, if they fail to commence the proceedings within six months of the death, then any one of the dependants can sue for the Fatal Accident claim.

In addition, consider whether any of the dependants could be in any way to blame for the accident (for example, road accident claim in which deceased was passenger in car driven by spouse). If so, ensure that the dependant in question is not appointed as a personal representative.

The proceedings will bear the name of the plaintiff, for example:

'ABC (Widow and Administratrix of the Estate of DEF Deceased)'.

Precedent writ indorsements for use in Law Reform and Fatal Accidents claims are printed in Precedent 1(3).

Difficulties can arise if there are disputes between the dependants. If one set of dependants bring the Fatal Accidents claim, and another claims to be joined as dependants, the solicitor will be in a difficult position. Quite simply, there will be a conflict between clients, and those who claim to be dependants. The correct procedure is for the solicitor to continue to handle the case, and the application will have to be heard by the trial judge. The courts have decided that it is not possible to have more than one firm of solicitors conducting the litigation on behalf of the plaintiff.

The inquest and inquest notes: Explain to the family that legal aid will not cover the cost of attending the inquest. Do they want to pay privately for the solicitor to attend? Bear in mind that the inquest notes can be obtained from the coroner, after the inquest, for a modest fee. However, those inquest notes will not be admissible at trial, unless the coroner is called to strictly prove them. To avoid this inconvenience, it is usual for the parties to agree an interlocutory order that the notes be admissible in evidence.

Limitation period: The limitation period in a fatal claim will usually be three years from the date of the death, although no claim can be brought if the deceased was statute-barred at the time of death. However, it is possible under the Limitation Act 1980 for the limitation period to be extended, although those provisions will not apply if the deceased was statute-barred at death. Generally, see Chapter 17, section 2.

When the plaintiff dies: If the death does not occur until some time after the accident, it is likely that the deceased will have commenced proceedings prior to death. If so, that action can be taken over by the deceased's personal representatives as the Law Reform claim, and they should apply for permission to the court, *ex parte* (see Procedural Table 3). An affidavit in support should be filed, setting out the nature of the action, the stage reached, the change that has occurred (ie death), their interest, the fact that the cause of action survives, and the order sought (CCR Ord 5, r 11 and RSC Ord 15, r 7). The personal representatives' written consent to act should also be produced. The order will be noted in the court records, and should be served on all the other parties to the action.

If there is also a Fatal Accidents claim arising on behalf of any dependants, the personal representatives should simultaneously seek the court's leave to amend the pleadings to include the new cause of action (the application could, of course, no longer be made ex parte), or alternatively, issue separate proceedings and consolidate the two actions at a later date.

Which court: Although the proceedings will have to be started in the county court if the cost is worth less than £50,000 (see Chapter 6, section 1) fatal cases are in the category of those considered suitable for trial in the High Court if they are worth over £25,000 and in these circumstances you should always consider transferring the matter up to the High Court (see Chapter 12, section 5).

5 Assessment of damages

The real difficulty lies in working out the size of the dependancy claim (under the Fatal Accidents claim).

The first stage of the calculation is to work out the net annual financial loss (that is the 'multiplicand'), which will then be multiplied to cover future loss.

The calculation of the dependancy is a purely financial calculation. It can be a distressing and difficult task for the dependants. However, the calculation must be accurate and comprehensive, and should be supported by all the bills and receipts of the year prior to death. Add up all the financial benefits received by the dependants from the deceased, such as housekeeping, rent, mortgage, community charge, gas, electricity, water, coal, holidays, clothes, school fees, insurance, television hire, hire purchase payments, gifts of a regular nature, the value of a motor car provided by the deceased or employers, and so on, but be sure to deduct that proportion of the expenditure which is attributable to the deceased (for example, that part of the total food bill that will now be saved). Also, calculate the value of services rendered to the dependants by the deceased which will now have to be paid for, such as house repairs and maintenance, or garden produce if the deceased was a keen gardener.

Wherever possible, support the dependancy figures with documentary evidence. If bills and receipts cannot be obtained, try writing to the deceased's bank for the return of all cheques and details of standing orders. Obtain copy tax returns from the Inland Revenue, and compare the total dependancy with the net income. In cases where no documentary evidence can be produced, it may be necessary to calculate the dependancy by taking a sum that can reasonably be attributed to the deceased's own expenses and benefit: the balance will be the dependancy. Additionally, be sure to take a detailed proof describing how the household was run and how expenses were met.

When calculating the children's dependancy, do not forget to take into account things like holidays, gifts, and clothes. This may well increase the dependancy by a considerable amount. Similarly do not forget to include the work that the deceased did towards maintaining and improving the home. The loss of a DIY enthusiast can result in a significantly increased dependancy. When the deceased was a homemaker, then one must take care when calculating the loss of those services. It is not good enough to simply take the cost of hiring a housekeeper. Bear in mind that the homemaker will have worked for much more than eight hours a day, and those additional lost services can be included in the dependancy claim.

Do not deduct the value of benefits (eg death benefit; insurance benefit) when calculating the dependancy.

It has to be accepted that this can often be an artificial calculation. Further, it can often be extremely difficult to apportion expenditure between various members of the family in any sort of realistic fashion. There is also the practical difficulty of collating the necessary information from the distressed dependants.

An alternative, and much more straightforward, approach is to simply take the deceased's net income, and deduct from that a figure to cover the money that the deceased spent on himself or herself. The balance will presumably be the dependancy for the rest of the family. Obviously, any other sums that would have been received by way of fringe benefits, etc (eg cheap mortgage; company car) will have to be added to the net earnings figures. In practical terms, this is a much easier approach. Even so, it may still be difficult to apportion items of expenditure between the deceased and the other dependants. When this is the case, the courts are generally prepared to accept a fairly rough and ready approach.

As a generalisation, one may say that if there is a husband and wife and the wife did not work, and the husband is killed, then the wife's dependancy will probably be in the region of 66 per cent of the husband's net income. If there is joint income then the dependancy is 66 per cent of the total joint net income and one deducts the continuing earnings to calculate the loss of dependancy. If there are children, then one may be thinking in terms of a dependancy of 75 per cent.

Authority for this comes from the judgment of O'Connor LJ in *Harris v Empress Motors* (1983)127 SJ 647 (CA). The judgment is not reported in full, but quotes from the transcript are useful: 'In the course of time the courts have worked out a simple solution to the ... problem of calculating the net dependancy under the Fatal Accidents Act in cases where the dependants are wife and children ... The modern practice is to deduct a percentage from the income figure to represent what the deceased would have spent exclusively on himself. The percentages have become conventional in the sense that they are used unless there is striking evidence to make the conventional figure inappropriate ... Where the family unit was husband and wife the conventional figure is 33 per cent and the rationale of this is that broadly speaking net income was spent as to one third for the benefit of each and one-third for their joint benefit ... No deduction is made in respect of the joint portion because one cannot buy or drive half a motor car ... Where there are children the deduction falls to 25 per cent ...' (ie 75 per cent dependancy).

So, the plaintiff's solicitor should normally adopt O'Connor's approach, unless you think that a detailed calculation of the dependancy in the old fashioned manner (as outlined above, going through all the items of expenditure, one by one) would be more advantageous or more appropriate.

The multiplier: Having calculated the dependancy, it is necessary to multiply that multiplicand by the appropriate multiplier, so as to cover losses in future years. The multiplier will vary with the age and health of the dependants, the age and pre-accident health of the deceased.

If the deceased was a person whose earnings could reasonably have expected to have increased over the years (for example, a professional person, or an apprentice), then it is fair to add a year or two to the multiplier. Similarly, if the deceased could reasonably have expected to continue working after the normal retirement age (for example, if self-employed) then the multiplier should be increased to reflect the fact.

In assessing the appropriate multiplier one must look at the reported awards and study publications such as Kemp and Kemp on the *Quantum of Damages, Current Law* and the monthly supplements to Halsbury's *Laws of England.* As a rough guide one can say that the multiplier will rarely exceed 18, and that a multiplier of more than 15 would only exceptionally be awarded in respect of a deceased who was over 35 at the time of death.

It must be emphasized that the multiplier will vary from case to case and that age is only one of the factors to be considered, for the courts do not calculate the multiplier on an actuarial basis and nor are they interested in arguments about the effects of inflation.

To illustrate the inconsistency of awards on an age basis, the following are all reported awards made in respect of deceased males (age is given first, followed by the multiplier): 46 × 17; 28 × 17; 43 × 14.5; 40 × 14.5; 41 × 14; 39 × 13.5; 49 × 12; 64 × 3; 38 × 14; 36 × 14; 42 × 13; 50 × 10; 24 × 16; 50 × 10; 24 × 17; 21 × 18; 24 × 16; 30 × 15; (see p 32 for more information on multipliers).

When assessing the multiplier one must ignore a widow's prospects of remarriage, and even ignore a remarriage that occurs prior to settlement or trial. But, you do not ignore the remarriage prospects of a widower, and nor do you ignore the mother's prospects of remarriage when considering the children's dependency. The court must take into account the benefit which the child is likely to receive from a stepfather but, even so, the court may well apportion more than is usual to the children, on the basis that if the mother remarries she will have a new husband with a duty to maintain her; also of course, the court will be conscious of the fact that the infants' funds will be under the control of the court, whereas those of the widow will not. As regards cohabitees, the court has to take into account the fact that there was no legal obligation on the deceased to maintain the cohabitee. The net effect is that a cohabitee can expect a lower multiplier than if he or she had been a spouse.

The defendants may request facilities for a medical examination of the dependants in the hope that a finding of poor health will enable them to argue for a lower multiplier; facilities should be refused and the defendants left to apply for an order.

Actuarial evidence: The use of actuarial tables is likely to lead to a higher multiplier than under the conventional approach. See Appendix E for the difference that the use of an actuarial table (such as that published by HMSO) can make. As suggested there, it might be worth suggesting to the defendants that actuarial evidence be admitted (in the form of those tables) without the need for an actuary to give evidence.

Funeral expenses: Funeral expenses should be recoverable (under the Law Reform claim is paid by the estate; under the Fatal Accidents claim, if paid by the dependants). However, funeral expenses must be reasonable. Generally insurers will try to save a few pounds by querying the funeral charges. Plaintiff's advisers might find it useful to bear two cases in mind.

(i) in *Gammell* v *Wilson* [1982] AC 27, the burial was in Ireland.

(ii) in *Quainoo* v *Brent and Harrow AHA* [1982] NLJ 1100 the funeral expenses were those of a member of the Ghanaian royal family, with the body being returned to Ghana. The cost of air fares for the relatives to return to Ghana, together with air freight for the coffin, London funeral director's expenses, and of the cars for the Ghanaian funeral procession were allowed. But, the costs of printing funeral cards, wreaths, photographer, hire of hall and party after funeral, and the funeral clothes, were disallowed.

6 Apportioning the settlement monies

If there is a Law Reform claim, and also a Fatal Accidents claim, then the defendant can make one payment into court in respect of both claims. If this global payment in is accepted, then the court will have to apportion the damages between the respective claims. Similarly, if there is a Fatal Accidents claim, and several dependants, then the court may have to apportion the payment in between the various dependants. Certainly, if any of the dependants are persons under a disability, then the court's approval (and apportionment of the monies) will be mandatory. Any settlement involving persons under a disability must be approved by the court (see Chapter 14).

Procedurally, the position is the same as with an infant approval. If proceedings have been begun, then one issues a summons (Notice of Application if county court). If proceedings have not been begun, then one commences proceedings by way of Originating Summons (Default Summons if county court). Specimen summonses and orders, are printed in Precedent 23. Refer to Chapter 14, section 2 for general guidance on infant approval settlements summonses, since the principles are the same.

If children are involved, and the court has to apportion between a parent and those children, then the court will probably begin by estimating the costs of maintaining that child from the date of the order (not the date of death) until the child reaches 18. The court will then apportion a sufficient sum to cover those maintenance costs, and also, if possible, allow the child a small capital sum with which to start life on attaining the age of 18. This exercise will be repeated for each child. Any balance will then go to the widow. In practice, of course, there is not enough money to go around; when that is the case, it will be necessary to reduce everyone's entitlement (including the children's), proportionately. Certainly, the courts do not approve of simply paying all the money to the widow, in the hope that she will utilise it properly towards maintenance, etc of the children. The courts take the view that this is too risky; they would prefer to have the minors' money invested, under control of the court. The point to appreciate is that minors' funds are controlled by the court, but widows' funds are not (until the mid-70s, widows' funds were also controlled by the court, but since that rule has been changed the courts have been less generous with their apportionments to widows).

Exceptionally, if there is a dispute between the dependants, or if there is a dispute between the widow and children, the court may allow other dependants to be joined as parties to the action. The court may also decide that the Official Solicitor should represent the children.

Chapter 16

Legal Aid Cases

This chapter collects together some of the more important considerations that arise if the plaintiff is legally aided. Reference should also be made to other relevant chapters in this book.

1 The application

The solicitor has a general duty to advise a client as to the availability of legal aid. Bear in mind that the financial limits are such that, for example, a married person with the usual commitments and family, and earning £20,000 per annum, could still be eligible for legal aid: although there may be a large contribution to pay.

If the client may be eligible, complete a Green Form at the initial meeting. This is a form of legal aid which is means-tested by the solicitor and can be used to give two hour's initial advice (more if extensions are obtained). Use this to cover the initial enquiries and the legal aid application, and to continue correspondence pending the grant of legal aid. Do not forget to apply for Green Form extensions if you will be carrying out over two hours' work or incurring disbursements. It is not necessary to have exhausted the initial limit before asking for an extension. However Green Form authority will not normally be given to obtain a medical report or incur other disbursements, and the Green Form cannot be used to start proceedings, so it is important to apply for legal aid as soon as possible.

When filling in the application form for legal aid, give the local office sufficient information to enable them to consider properly the merits of the application. Thus, they will need to know the extent of the injuries, special damage to date, the insurance position (or some evidence as to the means of the proposed defendant), and they must also be provided with some evidence as to liability, such as witness statements, a police report, or details of a relevant criminal conviction of the proposed defendant. Provide as much relevant information as possible. If the case is excellent on liability, then point this out in the hope that they will give an unlimited certificate. If the case is worth over £50,000 or is between £25,000 and £50,000 but comes within the special criteria, then argue for proceedings to be in the High Court, not county court (see Chapter 6, section 1(a) for the costs barrier in the High Court).

Restrict the amount of work that you do before the legal aid certificate is granted since you will not be paid by the Legal Aid Fund until the certificate is issued. Thus, in most cases the solicitor will try to get legal aid without having to write to witnesses, obtain a police report, or get medical evidence as the Legal Aid Board is reluctant to allow work under the Green Form which could be done under a legal aid certificate.

In practice, many solicitors wait too long before applying for legal aid; thus they run the risk of not being covered for the work they do. Apply as soon as you have the basis of the case (usually after your first meeting with the client), and leave the expensive work (eg obtaining medical reports, interviewing witnesses) until after legal aid has been granted. Do not run up disbursements which the client will have to pay for privately, when you could have had the work done under legal aid. If the case is nearing the end of the limitation period apply for emergency legal aid as there are usually long delays in processing an ordinary legal aid application.

Do not forget to explain to the client, verbally and in writing, the effect of the legal aid statutory charge. In deciding whether to grant a certificate, the area office will consider the merits of the case, and will not grant a certificate for a claim which, although sound in legal principle, will only bring a trivial advantage to the applicant. If an offer of legal aid is made, check whether a contribution is required.

Finally, remember that it is possible to reapply for legal aid. So, if the client is turned down on financial grounds do not be reluctant to submit a fresh application, at a later date, if the eligibility rates are increased, or if the client's finances change. If the client is turned down because the case has insufficient merit then reapply if fresh facts emerge or if your client privately obtains a counsel's opinion suggesting that the case is good on liability.

2 The certificate

Once the legal aid certificate is received, it should be checked for any limitations. If these are unduly restrictive, then it is possible to appeal to the local office, although in practice this is rarely done. Unless the certificate states to the contrary, the certificate will authorise High Court or county court proceedings and the normal work done prior to the commencement of proceedings. Thus it could, for example, cover the cost of an Originating Application for pre-action discovery in a medical negligence case (see Chapter 18, section 4), although the prudent solicitor would still safeguard the position by obtaining the local office's prior approval. Remember that a certificate cannot be back-dated or made retrospective, and accordingly cannot cover the cost of work done prior to its issue.

The certificate will often be limited. Check the wording of the limitation carefully. For instance, the phrase 'obtaining counsel's opinion only' means that no work or investigation can be carried out by the solicitor, and that the papers must be sent to counsel as they are; no investigatory work will be allowable on taxation, even if specifically requested by counsel. Thus, if any work has to be done it is advisable to ask counsel to make a written request for this evidence to be obtained, and the solicitor should then send a copy of counsel's opinion to the local office and ask that the certificate be extended (eg to 'all steps up to, but excluding, issue of the writ, but including obtaining counsel's opinion'). This would authorise the investigatory work. Another point to watch out for is a restriction on the number of experts' reports that can be obtained. For instance in a medical negligence case, the certificate frequently refers to an expert's 'report' in the singular; if more than one report is needed, then write to the local office explaining the position, and asking them for the authority to incur the additional disbursement.

Frequently, there will be a limited certificate which authorises the obtaining of counsel's opinion, etc. If the limitation period is about to expire, then protective proceedings must be issued. In such a case, ask for the certificate to be amended to cover the position by authorising steps 'up to and including the issue of the writ (but not service) and obtaining counsel's opinion'.

In personal injury cases it is extremely common to find that the certificate is limited to 'all steps up to but excluding setting down'. It is important to make a note to check this point before fixing a hearing date; if the certificate is limited, then legal aid authority must be obtained before the case can be taken any further. At this stage, it is usual to send the local office a copy of counsel's opinion (and any documents it refers to). Only in difficult cases should it be necessary to send other enclosures (eg medical reports, special damage calculations, etc). There is now a form to be used when applying for amendment; ensure that you explain in detail why the amendment is needed. There are often long delays in obtaining authority and in urgent cases you should apply for emergency authority by telephone.

Advising the client: Do not forget that you must advise the client as to the meaning of any limitations on the certificate. In addition, and probably more importantly, you must advise the client at the outset and when any settlement is discussed how the statutory charge works. Many solicitors have a standard leaflet (or letter) that they send to all clients who are awarded legal aid in addition to the leaflet provided by the Legal Aid Board when the application is made. It is important to explain how the statutory charge works, and how the client's damages can be used to meet any shortfall in costs. In a personal injuries claim, this is, in practice, likely to arise if a payment into court has not been beaten.

Green Form: Once legal aid has been granted immediately lodge any Green Form for payment. You do not need to await the end of the case.

3 Notifying the court and the other parties

Both the court and the other side must be told if the client is legally aided.

A defendant who is being sued by a legally aided plaintiff is at a disadvantage. Quite simply, it is less likely to recover his costs from a legally aided plaintiff than from a privately funded plaintiff. Thus, it is important to advise the other side of the fact that the plaintiff is legally aided.

Notice of issue of certificate: A Notice of Issue must be served on all parties to the proceedings. As soon as the proceedings are commenced (or when the certificate is issued, if proceedings have already been commenced) a Notice must be served on each of the defendants. A precedent Notice of Issue is printed in Precedent 35. Do not forget to keep a copy of the Notice of Issue, since it is one of the documents that has to be included in the bundle of papers when the case is set down for trial (see Chapter 12). The Notice of Issue must set out the scope of the client's certificate (eg 'to bring an action for personal injuries against the defendant arising from an accident on . . .'). But, it is not necessary to set out any limitation in the certificate. Many plaintiff's solicitors wrongly set out the limitation (eg that the certificate only authorises the case to be taken as far as setting down). It is wrong for the plaintiff's solicitor to disclose the limitations in his client's certificate; by doing so you weaken your client's position. The only time when a limitation must be stated is if the certificate relates to appeal proceedings. Otherwise, never reveal a limitation.

There is a different form to be used if a legal aid certificate is amended, discharged or revoked. See Precedent 35. Note that there is no need to serve a Notice of Amendment merely because the limitation on the client's certificate has been removed or amended (unless, of course, one originally referred to that limitation on the Notice of Issue, which, as we have seen, one is not advised to do). Often solicitors forget to serve a Notice of Issue until the proceedings are well under way. Failure to serve the Notice does not invalidate the client's legal aid certificate, or mean that the plaintiff automatically becomes liable for the other side's costs. However, in an extreme case, the plaintiff's solicitor could be held responsible for costs if the defendant has suffered serious prejudice. To avoid this difficulty, you should adopt the habit of asking the county court to serve the Notice of Issue with the proceedings (or serving it with the writ in the High Court).

Filing the certificate with the court: In the same way that the other side must be notified of the plaintiff being legally aided, so must the court. To do this, file one of the copy legal aid certificates with the court. You should prepare a backsheet (ie with title of action; stating it is a legal aid certificate; name and address of your firm, reference, phone number, etc). Note that there is no need for a copy of the legal aid certificate to be supplied to the other side, they receive a Notice of Issue (see above). However in the county court you must also file a copy of the Notice of Issue with the court (see above). In the High Court there is no need for a copy of the Notice of Issue to be filed with the court.

Once again, it is best to adopt the habit of filing the certificate when commencing proceedings. See Stock Letters 28 and 29.

Remember, it is all too easy to forget to lodge the certificate with the court, and to serve Notice on the other parties. Always double-check that this has been done.

4 The duty to the Legal Aid Fund

Apart from the duty to your client, a solicitor also has a duty to the Legal Aid Fund.

The general duty: There is a general duty on the solicitor not to take unjustifiable steps in the action; not to incur unjustifiable expenditure, and a duty not to continue litigation unjustifiably. In effect, if a solicitor continues with a hopeless case, which should have been brought to the attention of the Legal Aid Board, then the solicitor runs the risk of losing any entitlement to costs, and, in an exceptional case, being ordered to pay some of the other side's costs.

Recoupment of money: All money obtained from the defendant on behalf of the plaintiff, except interim payments, must be paid to the plaintiff's solicitor (not the client direct) and paid to the Legal Aid Board pending determination of the case and the plaintiff's solicitor's costs. This rule is designed to protect the statutory charge but is particularly inconvenient because there are often long delays in the Legal Aid Board paying the money out to the client at the end of the case and the interest rates paid are often lower than those that would have been obtained in a bank or building society deposit. The Legal Aid Board are considering amending the requirement that money be paid over to them (although it will still have to be paid to the solicitor rather than the client direct) but until they do so solicitors should at least try to alleviate the problem by always considering whether the money paid is more than any likely costs liability and, if so, sending an undertaking to this effect to the Legal Aid Board so that some money can be released to the client. If you decide to to this do not underestimate your costs!

To obtain costs: There is a general duty to obtain standard costs from the other side (whether by agreement or order). This is coupled with a general duty to safeguard the interests of the Legal Aid Fund on any *inter partes* taxation, and to take any steps that may seem necessary for a review of that taxation (although specific authority is needed before putting in a notice of objections to a taxation).

The duty to report to the area office: The solicitor must immediately notify the area office if any money is recovered or preserved for the client, and also the solicitor must account to the area office, not the plaintiff, if any money is received on behalf of the client (see above).

In addition, there is a general duty to report to the area office if there is:

(i) abuse by the client of legal aid (eg the client behaving unreasonably, such as telephoning frequently and so increasing the costs liability of the Legal Aid Fund).

(ii) when there are no reasonable grounds for continuing with the case. For instance, if there is new evidence that shows the client no longer has a cause of action, or if there has been a change in the prospects of success due to a payment into court, or if the defendant is shown to have no assets, or if there is now a CICB claim that will give the client full compensation, etc. If the solicitor is in doubt as to the position, report to the area office and let them decide.

(iii) the solicitor must provide the area office with a report of the progress in the proceedings, if requested.

(iv) the area office must be told if the client dies, or if a receiving order is made.

In addition, the solicitor has a discretion to report to the area office, for example, if you doubt your client's honesty. The solicitor who reports doubts and fears to the area office will not be in breach of the professional duty to the client, and the prudent solicitor will therefore, when faced with a difficulty, consult the area office and leave it to them to decide whether the case should continue or not.

When the defendant reports to the Legal Aid Board: An astute defendant may decide to take advantage of reg 73(2). This says that 'any party may disclose to an Area Director or an area committee communications in relation to the proceedings concerned sent to or by the assisted person's solicitor, whether or not they are expressed to be "without prejudice"'. In general, there is nothing to stop a defendant's solicitor writing to the legal aid authorities suggesting that a legally aided plaintiff is behaving unreasonably (eg in not accepting a payment in). If this happens then all the plaintiff's solicitor can do is to write a lengthy letter to the area office rebutting the allegations that have been made. However, the fact remains that area offices do occasionally allow themselves to be influenced by this tactical ploy on the part of defendants.

5 Disbursements

The necessity to obtain authority to incur expenditure, or take certain steps, can be either mandatory or discretionary. Authority is sought by way of letter to the area office, and it should be remembered that if the area office authorises the step or the expenditure, then the costs cannot be disallowed by the taxing officer on a legal aid taxation (although they may, of course, be disallowed *inter partes*).

Authority is *mandatory* if the intention is to:

(1) add a further party to the proceedings;
(2) defend a counterclaim or enter a cross-appeal;
(3) instruct more than one counsel (see below).

The solicitor has a *discretion* to seek the area office's authority (and thus cover the costs position) to:

(1) lodge an interlocutory appeal (cf an appeal to the Court of Appeal on judgment, which would require the issue of a new certificate);
(2) obtain a transcript (often the authority will be limited to obtaining only certain relevant parts of the transcript);
(3) take an unusual step, or incur unusually large expenditure;
(4) obtain expert evidence (see below).

If the solicitor does not obtain authority before taking any of the above steps, you run the risk that some (or all) of the expenditure, and of your costs, will not be allowed on taxation, in which case you will bear the loss since the money can neither be recovered from the client nor from the Legal Aid Fund. Accordingly, it is wise always to seek the Legal Aid Board's authority if there is any doubt as to the propriety of the step being taken. The authority will be given in a letter from the area office, and there is, of course, no need to serve a copy of that letter on the court or on the other parties to the action. If authority is refused there is no right of appeal, although there is no reason why a fresh application cannot be made.

(a) Counsel and counsel's fees

Authority must be obtained before instructing a second junior or before taking in a leader. When deciding whether to authorise a leader, the area office will consider such matters as the sum of money involved, the importance of the case to the client, whether the case involves a specialised field of law, and whether it raises a difficult point of law. However, the Legal Aid Board will not authorise a leader solely because, for example, the junior originally instructed has been taken ill, or because the other side has brought in a leader, or even if junior counsel is not sufficiently experienced (in such a case the application should be for authority to instruct a second junior). If a leader is authorised, the authority will only extend to the brief fee and any necessary consultation, such as consultation on *quantum*, but it will not cover such items as a written advice on evidence or *quantum*, or a consultation or advice on an interlocutory matter, unless specific authority is given. Junior counsel's fee will usually be allowed, but not always. These are the guidelines as to when junior counsel's fees will normally be allowed in legal aid cases:

Opinions: (written or in conference) will be allowed:

(*a*) on the merits, where any reasonable doubt exists;

(*b*) on the summons for directions;

(*c*) on *quantum* or on a proposed settlement.

Conferences will not usually be allowed for an interlocutory application, where counsel has already been allowed a fee for settling the application, or advising on it, or for settling the evidence in support of it. Nor will a fee usually be permitted for a conference on the settling of documents where these have already been settled by counsel, or where counsel has already given a written opinion on them.

Settling: counsel's fee will normally be allowed for the settling of:

(*a*) any pleading,

(*b*) particulars (or a request for particulars) of a pleading,

(*c*) interrogatories (or answers thereto).

Counsel's fee will not be allowed for settling an indorsement on a writ.

Summonses and interlocutory applications: counsel's brief fee will normally be allowed if the application involves interrogatories or particulars.

Fees for opinions, conferences and summonses not mentioned above may be allowed if the taxing officer is satisfied that they were 'necessary'. Fees for views of the locus by counsel will rarely be allowed. If in doubt, one should obtain authority.

(b) Experts' reports

When instructing an expert, be it doctor, engineer, or surveyor, there is always the risk that the fee will not be allowed on taxation, if it was 'unreasonable'. Some solicitors state in the letter of instruction to the expert that the fee cannot exceed the amount that will be allowed on taxation. By doing this, the solicitor seeks to avoid personal liability should the fee not be allowed. However it is prefered ie, if there is any doubt, for the solicitor to obtain prior authority from the local office. Such authority will usually be made subject to a maximum figure but often the area will refuse to give specific authority and instead state that the figure must be justified on taxation.

Ensure that the authority is obtained before the expenditure is incurred and remember that there can be long delays in obtaining such authority. When writing to the area office for authority, it is often convenient to ask for payment on account of that, and other, disbursements (see below).

(c) Obtaining the client's authority

If the client is legally aided, it is all too easy to forget that one must also obtain the client's authority for any unusual expenditure. Few solicitors will forget to obtain the area office's prior approval for such expenditure, but it is surprising how many forget to obtain the client's approval. The reason for consulting the client is that the client might, via the statutory charge, eventually have to meet the bill. Thus, the client should also be consulted.

It is not enough to simply advise the client of how the statutory charge works. One must also advise the client if one is going to incur expenditure that may not be recoverable. For instance, suppose one is thinking of obtaining actuarial evidence to support a future loss of earnings claim. In general, such evidence will not be admitted at trial and there is a likelihood that the costs of the actuary's reports would not be recoverable on an *inter partes* taxation. The legally aided plaintiff should therefore be advised that such expenditure may not be recoverable, since the client may well have to pay for it, through operation of the statutory charge. If the solicitor does not advise the legally aided client that such expenditure may not be recoverable, then you may find that you are unable to recover the disbursement under your common fund costs.

Recovering the cost of disbursements

The Legal Aid Board will reimburse the solicitor for any disbursements incurred. There is no need to wait until conclusion of the case. Accordingly, it should be standard practice to always request reimbursement of any disbursement as soon as you know that it is likely to be incurred. There is a standard form for this purpose CLA 28 available from the Legal Aid Board.

6 Payment into court

If the defendant makes a payment into court, check whether there is a limitation on the plaintiff's legal aid certificate requiring that the area committee be notified of all payments in (or offers of settlements). Such a limitation is not unusual.

The legally aided plaintiff should be advised of the risks of not accepting a payment into court. Do not be misled into thinking that the consequences are different merely because the client is legally aided. They are not, see Chapter 8, section 1. If the plaintiff fails to beat the payment in, then the statutory charge will apply as regards the plaintiff's own solicitor's common fund costs (as from the date of payment in). In addition, the court can take into account the damages the plaintiff is awarded (even if less than the payment in) in deciding whether the plaintiff should pay some of the defendant's costs. Thus, a legally aided plaintiff is not insulated against the effects of a payment in. For general advice on the payment in, see Chapter 8, section 1.

7 Discharge or revocation of the certificate

The certificate *must* be discharged if the assisted person:

(1) no longer has reasonable grounds for taking, defending, or being a party to, proceedings; *or*
(2) has required the case to be conducted unreasonably, or so as to cause an unjustifiable cost to the Legal Aid Fund; *or*
(3) should not, in the particular circumstances, continue to receive legal aid, since it would be unjustifiable to do so; *or*
(4) becomes financially ineligible.

The area office *may*, in its discretion, discharge the certificate:

(1) on request; *or*
(2) if the contribution is in arrears; *or*
(3) on the death of the assisted person, or on a receiving order being made; *or*
(4) at the conclusion of the case, or of the steps authorised.

Before a certificate is discharged, the assisted person will be given notice and afforded an opportunity to show cause why the certificate should not be discharged.

Discharge is not the same as revocation. If a certificate is revoked, it is as though the certificate had never been issued and so the client is responsible for all costs incurred. A certificate can be revoked (or discharged) if the assisted person:

(1) made untrue statements, or if there was material non-disclosure as to resources;
(2) knowingly made an untrue statement, or failed to furnish information, on other matters;
(3) failed to attend an interview or give information, when required.

If a certificate is revoked or discharged, then the plaintiff's solicitor must:

(1) serve notice of revocation or discharge on the other party (see section 3);
(2) notify counsel;
(3) file a copy with the court. A backsheet should be prepared. It should be endorsed 'we certify that reg 82(2) of Civil Legal Aid (General) Regulations 1989 has been complied with' (this confirms that notice of discharge/revocation has been served on the other parties, and that counsel has been notified). In addition, the backsheet should be endorsed 'we confirm the action has not been set down for trial' or 'the action has been set down for trial under Non-Jury Number . . . and accordingly we enclose a further copy of the certificate'. The endorsement on the backsheet should be signed and dated by the plaintiff's solicitor. There is no need for the solicitor to apply to go off the record; by filing the certificate, and serving notice on the other parties, the retainer is automatically terminated (see reg 83(2)).

8 Costs

Although it is likely that the Lord Chancellor's Department will bring in standard fees for civil cases, at present the basic rule in respect of legal aid costs is that they must be taxed. However, most solicitors acting on behalf of successful legally aided plaintiffs will wish to avoid the inconvenience, cost and delay of taxation by using the exception to this basic rule.

Assessment by area director: Under reg 105 of the Civil Legal Aid (General) Regulations 1989, the area director must assess the costs if proceedings have not yet been commenced (clearly, the court would not be able to tax the costs in such a case). In addition, the director also has the power to assess the costs of an action, if:

(*a*) solicitor and counsel think that they would not recover more than £1,000 in a legal aid taxation (taking their costs in aggregate and including disbursements but excluding VAT); *or*

(*b*) the case has been settled and the other side has agreed to pay a sum in respect of costs which the solicitor and counsel are prepared to accept. However, this exception will not be available if the court made a direction as to costs. The area director is entitled to refer a matter to a court taxing officer for assessment without a formal taxation;

(*c*) taxation would in the special circumstances be against the client's interests, and would increase the fund's expenditure.

Exception (*b*) is generally the method which solicitors will wish to use when trying to avoid taxation as assessments are calculated on a standard form which is shorter and simpler to complete than a full bill for taxation. Remember that costs may have to be taxed in an infant case (see Chapter 14, section 3), in which case the above exceptions cannot apply. On assessment of costs by the area director, the figure can be appealed to the area committee, by way of written representation.

If costs cannot be assessed by the area director (this will usually be when it has not proved possible to agree a figure with the other side), it will be necessary to prepare for a full taxation. The bill will be a three column bill, if the assisted person's costs are payable wholly out of the Legal Aid Fund, and six column if the order is for costs to be paid by another party (that is, three columns for *inter partes* costs and three columns for legal aid costs in excess of *inter partes* costs). You will normally wish to instruct a costs draftsperson to draw up this bill.

The client's liability for costs

The assisted party who loses a case will be liable for the defendant's costs up to the amount which the court thinks to be reasonable in all the circumstances, bearing in mind the means of the parties and their conduct in the action. The courts have stated that the contribution figure assessed on the issue of the legal aid certificate is not an appropriate guide when quantifying what is a reasonable amount for the losing assisted party to pay; however, in practice, the contribution figure is often the figure decided upon as being reasonable in the circumstances of the case.

It is for this reason that the knowledge that the plaintiff is legally aided may well induce a defendant to settle. For example, suppose that the plaintiff's claim is unsuccessful and so the defendant is entitled to tax costs at, say, £800, although its actual costs will be £900. If the plaintiff's maximum contribution was assessed at £200 then the defendant will be unlikely to recover more than that amount; thus the defendant will end up some £700 out of pocket.

Note that the other side can apply at any time within the next six years for the order as to costs to be varied if there is a change in the circumstances of the assisted person. Whether or not the successful non-assisted party will recover the balance of his costs from the Legal Aid Fund will depend upon whether the defendant can show that it will suffer financial hardship otherwise, and whether it would be just and equitable in the circumstances. It is for this reason that insurance companies are reluctant to incur heavy costs against a legally aided plaintiff.

9 Settling the case

The area office is always supposed to assess costs, even if they have been agreed between the respective solicitors. In practice, however, the local office will normally approve costs that have been agreed.

If costs have been agreed with the other side, then write to the local office notifying them of those costs and asking them to confirm that they agree them. In addition it will be necessary to confirm that there is no Green Form payment to be refunded (or to refund Green Form payments and any payments that have been made on account), that the client agrees to discharge the certificate, and that no further claim will be made on the fund. Use Stock Letter 45.

Chapter 17

The Limitation Period

The basic rule is that a personal injury claim must be commenced (ie the writ issued, or county court proceedings begun) within three years of the date of the accident. There are, however, exceptions to this:

- *Minors:* time does not run against a minor. Thus, the three year period begins to run when the minor reaches the age of 18;
- *Aircraft accidents:* here there is a two year, not three year, limitation period (Carriage by Air Act 1961);
- *Knowledge:* if the plaintiff did not know of the injury, or of the defendant's negligence, then the three year period will not start running until the date the knowledge was acquired (Limitation Act 1980, s 11);
- *Extending the three year period:* the court has a general discretion to extend the limitation period, if this would be 'equitable' (Limitation Act 1980, s 33).

1 When the three year period starts to run

In the vast majority of cases, time begins to run from the date of the accident. Quite simply, the plaintiff knows that there was an accident, and that someone else might be to blame. That being so, the limitation period will be three years.

In calculating the three years, the day of the accident (ie the date the cause of action accrued) is excluded. So, if a plaintiff was injured on 3 May 1992, the limitation will expire on 4 May 1995. In addition, if the three years and one day expire on a Saturday, Sunday, or Bank Holiday (ie when proceedings cannot be issued), then time is extended until the next day on which one can issue proceedings.

However, to apply the three year rule from the date of the cause of action, or injury, could produce hardship in some cases when the injured person does not know all the relevant facts. For instance, the person may not know of the injury until well after three years from the cause of action (as in an asbestosis claim, when the disease may not manifest itself until several years after the worker ceases to be in contact with asbestos). Similarly, the plaintiff may not be aware of evidence that shows that the proposed defendant was to blame for the accident (eg in occupational overuse injury cases ('RSI') the client may not link the symptoms to the work conditions). To deal with such situations, Limitation Act 1980, s 11 allows the three year period to run either from the date of the accident (ie cause of action accruing), or from the date when the plaintiff first had 'knowledge'.

Time starts running once 'knowledge' is acquired. This will be when the plaintiff first knew that the injury was:

(*a*) significant, *and*

(*b*) attributable to an act or omission of the prospective defendant.

Thus, the effect of s 11 is to extend the limitation period where the plaintiff did not have knowledge. However, it should be remembered that this will not help the plaintiff whose delay is his or her own fault, or who has delayed because of:

- ignorance of the law;
- unreasonable failure to use the known information to make further enquiries to find out what did happen;
- unreasonable failure to appreciate the significance of the injuries;
- unreasonable failure to take medical or legal advice.

In such circumstances, s 11 cannot apply. The plaintiff's only hope will be to rely upon the court's general discretion (ie under Limitation Act 1980, s 33, see below).

An illustration of how the 'knowledge' rules can be applied is given by *Davis* v *MoD* (1985) *The Times* 7 August (CA). In that case, an employee had been exposed to dermatitis between 1955 and 1971, when he left work. He first contracted dermatitis in 1969, and it became particularly serious in 1971. His GP had always felt that it was due to dust at work, and the plaintiff himself thought that this was so. Legal aid was obtained, and a writ was issued in 1973. But, the action was never prosecuted; this was because medical reports were obtained, and after obtaining two sets of counsel's opinion, he was advised that the dermatitis was not due to his working conditions. Some years later, he obtained contrary advice, and so a writ was issued in November 1981, with the writ being served in June 1982. The defendants applied for the action to be struck out under the inherent jurisdiction of the court. The court had to consider whether 'knowledge' had accrued prior to November 1978 (ie within three years of date of issue of writ). It was held that he did not have knowledge until that time, and the mere fact that his previous claim had not been prosecuted was not a bar to his proceeding with a second claim. Although he himself had always felt the dermatitis was attributable to his work conditions, it was accepted that there were no reasonable grounds for his continuing with his original claim (in view of the advice he had received).

Thus, if one is dealing with a case in which expert opinions are needed (especially medical evidence), then it may well be the case that 'knowledge' does not run until such time as the plaintiff gets positive advice, from such an expert, that there may be liability.

A more mundane, and less unusual case, was *Leadbitter* v *Hodge Finance* [1982] 2 All ER 167. In that case, the plaintiff's 'knowledge' was taken to be from the date when he received the police report, which indicated that another party might be liable. Thus, the date for joining that party as a second defendant ran from the date of the police report.

Medical negligence: The question of 'knowledge' is particularly relevant in medical negligence cases. It will often be the case that the plaintiff will not have the necessary 'knowledge' until he or she has received a firm indication (eg from a medical expert) that there was negligence. Thus, more often than not, the three year period in a medical negligence claim will not run from the date of the negligent treatment, but from the date when the client is told that there may well have been negligence. This is a point that is often overlooked by the inexperienced practitioner. However, if the medical negligence is obvious (eg the wrong limb is amputated!) then knowledge will accrue as from the date of the negligent treatment.

2 The court's discretion to extend the three year period

Under Limitation Act 1980, s 33, the court can extend the three year period if it would be 'equitable' to do so, but in reaching this decision it must have regard to any 'prejudice' to the defendant.

This discretion to extend the limitation period is completely separate from the 'knowledge' provisions in s 11. Under s 11, there is still a three year period, it is just that the date when the three years begins may be extended to the time when 'knowledge' accrued. Under s 33, it is the three year period itself that can be extended.

When deciding whether the s 33 discretion should be exercised, the court will, inter alia, consider the following matters:

(i) The length of the delay and the reasons for it. For instance, see *McCafferty* v *Metropolitan Police Receiver* [1977] 2 All ER 756 in which a plaintiff suffering from deafness due to noise was allowed to proceed out of time. Lawton LJ commented 'in my judgment the court should be understanding of men who, after taking an overall view of the situation, come to the conclusion that they would prefer to go on working rather than become involved with litigation';

(ii) the extent to which the evidence in the case will now be less cogent. For instance, if the defendants have dealt with other claims on the same facts, and have that evidence to hand, they will not be prejudiced by the delay, as in *Buck* v *English Electric* [1977] 1 WLR 806;

(iii) the conduct of the defendant. For instance, has it contributed to the delay by being obstructive? Has it unintentionally misled the plaintiff as to the question of legal liability?

(iv) the extent of the plaintiff's disability;

(v) the steps taken by the plaintiff to obtain advice. It may be relevant that the plaintiff will have a negligence claim against the advisers if the claim is not allowed to proceed out of time.

An example of how s 33 can be applied, in practice, is found in *Buck* v *English Electric* (above). This was a pneumoconiosis claim where the disease had first been contracted by the plaintiff in 1959. By 1963 he had become aware of his right to sue but his disability was only small at that time. By 1970, however, he was 100 per cent disabled and by 1973 he had been forced to give up work. The writ was issued in 1975. It was held that, although the claim was some nine years out of time, the court would allow it to proceed by virtue of its discretion under s 33. Despite the inordinate delay, the defendants had been involved in several similar claims in recent years and so it was unlikely that the delay would prejudice them since they had all the relevant information and evidence to hand.

It has to be said that there is some judicial conflict as to how s 33 should be applied. Does the court have a complete discretion, or must it be satisfied that the normal three year limitation period has 'prejudiced' the plaintiff? The answer seems to be that the court will want to look for prejudice to the plaintiff. Thus, for instance, if the plaintiff sues within the three year period, and then allows the action to lapse (eg fails to serve the writ in time; and the action is struck out), then the plaintiff cannot use s 33 to justify the commencement of further proceedings outside the limitation period. This is because it will not have been the three year period that would have prejudiced the plaintiff, but the plaintiff's own (or a solicitor's) default and inefficiency. The position seems to be that:

- if the plaintiff has begun proceedings within the three year limitation period, then the plaintiff cannot use s 33 to bring a second set of proceedings outside the period;
- if the plaintiff does not bring an action within the three year period, then the court has a discretion under s 33 to extend the time period, and allow the claim to proceed.

So, the plaintiff who has not yet sued will be better off than the plaintiff who has already tried to sue.

Adding a new defendant, out of time: The plaintiff may have begun proceedings within the three year period and then find, when the defence is served, that allegations are made against another party. At this stage, the plaintiff may well find that the three year period has expired, and so is apparently out of time for joining the third person as a defendant to the action. When this happens, the plaintiff may be in difficulty. However, it should not be forgotten that the three year period runs from the date of 'knowledge'; so, if the plaintiff did not realise that the third person might be to blame, then it can be argued that the three year period does not run until date of service of the defence. Alternatively, the plaintiff can simply proceed against the third person, and rely upon the court's general discretion under s 33. There are two alternatives. Either, the plaintiff can join the third person as a defendant (see p 74 for the procedure), or, can issue a second set of proceedings and then have the two actions consolidated (see Chapter 7, section 2(*b*)).

3 Fatal cases

The Limitation Act 1980 also applies to fatal cases. Thus, the three year period can run from the date of 'knowledge', and there is also a general equitable discretion to extend time.

As regards the acquisition of 'knowledge', s 12 sets out the rules. These are basically similar to those in s 11 (for non-fatal cases). The three year period runs from whichever is later of (*a*) the date of cause of action accruing (ie date of death), and (*b*) the date of the acquisition of the relevant knowledge (as defined above). In a fatal claim the 'knowledge' will be that of the personal representatives (in a Law Reform Claim) or the dependants (in a Fatal Accidents Claim). Note that different dependants may have acquired their knowledge at different times and thus will have different limitation periods for their claims, whereas in the case of personal representatives the date of the acquisition of knowledge will always be the date it was first acquired by any one of the personal representatives.

No claim can be brought if the deceased was statute-barred at the time of death. In deciding whether the deceased could have brought an action, one applies the test of whether the deceased died within three years of the accident or the date when the deceased acquired knowledge. If the death occurred more than three years after both those dates then no claim can be brought, for the court's equitable discretion under s 33 cannot be used to extend the limitation period for the deceased's claim. However, the s 33 discretion can be used to alter the limitation period for the statutory claim. Thus, if the deceased was not statute-barred at the time of death, but no claim was brought within the three years of death (or the necessary knowledge being acquired) then the court could exercise its discretion and allow a claim to proceed; but the contrary would not apply, for if the deceased was statute-barred at the time of death, no action could be brought under the Law Reform or Fatal Accidents Act, even if it was sought to do so within three years of the death.

4 Procedure

There is no set procedure for dealing with a limitation dispute. What happens is that the plaintiff issues proceedings in the usual way (the court staff should not refuse to deal with it because the three year period has expired) and the defendant should file a defence in a county court case or an Acknowledgment of Service in a High Court case. The defendant can issue a summons asking for the action to be stayed, or struck out under the court's inherent jurisdiction. Alternatively, the defendant may plead the limitation point in the defence, and allow the issue to be determined at trial. Thus, there are three ways of bringing the limitation question before the court:

(1) by hearing on an application or summons;
(2) by trial as a preliminary issue by the judge (ie as with a split trial). This might be appropriate if the matter is too complicated to be dealt with on an application or a summons (eg involves oral evidence and cross examination);
(3) at the trial. This would be the correct course of action if the limitation question is intricately bound up with the circumstances of the case, making a preliminary trial impracticable.

Note that when there is a limitation problem, the claim should not ignore it. The grounds on which the plaintiff relies (ie date of knowledge or entitlement to benefit of court's discretion) should be pleaded in full unless it is known that the defendant will not take the limitation point (eg has said so in correspondence).

Overall, the effect of the Act has been that very few personal injury claimants go without compensation due to limitation problems. Even if the Act does not allow the three year period to be extended, it will often be possible for the claimant to sue an adviser (usually a solicitor or trade union official for failure to issue a writ in time.

5 Dismissal for want of prosecution

Even if a plaintiff issues proceedings in time, the plaintiff can still face an application for the action to be dismissed for want of prosecution. In practice, many accident claims go to sleep, and take an unduly long time to proceed. In such cases, in addition to the risk that a county court action may be struck out for failure to apply to fix a date for trial within 15 months of close of pleadings, the plaintiff's solicitor is open to the risk of an application or summons to dismiss, and such applications should always be taken extremely seriously.

'When the delay is prolonged and inexcusable, and is such as to do grave injustice to the one side or the other or to both, the court may in its discretion dismiss the action straight away' (Lord Denning in *Allen* v *Sir Alfred McAlpine and Sons Ltd* [1968] 2 QB 229. In accident cases, the court will look to see whether:

(i) there has been inordinate and inexcusable delay; *and*

(ii) the delay has given rise to a substantial risk that it will not be possible to have a fair trial, or it is likely to cause serious prejudice to the defendants (eg unable to properly defend the claim, through fading memories of witnesses, etc).

When served with an application or a summons to dismiss for want of prosecution, the plaintiff's solicitor must prepare a comprehensive affidavit. This should explain why the case has taken so long to proceed, set out all the circumstances, exhibit all the relevant documents and generally give a full and satisfactory explanation. The affidavit should set out a full chronology of what has happened. There is no point in the plaintiff trying to gloss-over periods of undue delay. It is better to set out the circumstances in full and explain why the delay arose. If (as is often the case) the delay was partly due to the time that a doctor, or barrister, took to deal with the papers, then disclose the relevant correspondence. In short, do everything necessary to provide a full and frank account of what has happened, and try to deal with all possible criticisms. In addition, it is usually advisable to go through the file and update it immediately. For instance, if further medical reports have not yet been prepared, or lists of documents not exchanged, then the plaintiff should immediately press on with the action and do everything possible before the hearing of the application or summons. In effect, you should do everything possible to proceed with the action (as though the application or summons had never been served) so that you can state in your affidavit that all those steps have been taken. In practice, courts can be ruthless about striking out claims, and all applications to strike out must be taken extremely seriously by plaintiffs.

Obviously, if the action is struck out within the three year limitation period (which would be unlikely) then there is nothing to stop the plaintiff simply issuing a second set of proceedings, although there is authority for saying the defendant might be able to get the second action struck out as an abuse of the court process!

Bear in mind that if the claim is struck out, the plaintiff's solicitor may well be liable to the client, since, more often than not, the delay is the fault of the plaintiff's solicitor, not the plaintiff. Applications to strike out are becoming more and more common. Plaintiffs' solicitors should be aware that an astute defendant might use this tactic; it is therefore advisable always to ensure that there is never a long period of silence in the correspondence. If there is a problem with the case (eg the doctor is taking six months to prepare a medical report) then it might be better to write to the other side bringing them up to date on the position and explaining why the delay is arising. Should they subsequently issue an application or summons to strike out, then the court is likely to be impressed by the plaintiff's openness, and having kept the defendant informed of the position. The main point is that the defendant should be reassured that the plaintiff is proceeding with his or her claim and that you too regret the delay that is occurring. Exceptionally, therefore, the astute plaintiff will be writing letters to the defendant in anticipation of a possible application to strike out: indeed, writing letters when you would not otherwise have done so. In an old or stale case, it can often be worth doing this.

For general information on the criteria that justify dismissal, see the notes to White Book Ord 25 r 1(3)A.

6 Dismissal for failure to fix a date

As stated above, in the county court the automatic directions (CCR Ord 17, r 11) provide that the case will automatically be struck out if the plaintiff does not apply to fix a hearing date within 15 months of close of pleadings. If such an action is struck out after the end of the three year limitation period it is very unlikely that an application to restore would succeed and you may find yourself faced with a negligence action.

Chapter 18

Medical Negligence Claims

1 Introduction

It is well known that medical negligence cases are difficult. There are several reasons for this. First, there is the difficulty of finding a suitably qualified expert who is prepared to stand up in court and say that another doctor was negligent. Secondly, there is the cost. Merely investigating the claim, to see whether it is worth issuing a writ, is likely to cost £750 or more. Medical negligence cases revolve around expert evidence, and this is expensive. Thirdly, there is the well known reluctance of the medical profession (and its representative bodies) to admit negligence; the result is that a higher percentage of medical negligence claims go to trial than for a corresponding number of straightforward personal injury claims. Fourthly, and most importantly, the standard of proof required of a plaintiff is extremely high.

In theory, there could be as many as four different types of action that could be brought by a complaining patient: trespass (ie assault and/or battery); misrepresentation (ie if patient is given misleading information by the doctor); contract; and negligence. In practice, of course, it is in negligence that the action is likely to lie.

To win a case, the plaintiff in a negligence action must show that the doctor followed a course of action that is not supported by any responsible body of medical opinion. The classic test was laid down in *Bolam* [1957] 2 All ER in which it was said that a doctor 'is not guilty of negligence if he has acted in accordance with a practice accepted as proper'. Similarly, it has been said that 'the true test for establishing liability in diagnosis or treatment on the part of a doctor is whether he has been proved to be guilty of such failure as no doctor of ordinary skill would be guilty of' (*Hunter* 1955 SLT 101). In practice, this is likely to mean that if the defendant can produce a reasonably qualified doctor to support the treatment that was given, or can refer to a leading textbook, then the doctor is likely to be able to successfully defend the claim. The vital point to appreciate is that it is not sufficient for the plaintiff merely to be able to show that many other doctors would have behaved in a different manner.

Similarly, it is now established that there is no general duty to advise a patient of all the risks involved in a course of treatment: unless the patient specifically asks *(Sidaway* [1985] AL871).

Anyone handling plaintiff medical negligence claims should join AVMA (Action for Victims of Medical Accidents) Bank Chambers, 1 London Road, Forest Hill, London, SE23 3TP. Tel 081–291 2793.

2 Taking instructions

The first step will be to take the client's statement. Make sure that you have a full chronological record of all the treatment given; the names of the doctors (if known); the addresses of the hospitals concerned; the patient or hospital record numbers; the name and address of the client's GP; etc.

In many cases, this preliminary statement will be used to support an application for legal aid. The area office will want to see that there is an indication of negligence. Concentrate on trying to get some indication of this. For instance, has the client's GP made off the cuff remarks that indicate that all is not well; why does the client think that the treatment was not satisfactory? Bear in mind that you are not required to prove your case at this stage. In practice, legal aid offices are ready and willing to grant a limited legal aid certificate if it can be shown that there is some indication of negligence. Do not feel that you have to produce expert evidence to them before legal aid will be granted. In fact a green form extension will not usually be given to cover the cost of an initial medical report.

Point out to the client that medical negligence cases present difficulties. Explain the standard of proof that will be needed to win the case. Emphasise the likely costs, especially if the case is to be privately funded. Because of the costs, it follows that it is well worth the client accepting an offer of legal aid, even if the contribution is high.

3 Legal aid

Avoid doing any work on the file until the legal aid certificate has been granted. In practice, the certificate is likely to be limited to the obtaining of the medical notes and records, the instruction of an independent expert, and the sending of papers to counsel to advise. In short, the certificate is likely to cover the obtaining of counsel's opinion as to whether proceedings are justified. As mentioned above, it will usually be found that a legal aid application will be considered on the basis of a short statement from the client, together with a covering letter from the solicitor.

4 The letter of claim

It is usual to claim against the local authority or hospital trust responsible for the hospital involved rather than the individual doctor. To find out whether the hospital is run by the local authority or has 'opted-out' and is run by a trust, telephone the hospital concerned or consult the Hospital Year Book published annually by the Department of Health.

The general rule in personal injury claims is to make the initial letter of claim short and to the point (see Chapter 4, section 3). However, it is suggested that medical negligence cases should be an exception to this rule. This is because the letter of claim will normally be going to a hospital administrator or other professional, rather than to a lay person (as is the case with the typical road accident or workplace accident case). Also there is a greater likelihood of the initial letter of claim being seen by a judge, especially if proceedings have to be brought for discovery of the notes and records. A court is more likely to be impresssed by a plaintiff who has made requirements clear and specific from the outset.

Use Stock Letter 27. It will be seen that this does more than merely make the claim. In particular:

(*a*) there is a brief description of what happened. Do not provide too much information at this stage, but do set out those facts over which there cannot be any dispute. If individual doctors or nurses can be identified, then it is best to name them so that the health authority or hospital trust can liaise with the relevant medical defence body. One must give a general indication of what the negligence is that is being alleged: one cannot simply make a claim for negligence. In a suitable case, do not be reluctant to rely upon *res ipsa loquitur* (eg if the client was under a general anaesthetic and cannot be expected to have any knowledge as to what happened);

(*b*) do not simply ask for the 'medical notes and records'. These need to be specified in full (see below). Make it clear that you want the notes to be disclosed to yourself, rather than to your nominated medical expert (see below);

(*c*) ask for disclosure of all witness statements (eg statements by doctors and nurses to the area health authority). Whilst this may be premature, there is no harm in asking;

(*d*) anticipate points that may be raised by the health authority or hospital trust—confirming you will meet reasonable photocopying charges; confirm that the records and notes will not be publicised elsewhere;

(*e*) make it clear that an application for pre-action discovery will be made, if the notes are not disclosed. If legal aid has been granted, then say so.

If the legal aid certificate is limited to obtaining the notes and records, and then getting counsel's opinion, this should cover the costs of an

Originating Application or Summons. In practice, it will occasionally be found that the local office will query this and say that specific authority should have been obtained. It seems clear there is no authority for that suggestion, but some practitioners prefer to avoid doubt and write to the area office stating that an application for pre-action discovery is being made (by Originating Summons) and that it is believed this comes within the scope of the certificate.

5 Disclosure of the medical notes and records

The proposed defendant will probably agree to the release of medical notes and records, but may offer that they be forwarded direct to the plaintiff's medical experts.

You should always refuse such a suggestion. It is well established that such a restriction cannot be forced on the plaintiff (See *McIvor v Southern Health and Social Services Board* [1978] I WLR 757) and a patient is entitled to see copies of all medical records under the Access to Health Records Act, 1990.

The disadvantage of having the notes go direct to the expert is that you, as solicitor, will not see them. Nor will your client. It is possible that either you or your client may be able to draw specific points to the expert's attention, if you have an opportunity of going through the records. Another problem is that the plaintiff's medical expert may not realise that important documents have not been disclosed, whereas the client may (by recalling certain courses of treatment which are perhaps not referred to in the disclosed notes). Thus, disclosure to the solicitor (and the client) is a vital check on the accuracy and comprehensiveness of the notes. Perhaps more importantly, if the notes are disclosed to the solicitor (and thus, to counsel) it means that the expert can be closely cross-examined in conference as to the strength of the opinion expressed. It may also mean that counsel is able to draft a stronger Statement or Particulars of Claim than would otherwise have been the case.

You should therefore always insist on full disclosure to you and should read the records carefully and critically, noting any omissions or anomolies which should be brought to the attention of the client and counsel.

The Originating Application or Summons: If agreement cannot be reached on disclosure of the medical notes and records, then issue an Originating Application or Summons. Follow Procedural Table 16 and Precedent 7.

Usually, the defendant's solicitor will concede the point, and agree to the release of the medical notes and records to the plaintiff, and the plaintiff's solicitor, before the Originating Application or Summons is heard. They will probably want their costs; resist this suggestion. It may be worth writing a letter pointing out that the costs to date have been incurred through their unreasonable action, and if they insist on their costs being paid then you will take the matter before the court (on the Originating Application or Summons) and ask that they pay all the costs incurred. It may be worth reminding the defendants of the case of *Hall* v *Wandsworth HA* (1985) *The Times* 16 February. In that case, Tudor Price J awarded costs to the plaintiff in a pre-action discovery case. He held that he had a general discretion to override Ord 62, r 3(12) (ie the defendant has costs of the application unless court orders otherwise). It was held that the documents should have been produced given that an appropriately worded letter before action had been provided by the plaintiff's solicitors. Thus, be prepared to argue for the costs of discovery if the defendants insist on the Originating Application or Summons being taken to a hearing. It is at this stage that the value of a well-written, and comprehensive, letter of claim will become apparent.

Exchange of witness statements: Do not forget that you can now apply to the court for an order that the parties exchange witness statements (ie statements as to fact). This is now the norm in all personal injury cases (including medical negligence). In the county court this will be one of the automatic directions. In the High Court, given that there are no automatic directions in medical negligence cases, the obvious occasion on which to ask for exchange of witness statements is on the summons for directions. However there is no harm in either the High Court or county court in asking for it at an earlier stage—especially if those statements are crucial to the plaintiff being able to evaluate the prospects of success.

In many ways, it can be said that the power to obtain witness statements can completely alter the whole approach to medical negligence litigation. As a matter of principle, plaintiffs should pursue full exchange and disclosure of witness statements in all medical negligence cases. Bear in mind that medical staff will have made statements to the area health authority (and perhaps to defence organisations). Inevitably, the defendants' experts will be relying upon those statements of facts by preparing their statements as to opinion. Thus, you no longer have to rely solely upon disclosure of notes and records; now, you should go for full disclosure of all statements made. From the plaintiff's point of view, it is best to ask for these at an early stage, even if it may seem premature.

6 Choosing the expert

The choice of expert is crucial to the prospects of success. The real skill of running a medical negligence case is to choose the correct expert. In practice, there are relatively few medical experts who are sufficiently well qualified, and who are willing to give evidence in medical negligence claims. The practitioner with an interest in medical negligence claims would be well advised to join AVMA. Members can have access to their list of suggested experts, and will be given informal advice as to the merits of individual experts. This advice can be invaluable.

Send a full set of the medical notes and records to the client. Ask the client to make detailed comments. Usually, in view of the bulk of the records, it is easier if the client annotates comments directly onto the copy notes. Those annotated notes should then be included in the bundle of papers sent to the expert. Do not forget to go through the records yourself, and be sure to make an attendance note on the file, recording the time spent in perusing and reading the notes.

The legal aid certificate will probably cover the cost of having counsel draft the letter of instructions to the medical expert. In practice, most solicitors are happy to draft the letter themselves. Presumably, one is going to an expert who has some knowledge of medical negligence matters, and who therefore realises the issues that have to be attended to, and knows the legal tests that apply. Stock Letter 17 can be used as the basis of the letter to the medical expert. Alternatively, one can send the papers to counsel to draft the letter, but this will usually result in yet more delay.

When the expert's report is received, a copy should be sent to the client. Remember that the legal aid certificate will probably only cover the obtaining of one report. Thus, if further reports are needed (or supplementary reports, should it be necessary to clarify points with the expert) then it is advisable to obtain prior clearance from the area office. Write to them explaining why the additional disbursement is necessary. If the second report is being obtained from the same doctor, it often helps to describe it as a supplementary report to the previous report, rather than as a separate report!

If the expert's report is not favourable to the client, then the client may wish to go to a different expert. That is the client's right. But, if the client is legally aided, there is a complication. You must first apply for authority to obtain a second report. If this is not granted and the client wishes to obtain a further report, it would be necessary to arrange for the certificate to be discharged, and for the client to then go on an independent basis to the expert. If that second report was favourable, one could then reapply for legal aid, on the basis of that report. What one cannot do is obtain a second report, not authorised by legal aid, whilst one still has a legal aid certificate.

If the report is favourable, then one will normally wish to go back to the area office for the legal aid certificate to be amended, so as to cover the commencement of proceedings, etc. The initial legal aid certificate (limited) will probably have covered the obtaining of counsel's advice, after having received the expert's report. In many cases, there will be little point in going to counsel. It will usually be clear from the expert's report whether the claim is worth pursuing or not. Obviously, if the case presents difficulties, then go to counsel. Otherwise, if the case looks sound, it is probably easier to go directly to the area office and ask for the legal aid certificate to be extended.

7 Commencing proceedings

As regards the three year limitation period, remember that this may well be extended in medical negligence cases. This is because the three years can run from the date 'knowledge' was acquired, which will often be when the plaintiff was first advised that there may well have been medical negligence. Sometimes, that will be as late as the date on which an expert's report was obtained. Generally, for limitations, see Chapter 17.

As with the choice of medical expert, so it is important to choose a suitably experienced counsel. Relatively few counsel specialise in medical negligence claims, but it is well worth making enquiries to find such a counsel. If the client did not get the costs of an Originating Application or Summons, then suggest to counsel that these costs might be pleaded as special damage in the Particulars or Statement of Claim.

After proceedings have been commenced, the action will probably proceed in a similar manner to any other personal injury claim but note the following:

Which court? Cases worth under £50,000 will have to be started in the county court (see Chapter 6) but a medical negligence claim may be considered suitable to transfer up to the High Court under the criteria set out in Art 7(5) of the High Court and County Courts Jurisdiction Order 1991 and if it is worth over £25,000 you should consider applying to transfer up immediately after issue of proceedings. This is done by notice of application in the ordinary way.

Medical report: The plaintiff has to serve with the Particulars or Statement of Claim a medical report. This medical report must substantiate all personal injuries alleged in the pleading but need not contain the expert's views on liability. Because of the need to differentiate between the expert's report on liability and the report on condition and progress you should consider asking the expert to write (or rewrite) the report in two parts; one for disclosure at the beginning of the case and the other for later disclosure.

Discovery: Since the medical notes and records have already been disclosed, the defendant's solicitor may well suggest that the preparation of lists be dispensed with. The plaintiff should normally resist this suggestion. If it is to be agreed, then the plaintiff should ask the defendant to confirm in open letter that there are no 'documents, including obstetric, surgical, medical, nursing, drug, and other treatment and investigative notes and records, laboratory test reports, x-ray plates and reports, patient consent forms. and clinical correspondence, and computer data, relating to the plaintiff' other than that previously disclosed. This will ensure that discovery has been complete.

It is preferable to have a list of documents served by the defendant. Schedule 1, Part 2 should set out the documents that the defendant regards as being privileged. See what documents are referred to; is there just a general phrase referring to privileged documents, or are specific documents listed? If there is no list of specific documents, then ask the defendant to confirm what documents are being referred to in Sched I, Part 2. Bear in mind there may well have been an internal hospital enquiry report. If necessary, refer the defendants to Ministry of Health Circular HM (55) 66. This was issued in 1955, and requires that a report be prepared whenever a patient suffers injury as a result of a mishap in the course of hospital treatment. The 1955 circular takes the view that such a report has legal privilege, as having been prepared for the purposes of litigation. But, this is not necessarily correct. In *Waugh* [1980] AC 521, the House of Lords laid down the 'dominant purpose' test (ie what was the dominant purpose in preparing the report, for litigation, or for ascertaining the lessons to be learnt, so that accidents might be avoided in the future?). See Chapter 9, section 2. Since this circular specifically states 'without a contemporaneous report it may not be possible to take action urgently needed to prevent the occurrence of the same mishap again' does this not expose the dominant purpose as having been accident prevention investigation, rather than litigation? So, it may well be worth asking if such a report was prepared, and, if so, whether privilege is claimed.

Order for directions: In the county court the Automatic Directions will apply (CCR Ord 17, r 11) in the High Court. Automatic Directions do not apply to medical negligence cases (RSC Ord 25, r 8(5)(*b*)). Thus, a Summons for Directions will be needed but in either court you should consider carefully what orders are needed and, if necessary make an application. In particular you may wish to call more than two medical experts or require an exchange of witness statements (see below). In practice, it will often be possible to agree the order for directions, which will thus obviate the need for the parties to attend court.

Since *Naylor* (1987) it has become normal in medical negligence cases for all reports (including experts' reports on liability) to he disclosed. The old rule that liability reports need not be disclosed has been scrapped. The defendants may suggest that the plaintiff discloses a list of references (ie from published journals and books) in support of the case. It is unwise for the plaintiff to disclose such references until after service of the defence, although it is often found pleading to include a basic reference (eg from a well known student text book) in the claim. Otherwise, one should not disclose one's references at an early stage, and one should only agree to disclose them on a mutual basis with the defendants (for which an order will be needed).

Exchange of witness statements: Remember that the court can now order the compulsory exchange of witness statements (ie statements of fact), RSC Ord 38, r 2(*a*), and this will be an automatic direction in the county court; see Chapter 11, section 7. This is most important in medical negligence cases, given that the defendants' medical staff will inevitably have made statements of fact and these will have been recorded in writing. If any of those witnesses are to give evidence on behalf of the defendant, then it will be helpful for their statements to be disclosed to the plaintiff. Accordingly, the plaintiff should normally seek a full order for exchange of all witness statements at an early stage.

Chapter 19

The Motor Insurers' Bureau

The MIB will deal with two types of claims: those in which the defendant motorist is uninsured, and those in which the defendant cannot be traced (ie 'hit and run' cases). If the motorist's identity was never known (because, for example, the motorist gave a false name) then it is treated as a hit and run case, with the motorist being untraced, rather than uninsured.

The liability of the MIB to deal with these claims is set out in two separate agreements; the texts of both agreements, and the explanatory notes that accompany them, are set out in Appendix F.

1 The uninsured defendant

Broadly speaking, the MIB must meet any judgment obtained against any uninsured motorist. But this is subject to two major conditions:

(i) The MIB must have been given notice, *either* before proceedings were started that it was intended to sue the uninsured motorist *or,* within seven days of proceedings being commenced. (Note that if insurers are dealing with the claim for some reason, the notice is given to them, not the MIB, see below.) Use Stock Letter 33.

(ii) The MIB's liability only extends to damages for those risks that must be compulsorily insured for under the Road Traffic Acts. It is worth noting that since 1989 this extends to property damage (up to £250,000), but there is an 'excess' of £175 which is irrecoverable.

The full list of conditions that must be met for a claim are set out in clause 5 of the Uninsured Motorists' Agreement; see Appendix F. But, from the plaintiff's point of view, the essential requirement is that notice of proceedings be given within seven days after proceedings are issued. Often, though, the notice will be given to an insurance company and not to the MIB. This happens when the defendant had a policy of insurance but the insurers have been able to repudiate it, thus leaving the defendant uninsured (eg if there has been the unauthorised use of a vehicle for business purposes; false statements made on the proposal form etc). In these circumstances the insurer concerned will have to deal with the claim, and therefore the plaintiff should give notice to the insurance company, not the MIB. This is because the insurers would be liable to deal with the claim, for ss 151 and 152 of the Road Traffic Act 1988 make them responsible for claims made against their insured, even if the policy has been repudiated; this is called the 'RTA liability' and is completely separate from the MIB scheme.

Note that the MIB take full advantage of the seven days' notice rule; if notice is given out of time they will probably refuse to accept liability. When that happens, consider abandoning the proceedings and instead issue new proceedings and give proper notice of issue.

Note also that the scheme does not cover:

(i) Crown vehicles (but, in practice, the government department concerned will deal with the claim in the usual way);

(ii) cases in which the applicant was a passenger who knew that the vehicle was being driven without the owner's consent (see clause 6(1)(*c*)(i));

(iii) situations when the applicant knew that there was no policy covering the vehicle (see clause 6(1)(*c*)(ii)).

In practice, an MIB uninsured motorist claim proceeds like any other claim. As soon as the MIB are notified of the claim they will nominate an insurance company to deal with it on their behalf. Thereafter the plaintiff will correspond with the insurance company, and the case will proceed in the usual way, often being settled without judgment being obtained. Legal costs will form part of the claim to be met by the MIB in the usual way.

Finally, if the name and address of the driver are known but the driver later becomes untraceable, the correct procedure is to apply for substituted service on a known insurer or on the MIB (see *Gurtner* v *Circuit* [1968] 2 QB 587).

The text of the Uninsured Motorists' Agreement is set out in Appendix F; the notes at the end of the text provide a useful summary of the main provisions.

2 The untraced motorist (the hit and run cases)

A separate MIB agreement, the Untraced Motorists' Agreement, deals with liability for untraced motorists. Broadly speaking, the MIB must deal with a claim arising out of the negligence of an untraced motorist if:

(i) the applicant cannot trace the person responsible for the accident;

(ii) the accident happened in circumstances that would make the untraced person liable to pay damages for negligence;

(iii) the liability should have been covered by insurance (ie the agreement only relates to 'death or bodily injury'—see Road Traffic Act 1988, s 145).

This agreement has not yet been extended to cover property damage.

The claim to the MIB must be made within three years of the accident. There are no provisions for the three year limitation period to be extended; as would be the case with a civil claim (ie under the Limitation Act).

On being notified, the MIB will investigate the claim, and ask for medical reports etc. Eventually, the MIB will give its written decision which can be appealed against (on either liability or *quantum*) within six weeks. The grounds of appeal are set out in clause 11 (see Appendix F). The appeal lies to an arbitrator (who will be a QC) who looks through the papers, and who can, if considered necessary, call for further information before giving a decision. The arbitrator's fees will be paid by the MIB unless the arbitrator states that they should be borne by the applicant because there was no reasonable ground for the appeal. There is no appeal from the decision of the arbitrator.

An alternative, less formal, procedure was introduced in 1977. This allows the MIB to make an offer in settlement in straightforward cases of up to £50,000. The applicant is furnished with a statement of the circumstances and evidence on which the offer is based. If the applicant accepts the offer, the normal right of appeal will be foregone. If the applicant rejects the offer, then the normal procedures apply. This procedure allows for a speedier settlement of claims. Full details are set out in the text of the 1977 Supplemental Agreement, printed in Appendix F.

Solicitors should note that the MIB will only pay £150 profit costs (plus VAT and reasonable disbursements) to the successful applicant's solicitors. This is so whether the claim is dealt with under the 1972 Untraced Motorists' Agreement or the 1977 Supplementary Agreement.

If the solicitor acted for more than one applicant in claims arising out of the same accident, then an additional fee of £75 will be paid for each extra claimant. An applicant should always be told that the MIB will not pay:

(i) vehicular damage, damage to property, towage charges and the like, since these items are not compulsorily insurable;

(ii) legal costs (other than as set out above);

(iii) the sick pay loaned by an employer whilst the claimant was off work (with a civil claim, this would be recoverable).

The text of the Untraced Motorists' Agreement and the Supplementary Agreement is set out in Appendix F; the notes at the end of the text provide a useful summary of the main provisions. The procedure for making a claim on the MIB is by letter addressed to 'the Secretary', setting out the claim and enclosing any supporting documents. Further details to be obtained from the MIB at 152 Silbury Boulevard, Central Milton Keynes, MK9 1NB. They have an extremely helpful telephone advice service on 0908 240000.

Appendix A

Client's Accident Questionnaires

Contents

1 Road accident questionnaire
2 Workplace accident questionnaire
3 Fatal accident questionnaire

* * *

1 Road accident questionnaire

Personal details

1 Full name
2 Address
3 Telephone number
  Work:
  Home:
4 Date of birth
5 Do you live alone or with a partner?
  Partner's name and relationship
6 Children:
  Names
  Sex
  Ages
  Dates of birth
7 Next friend if infant
8 Employment details
9 Professional qualifications and job history (Please attach CV)
10 Present employer
  Employer's name
  Employer's address
  Occupation (job title)

Place of employment
Date commenced
(*a*) this employment
(*b*) this particular job

11 Normal earnings per week
(*a*) gross salary
(i) basic
(ii) overtime
(*b*) net take home

12 Dates of time lost from work due to accident. Have you yet returned to work?

13 Details of accident
Date
Time
Full description of how accident occurred and sketch showing position of witnesses etc. Please enclose photographs of the accident site if you have any.
Place of accident
Names and addresses of witnesses
Details of any other person hurt in the accident

14 Injuries received (please attach any doctor's reports).
Details of any previous accidents or injuries
Details of activities unable to complete due to accident including leisure activities

15 Name and address of general practitioner

16 Name and address of hospital(s) where treated

17 What is your hospital record number?

18 Name and address of any counsellor or social worker?

19 Welfare benefit(s)
National Insurance number
Address of local DSS office
Amount of Statutory Sick Pay received
Amount and description of other welfare benefits received (eg income support, disability living allowance, disability working allowance).

20 Other losses and expenses
Clothing lost in accident
Prescription charges
Cost of home help
Taxis and other transport expenses
Any other losses or expenses

21 Vehicle details
Name and address of driver responsible for accident
Name and address of driver's insurers
Name and address of owner of vehicle responsible for accident (if different)
Registration number, make, insurers of vehicle responsible for accident,
Registration number, make, insurers of your vehicle and extent of insurance cover
Police station accident reported to
Notice of intended prosecution received?
Seat belts fitted and worn by client?
Previous convictions, endorsements

Extent of damage to client's vehicle
Estimated cost of repair or pre-accident value
Towage charges
Hire charges
Where client's vehicle is stored and whether it can be examined
Storage charges

Please enclose copies of all documents which may be relevant to the accident.

2 Workplace accident questionnaire

Questions 1 to 20 in the above road accident questionnaire should be answered and in addition:

1 Client's status *vis-à-vis* other employees
2 Who in immediate authority over client?
3 Was protective clothing available and offered?
4 Was the client given any training which could have prevented accident?
5 Who was responsible for the accident?
6 Details of previous similar accidents
7 Details of earlier relevant complaints to employers
8 When was accident reported and to whom?
9 Has accident been entered in accident book?
10 Did company doctor see client?
11 Have any union memoranda been sent regarding accident or similar incident?
12 Has there been a factory inspection following accident?
13 Has accident been reported under Riddor Scheme?
14 Full details of equipment which caused accident?

Again all relevant documents should be sent.

3 Fatal accident questionnaire

Complete the appropriate accident questionnaire and in addition:

1 Date of death
2 Legal relationship of deceased to client
3 Name, address, age, sex and relationship to deceased of any dependants
4 Coroner's court address
5 Date of inquest
6 Is the client the executor/proposed administrator?
7 Does client wish Letters of Administration to be taken out by firm?
8 Birth certificate of defendants
9 Birth and marriage certificates of spouse
10 Death certificate of deceased
11 Loss and expense to date
12 Receipt for funeral, flowers, grave, press notice, etc
13 Dependant's earnings prior to and since the date of accident
14 Dependancy calculation: amount spent prior to death on the following items and the extent to which this expense related to the deceased:

Food
Clothing
Rent/mortgage
Entertainment
Alcohol/cigarettes
Hire purchase
Insurance
Holidays
Value of services rendered by deceased to dependants
Travel and motoring

Appendix B

Stock Letters

Contents

1 Investigating the accident (letters (1) to (9))
2 Medical matters (letters (10) to (18))
3 Special damage (letters (19) to (22))
4 The action (letters (23) to (45))

* * *

1 Investigating the accident

(1) *To client on being instructed*

Dear

RE: YOUR CLAIM FOR PERSONAL INJURY

I confirm that we shall be meeting to discuss your proposed claim for personal injury at [these offices] at o'clock on [date].

To succeed in a claim for damages for personal injury you will have to prove that you have suffered injury, that someone else was negligent and that this negligence caused your injury. It is not sufficient only to prove that you have been injured. We shall discuss this further in our meeting.

It would be extremely helpful if you would do the following before our meeting.

1 I enclose a questionnaire which I should be grateful if you would complete.

2 Please prepare a written statement of what happened together with your opinion of the cause of the accident.

3 Please draw a sketch plan showing your position and the position of any witnesses.

If for any reason you are unable to complete the questionnaire fully do not worry as we can discuss this further at our meeting.

I enclose a standard letter which sets out the basis on which this firm charges in private matters, various information you will need in Legal Aid matters including the operation of the Legal Aid Board's statutory charge, and this firm's complaints procedure. Please read the letter carefully as it contains much information which will be important throughout your claim.

I look forward to meeting you on . Please make sure that you mark all letters to me with the reference which appears at the top of this letter otherwise delay is likely to occur.

(2) *To witness of street accident*

Re (*name and address of client*)

I am acting for in connection with the accident which took place on the (*date*) at (*place*).

I believe you witnessed this accident and accordingly I should be most grateful if you would send me a short statement describing what happened, who was to blame, and how you think the accident could have been avoided. A sketch plan would be most helpful.

Your assistance in this matter would be greatly appreciated; I look forward to hearing from you and enclose a stamped, addressed envelope. If you wish to telephone me to discuss the matter please do not hesitate to do so.

(3) *To witness of workplace accident*

Re (*name and address of client*)

I am acting on behalf of (*name*) in connection with the accident which took place on the (*date*) at (*place*).

I believe you witnessed the accident. If that is correct, I should be most grateful if you would send me a short statement describing what happened, who was to blame, and how the accident could have been avoided.

Even if you did not witness the accident it may be that you will still be able to help; if you know the background to the accident or know of anyone who has had a similar accident perhaps you would let me know.

Your assistance in this matter would be greatly appreciated; I look forward to hearing from you and enclose a stamped, addressed envelope. If you wish to telephone me to discuss the matter please do not hesitate to do so.

(4) *For police report*

To Chief Constable or Metropolitan Traffic Commissioner

Re: Road Traffic Accident on (*date*) at (*place*)

We act on behalf of (*name*) of (*address*) in connection with the above street accident. We enclose a map showing the accident location.

We enclose a remittance of £* , and should be obliged if you would forward us a copy of the police report and statements. If proceedings are pending we should be grateful if you would let us know the name and address of the accused, the charge, and details of insurers.

[*Fees are: full accident report £41; minor accident report £18.50; statements £18.50, two or more £24; sketches £18.50; interviews £42; black and white photographs £1.65.]

(5) *To trace vehicle's registered owner*

To Record Section, Vehicle Enquiry Unit, DVLC, Swansea, SA99 1AJ
We act on behalf of (*name*) of (*address*) in connection with an accident involving vehicle registration No .

I should be grateful if you would let me know the name and address of the vehicle's registered owner. I enclose a remittance of £*

[*Fee is £3.50 per vehicle.]

(6) *For inquest depositions*

To: The Coroner's Office
Re: (*name*) Deceased
We act for the dependants of the above named deceased, and should be obliged if you would note our interest and inform us of the date of the inquest.

If the inquest has already been held we should be grateful for a copy of the evidence and depositions, for which we undertake to pay the appropriate fee.

(7) *To Health and Safety Executive*

We act for (*name*) of (*address*) in connection with an accident at work on (*date*) at (*place*) whilst in the employ of (*name of employers*).

Would you please let us know if the accident was investigated and, if so, please forward us a copy of the report, with any accompanying statements, photographs, etc. We enclose a cheque for the fee of £71* (plus VAT of £).

*The fee is £71 for a factory or quarry or agricultural inspector's report; £117 for a HSE specialist inspector; £87 for a mines inspector.

(8) *Advising client to abandon claim*

(*Set out reasons for abandoning claim, enclose bill of costs, and include the paragraph below.*)

It is my professional duty to remind you of the three-year limitation period which arises in a case such as yours; accordingly, if you wish to pursue the claim further you should ensure that proceedings are commenced within three years of the date of the accident, otherwise you will probably be barred from bringing a claim.

(9) *To insurers accepting negotiated offer*

Our client is prepared to accept your offer of £ .

This acceptance is, of course, subject to the payment of our costs. We enclose a schedule setting out our profit costs which is sent to you on a without prejudice basis for possible agreement. Our disbursements were £( ). We would accept a profit cost figure of £ , which will attract VAT of £ , making a total costs figure of £ inclusive of the VAT.

We await receipt of both cheques.

The offer in respect of our costs will remain open for 14 days after which it will be withdrawn and we shall have our costs assessed by a costs draftsman, for taxation. We shall not then consider ourselves bound by the lower offer.

2 Medical Matters

(10) *To general practitioner for report*

Re (*client's name and date of birth*).

We act on behalf of (*name*) of (*address and telephone number*), a patient of yours, in connection with injuries received in an accident on (*date*).

Please prepare a report on the injuries received by our client, the treatment given, present condition and prognosis for recovery.

We enclose a Release in respect of our client's medical records and should be grateful if you would contact our client direct at the address and telephone number set out above to make an appointment to enable you to carry out an examination.

We confirm that we shall be responsible for your reasonable fee and look forward to receiving the report.

(11) *To inform client of general practitioner's examination*

I have today written to doctor (*name*) requesting a report on your injuries.

The doctor will contact you direct to arrange a convenient date for the examination. It might also be helpful if you were to contact the surgery to arrange a convenient date. Please let me have a note of your losses and expenses in attending the surgery so that they may be included in your claim.

(12) *To hospital for report*

To medical records officer: re (*client's name*) Patient Number , Date of Birth .

We are instructed by (*client's name*) of (*client's address and telephone number*) in connection with injuries received in an accident on (*date*) and for which our client received treatment at your hospital.

We should be grateful if the consultant who treated our client would examine him/her and prepare a report on the injuries received, treatment given, present condition and the prospect of a full recovery.

We enclose a medical release form. The appointment should be made direct with our client whose address and telephone number are set out above. We confirm that we shall be responsible for your reasonable fee.

(13) *To client notifiying of the hospital examination*

I have today written to the (*name hospital*) requesting a report on your injuries. The hospital will send you an appointment and it is important that you attend when requested.

Please co-operate fully with your doctor and let me have a note of your losses and expenses in attending the appointment so that they may be included in your claim.

(14) *To independent consultant*

Re (*client's name and date of birth*)

We act for (*name*) of (*address and telephone number*) in connection with injuries sustained in an accident on (*date*).

We should be grateful if you would arrange to examine our client and prepare a report on the injuries received, treatment given, present condition and prognosis for the future.

Our client has received treatment from (*name of hospital and patient number*). Our client's GP is Dr (*name and address*). We enclose releases in respect of our client's medical records and should be grateful if you would write direct to the doctors to obtain the records.

The appointment should be made direct with our client. We confirm that we shall be responsible for your reasonable fee.

[*Note*: consider detailing the injuries for the doctor, and perhaps enclose a copy of the client's statement. If there have been any previous medical reports you may consider sending these.]

(15) *To client notifying of the examination by other side*

The defendant's insurers have requested permission to have you medically examined by doctor (*name*) of (*address*).

This is a reasonable request and you should therefore attend any convenient appointment the doctor may give you. The doctor will wish to have details of your medical condition but you should not discuss the facts of the accident or liability for it; you should not sign any documents without first sending them to me for approval.

Please let me have a note of your losses and expenses in attending the examination and I shall arrange for these to be refunded.

(16) *To other side agreeing to examination*

You may have our client examined by Doctor (*name*).

Please ensure that a convenient appointment is made direct with our client whose address and telephone number are (*address and telephone number*).

Facilities for this examination are granted on the basis that Doctor (*name*) has not previously treated our client; in addition you will be required to reimburse our client for any losses and expenses in attending the examination.

(17) *To consultant in medical negligence case*

Re (*Client's name and date of birth*).

We act on behalf of (*name*) of (*address and telephone number*) in connection with a proposed negligence claim against (*hospital trust/health authority*).

We should be grateful if you would provide expert medical evidence and advise us to whether it seems the standard of care received by our client was of a lower standard than that which can reasonably have been expected. If you are prepared to assist then we confirm that we shall be responsible for your reasonable fee [if legal aid has specific maximum authority then state that amount] [if limitation period is approaching or report is needed urgently for other reasons state date by which report is required]. The appointment should be made direct with our client whose address and telephone number are set out above.

To assist we enclose the following copy documents:

1 Our client's statement
2 Relevant correspondence with our client
3 Medical notes and records as disclosed by the Health Authority
4 Medical notes and records as disclosed by general practitioner
5 Relevant correspondence with the Health Authority (including initial letter of claim)

Specifically would you please report on the nature of the illness or complaint that our client was being treated for; the treatment given and recovery since then. If appropriate would you also give a prognosis. In addition would you kindly let us have your comment on the nature of the treatment provided, and your criticims of the standard of care and treatment. [It might be appropriate to set out briefly the type of negligence which is alleged].

As you are no doubt aware, the approach of the Courts to medical negligence claims was summarised in *Bolam* [1957] 1 WLR 582, and in particular it was said [give relevant quotes as set out in Chapter 18, section 1].

If you should conclude that there was negligence on the part of the Health Authority/Hospital Trust or its servants or agents please particularise each and every allegation of negligence since it would be extremely helpful to counsel when settling the Statement of Claim. In addition we should be grateful if you could refer to any reference books that give support to your criticism. If possible we would wish to include references from contemporary well known medical texts (eg student text books) as well as references in any of the more specialist periodicals or journals.

If you feel that there are any specific points that need to be discussed with counsel before you finalise the form of your report or if you need any further information before writing the report please do not hesitate to contact us.

Should this matter proceed to litigation, then it is probable that the contents of your report relating to our client's present condition and the prognosis will be disclosed to the other side initially. However those parts of your report relating to the question of liability and negligence might not be disclosed until later. It would therefore be convenient if you could deal with those two aspects separately so that, if necessary, it is possible to disclose those parts of the report that relation to condition and prognosis only.

(18) *Client's consent to release of medical records to the other side*

Re (*Name, address, date of birth, hospital number*).

I, (*name*) of (*address*) authorise you to forward direct to Doctor [ ] all medical notes and records in your possession relating to my treatment subsequent to my accident on (*date*). This authority does not extend to the disclosure of any medical reports that may have been obtained at the request of my solicitors.

(19) *Client's consent to release of medical reports to you and your own doctor*

TO WHOM IT MAY CONCERN:

I, (*name*) of (*address*) (*date of birth*) hereby request and authorise you to release all your surgical, medical, nursing, drug and other treatment, investigation notes, records, laboratory test reports and contractual documents relating to treatment for surgical, medical and nursing purposes and including X-rays to my solicitors (*name and address*) for such purposes as they may require.

(19)(A) *Client's consent to release of medical notes to hospital in medical negligence case*

I, (*name*) of (*address*) (*date of birth*) Hospital Record Number hereby request and authorise you to release all your surgical, medical, nursing, drug and other treatment and investigation notes and records, laboratory test reports and contractual documents relating to treatment for surgical, medical and nursing purposes to include:

1 Accident and emergency department record card
2 General practitioner's referral letter
3 Admitting doctor's notes and examination
4 Patient consent forms
5 Ward doctor's clinical notes
6 Operating records
7 Anaesthetic records
8 Intensive therapy records
9 Daily nursing notebook
10 Laboratory requests and report on blood and other bodily samples
11 Ultra sound scans, reports, photographs and video tapes
12 Electrocardiograms (ECG) and reports
13 Echocardiograms and reports
14 Electroencephalograms (EEG) and reports
15 Temperature, pulse, blood pressure and respiration charts
16 Prescription records
17 Fluid balance charts
18 Blood balance charts
19 Blood transfusion records
20 Heart injury charts
21 X-ray plates, requests and reports
22 Theatre registers
23 Casualty registers
24 Health visitor records
25 Cardiac cerebral function records
26 Perfusionist records
27 Correspondence, including correspondence to and from other hospitals involved in treatment and with the general practitioner
28 Internal memoranda
30 Doctor's own files relating to treatment of the patient and the type of treatment generally
31 Documents relating to any untoward incident or accident investigation by the hospital, district or regional health authority or DSS

Obstetrics

32 Partogram
33 CTG traces
34 Progression of labour chart
35 Community midwifery records

SIGNED ....
DATED ....

3 Special damage

(20) *To employer (not defendant) for wage details*

Re (*client's name and address*)
Payroll No:

We are instructed by (*name*), an employee of yours, in connection with an accident on (*date*).

In order that we can calculate our client's wage losses arising out of the accident we should be grateful if you would forward to us:

(*a*) details of our client's net and gross earnings for the 26 weeks prior to the accident differentiating between basic pay and overtime;
(*b*) details of our client's net and gross earnings since returning to work differentiating between basic pay and overtime;
(*c*) the amount of Statutory Sick Pay received;
(*d*) details of any other sick pay, if any, which you have forwarded to our client and which is refundable to you, should damages be recovered from a third party;
(*e*) any other employment losses (for example, lost bonus or promotion) arising from the accident.

Your assistance in providing this information would be greatly appreciated by our client and by us. We look forward to hearing from you.

(21) *To Inland Revenue for client's tax returns*

Re (*name and address of client*)
Ref No:

We are instructed by (*name*) in connection with an accident on the (*date*).

We should be grateful if you would let us know:

(*a*) names and addresses of our client's employers during the (*time period*) prior to the accident and also since that time;
(*b*) the dates of these periods of employment and the net and gross earnings during each period;
(*c*) our client's code number throughout this time.

We look forward to hearing from you; We enclose our client's signed authority.

(22) *Client's consent for Inland Revenue*

I (*name and address of client*)
authorise Messrs (*name and address of solicitors*) to be provided with such information as they may require in connection with my financial affairs. I confirm that they are instructed by me in connection with my accident of the (*date*).

Signed Date

4 The action

(23) *Initial letter of claim—road accident: (a) to driver*

We act on behalf of (*name*) of (*address*) in connection with an accident which occurred on (*date*) at (*place*).

This accident was caused through your negligent driving of a motor vehicle and accordingly our client claims damages for the personal injury, losses, expenses, and inconvenience arising.

Please forward this letter to your insurers or the owner of the vehicle you were driving and let us know their names and your insurance policy number so that we may correspond with them direct.

(24) *Initial letter of claim—road accident: (b) to owner*

We act on behalf of (*name*) of (*address*) in connection with an accident which occurred on (*date*) at (*place*).

This accident was caused by the negligent driving of your servant or agent in a motor vehicle owned by you, and accordingly our client claims damages for the personal injury, losses, expenses, and inconvenience arising.

Please pass this letter to your insurers and let us know their name and policy number so that we may correspond with them direct.

(25) *Initial letter of claim—road accident: (c) to insurers*

We act on behalf of (*name*) of (*address*) in connection with an accident which occurred on (*date*) at (*place*).

This accident was caused through the negligent driving of a (make of car) motor car, registration No , owned by (*name and address*) which we understand is insured with you under Policy No .

Our client claims damages for the personal injury, losses, expenses and inconvenience arising from this accident.

Please confirm that this matter has been reported to you, and that, in view of this letter, there will be no need for us to send a letter of claim direct to your insured.

Our client's vehicle is registration No and is insured with the (*name and address of the insurers*) under Policy No with a (*type of cover*) policy.

(26) *Initial letter of claim—workplace accident*

We act on behalf of (*name*) of (*address*) a/an (*occupation*) in your employ in connection with an accident which occurred on (*date*) at (*place*).

This accident was caused through the negligence of your servants or agents and/or breach of statutory duty, and accordingly damages are claimed for personal injury, losses, expenses, and inconvenience.

We look forward to hearing from your insurers or solicitors. Please let us know their name and reference so that we may correspond with them direct.

(27) *Initial letter of claim—medical negligence case*

We act on behalf of (*name*) of (*address*) who sustained personal injury, losses, expenses, and inconvenience as a result of negligent treatment received during the time of care as a patient at the hospital in (*approximate date*).

Briefly, the facts of this matter are as follows. (*Set out brief summary of sequence of events and basic allegations of negligence*).

Further, and more detailed, allegations of negligence will be provided in due course when we have been allowed access to the full medical notes and records, and taken independent expert medical advice. Please send us copies of all medical notes and records, together with all surgical, nursing, drug, and other treatment and other investigation notes and records, laboratory test records, x-ray plates and reports, patient consent forms, and clinical correspondence, and any computer records, relating to the plaintiff in accordance with the attached authority signed by our client. In addition please confirm that you will disclose any documents or other records relating to any incident involving our client, or any accident investigation by the hospital, Hospital Trust, District, Regional Health Authority, or the Department of Health as well as disclosure of all such items in your possession. Please provide us with a list of any other such items that are no longer in your possession, custody or power, and state the believed present location of such items.

To avoid any misunderstanding, we should like to make it clear that it is not our practice to accept disclosure of such records, etc to a nominated medical adviser.

We shall of course be responsible for your reasonable photocopying fees (including the cost of taking copies of x-rays and computer records); alternatively, if you wish to forward the original documents to us, we undertake to hold them to your order and keep them in a safe place. They will be returned on demand, after we have taken copies.

In the meantime, would you confirm that all such medical notes and records, etc will be preserved pending their production, and inspection by our independent expert, and pending trial of the proposed proceedings.

If we do not hear from you in reply within the next four weeks we shall have to assume that you are not prepared to accept such unconditional release of the medical notes and records. Accordingly, proceedings will be commenced for pre-action discovery without further notice. Please let us know whether you wish to nominate solicitors to accept service of any proceedings.

(28) *Requesting county court to issue proceedings*

We enclose the documents listed below. Please issue these proceedings:

—summons (Form N201);
—fee of £43;
—Particulars of Claim (in duplicate)*;
—medical report (in duplicate);
—statement of special damage (in duplicate);
—legal aid certificate for filing†;
—notice of issue of legal aid certificate to be served on Defendant†;
—authority of minor's next friend†;

Please serve the proceedings direct on the defendant's (solicitors, *Messrs* of who have agreed to accept service.†)

We look forward to receiving the plaint note and notification of the date of service.

[*Enclose copy for court, with copy for each defendant.]
[†If applicable.]

(29) *Requesting High Court to issue writ*

We enclose:
(*a*) original writ; } endorsed with certificate of value
(*b*) copy writ, duly signed;
(*c*) copy writ for each defendant;
(*d*) cheque for £70 payable to HM Paymaster General;
(*e*) legal aid certificate for filing*

Please issue the writ and return the original and defendant's copies to us to service.
[*If applicable.]

(30) *To solicitor nominated to accept service for insurers (High Court)*

We enclose sealed copy writ, Acknowledgment of Service form, Statement of Claim* with medical report* and statement of special damage* and Notice of Issue of Legal Aid Certificate* in this action, service of which please accept and acknowledge.

We are informed by (*name of defendant's insurers*) who are dealing with this matter from their office at (*address*) under Reference that you will accept service on behalf of their insured.

We look forward to receiving your defence within 28 days.

[*If applicable.]

(31) *Service on limited company* [send to registered office]

We enclose sealed copy writ, Acknowledgment of Service form, Statement of Claim with medical report* and statment of special damage*, and Notice of Issue of Legal Aid Certificate. *Please acknowledge receipt.

We suggest you forward these documents to your insurers or solicitors and confirm to us that you have done so.
[*If applicable.]

(32) *Advising insurers of issue against their insured*

Please note proceedings in [ ] court writ were issued on (*date*) against your insured; this notice is given to you for the purposes of s 151 of Road Traffic Act 1988.

(33) *Advising Motor Insurers' Bureau of issue against uninsured defendants*

Write to: The Secretary, Motor Insurers' Bureau, 152 Silbury Boulevard, Central Milton Keynes, MK9 1NB.
Please note that legal proceedings in [ ] court were issued on (*date*) against the uninsured motorist (*name*) of (*address*); this notice is given to you for the purposes of clause 5(1)(*a*) of the 1988 Uninsured Drivers' Agreement.

(34) *Payment into court—advising client to accept*

The defendants have now paid the sum of £ into court in full and final settlement of your claim.

You have a period of twenty-one days in which to accept this sum. If you accept the payment in then that will be the end of the case and the bulk of the costs and fees will be paid by the defendants. If you decide not to accept it then the case will proceed, if necessary, to trial. The trial judge will not be told of the payment in and if you are awarded less, then you will receive the lesser figure; similarly, if you are awarded more than the payment in then you will receive the larger sum.

Should you not accept the payment in and should the trial judge not award you more than the payment in, then you would have to pay *all* the costs arising from the date of payment in. Since that would include the costs of trial, for both parties, it would be a considerable sum.

[This would probably happen even though you are on legal aid. Normally, if you did not beat the payment in, the other side's costs, if you were ordered to pay them, and your own unpaid legal costs would be deducted from your damages (and, if necessary, from the legal aid contribution you have been paying).] (*omit if not legal aid case*)

(*Describe client's own case and counsel's advice.)*

My opinion is that you should accept the payment into court, rather than risk recovering less damages and incurring the heavy costs that would arise. Please let me have your instructions.

(35) *Payment into court—advising client to reject*

(As letter (34), except for final paragraph, then continue as below.)

Litigation is uncertain and I can give no guarantee that you will recover more than has been paid into court. My own opinion is that there are reasonable prospects of your recovering a greater sum and accordingly I would advise you not to accept the payment in. However, the decision must be yours alone for if you are awarded less than the payment in then you will have to bear the costs arising between now and judgment.

Please consider the matter carefully and let me have your instructions. Obviously you are welcome to discuss the matter with me.

(36) *To court accepting payment in within twenty-one days*

We enclose Notice of Payment into Court, Notice of Acceptance and form of request for payment out.

No order has to be made as the notice of acceptance is within twenty-one days of the payment in. We look forward to receiving the money in due course.

(37)(A) *Advising client of forthcoming trial (fixed date)*

I have now arranged a fixed hearing date in your case. It will be heard at the Court at (*address*) on (*date*) at (*time*). I shall write to you much nearer the time to set out arrangements for meeting on the date of trial. I shall be grateful if you would formally confirm that you are able to attend the trial. I have written to your witnesses to inform them of the date.

(37)(B) *Advising client of forthcoming trial (floating date)*

I have now arranged for your case to be set down for trial at the court in (*place*). You will probably have little warning of the date of trial and should therefore be prepared to attend at short notice.

It is therefore most important that you do not go away; please confirm that you have received this letter and remember to tell me of any temporary change of address between now and the date of trial.

(38)(A) *Advising witness of forthcoming trial (fixed date)*

You will recall that you kindly provided a statement in connection with our client's accident on (*date*) and I wrote to you recently regarding available dates when you could attend the trial.

A time has now been fixed for the trial and it will be heard at (*address*) on (*date*).

I am sorry to inconvenience you by requiring your attendance at the hearing but I can assure you that your evidence is necessary. You will be reimbursed your losses and expenses.

I am arranging for a Witness Summons to be served on you personally by my agent. This is a formal step in respect of your attendance and may also avoid any problems with your employer.

Please use the attached pre-paid envelope to acknowledge receipt of this letter and confirmation that you will be able to attend the trial. It is important that you notify me of any change of address between now and the trial, however temporary.

Finally I enclose copy of the evidence which you provided. [*If witness statements have been exchanged*—a copy of this has now been sent to the other side and you will not be able to raise any matters of fact which are not in the statement. It is therefore important that you re-read the statement shortly before trial since you will be asked questions covering the point raised in the statement]. [*If witness statements have not been exchanged*—I am enclosing a copy of the evidence which you provided. This will not be read out at the hearing but you will be asked questions covering the points raised in your statement.] I look forward to hearing from you.

(38)(B) *Advising witness of forthcoming trial (floating date)*

Re (*client's name*)

As you will recall, you kindly provided a statement in connection with my client's accident on the (*date*).

My client's case is now proceeding to trial and it will be necessary for you to attend as a witness.

I am unable to give the exact date of the hearing but I will notify you at least twenty-four hours beforehand. The court is at (*address*).

I am sorry to inconvenience you but can assure you that your evidence is necessary. You will be reimbursed your losses and expenses.

I am arranging for a subpoena to be served on you personally by my agent so as to avoid any problems with your employer.

Please use the attached pre-paid envelope to acknowledge receipt of this letter. It is important that you notify me of any change of address between now and the trial, however temporary.

Finally, I am enclosing a copy of the evidence which you provided. This will not be read out at the hearing but you will be asked questions covering the points raised in your statement [*Or (if witness statements have been exchanged)* —This will be shown to the court and will form the basis of your evidence. You will be asked questions on the points raised in the statement.] I look forward to hearing from you.

(39) *To process server to serve subpoena on witness*

I enclose original and copy subpoena for service on (*name and address of witness*). [Explain where and when the witness can be found and include a photograph if possible.] Please effect service and return the subpoena to me. In addition please pay the witness any conduct money that may be due and include the amount paid in your bill to me.

(40)(A) *Advising doctor of date of trial (fixed date)*

Re (*Client's name and address and date of birth*)
— Your ref
I refer to the report(s) which you kindly prepared on my above named client and our recent correspondence regarding the trial date.

I regret that it has not been possible to agree the medical evidence with the defendant's solicitor and it will therefore be necessary for you to attend the court at (*address*) on (*date*) to give evidence.

I apologise for any inconvenience this may cause you. It will be helpful if you would let me have an estimate of your fee for attending at the trial.

(40)(B) *Advising doctor of date of trial (floating date)*

Re (*Client's name and address and date of birth*)
I refer to the report(s) which you kindly prepared on my above named client.

I regret that it has not been possible to agree medical evidence with the defendant's solicitor and it will therefore be necessary for you to attend court on a date which will not be fixed until shortly before the trial. I apologise for any inconvenience this may cause you. I shall endeavour to give you ample warning of the likely date of trial and if there are exceptional circumstances that make it impossible for you to attend on certain dates please provide me with full details as soon as possible since it may be necessary for me to make an application to the court for the hearing to be postponed.

(41)(A) *Advising expert of date of trial (fixed date)*

I refer to your report in this matter. My client's case has now been set down for hearing at the court at (*address*) on (*date*) to give evidence.

I apologise for any inconvenience this may cause you. It will be helpful if you would let me have an estimate of your fee for attending at the trial. If you wish to be served with a Witness Summons please let me know and confirm that it may be served on you by post.

(41)(B) *Advising expert of date of trial (floating date)*

Re (*Client's name and address*)
— Your ref:
I refer to your report in this matter. My client's case has now been set down for hearing at the court at (*address*).

It will be necessary for you to attend and give evidence and I shall endeavour to give you ample warning of the hearing date. If you wish to be served with a Witness Summons please let me know and confirm that it may be served on you by post.

(42) *Advising counsel's clerk on setting down (High Court—floating date)*

Re (*plaintiff* v *defendant*)
(*court*)

This action has now been set down for trial. I should be obliged if you would watch the list and let me know as soon as the case appears.

(43) *Advising other side of setting down (High Court)*

This action was set down for trial in the (*place of trial*) non-jury list, on the of 199 , under reference number

(44) *To witness after case heard*

Many thanks for attending court. I am grateful to you for your co-operation and trust that you were not unduly inconvenienced.

£ (*amount*) conduct money was served on you with the [witness summons/subpoena] and since your losses and expenses amounted to £ (*amount*) there is the sum of £ (*amount due*).

I enclose a cheque for that sum and should be obliged if you would acknowledge receipt using the enclosed pre-paid envelope.

(45) *To Legal Aid Area Committee for approval of approved costs*

Certificate No:

We write to advise you that this matter has now been settled between the parties on the following terms . . . We have provisionally agreed our costs with the other side, as follows:

profit costs (standard *inter-partes* basis)	£
VAT	£
disbursements (*detail*)	£
Total	£ ......

We are prepared to accept these figures and should be grateful if you would confirm that you will assess our costs accordingly. We confirm that:

—no final order has been made in the action; [or final order is enclosed]

—the profit cost figures referred to above are standard *inter-partes* costs only. We agree to waive any entitlement we may have to common fund costs and you may take this letter as our undertaking not to make any further claim on the Legal Aid Fund in respect of this matter;

—we have not advised under the Green Form in connection with this matter (or, say that if a Green Form has been completed but not submitted then it will not be submitted; or, enclose refund of any costs to you under the Green Form);

—our client now consents to the discharge of the certificate.

In anticipation of your agreement, we enclose our cheque for £ being a refund of disbursements (and/or profit costs) previously paid to us. Kindly confirm that we may account to our client direct for the damages recovered.

Appendix C

Precedents

Contents

1 Writ indorsements (including indorsement of value)
2 Renewing proceedings
3 Defendant failing to file Acknowledgment of Service, Notice of Intention to Defend, or a Defence
4 When there is no Defence save as to quantum (CCR Ord 9, RCJ Ord 14)
5 Extension of time
6 Form of application for a special appointment before the master [High Court only]
7 Discovery
8 Inspection of property prior to the commencement of proceedings
9 Inspection of property after the commencement of proceedings
10 Notice to Admit facts
11 Further and Better Particulars
12 Interrogatories
13 Amendment of pleadings
14 Amendment of pleadings to join a new party to the action
15 Obtaining an interim payment
16 When the plaintiff changes name
17 Consolidation
18 To obtain a split trial
19 Next friend
20 Infant: Notice of Adoption
21 Infant approval: county court
22 Infant approval: High Court
23 Infant approval: in a fatal claim
24 Notice to be served after one year's delay [High Court only]
25 Notice of appeal to judge in chambers
26 Hearsay evidence
27 Witness Summons or Subpoenas
28 Consent to action being stood out of the list
29 Notice of discontinuance

30 Compromise or settlement of the action
31 To change solicitors
32 To transfer High Court proceedings to the county court
33 Legal Aid: Notice of Issue and Revocation/Discharge

* * *

1 Writ indorsement (High Court)

(A) *Indorsement of Value–all cases*

This writ includes a claim for personal injury but may be commenced in the High Court because the value of the action for the purposes of Art 5 of the High Court and County Courts Jurisdiction Order 1991 exceeds £50,000.

(B)(1) *Road accidents*

(a) When defendant is both owner and driver

The Plaintiff's claim is for damages for personal injuries suffered and for losses, expenses and inconvenience incurred (together with interest thereon pursuant to s 35A of the Supreme Court Act 1981) as a result of an accident which occurred on or about   at   through the negligent driving management and/or control of a motor vehicle owned and driven by the Defendant.

(b) When two defendants—ie different owner and driver

As above, except '... of a motor vehicle owned by the First Defendant and driven by his servant or agent the Second Defendant'.

(2) *Workplace accident (against employer)*

The Plaintiff's claim is for damages for personal injuries suffered and losses and expenses incurred (together with interest thereon pursuant to s 35A of the Supreme Court Act 1981) as a result of an accident which occurred on or about the   at the Defendant's premises at   arising out of the negligence and/or breach of statutory duty of the Defendants, their servants or agents.

(3) *Fatal cases*

(a) Road accident

THE PLAINTIFF is the Administrator and Testator of the estate of [*name*] deceased ('the deceased') and claims:

(1) Damages under the Law Reform (Miscellaneous Provisions) Act 1934, on behalf of the estate of the deceased

—and—

(2) Damages under the Fatal Accidents Act 1976 on behalf of the dependants of the deceased

(together with interest thereon pursuant to s 35A of the Supreme Court Act 1981) in consequence of the death of the deceased as a result of an accident which occurred on or about at through the negligent driving management and/or control of a motor vehicle owned by the First Defendants and driven by their servant or agent the Second Defendant.

(b) Workplace accident

As above except 'at arising out of the negligence and/or breach of statutory duty of the Defendants, their servants or agents'.

(4) *Minor cases*

Writ indorsement remains as if it was an adult but the statement of parties has '(a minor suing by his/her next friend and (*eg mother*)' inserted after the plaintiff's name.

2 Renewing proceedings

(A) *County Court*

To renew a summons, apply *ex parte* to the district judge of the court by application giving the reasons why you want the summons renewed. *NB* if the summons is near its expiry period apply in person, not by post.

(B) *High Court*

To renew a writ (ie extend the time for service) take (or post) the original writ, together with an affidavit in support, to the Master's Secretary Department. State that you want the writ to be renewed under Ord 6, rule 8. The papers will be ready for collection on the next working day. Note that there is no need to issue a summons; the application is made ex parte, by simply lodging the documents referred to.

3 Defendant failing to file Acknowledgment of Service, Notice of Intention to Defend, or a Defence

(A) *County Court*

Plaintiff obtains judgment by completing and submitting Form N234 to the Court if no defence is received within 14 days of service. If the proceedings were served by the plaintiff rather than the Court, then an affidavit of service will also be required.

(B) *High Court*

Plaintiff obtains judgment either:

(a) By postal application

Send the following documents to the Action Department, Postal Section, Central Office, Royal Courts of Justice. Strand, London WC2, or to the DR:

(1) letter requesting that judgment be entered;
(2) stamped addressed envelope for use by court when sending judgment to plaintiff;
(3) original writ (with affidavit of service or Acknowledgment of Service, as appropriate);

(4) affidavit of service (Form No PF 122A–122E in White Book) if failure to give notice of intention to defend; original statement of claim if failure to file a defence; original Acknowledgment of Service, if failure to give notice of intention to defend;

(5) three copies of judgment form (Oyez Form No D1). Do not send carbon copies. Complete the form as follows:

'The day of 19

No Notice of Intention to Defend having been given (or No Defence having been served) by the Defendant herein, it is this day adjudged that the Defendant do pay the Plaintiff damages to be assessed.

The amount found due to the plaintiff under this judgment having been certified at £ as appears by the master's certificate filed the day of 199 .

It is adjudged that the defendant do pay the plaintiff £ and costs to be taxed [and that there be legal aid taxation pursuant to the Legal Aid Act 1988].

The above costs have been taxed and allowed £ as appears by a taxing officer's certificate dated the day of 199 .'

The parts of the form below the line will be completed once the damages have been assessed, and the costs taxed.

If the application is for judgment in default of defence, the back of the judgment form should be indorsed by the plaintiff: 'I/We, solicitors for the plaintiff, certify that the time for service of the defence by the defendant prescribed by the Rules of Court or extended by order of the court or the consent of the parties has expired and that the defendant is in default in serving a defence within such time.

Dated Signed '

(b) By personal attendance

Attend Action Department or DR, with documents (3), (4) and (5) above. The sealed judgment will be handed to the plaintiff.

(C) *Provisional damages*

If the plaintiff has included a claim for provisional damages, then there is a slightly different procedure for entering Judgment in Default. In essence, the Statement or particulars of Claim has to be served (if not already served), and a Summons for Directions or pre-trial review issued. The full procedure is in a Practice Direction (1988) 2 All ER 102.

4 When there is no Defence save as to quantum (CCR Ord 9 r 14; RCJ Ord 14)

Plaintiff (or solicitor) swears an affidavit in support, which must (1) verify the facts on which the claim is based, and (2) state the deponent's belief that there is no defence save as to quantum. The affidavit can be based on information and belief if the sources and grounds are stated.

The plaintiff issues a summons or County Court application completed as follows:

'for interlocutory judgment in this action for damages to be assessed and costs to be taxed

AND take notice that a party intending to oppose this application or to apply for a stay of execution should send to the opposite party or its solicitor, to reach it not less than three days before the date above mentioned, a copy of any affidavit intended to be used.'

For the steps to be taken, refer to Procedural Table 1, but note that the summons or application and the affidavit in support must be served on the other side at least ten clear days (weekends and holidays count as clear days) before the return date; this is instead of the usual two days. If the defendant wishes to produce an affidavit in reply, it should be served on the plaintiff at least three clear working days (excluding weekend and holidays) before the hearing. See Procedural Table 11 for the form and layout of an affidavit.

If the application is successful the form of judgment will be as follows:

'THE Defendant having given notice of intention to defend herein and the Court under [CCR Ord 9 r 14, or Ord 14, r 3] has this day Ordered that judgment as hereinafter provided be entered for the plaintiff against the defendant.

It is this day adjudged that the defendant do pay the plaintiff damages to be assessed and costs to be taxed.

[*High Court only*

THE amount found to be due to the Plaintiff having been assessed at £ as appears by the finding of the Master dated

It is adjudged that the Plaintiff recover the sum of £ against the Defendant and that costs be taxed.'

The last two paragraphs need not be inserted at this stage since they are for use after the damages have been assessed. When entering the judgment refer to Procedural Table 5 (but using Oyez Form D5, not D6). To have the damages assessed, refer to Procedural Table 7.]

5 Extension of time

The party seeking the extension of time issues an application or summons (see Procedural Table 1) completed as follows:

'that the may have until the day of 19 in which to serve .'

(A) *In the County Court*

The hearing of the application will be in the normal way before the district judge. The Court will draw up the order. There may be a long delay before the hearing date and it may be necessary to apply *ex parte* for a stay pending the hearing.

(B) *In the High Court*

The time summons will be issued for hearing before the Practice Master at 10.30 am two working days later. The summons should be served on the other side at least one clear day before the hearing.

If the application is successful there is no need to have the order drawn up; just notify the other side that the order has been made. However, the order can be drawn up if the applicant so desires (see Procedural Table 1 on p 259 for the steps to be taken), in which case the order will read as follows:

'It is Ordered that the shall have until the day of 19 in which to serve and that the costs of this application be .'

6 Form of application for a special appointment before the master (High Court only)

A special appointment will be needed for a lengthy hearing (eg if it seems likely that it will last more than twenty minutes) or for the assessment of damages. Application can be made by personal attendance at the court office, but it is easier to apply by post to the Action Dept (Postal Section), enclosing original summons (or copy judgment and fee if applying for the assessment of damages), letter requesting the special appointment, a stamped addressed envelope and the following form. To apply in person, leave the form (plus the summons) at the Master's Secretaries Department for collection on the next working day.

APPLICATION FOR APPOINTMENT BEFORE A MASTER

Master
Parties in action
Type of summons (or, if assessment of damages, nature of claim)
Estimated length of hearing
Dates convenient to all parties
Dates to be avoided
Are counsel attending?
Names of counsel (if known)
Date application made
Solicitor making the application
Note: this form has no heading and is not served on the other parties.

7 Discovery

(1) *Discovery of documents before the commencement of proceedings*

The proposed plaintiff should issue an Originating Application or Summons (see Procedural Table 16) against the proposed defendant. The Originating Application or Summons should be typed out so as to comply with the requirements of a pleading (see Chapter 5, section 6), using the specimen printed in Appendix G as a precedent, with the wording below inserted into the main body of the form;

IN THE MATTER of an application under [CCA 1984, s 52(2) *or*] [section 33(2) of the Supreme Court Act 1981]
BETWEEN
To
[Insert formal parts]
the Plaintiff claims against the Defendant Orders that the Defendant do within 14 days from the date of this Order:

(*a*) make and serve on the Plaintiff's solicitors a list (verified by affidavits sworn by its administrator or other responsible officer) stating whether any medical records and documents, including all obstetric, surgical, medical, nursing, drug, and other treatment and investigation notes and records, laboratory test reports, x-ray plates and reports, patient consent forms, clinical correspondence, and computer data, relating to the Plaintiff are in the possession, custody or power of the Defendant AND if any such documents were once but are not now in the possession, custody or power of the Defendant then to itemise such documents and state in whose custody, power or possession they are now believed to be,

AND

(*b*) produce such of those documents and other records above-referred to as are in the custody, possession or power of the Defendant to the applicant (or the plaintiff's solicitor) with liberty to disclose them limited to the Plaintiff's legal, medical, and other professional advisers, and limited to the purpose of the subsequent proceedings in this court which the Plaintiff is likely to bring against the defendant in respect of personal injury.

AND that the costs of and incidental to this Application be the Plaintiff's in any event.

If the Defendant does not acknowledge service such judgment may be given or Order made against or in relation to it as the Court may think just and expedient.

DATED THIS day of 199

[Insert formal parts]

The affidavit in support of the Originating Application or Summons must comply with the following requirements, namely, it must:

(1) describe or specify the documents;

(2) show, if practicable by reference to any pleading which it is intended to serve, that such documents are relevant to an issue likely to arise out of a claim for personal injuries in subsequent proceedings;

(3) show that the party is likely to have, or have had, such documents in its possession, custody, or power;

(4) state the grounds on which it is alleged that the parties are likely to be parties to subsequent personal injury proceedings; thus, the circumstances of the accident will need to be stated and the letter before action (or the proposed pleadings) should be exhibited if possible, although this may not always be essential.

Such an affidavit may well commence by setting out the deponent's name, address, status and occupation, who the client is, and how the claim arises.

In a medical negligence case it might, for example, continue:

'3 A copy of the plaintiff's statement, which I have prepared, is now produced and shown to me as exhibit 1. On the basis of what the plaintiff has told me, I believe that the medical treatment afforded to the plaintiff at the Hospital fell below the standard which might reasonably have been expected and accordingly I verily believe that the plaintiff has a claim for personal injuries arising therefrom, and that the parties to this action are likely to be party to subsequent court proceedings.

4 In my belief the defendants have or have had in their possession custody or power, surgery records, x-rays, medical notes, memoranda between staff, circulars and other written records and materials and computer records concerning the treatment of the plaintiff in the hospital. It is my belief that it would be normal hospital practice (in accordance with National Health Service procedures and Department of Health recommendations) for such documents to exist.

5 These documents are relevant to some or all of the issues in this case. Without such documents the medical advisers instructed on behalf of the plaintiff cannot properly report on the treatment received by the plaintiff, or on the complaints made by the plaintiff.

SWORN etc.'

In a workplace accident case, paragraph 4 might read as follows:

'4 In my belief the defendants have or have had in their possession custody or power, surgery records, entries in an Accident Book (pursuant to the duty laid down in the Social Security (Claims and Payments) Regulations 1979), Form B176 completed for the Department of Social Security by virtue of the plaintiff having claimed industrial injuries disablement benefit, and Form F2508 (pursuant to the Notification of Accidents and Dangerous Occurrences Regulations 1980). I also believe that the defendants have or have had in their possession custody or power documents relating to the repair and maintenance of the forklift truck being driven by the plaintiff at the time of his accident, such records being from the date of purchase until the present time, since it would be normal commercial practice for such documents to exist.'

If the application is successful the order will be drawn up by the County Court, or in the High Court should be drawn up in the usual way (see Procedural Table 16 on p 277). Note that the order should state the specific documents to be disclosed and, as such, will be similar to an order for Specific Discovery (generally, see Ord 24, r 7A). See Procedural Table 11 for the form and layout of an affidavit.

(2) *When defendant fails to serve a list of documents*

The plaintiff issues a summons or application (see Procedural Table 1) completed as follows:

> 'that the Defence be struck out and the Defendant be placed in the same position as though it had never defended and interlocutory judgment be signed on behalf of the Plaintiff with damages to be assessed, the Defendant having failed to serve a List of Documents pursuant to CCR Order 17, Rule 11(7) or RCJ Order 24, Rule 2 (*or* "the Order dated ") AND that the costs of this Application to be the Plaintiff's in any event.'

Frequently, the order made will be in the following terms:

> 'that the Defendant do within 14 days serve a List of Documents on the Plaintiff failing which the Plaintiff be at liberty to enter judgment with damages to be assessed and that the costs of this Application be the Plaintiff's in any event.'

(3) *Notice requiring an affidavit verifying a list of documents*

The layout, heading and style of the notice will be as for a pleading (see Chapter 5, section 6). The notice should read as follows:

> 'TAKE NOTICE that you the above named defendant are required within 14 days after the service of this Notice on you to make and file an Affidavit verifying the List of Documents you have made under CCR Order 17, Rule 11(7), or RSC Order 24, Rule 2(1) (*or* "pursuant to the order of dated ").'

Application for an order that an affidavit verifying the list be filed can be made by issuing an application or summons (see Procedural Table 1, completed as follows:

> 'that the within days file an affidavit verifying its list of documents.'

For the form of affidavit, see Form No 27 (para 22, Vol 2, White Book). In the county court, use Form N265(i). See Procedural Table 11 for the form and layout of an affidavit.

(4) *Discovery of specific documents*

This procedure is used to obtain disclosure of specific documents which have not been disclosed in the other side's list of documents, even if the other side has filed an affidavit verifying the list. The applicant should issue an application or summons (see Procedural Table 1), supported by an affidavit. The affidavit must state:

(1) the deponent's belief that the other party has the documents sought, and

(2) the deponent's belief that the documents are relevant to matters in the action.

The specimen affidavit printed below is for use in a workplace accident case in which the defendant has failed to disclose certain documents; the wording can, of course, be altered to meet the requirements of individual cases.

Application or summons:

> 'that the Defendant do within 14 days serve a List of Documents and file an Affidavit verifying such list limited to the classes of documents referred to in Paragraph   of the Affidavit of   served with this (Application or Summons) and that the costs of this Application be the Plaintiff's in any event.'

Affidavit: set out in the usual form, with the opening paragraphs stating how the deponent is authorised to swear the affidavit, when the accident occurred, when the writ was issued, when the proceedings were served, and when the Defence was served.

The specimen affidavit in Precedent 6(1) can be adapted as necessary. It is a good idea to conclude the affidavit with a final paragraph stating 'the documents are relevant to the issues raised by the defence and could be produced at the trial by means of a (witness summons or writ of Subpoena Duces Tecum)'. See Procedural Table 11 for the form and layout of an affidavit.

If the application is successful the order should be drawn up in the usual way (see Procedural Table 1). The order might read as follows:

> 'THAT the Defendant do within 14 days serve a List of Documents on the Plaintiff limited to the following:
>
> (*set out classes of documents*)
>
> AND that the Defendant do also file an Affidavit verifying such List within 14 days of the service thereof AND that the costs of this Application be   .'

(5) *Discovery against a person who is not a party to the action*

The applicant should issue an application or summons in the usual way (see Procedural Table 1) completed as follows:

> FOR AN ORDER pursuant to (Section 53 of the County Courts Act 1984 and CCR Order 13, Rule 7(1)(*g*) or Section 34(2) of the Supreme Court Act 1981 and RSC Order 24, Rule 7A(2)) that   (*name and address of non-party*) do make an Affidavit stating whether any documents of the following classes:
>
> (*set out classes of documents*)
>
> are or at any time have been in the possession, custody or power of the said   and if not in its custody at present, when it parted with them and what has become of them AND that the COSTS of and occasioned by this Application may be provided for.'

The application or summons should be served on the parties to the action in the usual way, but should be served on the non-party as if it were an Originating

Application or Originating Summons or Writ (eg personal service, for the rules on service, see Chapter 6, section 3). An affidavit in support should also be served with the application or summons; this affidavit must comply with the following requirements:

(1) specify or describe the documents,

(2) show, if practicable, by reference to a pleading in the action, that the documents are relevant to an issue arising or likely to arise in the personal injuries action, and that the non-party has them in its possession, custody or power.

See Procedural Table 11 for the form and layout of an affidavit.

If the application is successful the order should be drawn up in the usual way (see Procedural Table 1) and might read as follows:

> 'UPON HEARING for the parties and for (*name and address of non-party*) AND upon reading the Affidavit of IT IS ORDERED that the said do within 14 days make an Affidavit stating what documents of the following classes:
>
> (*set out classes of documents*)
>
> are or at any time have been in its possession, custody or power, and if not in its custody at present, when it parted with them and to whom AND that the do pay the costs of the said occasioned by this Application, to be taxed if not agreed,
>
> AND that the costs of this Application including the costs paid to the said be .'

8 Inspection of property prior to the commencement of proceedings

The proposed plaintiff should issue an Originating Application or Summons against the proposed defendant (see Procedural Table 16). The Originating Application or Summons should be typed out so as to comply with the requirements of a pleading (see Chapter 5, section 6), using the specimen printed in Appendix G as a precedent, with the wording below inserted into the main body of the form.

Refer to the specimen wording in Precedent 6(1) which can be amended as follows:

> 'IN THE MATTER of an application under (Section 52(1) of the County Courts Act 1984 or Section 34(2) of the Supreme Court Act 1981)
>
> BETWEEN: (*etc*)
>
> ... an Application by the Plaintiff for an Order that the Defendant do upon seven days' notice give inspection to the Plaintiff, his/her solicitor, and engineering expert of (*property in respect of which the Order is sought*) and do allow the making of any drawing and the taking of any photograph or video film of the same by the Plaintiff, his/her solicitor, and engineering expert.
>
> AND that the costs of this Application be the Plaintiff's in any event. (*etc: continue as in pre-printed form*).'

The affidavit in support of the application must comply with the following requirements:

(1) describe or specify the property,

(2) show, if practicable by reference to a pleading which it is intended to serve, that the property may become the subject matter of proceedings.

Such an affidavit might commence by setting out, in the usual way, who the deponent is and how s/he is authorised to swear the affidavit, who the client is, and how and when the accident occurred.

This is an extract from an affidavit that was used in a workplace accident case (the plaintiff said that a shelf had fallen on him):

> '2 I received the plaintiff's instructions to act on his behalf on and on the I wrote to the defendants claiming damages. Since then I have been in correspondence with the defendants' insurers and solicitors and have informed the former that the plaintiff alleges that the shelf which fell on him was inadequately secured to the adjoining wall.
>
> 3 I am of the opinion that the defendants were in breach of their common law duty to provide a safe place of work and a safe system of working for the plaintiff, their employee, and that they were also in breach of their statutory duty to the plaintiff, including that under s 28(2) of the Factories Act 1961.
>
> 4 Although the defendants' insurers and solicitors have denied these allegations I am of the opinion that the defendants are likely to be made party to an action for damages for personal injuries.
>
> 5 On the I wrote to the defendants' insurers and asked for facilities for an inspection by myself and/or a qualified engineer of the scene of the accident. Subsequently, I made further requests for permission to inspect but such permission has not been forthcoming.
>
> 6 There is now shown to me and produced as exhibit No**, a bundle of correspondence which has passed between the defendants' insurers and/or solicitors and myself.
>
> 7 I am informed by the plaintiff and believe that the said shelf and the method by which it was attached to the adjoining wall will be the subject matter of the intended proceedings referred to in paragraph 4, above. Accordingly, I request that the plaintiff, his solicitor and engineering expert be granted permission to inspect and photograph the site of the accident, and the shelf which fell on the plaintiff.
>
> SWORN etc.'

If the application is successful in the County Court, the court will draw up the order. In the High Court the order should be drawn up in the usual way (see Procedural Table 16); the wording of the order would be similar to the wording used in the Originating Application or Summons to describe the order sought.

See Procedural Table 11 for the form and layout of an affidavit.

9 Inspection of property after the commencement of proceedings

(1) Against the defendant

The plaintiff should issue an application or a summons (see Procedural Table 1) completed as follows:

> 'THAT the Plaintiff, his/her solicitor and engineering expert may at all reasonable times upon giving seven days' previous notice to the Defendant be at liberty to enter upon the Defendant's premises at
> to inspect machinery the subject matter of this action, namely,
> and to make any drawings, to take photographs or video films of the same and that the Defendant be ordered to permit the Plaintiff, his/her solicitors, and engineering expert, to enter and be upon the said premises for these purposes, AND that the costs of this Application be the Plaintiff's in any event.' Refer to Procedural Table 1 for the steps to be taken.

If the application is successful in the County Court, they will draw up the order, or, in the High Court the order should be drawn up using similar wording.

(2) *Against a person who is not a party to the action*

The applicant should issue an application or summons (see Procedural Table 1), completed as follows:

> 'FOR AN ORDER pursuant to CCR Order 13, Rule 17(*g*) or RSC Order 29 Rule 7A that (*name and address of non-party*) do upon seven days' notice give inspection of to the Plaintiff, his/her solicitor, and engineering expert and do allow the making of any drawings and the taking of any photographs or video films of the same by the Plaintiff, his/her solicitor, and engineering expert AND that the costs of and occasioned by this Application may be provided for.'

The application or summons should be served on the parties to the action in the usual way, but should be served on the non-party as if it were an Originating Application or Summons or Writ (eg personal service—for the rules on service, see Chapter 6, section 3). An affidavit in support should also be served with the application or summons; this affidavit must comply with the following requirements:

(1) describe or specify the property;

(2) show, if practicable by a reference to a pleading in the action, that the property is the subject matter of the personal injuries action, or is property as to which any question arises in the action.

See Procedural Table 11 for the form and layout of an affidavit.

If the application is successful in the County Court, they will draw up the order or, in the High Court the order should be drawn up in the usual way (see Procedural Table 1) and might read as follows:

> 'UPON HEARING for the parties and for (*name and address of non-party*) AND upon reading the Affidavit of IT IS ORDERED that the do upon seven days' notice give inspection of to the plaintiff, his/her solicitor, and engineering expert, and do allow the making of any drawings and the taking of any photographs of the same by the Plaintiff, his/her solicitor, and engineering expert AND that the do pay the costs of the occasioned by this Application, to be taxed if not agreed AND that the costs of this Application including the costs paid to the be .'

10 Notice to Admit Facts

Prepare the layout, heading and style of the notice as though it were a pleading (see Chapter 6, section 6). The notice should read as follows:

> 'TAKE NOTICE that the in this Action requires the to admit for the purposes of this Action only the several facts specified below and the is hereby required to admit the several facts saving all just exceptions as to the admissibility of such facts as evidence in the Action.
>
> Dated the day of 19 .
>
> Solicitor for the

To Solicitor for the . The facts, the admission of which is required, are:

1
2
3

(*etc*).'

If the other side decide to file an admission (or qualified admission), they should do so using Form PF 61. In the county court, the Notice to Admit is in Form N281.

11 Further and Better Particulars

The applicant should issue an application or summons in the usual way (see Procedural Table 1) having previously requested the Further and Better Particulars by letter. The form of application summons should be completed as follows:

'for an Order that the do within 14 days serve on the the Further and Better Particulars of the requested in a letter dated and a copy of which is served with this [Application or Summons] AND that the costs of this application to be 's in any event.'

If the application is successful, the order will read as follows:

'IT IS ORDERED that the do within 14 days serve on the the Further and Better Particulars of the as initialled by the court AND that the costs of the application be .'

12 Interrogatories

The applicant should issue an application or a summons in the usual way (see Procedural Table 1), completed as follows:

'For an Order that the be at liberty to serve on the the Interrogatories served with this [Application or Summons] and that the do within 14 days answer the questions in writing by Affidavit AND that the costs of this Application be the 's in any event.'

If the application is successful the order might read as follows:

'IT IS ORDERED that the be at liberty to serve on the Interrogatories in writing as initialled by the court and that the do within 14 days answer the said Interrogatories AND that the costs of this Application be

The affidavit giving the Answer to the Interrogatories, should be set out in the usual way. Have a separate paragraph for each Interrogatory (reciting the Interrogatory in full, and then giving the Answer). See Procedural Table 11 for the form and layout of an affidavit.

13 Amendment of writ and/or pleadings

The precedents below are for use when amending the writ and the Statement of Claim; they can be amended as necessary for use in the County Court or for pleadings other than the Statement of Claim. First refer to Chapter 10, section 6 for notes on when leave is needed to amend writ and/or pleadings.

The applicant should issue a summons (see Procedural Table 1), completed as follows:

'For an Order that the Plaintiff have leave to amend the Writ as marked in red on the copy served with this Summons and that the service of the Writ and the Defendant's Acknowledgment of Service and Notice of Intention to Defend stand AND that the Plaintiff have leave to amend the Statement of Claim as marked in red on the copy served with this Summons with leave for the Defendant to re-serve an amended Defence (if so advised) within 14 days thereafter AND that the costs reserved and thrown away by the amendments be   and that the costs of this Application be   .'

In the County Court the court will draw up the order. In the High Court if the application is successful there is no need to have the order drawn up, but simply notify the other side that the order has been made. However, the order can be drawn up if the plaintiff wishes or the other party demands, in which case the order should be drawn up using wording similar to that used on the summons.

Refer to Procedural Table 1 for how to draw up the order.

Both the Writ and the Statement of Claim (in their amended form) should have the words 'amended by order of the court   dated the   day of   199   ' typed in red across the top left (or, typed in black, underlined in red). Both documents should then be re-served. Generally, see Chapter 6.

14 Amendment of proceedings to join a new party to the action

The applicant should issue an application or summons in the usual way (see Procedural Table 1), completed as follows:

'For an Order that the Plaintiff be at liberty to amend the [Proceedings/ Writ and Statement of Claim] in this Action by adding the name of   as a Plaintiff (*or* Defendant) and to amend the indorsement on the [Writ] [Summons] as marked in red on the copy served with this Application and to amend the [Particulars/Statement of Claim] as marked in red on the copy served with this Summons AND that the costs of this Application be   .

If the application is successful, the order might read as follows:

'It is Ordered that the Plaintiff be at liberty to amend the [Proceedings/ Writ and Statement of Claim] as marked in red on the copies initialled by the court and it is Ordered that the amended proceedings be served within 14 days of the date of this order with leave to the Defendant to serve an amended Defence (if so advised) within 14 days thereafter AND that the costs incurred and thrown away by the amendments be   and that the costs of this Application be   .

A County Court Order will be drawn up and served by the court. In the High Court refer to Procedural Table 1 or 2 for how to draw up the order.

Both the County Court Summons/Writ and all pleadings (in their amended form) should have the words 'amended by order of the court   dated the   day of   199   ' typed in red across the top left (or, typed in black, underlined in red). Both documents should then be re-served. Generally, see Chapter 6.

15 Obtaining an interim payment

The plaintiff's solicitor should issue an application or summons in the usual way (see Procedural Table 1), completed as follows:

'For an Order that pursuant to (CCR Order 14, Rule 12 *or* RSC Order 29 Rule 10) the Defendant do make to the Plaintiff as an Interim Payment such sum as the Court thinks just (together with interest thereon) and that any such payment so made be on account of any damages which the Defendant may subsequently be held liable to pay to the Plaintiff AND that the costs of this application be costs in the cause.'

The summons must be supported by an affidavit; this affidavit should comply with the following requirements:

(1) verify the special damage to date;

(2) exhibit hospital and medical reports relied on in support of the application;

(3) in a fatal case give details of the dependants, their ages, and relationship to the deceased.

The wording of the affidavit will vary with the individual case, but it will usually commence by stating the deponent's name, address, marital status, occupation, and connection with the case, who the plaintiff is, how and when the accident occurred, when the writ was issued and when the writ and pleadings were served, and whether the Defence denies liability. It can refer to payments in. The affidavit might well continue (for example) as follows:

'5 On the   of   19   at   Magistrates' Court the defendant pleaded guilty to and was convicted of driving a motor car without due care and attention at the time of the plaintiff's accident, contrary to section 3, Road Traffic Act 1988 and was fined £   , with his licence endorsed, and two penalty points imposed, and an order to pay £   costs.

6 On the basis of the evidence before me I believe that the plaintiff has a good cause of action and that his/her accident was caused solely by the defendant's negligent driving.

7 The Defendant is insured with the   Insurance Company Limited.

8 I have calculated the special damage to date at the sum of £   in accordance with the calculations annexed hereto and which I now produce as Exhibit A.

9 I have obtained a medical report from M   who is consultant   to the   Hospital and I now produce that report which is annexed hereto as Exhibit B.

10 I humbly ask this honourable Court to make an Order for an Interim Payment.'

The plaintiff's solicitor (if swearing the affidavit) should state that you are authorised by the plaintiff to swear the affidavit on his/her behalf. See Procedural Table 11 for the form and layout of an affidavit.

If the application is successful in the County Court, they will draw up the order. In the High Court the order should be drawn up in the usual way (see Procedural Table 1). The order will be worded as follows:

'IT IS ORDERED that the Defendant do pay to the Plaintiff within 14 days the sum of £   as a payment on account of any damages which the Defendant may subsequently be held liable to pay to the Plaintiff AND (*the court may treat the hearing of the summons or application as an opportunity to make other orders*) AND that the costs of the Application be   .'

If the payment is to come out of money already paid into court, then the wording would be along the lines of 'the sum of £ out of the monies now standing in court to the credit of this action be paid out to the Plaintiff as a payment on account of any damages *etc.*'

16 When the plaintiff changes his/her name

If the plaintiff marries and changes his/her name, or changes his/her name for some other reason, there is no need to apply for leave to amend the proceedings or writ and/or pleadings. A Notice in the usual style, format and layout of a pleading (see Chapter 6, section 6) is filed with the court and a copy sent to the other parties. The action continues in the new name.

The Notice should state the plaintiff's new and old names (eg XYZ (formerly ABC) plaintiff) and state:

'TAKE NOTICE that the Plaintiff in this action, ABC, is now known as XYZ.'

17 Consolidation

The applicant should issue an application or summons in the usual way (see Procedural Table 1) with the full titles, numbers, and parties of all the actions to be consolidated appearing thereon (as in the example, below). Alternatively, separate applications or summonses should be simultaneously issued in all the actions. Complete the form of application or summons as follows:

'FOR AN ORDER that Actions 19 No and 19 No and 19 No be consolidated AND that the costs of this Application be costs in the cause.'

If the application is successful in the county court, they will draw up the order, or in the High Court you should draw it up in the normal way. The order should be drawn up as follows:

'IT IS ORDERED that Actions 19 No and 19 No and 19 No be consolidated and that the three Actions be carried on as one Action AND that the costs of all the parties to the said Actions including the costs of this Application shall be costs in the cause in the consolidated Action.'

When drawing up the order it is important that the heading should include the titles, numbers, and parties to all the actions and state 'Consolidated by order of dated ' and that this full new heading be used henceforth throughout the action. Refer to Procedural Table 1, for how to draw up the order.

In the High Court, once the order has been drawn up, it must be lodged with the Action Department, so that the court record (ie cause book) can be amended to record the fact that the actions are consolidated. Do this by posting a copy of the order to the Action Department.

After consolidation the title of the action appears as:

		19 , No
Between	*A B*	Plaintiff
	and	
	C D	Defendant
		19 , No
And between	*E F*	Plaintiff
	and	
	C D	Defendant

(Consolidated by Order of dated the day of 19).

18 To obtain a split trial

The applicant should issue an application or summons in the usual way (see Procedural Table l) completed as follows:

'FOR AN ORDER that the question of liability of the Defendant to the Plaintiff in this Action be tried as a preliminary issue before the question or issue of any damages, and that subject to the Defendant being found liable to the Plaintiff, the issue of damages be tried subsequently as may be directed by the trial judge AND that the costs of this Application be costs in the cause.'

If the application is successful in the County Court, they will draw up the order or, in the High Court you should draw it up in the normal way. The order may be drawn up as follows:

'IT IS ORDERED that the question or issue of the liability of the Defendant to the Plaintiff be tried as a preliminary issue before the question or issue of the quantum of damages if any, and that subject to the Defendant being found liable to the Plaintiff the issue of damages be tried subsequently in such manner as may be directed by the trial judge AND (*usually orders will be made as to discovery limited to liability*) AND that the costs of this Application be costs in the cause.'

Refer to Procedural Table 1 for how to draw up the order in the High Court.

19 Next friend

(1) *County court: next friend's consent, and undertaking for costs*

This form should be set out with the title to the action. Note that it must be signed in front of a solicitor (or court officer).

'I, the undersigned, (*name and address*) being the next friend of (*minor*) who is a minor [or a patient], and who wishes to commence an action in this court, against (*defendant*) hereby undertake to be responsible for the costs of (*minor*) in those proceedings, as follows, namely, if (*minor*) fails to pay to (*defendant*) when and in such manner as the court shall order, all such costs of the proceedings as the court directs the minor to pay to (*defendant*) I will forthwith pay the same into the office of the court.

dated

Signed by the above-named
in my presence
(Solicitor or Officer of Court)

In the High Court the minor's solicitor signs a different form; see (2) and (3) below.

(2) *High Court: consent of proposed next friend*

The Notice should be set out with the style, heading, format, and layout of a pleading (see Chapter 6, section 6). The wording will be as follows:

'I, XYZ of , consent to be next friend [guardian ad litem] of the above-named plaintiff, a minor [a patient] in this action, and I authorise (*name of solicitor*) to act on my behalf
(*signed and dated*).'

In a county court case, a minor's next friend signs a different form, see (1) above.

(3)(a) (High Court only) Solicitor's certificate in a minor claim

The Notice should be set out with the style, heading, format, and layout of a pleading (see Chapter 6, section 6) (or it can be endorsed onto the writ). The wording might be as follows:

'I (*name and address of solicitor*) hereby certify that I believe that XYZ is a minor and that the above-named (*next friend*) has no interest in the cause or matter in question adverse to that of the minor.

(*signed and dated*) solicitor for the .'

(b) (High Court only) Solicitor's certificate in patient's claim

The Notice should be set out with the style, heading, format, and layout of a pleading (see Chapter 5, section 6). The wording might be as follows:

'I (*name and address of solicitor*) hereby certify that I believe that XYZ is a patient (*give grounds of knowledge or belief*) and that the above-named has no interest in the cause or matter adverse to that of the patient. And I further certify that no person has been authorised under Part VII of the Mental Health Act 1983 to conduct the proceedings in this cause or matter in the name of the patient or on his behalf.

(*signed and dated*) solicitor for the

If the next friend or guardian has been authorised to sue under Part VII of the 1983 Act, then this certificate is not needed.

20 Minor: Notice of Adoption

When the minor reaches age 18, a Notice of Adoption can be filed.

The Notice should be set out with the style, heading, and format of a pleading (see Chapter 6, section 6). The wording will be as follows:

'TAKE NOTICE that of attained the age of eighteen years on the day of 19 and hereby adopts the above proceedings and appoints me as his solicitor.'

This is filed with the court.

Thereafter the minor will appear as 'ABC (late a minor but now of full age)'.

21 Minor Approval: County Court

(a) Minor Approval: when proceedings have not been commenced

The plaintiff should commence proceedings in the usual way by issuing an ordinary summons against the defendant. The Particulars of Claim will be in the following form:

'1 The Plaintiff is a Minor born on the day of 19 whose claim against the Defendant is for damages in respect of (*set out claim as on a writ indorsement*) and who sues by his next friend.

2 (*set out any fatal accident particulars, if applicable. See Precedent 23*)

3 By way of settlement of the Plaintiff's said claim the Defendant has agreed to the following terms:

(*set out terms of settlement, which will be similar to those in the above precedent*)

AND the Plaintiff requests that this honourable Court do approve the said settlement.

Do not forget that the next friend's consent (and undertaking for costs) must be lodged, see Precedent 19(3).

(b) Minor approval: when proceedings have already been commenced

The plaintiff should issue a notice of application in the usual way, completed as follows:

TAKE NOTICE that the Plaintiff intends to apply to the at on day the day of 19 at in the noon for an Order that the following terms of settlement of this action having been agreed between the parties: (*set out terms of proposed settlement in similar terms to those in Minor Approval Originating Summons, below*) the said terms be approved by this honourable Court.'

The Order will be on Form N292—and see examples under 22 below.

22 Minor approval: High Court

(a) Minor approval: when proceedings have not been commenced

The minor plaintiff should issue, by his next friend, an originating summons. For the procedure in an Infant Approval Originating Summons, see Procedural Table 17. The form below is Form PF 167 (para 38, of Vol 2, White Book). Note that the blank spaces in the form should be left blank, so the court does not know the figures when it is going through the papers.

'Normal Form of Originating Application by the plaintiff whose claim against the defendant is for (*set out nature of claim, use Precedent 1 writ indorsements*) for an order that the terms of compromise agreed by the parties in the form of the draft hereinafter set out be approved and be made an order of the court and that by consent, all proceedings be stayed save for the purpose of carrying the said terms into effect and that there be liberty to apply for that purpose and generally.
[Formal parts]

(*On reverse side of the sheet of paper, type the following*)

Draft Order

Upon hearing the [solicitors] for the plaintiff and the defendant the following terms of settlement arrived at between the parties are approved by and made an order of the Court and by consent it is ordered that all further proceedings in this action be stayed save for the purpose of carrying the said terms into effect and that there be liberty to apply for that purpose and generally:

*1 That the plaintiff be at liberty to accept the sum of £ in satisfaction of the claim herein in the manner hereinafter provided.

2 That the said sum be satisfied as follows:

(1) the sum of £ at present in Court shall be allocated [in satisfaction] [or on account] thereof.

(2) The defendant within 14 days do [further] pay: (a) £ to (b) £ into Court for the benefit of the plaintiff.

3 That the fund of the plaintiff be invested, applied or otherwise dealt with [as set out in the Directions initialled by the Court].

OR [For use if the fund is to be administered locally.]

[3 That the said fund be invested and accumulated in Short Term Investment Account for the benefit of the plaintiff pending further order, and that all further proceedings relating to the investment and application of the said fund be transferred to the District Registry].

4 That the defendant do pay the plaintiff's costs to be taxed upon the standard basis, the plaintiff's solicitor waiving claim to any further costs.

[5 That in addition the costs of the plaintiff be taxed in accordance with the Legal Aid Act 1988].

6 That [there be liberty to apply that] taxation of the plaintiff's costs be dispensed with.

7 That upon payment by the defendant of the several sums and costs before mentioned he be discharged from liability in respect of the claims in this action.

8 That any interest accumulated to the date hereof on the sum in Court be paid out to the defendant's solicitors and any interest accruing thereafter be applied [proportionately] as directed for the capital [or as may be].

Dated the day of 19 .'

Obviously, the wording of the order will vary from case to case. Refer also to Precedent 30 for further specimen clauses that can be used on a settlement. By way of illustration, these were the orders made in one infant case:

1 'That the defendant do within 21 days pay to ABC the father and next friend of the minor plaintiff the sum of £ ;
2 That the defendant do within 21 days pay the further sum of £ to the plaintiff's solicitors upon their undertaking to pay the sum of £ into a national savings account and the sum of £ into a building society account in the plaintiff's name;
3 That the defendant do pay to the plaintiff his costs of this action, such costs being agreed with the approval of the court at £ and the plaintiff's solicitors waiving any claim to any further costs. Taxation between solicitor and own client being dispensed with;'

Once the order has been made, it should be drawn up by the County Court or, in the High Court by the solicitor. Refer to Procedural Table 17.

(b) Minor Approval: where proceedings have already been commenced

The plaintiff should issue an application or summons in the usual way. Since it will be to approve a settlement, it will be a consent application or summons, use Procedural Table 2 but note that the court's approval will be needed. The form below is Form PF 165 (para 376, of Vol 2. White Book). Leave the blank spaces blank, so the court does not know the figures when going through the papers. The wording to be inserted into the summons will be as in the precedent Infant Approval Originating Application (Precedent 20(1)(*a*), above). Referring to that Precedent, insert into the application or summons the nature of the order sought (this will be done by using the following part of that Precedent 'For an order that the terms of compromise ... to apply for that purpose generally'). On the reverse side of the form, type out the draft order. This will be identical to the form of draft order in the Infant Approval Originating Application or Summons. Thus, type out the reverse side of that form (as in the Precedent above), namely 'Upon hearing ... dated the day of 199 .'

Once the order has been made the court will draw it up in the County Court in Form N292. In the High Court it will need to be drawn up. The wording will be similar to that used in an Originating Application or Summons (ie Back of Form PF 165, see above). See Procedural Table 2, for how to draw up the order.

(c) Form giving directions over minor's monies

If the sums are large, the court may well give detailed directions as to the application and investment of the damages. The two precedent forms (above) refer to Form PF 169, which is this form (alternatively, use Oyez Form H20):

Directions as to the Application and Investment of Monies Awarded to

[ ]

In Court

19 No

[*Short title of action*]

1 AMOUNT OF AWARD £

2 PAY to for the benefit of the minor

3 Subject to a first charge under s 9(6) of the Legal Aid Act 1974

4 INVEST:

£ in in Stock* 19
£ in Gross Income Fund Units
£ in Capital/High Yield Fund Units
£ in a Short Term Investment Account
£ in

*Indicate whether Stock is on National Savings Stock Register

5 DIRECTIONS AS TO INCOME FROM INVESTMENT

Either (i) Re-invest in
OR (ii) Place to a Short Term Investment Account and accumulate
OR (iii) Pay income during minority to
or until
OR (iv) Pay from Short Term Investment Account £
[Monthly] [Quarterly] to
commencing on until

6 DIRECTIONS AS TO INCOME TAX

Either (i) Recovered income tax to be paid by the next friend into the minor's fund in Court and to be invested in or placed to Short Term Investment Account
OR (ii) Recovered income tax to be retained by the next friend for the benefit of the minor

7 Upon the minor attaining the age of 18, the fund be transferred to her or sold and proceeds paid to her or as she may direct.

Dated

A Master of the Queen's Bench Division

Note—This form must be handed to the Master at the appointment to approve the terms of settlement. Copies may be obtained from Room 122. The plaintiff's solicitor should insert the title of the action before the hearing.

23 Minor Approval: in a Fatal Claim

If a fatal case involves apportionment of money to a minor, then the settlement will have to be approved by the court. Similar principles apply as in an ordinary Minor Approval.

(a) County Court

The procedure is the same as for a Minor Approval in the County Court (see Precedent 21). Adapt the High Court Precedent (below) as necessary, for how to apportion the monies between the various claimants.

(b) High Court

For the procedure, see Precedent No 21, above.

- *if proceedings have not been commenced*

Issue an Originating Summons. Refer to Precedent 21(1)(*a*), Minor Approval Originating Summons. The wording will be identical, except that after the reference (in italics) to the writ indorsement, insert the following: 'The particulars required pursuant to section 2(4) of the Fatal Accidents Act 1976 are: (*state names, ages and relationship to deceased of all the persons on whose behalf the proceedings are brought*)'. The reverse side of the Originating Summons is similar to that in Precedent 21(1)(*a*) except that the printed paragraphs 1, 2 and 3, are replaced with the following (and subsequent paragraphs are obviously renumbered):

*1 That the plaintiff be at liberty to accept the sum of £ in satisfaction of the claims herein in the manner hereinafter provided, such sum being apportioned as follows:

(*a*) to the claim of the plaintiff under the Law Reform (Miscellaneous Provisions) Act 1934 £ ;

(*b*) to the personal claim of the plaintiff under the Fatal Accidents Act 1976 £ ;

(*c*) to the personal claim of the minor under the Fatal Accidents Act 1976 £ .

(*and so for each minor*)

2 That in satisfaction of the several sums apportioned to the plaintiff:

(*a*) there be paid out to her solicitors from the sum of £ at present in the Court, the sum of £ ;

(*b*) there be paid to her solicitors by the defendant within 14 days the [further] sum of £ .

3 That in satisfaction of the sum apportioned to the minor

(*a*) there be allocated thereto from the sum of £ at present in Court the sum of £ ;

(*b*) there be paid into Court by the defendant within 14 days the [further] sum of £ .

(*and so for each minor*)

4 That the fund[s] of the said minor child[ren] be invested, applied or otherwise dealt with [as set out in the PF 169 Directions initialled by the Master].

This is Form PF 166 (para 377, of Vol 2, White Book).

- *if proceedings have already been commenced*

Issue a consent summons. The form of consent order will be based on Form PF 171 (para 382, Vol 2, White Book). The form of summons is similar to that for Minor Approval Summons (refer to Precedent 21(1)(*b*). Complete the front of the summons using identical wording. The reverse side of the summons is completed using identical wording to that in a Fatal Accidents Originating Summons, see above. Type out the wording (above) on the reverse side of the summons.

24 Notice to be served after one year's delay [High Court only]

The notice should be set out with the style, heading, and format of a pleading (see Chapter 6, section 6). The wording should be as follows:

> 'TAKE NOTICE that pursuant to Order 3 Rule 6 of the Rules of the Supreme Court 1965 the Plaintiff intends to proceed in this Action after the expiration of one month from the date of this Notice.'

25 Notice of appeal to judge in chambers

(a) County Court

The notice of appeal should be made on a normal notice of application form. It should be set out with the style, heading and format of a pleading (see Chapter 6, Section 6). The wording should be as follows:

> 'The above-named appeals to the judge against the decision of district judge given on the
> (*date*) Ordering (*or* refusing to Order)
> [set out order made]
> On the following grounds [set out grounds]
> Signed '

(b) High Court

The notice of appeal should be set out with the style, heading, and format of a pleading (see Chapter 6, section 6). The wording should be as follows:

> 'TAKE NOTICE that the above-named intends to Appeal against the decision of Master (*or* "Mr Registrar ") given on the day of
> 19 Ordering (*or* "refusing to Order") .
> AND further take Notice that you are required to attend before the Judge in Chambers, at the Central Office, Royal Courts of Justice, Strand, London, WC2 (*or address of district registry where judge sits in chambers*) on day the day of 19 at o'clock in the noon on the hearing of an Application by the said that AND further take Notice that it is the intention of the said to attend by Counsel (*if applicable*).'

26 Hearsay evidence (ie Civil Evidence Act notices)

(1) *Evidence such as a proof or statement*

The notice to be served on all the parties to the action (including third parties) should be set out with the style, heading, and format of a pleading (see Chapter 6, section 6) and should have a copy of the proof or statement attached.

The notice must state:

(*a*) the time, place, and circumstances of the statement or proof, by and to whom it was made, the substance of what was said, or, if material, the actual words used (ie attach a copy if possible);

(*b*) the reason why the witness cannot, or should not, attend, which can be for any one of the following reasons, *viz*, that the witness is dead, beyond the seas, unfit, cannot be found or identified, or cannot be expected to have any recollection of matters relating to its accuracy.

Any counter-notice must be served within seven days in the County Court or in the High Court twenty-one days of service of the notice and be set out in a similar form. It should formally require the witness to attend and should specifically deny any reason stated in the notice as to why the witness cannot, or should not, attend.

A summons issued in reply to a counter-notice should be issued in the usual way (see Procedural Table 1), completed as follows:

> 'FOR AN ORDER that   cannot (*or* "should not") be called as a witness at the trial of this Action, on the ground that
> AND that the costs of this Application be the   's in any event.'

(2) *Evidence such as hospital records and DSS benefit record*

The notice to be served on all the parties to the action (including third parties) should be set out with the style, heading, and format of a pleading (see Chapter 6, section 6) and have a copy of the record, etc, attached thereto.

The notice must state:

(*a*) the person who compiled the record, the duty under which it was compiled, the person who supplied the original information from which the record was compiled, persons through whom the information was supplied to the compiler and the duty under which it was supplied, and the time, place, and circumstances of the compilation;

(*b*) the reason why the compiler cannot, or should not, attend, which can be for any one of the following reasons, *viz*, that the compiler is dead, beyond the seas, unfit, cannot be found or identified, or cannot be expected to have any recollection of matters relating to its accuracy.

Any counter-notice will be similar to the one in precedent (1) above.

27 Witness Summons or subpoena

The form of witness summons or subpoena (Form N286 (county court) or High Court Oyez Form G5 or G6) is self-explanatory; however, if applying for witness summons for documents to be produced or subpoena *duces tecum* the court requires a detailed description of the documents to be produced, and the following precedents are suggested:

For a policeman or factory inspector—

'(1) official note book,
(2) rough notes taken at scene of accident,
(3) any other relevant documents,
(4) a plan or sketch plan.'

For a Job Centre official—

'all notes, memoranda, and other writing relating to the accident the subject of these proceedings.'

For a hospital administrator—

'all case notes, records, x-rays and other material relating to the treatment of the plaintiff.' (Or use the list set out in Appendix B(19) above.)

28 Consent to action being stood out of the list [High Court only]

The notice should be set out with the style, heading, and format of a pleading (see Chapter 6, section 6). It is addressed 'To the Associate' and can be signed on behalf of the other party's solicitors they have written a letter of authority. The notice should read as follows:

'We the Solicitors for the Plaintiff and Defendant respectively hereby consent to this Action being stood out of the list, with liberty to restore, on the grounds that .'

29 Notice of discontinuance

The notice should be set out with the style, heading, and format of a pleading (see Chapter 6, section 6); it has the following wording:

'TAKE NOTICE that the Plaintiff hereby wholly discontinues this Action.
[and that each party will bear their own costs (*if applicable*)].'

30 Compromise or settlement of the action

The parties should apply for an order, by consent, which embodies the agreed terms of settlement; rather than issuing an application or summons in the usual way, it is normal to draw up the actual form of order required and have this signed by solicitors for all parties. This can then be sent to the court with a request that it be initialled by the district judge or master, stamped by the court and returned to the parties. The normal form is for an order to stay the action, but with a 'Tomlin Order' attached, which allows the court to enforce the terms of settlement—

'It is ordered by Consent all further proceedings in this Action be stayed upon the terms set out below, except for the purpose of carrying those terms into effect, with liberty to apply for that purpose:
(*set out the agreed terms*) .'

Often, the stay is incorporated in an order authorising money in court to be paid to the defendant. The wording of a typical summons might be:

1 The plaintiff do accept the sum of £ in full and final satisfaction of the claim herein.
2 Credit against that sum be given to the defendant in respect of interim payments totally £ (made of £ in 199 , and as to £ in 199) the latter interim payment being paid to the plaintiff out of the monies then standing in court.
3 The sum of £ now standing in court to the credit of this action be paid out to the plaintiff's solicitors without further authority in further part satisfaction of the sum referred to in paragraph 1 hereof.
4 The balance of £ due in respect of the sum mentioned in paragraph 1 hereof be paid to the plaintiff's solicitors within 14 days.

5 The defendant do further pay to the plaintiff costs of this action to be taxed in default of agreement on the standard basis within 28 days of taxation or agreement OR
The defendant do further pay to the plaintiff costs of this action and costs incidental to the claim herein and consequent thereon, such costs being on the standard basis and agreed at £ (being £ profit cost; £ disbursements; £ VAT).
6 Any interest accrued to the monies standing in court be paid out to the defendant's solicitors without further authority.
7 Upon payment of the aforesaid sums the defendant be discharged from all further liability arising out of or in any way connected with the accident the subject matter of the plaintiff's claim.
8 The plaintiff's costs be further taxed pursuant to the Legal Aid Act 1988.
9 That there be liberty to apply for the purpose of enforcing the terms of this order.

See Procedural Table 13(*b*) for the steps needed to have the money in court paid out.

31 To change solicitors

The newly instructed solicitor should complete Oyez Form No BSl, or type out a Notice in the style, format, and layout of a pleading (see Chapter 6, section 6) as follows:

'TAKE NOTICE that of has been appointed to act as the Solicitor of the above named Plaintiff in the place of . The address for service of the above named is *(dated and signed)*.'

Certify on the back whether or not the action has been set down for trial. The Notice should be lodged and filed at the court. A copy should be sent to the other parties to the action, indorsed with the words 'TAKE NOTICE that this Notice was filed with the on the day of 19 .
(dated and signed).'

32 To transfer High Court proceedings to the county court

Normally, summons will be issued by the Court. When an order has been made transferring the case to the County Court, procedure is that the Plaintiff attends the filing department of the Central Office with the order and files:

(1) Copy order.
(2) Statement of the names and address of the parties and their solicitors.
(3) Copies of any pleadings served.
(4) Copy of any notice of payment into court.
(5) Statement of the index numbers of any affidavits already filed.

The Court will then send these documents (plus the Writ, acknowledgement of service, and any orders) to the County Court.

This procedure should not be confused with the situation in which one of the parties (or both parties) wants the action transferred to the County Court because it has become clear that it is not suitable for the jurisdiction of the High Court (usually because it has become clear that the case is worth considerably less than originally envisaged). If both parties consent, then it can be by consent summons (see Procedural Table 2); it can be obtained through the post. The wording of the summons and Order will be (by consent) 'that this action be transferred to County Court sitting at under s 40 County Courts Act 1984 and that the costs of this application be costs in the cause'. Once the Order has been made follow procedural steps set out above.

33 Legal aid: Notice of Issue and Revocation/Discharge

The Notice should be typed out in the form of a pleading (see p 49) with the heading of the action, and the names of the parties, etc.

A Notice of Issue will read:

'TAKE NOTICE that a Legal Aid Certificate No dated the day of 199 has been issued in Area No to in connection with the following proceedings:

TAKE further notice that, in consequence thereof, the Plaintiff in these proceedings is and has been from that date an assisted person.
(*Signed and dated*) .'

With a Notice of Amendment, Discharge, or Revocation, the certificate will be similar. Set out the heading in the usual way and then the main body of the form will be:

'TAKE NOTICE that a Legal Aid Certificate dated the day of 199 issued to the above named Plaintiff has, on the been [amended] [discharged] [revoked].

[The amendment provides: that the certificate shall [not] extend to the following proceedings:

[*Signed and dated*) .'

Appendix D

Procedural Tables

Contents

1 Issuing proceedings in county court
2 Issuing a writ
3 Obtaining an order: by application or summons
4 Obtaining an order: by consent application or summons
5 Obtaining an order: *ex parte* application
6 Appealing district judge or master's order to judge in chambers
7 Entering judgment pursuant to an order
8 Entering judgment when no defence
9 Assessment of damages (after judgment)
10 Entering judgment after trial by judge
11 Preparing an affidavit
12 Paying money into court: High Court
13 Acceptance of money paid into court: High Court
14 Paying money into court: county court
15 Acceptance of money paid into court: county court
16 Originating Summons or Application
17 Originating Summons or Application: minor approval
18 Provisional damages
19 Fixing a date for trial or setting down for trial
20 Trial bundles

* * *

1 Issuing proceedings in county court

(i) Prepare the Particulars of Claim (see Chapter 6, section 2).

(ii) Complete request for Default Summons (Form N201). This is largely self-explanatory. The first page requires name and address of both plaintiff and defendant; also name and address of next friend if plaintiff is minor. The 'amount claimed' will normally be left blank; 'issue fee' is the court fee; in the space for 'solicitor's costs' insert 'to be taxed'. Delete the request for referral to arbitration.

(iii) Send to the court (use Stock Letter 28):
(*a*) form N201;
(*b*) Particulars of Claim (one copy for the court; one copy for each defendant);
(*c*) medical report(s) (one copy for the court, one copy for each defendant);
(*d*) Statement of Special Damage (see Chapter 5) (one copy for the court, one copy for each defendant);
(*e*) court fee. Will normally be £43 (less, in unlikely event of claim not exceeding £500);
(*f*) legal aid certificate (if plaintiff legally aided). Court will also serve notice of legal aid certificate on the defendant, so include this as well;
(*g*) if plaintiff is a person under a disability, include next friend's authority (see Precedent 19(3));

(iv) Court will issue the proceedings. Summons, Particulars of Claim and all reports and notices will be served on defendant by first class post (unless personal service arranged by plaintiff). Service will be presumed to take effect seven days after posting. If proceedings to be served on defendant's solicitors, then mention this in covering letter.

(v) Court will send plaint note to plaintiff (giving number of case which must be quoted in future; also will notify of date proceedings were issued and date when service is presumed to take effect).

2 Issuing a writ

A writ can be issued by post or by personal attendance at the court office. Whichever procedure is used, you:

(*i*) complete the writ of summons (Oyez Form A1). Prepare good photocopies (no carbons); one for the court and one for each defendant. Then sign the copy for the court. Ensure that the writ contains an endorsement of value.

(*ii*) complete the Acknowledgement of Service form. This is not needed for issuing the writ; it is only needed when serving the writ (but it is convenient to complete it at the same time as preparing the writ). There must be one form for each defendant; there is no need to supply a copy for the court. Check that the form is completed correctly (ie division; district registry if applicable; names of parties as on the writ; name and address of solicitor issuing the writ). The form is not produced when issuing the writ and is not stamped by the court.

(a) Issuing by post

1 Send stock letter 29 to DR or Action Department, Postal Section, RCJ, Strand, London WC2. Ensure that all the necessary documents are enclosed together with the writ fee of £70. The cheque should be made payable to 'HM Paymaster General'.

2 Court officer will:
(*a*) allocate an action number which will be marked on all the documents;
(*b*) seal each copy of the writ in red;

(*c*) retain the copy of the writ signed by the solicitor, to be placed in the court's file;
(*d*) stamp the original writ with the word 'original'. This is now the original writ to be retained throughout the action by you, as plaintiff;
(*e*) post original and copy writs (save for copy retained by court) to you.

Note that postal issuing is at the risk of the solicitor. Accordingly a writ should be issued personally if a limitation period is about to expire.

(b) Issuing in person

1 Plaintiff attends writ room or district registry, with:
(*a*) original writ plus copy for court (signed by the solicitor) and copy for each defendant;
(*b*) fee of £70.

2 Court officer will:
(*a*) allocate an action number which will be marked on all the documents;
(*b*) seal each copy of the writ in red;
(*c*) retain the copy of the writ signed by the solicitor, to be placed in the court's file;
(*d*) stamp the original of the writ with the word 'original'. This is now the original writ to be retained throughout the action by you, as plaintiff;
(*e*) hand back to you all the documents (save for copy retained by court).

3 Obtaining an order: by application or summons

This procedural table explains how to issue an application or summons, and how to obtain an order after an interlocutory hearing. There are, however, two other alternatives:

- *Consent order:* if the other side will consent to the order being made, then the procedure is simplified. Use Procedural Table 4, not this procedural table.
- *Ex parte application:* a few orders can be obtained *ex parte*. A simplified procedure applies; use Procedural Table 5 not this procedural table.

(a) County court

(i) Prepare Notice of Application with a copy for each party to the action using Form N244. Refer to Chapter 9, section 2 for general advice on preparing a notice of application. Use the appropriate precedent for the order sought, using precedents in Appendix C. Endorse the application with a time estimate.

(ii) Apply to the court by post to issue the application. There is no fee. Inform the court if the hearing is likely to take more than five minutes.

(iii) Court officer will:
(*a*) insert a return date for hearing the application;
(*b*) return one copy of the application to you endorsed with the hearing date;
(*c*) serve the application on the other parties (unless you have requested that the application be returned to you for personal service).

(iv) Draft and swear any affidavit that is to be used in support. File a copy with the court together with a further copy for each party which they will serve. Alternatively you may serve the other party direct. For the style and layout of an affidavit (and in particular the details that go on the front and back page) see Procedural Table 11.

(v) If you requested the pages to be returned to you for service then serve a copy of the notice of application (and any affidavit) on all other parties, not less than two days before the hearing of the application.

(vi) Parties attend before the district judge on hearing of the application. The district judge will read the affidavit, listen to the arguments of both parties and make the order.

(vii) The court will draw up the order and serve it on all parties.

(b) High Court

(i) Prepare summons applying for order, with copy for each party to the action. Oyez Form S1A can be used (SlB for DR cases) or a typed copy. Refer to Chapter 9, section 2 for general advice on preparing the form of summons. Insert appropriate precedent for the order sought, using precedents in Appendix C. If a master has been assigned to the action, insert that master's name; if this is the first summons in the action no master will have been assigned so leave that part of the form blank.

(ii) Apply to the court for the summons to be issued. There is a £10 fee. If the hearing of the summons is likely to take more than 20 minutes, then a special appointment will be needed (complete the form in Precedent 6). The summons can be issued either by post or in person:
By post—This is the usual way of issuing a summons.
Send the following documents to the Action Department, Postal Section, Central Office, Royal Courts of Justice, Strand, London WC2, or to the DR:
(*a*) letter requesting that summons be issued; and £10 fee.
(*b*) top copy summons (no need to send a copy).
In person—Attend Action Department or DR, with top copy summons (no copy needed).

(iii) Court officer will:
(*a*) insert a return date for the hearing of the application;
(*b*) assign the action to a particular master if it is the first summons in the action;
(*c*) stamp the summons and return it to you (by post if the application was made by post).

(iv) Draft and swear any affidavit that is to be used in support. The affidavit need not be filed with the court, since it will be handed to the master at the hearing of the application, and then returned to you for filing. For the style and layout of an affidavit (and, in particular, the details that go on the front and back page) see Procedural Table 11.

(v) Serve the copy summons (and any affidavit) on all other parties to the action, not less than two clear days before the return date.

(vi) Parties attend before the master on hearing of the application. Hand the stamped summons and a set of the pleadings to the master, along with any affidavit in support. The master will listen to the arguments of both sides and indorse the order on the stamped summons; he will then hand it back to you with the other documents.

(vii) Draw up the order (even if the order made was not as you requested). Oyez Form H2 can be used (H2A if DR case), and insert the appropriate precedent of order, from Appendix C. See Chapter 9 for general advice on drawing up the order. Note that there are a few orders that do not have to be drawn up.

(viii) If an affidavit is to be included in the order, take the order to the Action Department (Filing Department), where it will be indorsed on the back with the index number of the affidavit and returned to you.

(ix) Ask the court to draw up the order. No fee is payable.
This is usually done by post, although it can be done by personal attendance:
By post—Send the following documents to the Action Department, Postal Section, Central Office, Royal Courts of Justice, Strand, London WC2, or to the DR:
(*a*) letter requesting that order be drawn up;
(*b*) the top copy (stamped) summons, initialled and dated by the master;
(*c*) proposed form of order, plus copy (not a carbon copy);
(*d*) any affidavit that was used in support of the application, plus confirmation on the backsheet that it has been filed with the court.
In person—Attend Action Department, or DR and lodge:
(*a*) the top copy (stamped) summons, initialled and dated by the master;
(*b*) proposed form of order, and copy (not a carbon copy);
(*c*) any affidavit that was used in support of the application, plus confirmation on the backsheet that it has been filed with the court.

(x) The court officer will:
(*a*) approve the draft order;
(*b*) initial and seal the original and copy order;
(*c*) file copy order and enter it in the Cause Book;
(*d*) return the original order to you (by post if the application was made by post).

(xi) Serve copy order by post on other parties to the action.

4 Obtaining an order: by consent application or summons

If the other side will consent to the order being sought, then it may be possible to issue a consent application or summons. If the other side will not consent, then follow the steps set out in Procedural Table 3. Remember that a few orders can be obtained by *ex parte* application—in which case, use Procedural Table 5.
Is court approval needed for the consent summons? Most consent orders can be obtained without the need to go before a master or district judge. But, this is not always the case. In certain instances (eg infant approval, and out of time acceptance of money paid into court) the court's approval must be obtained. This means attending before the court.

There is no need to obtain the court's approval if the consent application or summons:

- involves settlement of the case (eg consent Tomlin Order)
- pays money out of court
- Time Summons
- transfers case to county court (but permission is needed for a transfer from county court to High Court)
- gives judgment with damages to be assessed
- sets aside judgment in default
- relates to cost.

If the order is in the list, follow the procedure in *(b)* below. But, if the order does not come within any of these categories (for instance if it is infant approval; interim payment; interrogatories) then the order must be approved by the court—follow the procedure in (*a*) below.

(a) When the court must approve the consent application or summons

(i) Prepare application or summons applying for order, with copy for each party to the action. Refer to Chapter 9, section 2 for general advice on preparing the form of application or summons. Insert appropriate precedent for the order sought, using precedents in Appendix C. The wording on the application or summons will say 'that by consent . . .'. Note that many solicitors do not bother to prepare an application or summons if it is a consent order. Instead, they prepare the consent order straight away (ie step (v) below) on the basis that the court will almost certainly approve the order as sought. The court will normally accept this practice.

(ii) Send top copy application or summons to the other parties for them to indorse their consent on the application or summons. They should write 'We consent to an order on the terms set out herein, signed . . . solicitor for . . .'. This should be inserted in the margin of the application or summons. Note, once again, that many solicitors dispense with a draft application or summons—they simply forward a draft order to the other parties, for the indorsement to be marked on.

(A) *County court*

(iii) Attend before the district judge who will read the order (and any affidavit in support) and consider whether to make it. The district judge can order both parties to attend or may make the order straight away.

(iv) Once the court has made the order, it will arrange to draw it up and serve it on all parties.

(B) *High Court*

(iii) Attend before the master assigned, or the practice master, who can then order both parties to attend. Alternatively, he may make the order straight away.

(iv) The master makes the order by indorsing it on the summons, or draft order, which he then returns to the applicant.

(v) Draw up the order. Use Oyez Form H2 (H2A if DR case) and insert appropriate precedent of order, in Appendix C. If you dispensed with preparing a draft summons, and instead had a draft order indorsed by the parties and approved by the master, then obviously there is no need to redraw the draft order. This step can therefore be skipped.

(vi) If an affidavit is to be included in the order, take the order to the Action Department (Filing Department), Room 126 (or DR) where it will be indorsed on the back with the index number of the affidavit and returned to you.

(vii) Ask the court to draw up the order. No fee is payable. This is usually done by post, although it can be done by personal attendance:
By post—Send the following documents to the Action Department, Postal Section, Central Office, Royal Courts of Justice, Strand, London

WC2, or to the DR:
(*a*) letter requesting that order be drawn up;
(*b*) the top copy (stamped) summons, initialled and dated by the master with proposed form of order and copy (not a carbon copy). If you did not bother to issue a draft summons, but had a draft order indorsed by the other parties and initialled by the master, then simply enclose that draft order, with copy;
(*c*) any affidavit that was used in support of the application, plus confirmation on the backsheet that it has been filed with the court.
In person—Attend Action Department or DR and lodge:
(*a*) the top copy (stamped) summons, initialled and dated by the master with proposed form of order and copy (not a carbon copy). If you did not bother to issue a draft summons, but had a draft order indorsed by the other parties and initialled by the master, then produce that draft order, with copy;
(*b*) any affidavit that was used in support of the application, plus confirmation on the backsheet that it has been filed with the court.

(viii) The court officer will:
(*a*) initial and seal the original and copy order;
(*b*) file copy order and enter it in the Cause Book;
(*c*) return the original order to you (by post if the application was made by post).

(ix) Serve copy order by post on other parties to the action.

(b) When the court need not approve the consent order

(A) *County court*

(i) Prepare Notice of Application with a copy for each party to the action using Form N244. Refer to Chapter 9, section 2 for general advice on preparing a Notice of Application. Use the appropriate precedent for the order sought using precedents in Appendix C. The wording on the application will say 'by consent'. Note that many solicitors do not bother to prepare an application if it is a consent order. Instead they prepare the consent order straight away on the basis that the court will almost certainly approve the order as sought. The court will normally accept this practice and it is recommended.

(ii) Send top copy of the application or order for the other parties for them to endorse their consent to the application. They should write 'we consent to an order to the above terms. Signed. . . . .Solicitor for. . . . .'
Note once again that many solicitors dispense with the draft Application: they simply forward a draft order to the other parties for the endorsement to be marked on it.

(iii) Send the signed application or signed consent order to the court with a request that it be sealed by the court.

(iv) The court will stamp the order and arrange a copy of it to be served on all parties.

(B) *High Court*

(i) Prepare summons applying for order, with copy for each party to the action. Oyez Form S1A can be used (SIB for DR cases) or a typed copy. Refer to Chapter 9 for general advice on preparing the form of summons. Insert appropriate precedent for the order sought, using precedents in Appendix C. If a master has been assigned to the action, insert his name; if this is the first summons in the action no master will have been assigned so leave that part of the form blank. The wording on the summons will say 'that by consent . . . '. Note that many solicitors do not bother to prepare a draft summons if it is a consent order. Instead, they prepare the consent order straight away (ie step 3 below) on the basis that the master will almost certainly approve the order as sought. The court will normally accept this practice and it is recommended.

(ii) Send top copy summons to the other parties for them to indorse their consent to the summons. They should write 'We consent to an order on the terms set out herein, signed . . . solicitor for . . .'. This should be inserted in the margin of the summons. Note, once again, that many solicitors dispense with a draft summons—they simply forward a draft order to the other parties, for the indorsement to be marked on.

(iii) Draw up the order. Use Oyez Form H2 (H2A if DR case) and insert appropriate precedent of order, in Appendix C. If you dispensed with preparing a draft summons, and instead had a draft order indorsed by the parties and approved by the master, then obviously there is no need to redraw the draft order. This step can therefore be skipped.

(iv) If an affidavit is to be included in the order, take the order to the Action Department (Filing Department), Room 126 (or DR) where it will be indorsed on the back with the index number of the affidavit and returned to you.

(v) Ask the court to draw up order. No fee is payable. This is usually done by post, although it can be done by personal attendance:

By post—Send the following documents to the Action Department, Postal Section, Central Office, Royal Courts of Justice, Strand, London WC2, or to the DR:

(*a*) letter requesting that order be drawn up;

(*b*) the top copy (stamped) summons, initialled and dated by the master with proposed form of order and copy (not a carbon copy). If you did not bother to issue a draft summons, but had a draft order indorsed by the other parties and initialled by the master, then simply enclose that draft order, with copy;

(*c*) any affidavit that was used in support of the application, plus confirmation on the backsheet that it has been filed with the court.

In person—Attend Action Department or DR and lodge:

(*a*) the top copy (stamped) summons, initialled and dated by the master with proposed form of order and copy (not a carbon copy). If you did not bother to issue a draft summons, but had a draft order indorsed by the other parties and initialled by the master, then produce that draft order, with copy;

(*b*) any affidavit that was used in support of the application, plus confirmation on the backsheet that it has been filed with the court.

(vi) The court officer will:

(*a*) initial and seal the original and copy order;

(*b*) file copy order and enter it in the Cause Book;

(c) return the original order to you (by post if the application was made by post).

(vii) Serve copy order by post on other parties to the action.

5 Obtaining an order: *ex parte* application

For a list of the occasions when an application can be made *ex parte,* see Chapter 9.

(a) *County court*

(i) Issue a Notice of Application in the ordinary form using N244. Refer to Chapter 9, section 2 for general advice on preparing an *ex parte* application. Use the appropriate precedent for the order sought using precedents in Appendix C. Endorse the application with a time estimate.

(ii) Draft and swear any affidavit that is to be used in support. For the style and layout of an affidavit (and in particular the details that go on the front and back page) see Procedural Table 11.

(iii) Apply to the court to make an order either by post or in person.

By post:

Send the court the following documents:

(*a*) Letter requesting that the order be made;

(*b*) Notice of application;

(*c*) Sworn affidavit in support. The district judge will make the order and the court officer will file the affidavit, draw up the order and send a copy to you and, if requested, to the other party or will return both copies to you for service.

In Person

(*a*) Apply to the court by post to issue the application for a hearing date (ask for an early hearing date if the matter is urgent) and inform them that the application is *ex parte*. Send a copy of the affidavit. The court officer will insert a return date for the hearing of the application. You should then attend on that hearing date and argue the matter before the district judge. The district judge will make the order and the court officer will draw up the order sought and serve it on all parties (or on you to serve on the other parties if you have requested this).

(b) High Court

(1) Swear and stamp any affidavit that has to be sworn in support of the application. There is no form of summons to be used when seeking an *ex parte* order; there is no fee payable.

(2) Apply for order either by post or in person:

By post:

Send the following documents to the Action Department, Postal Section Central Office, Royal Courts of Justice, Strand, London WC2 (or to the DR);

(*a*) letter requesting that order be made;

(*b*) sworn affidavit in support;

(*c*) draft order, plus copy (not a carbon copy), completed as far as possible, leaving blank those parts of the form that must necessarily be completed by the master. Remember that it is not always necessary to draw up an order.

(3) Master will indorse order on summons.
(4) Court officer will:
(*a*) complete copy order;
(*b*) file affidavit;
(*c*) file copy order;
(*d*) seal order;
(*e*) send sealed order to you.
In person:
(i) Leave affidavit with Master's Secretaries' Department.
(ii) Master will indorse order on the affidavit.
(iii) Collect indorsed affidavit from Masters' Secretaries' Department.
(iv) Draw up the order (if necessary) as if it was an order made by way of summons (see Procedural Table 1, steps (ix)-(xi) above).

6 Appealing district judge or master's order to judge in chambers

(a) County court

(i) Prepare Notice of Appeal using Precedent 25.
(ii) The notice must be filed with the court and served on the opposite party within five days of the order appealed from or such further time as the judge will allow. The appeal can be lodged by post or in person. Send to the chief clerk of the county court by following:
(*a*) Letter requesting that Notice of Appeal be filed. Also give an estimate of the length of the hearing.
(*b*) Notice of Application for Appeal.
(iii) Serve the Notice of Appeal on all other parties within five days of the order appealed from (even though you do not have a hearing date for the application).
(iv) The court office will insert return date for the hearing of the appeal before the judge and will serve it on all of the parties at least two days before the return date.
(v) The parties attend before the judge in chambers. The appeal will be in the form of a rehearing with you (as appellant) opening the case; further affidavits may be admitted.
(vi) The judge will make the order and arrange to draw it up and have it served on all parties.

(b) High Court

(i) Prepare a Notice of Appeal (Oyez Form B56 can be used, or type out Precedent 25).
(ii) Notice must be issued within five days of order that is being appealed. Appeal can be lodged by post, or in person.
By post—Send to Action Department, Postal Section, Central Office Royal Courts of Justice, Strand, London WC2, or to the appropriate DR appeal court:
(*a*) letter requesting that Notice of Appeal be lodged. Also, give an estimate of the length of the hearing;
(*b*) solicitor's cheque for £15 made payable to 'HM Paymaster General';
(*c*) Notice of Appeal, plus a signed copy (not a carbon copy);
In person—Attend Action Department, or appropriate DR appeal court, with documents (*b*) and (*c*) above, together with certificate stating

estimated length of the hearing (no prescribed form—letter will do).

(iii) Court office will insert return date for hearing of appeal. In London, this will usually be in the ordinary list, on Tuesday and Thursday mornings (10.30 am if counsel; 12 noon non-counsel). But, if application is likely to last more than 30 minutes it will be given a special appointment. This is a floating list (no fixed dates) but parties will generally be given at least seven days notice before hearing. In practice, you may have the Notice of Appeal returned to you with a date (in the ordinary list) inserted. If the hearing is likely to last more than 30 minutes send a copy to the other side, and get them to consent to the matter being transferred to the special appointment list. The court should then be notified. The hearing will be taken out of the general list. Solicitors should then get counsels' clerks to liaise as to convenient dates; counsels' clerks should then contact the Action Department direct.

(iv) Serve copy notice on other parties to the action at least two clear days (three days in DR case) before the return date.

(v) Parties attend before judge in chambers. Appeal will be listed in chambers cause list and in daily cause list. The appeal will be in the form of a rehearing with you (as appellant) opening the case; further affidavits may be admitted.

(vi) Judge will indorse his order on the Notice of Appeal, and return this to you.

(vii) Draw up order as though it was a master's (but use Oyez Form H1). Order is drawn up either by postal application or by personal attendance; see steps (ix), (x) and (xi) in Procedural Table 1.

7 Entering judgment pursuant to an order

(a) County court

(i) Where defendant is debarred from defending altogether or the whole of the defence is struck out the plaintiff may have judgment entered for the amount of the claim and costs on filing a request. This is very unusual in the county court. File form N234 (Request for Interlocutory Judgment for Damages to be Assessed).

(ii) Send this to the court with a request that they draw up the judgment and serve it on all parties (there is no fee).

(iii) See Procedural Table 9 for how to get damages assessed.

(b) High Court

(i) (i) As plaintiff, you draw up judgment in duplicate. For interlocutory judgment, with damages to be assessed, use Precedent No 3 (modify, so refers to master's order), or Oyez Form D12. The draft can be left with the Judgment Room in the Action Department for approval.

(ii) Attend Judgment Room with:
(*a*) master's indorsed order on summons;
(*b*) judgment and copy;
(*c*) pleadings;
(*d*) original writ.

(iii) The court officer will:
(*a*) seal judgment and copy judgment;

(*b*) file original judgment and pleadings;
(*c*) return copy judgment and master's copy;
(*d*) enter judgment in Cause Book.
No fee is payable.

(iv) Serve judgment on other side.

(v) Judgment will have been interlocutory with damages to be assessed. See Procedural Table 7, below, for how to get the damages assessed.

8 Entering judgment when no defence

(a) County court

(i) If the only dispute is as to *quantum* the defendant may fail to file a defence. In those circumstances you should complete Form N234 requesting judgment against the defendant by default for damages to be assessed and costs.

(ii) The court office will draw up the order and judgment and arrange to serve it on all parties.

(iii) See Procedural Table 9 below for how to get the damages assessed.

(b) High Court

(i) Request court to enter judgment.
If the only dispute is as to *quantum*, the defendant may file an Acknowledgment of Service, but complete it without giving the necessary notice of intention to defend or may fail to serve a defence. In such a case, interlocutory judgment can be entered with damages to be assessed. This can be done by post, or in person.
By post:
Send to Action Department, Postal Section, Central Office, Royal Courts of Justice, Strand, London WC2, or to the appropriate DR:
(*a*) original writ:
(*b*) the Acknowledgment of Service form;
(*c*) judgment (and copy—not carbon copy).
In person:
Attend Judgment Room in the Action Department (Rooms 119 and 129) with:
(*a*) original writ;
(*b*) the Acknowledgment of Service form;
(*c*) judgment (and copy—not carbon copy).

(ii) The court office will:
(*a*) seal judgment and copy judgment;
(*b*) file original judgment;
(*c*) enter judgment in Cause Book;
(*d*) return copy judgment (with writ and acknowledgment of service form). This will be done by post, if the application was made by post.
No fee is payable.

(iii) Serve judgment on other side.

(iv) Judgment will have been interlocutory with damages to be assessed. See Procedural Table 9 below, for how to get the damages assessed.

9 Assessment of damages (after judgment)

(a) County court

(i) Apply by Notice of Application to the plaintiff to fix a date for such assessment. Give a time estimate and state dates that you will be unavailable.

(ii) The court will fix a date for the application (which will be held before a district judge) and will give the defendant at least seven days notice of the hearing of the assessment.

(iii) After the hearing of the assessment the district judge will make the order and the court will draw it up and serve it on all parties.

(b) High Court

(i) The appointment can be obtained through the post, or by personal attendance at the court.
By post:
Send to the Action Department, RCJ, Strand, London WC2:
(*a*) letter requesting special appointment for assessment of damages;
(*b*) photocopy of the judgment sealed by the court, or a plain copy (or photocopy) certified by the solicitor to be a true copy;
(*c*) fee of £15. Cheques should be payable to 'HM Paymaster General';
(*d*) Special Appointment form (use Precedent 5);
Court sends notice of appointment to application.
In person:
Attend DR or Queen's Bench Masters' Secretaries' Dept with documents (*b*), (*c*) and (*d*) above. Court officer will impress a form of appointment on the copy judgment. Take the form to the master to whom action has been assigned, for date of appointment to be inserted.

(ii) Serve copy notice of appointment on other parties to the action (at least seven days' notice).

(iii) After the hearing of the appointment, the master will indorse his order on the copy judgment.

(iv) Attend court (or DR) with copy judgment. The amount of damages will be inserted in the order for judgment at the Judgment Section.

10 Entering judgment after trial by judge

(a) County court

The county court will draw up the order and arrange to serve it on all parties.

(b) High Court

(i) Associate draws up the certificate of judgment.

(ii) The associate's certificate, pleadings and exhibits are:
(*a*) in London cases: sent by the Crown Office and Associate's Department to the party entitled to enter judgment; or
(*b*) in DR cases: collected from the court officer immediately after the trial by the party entitled to enter judgment.

(iii) Judgment is drawn up in duplicate (Oyez Form D11 can be used). Draft can be left with Action Department (Judgment Room: A–K: Room 119 and L–Z: 129) for approval.

(iv) Attend Judgment Room with:
(*a*) judgment and copy;
(*b*) associate's certificate;
(*c*) pleadings;

(*d*) original writ;
(*e*) list of exhibits.

(v) The court officer will:
(*a*) seal judgment and copy;
(*b*) file judgment, associate's certificate and pleadings;
(*c*) return copy judgment;
(*d*) enter copy judgment in Cause Book.

No fee is payable.

(vi) Serve copy judgment on other side.

11 Preparing an affidavit

The courts are particular about the form in which affidavits are presented to them. You should ensure that:

- each affidavit (and each exhibit) is marked on the top right hand corner, of the first page, with a summary. The summary should include the party on whose behalf it is filed; the initials and surname of the person making the affidavit; the number of the affidavit being sworn by that person; the date when it was sworn. For instance:
  'Plt; JM Pritchard; First; 21.1.93'
  '2nd Defndt; JM Pritchard; Third; 28.5.93'
  Make sure this appears in the top right hand corner of the first page of every affidavit and every exhibit and on the backsheet.
- do not use plastic bindings. Staples are frowned upon (but sometimes accepted); ideally, the courts like green binding.
- do not exhibit original documents; good photocopies will do. If correspondence is being exhibited, then put it into one bundle (ie not several different exhibits) and make sure that they are in chronological order—earliest letters at the top. Number the pages (the number should go in the centre bottom). If the bundle is lengthy, then the front page should include an index.
- the exhibits should be numbered sequentially, eg if your first affidavit has exhibits 1–3 then the first exhibit to the second affidavit by the same deponent will be numbered 4.

12 Paying money into court: High Court

Payment in can be either by post or by personal attendance at court.

By personal attendance

(i) Defendant attends Court Funds Office, (or attends the DR) with;
(*a*) Request for Lodgment of money in court. Use CFO Form 100, printed in the White Book, Vol 2, para 1202;
(*b*) cash, cheque, or banker's draft, in favour of 'Accountant General of the Supreme Court';
(*c*) copy writ;
(*d*) Notice of Payment In (Form 23 in Appendix A of the White Book) which will be served on the plaintiff;
(*e*) if the payment in is made pursuant to an order, a copy of the order;

(ii) The Court Funds Office will stamp the Notice of Payment In and this will serve as a receipt since it is handed back to the defendant. In addition the defendant is given a receipt.

(iii) Defendant sends stamped Notice of Payment In to the plaintiff and copy to other defendants.

(iv) Plaintiff sends written acknowledgment to defendant within two days of receipt of the Notice of Payment In.

(v) The defendant can increase the amount of the payment in by repeating the above procedure.

By post

(i) Defendant sends to the DR, or the Court Funds Office, RCJ, Strand London WC2 (can be sent to RCJ even if DR case):
(*a*) Request for Lodgment of money in court. Use CFO Form 100, printed in Vol 2 of the White Book, para 1202;
(*b*) cheque or banker's draft in favour of 'Accountant General of the Supreme Court';
(*c*) copy writ;
(*d*) notice of payment in (Form 23 in Appendix A of the White Book; Oyez Form BS) which will be served on the plaintiff;
(*e*) if the payment in is made pursuant to an order, a copy of the order;
(*f*) sae for return of documents and receipt.

(ii) On receipt by the court, the postal application will be dealt with in the same way as a personal lodgment made on the same date. If the remittance is by way of a cheque, the date of the lodgment will be the date that notification of clearance of the cheque is received by the court. A banker's draft will be treated as cash and will not need to be cleared.

(iii) The Court Funds Office will stamp the Notice of Payment In and this will serve as a receipt since it is handed back to the defendant. In addition the defendant is given a receipt for its own use.

(iv) Defendant sends stamped Notice of Payment In to the plaintiff and copy to other defendants.

(v) Plaintiff sends written acknowledgment to defendant within two days of receipt of the Notice of Payment In.

(vi) The defendant can increase the amount of the payment in by repeating the above procedure.

There is no need for the defendant to ask for the money to be put on deposit—it goes on automatically after 21 days.

13 Acceptance of money paid into court: High Court

(a) within 21 days of payment in

(i) Plaintiff sends notice of acceptance Form 24, App A, the White Book, to all defendants within 21 days of receipt of the notice of payment in. If action set down for trial, send copy to clerk of the lists. Form is typed out in style of a pleading, is headed 'Notice of Acceptance' and reads 'take notice that the plaintiff accepts the sum of £
paid into the court by the Defendant in satisfaction of the cause(s) of action in respect of which it was paid in and in respect of which the Plaintiff claims [against that defendant] [and abandons the other causes of action in respect of which the Plaintiff claims in

the action]. Dated .'

(ii) Ask for money to be paid out of court. Write to (or attend) Court Funds Office:

By post

(*a*) stamped Notice of Payment In (ie the form received from the court);
(*b*) copy of notice of acceptance. If action set down for trial, enclose second copy (state in letter action is set down, and second copy is for Crown Office);
(*c*) request for payment out. This will be on CFO Form 201, the White Book, para 1210;
(*d*) two copies of the payment schedule. Use Form 200 the White Book, para 1209;
(*e*) original receipt given to defendant.

(iii) Cheque is sent to plaintiff.
(iv) Plaintiff can tax costs four days after the date of payment out.
(v) Plaintiff can enter judgment for taxed costs two days after judgment:

But

(i) If payment in is not made by all the defendants, the plaintiff must:
(*a*) serve notice of discontinuance (Oyez Form B19, or Precedent 30) on other defendants and obtain their consent to payment out; or
(*b*) issue a summons for an order that the money be paid out (see below).

(ii) If payment out can only be made with the leave of the court (ie minor plaintiff, more than one plaintiff in fatal accident claim, or if hearing of the action has begun) the plaintiff should apply to the trial judge or issue a summons for application to the master (see below).

(b) more than 21 days after payment in

(i) Plaintiff prepares draft summons (eg use wording of Precedent 32). This will be for settlement of the action (eg stay of proceedings; payment out; taxation of costs—unless figures have been agreed, etc);
(ii) Issue consent summons. Note that the court's approval will not be required for this summons (unless minor case), and so the consent order can be obtained by post. Refer to Procedural Table 4, for the steps to be taken.
(iii) Once the order has been made, the plaintiff can have the money paid out. Plaintiff posts to court funds office:
(*a*) stamped Notice of Payment In (ie form received from court);
(*b*) consent order (initialled by master). If action set down for trial, enclose second copy of consent order (state in letter action is set down, and second copy is for Crown Office);
(*c*) request for payment out. This will be on CFO Form 201, the White Book, para 1210;
(*d*) two copies of the payment schedule. Use Form 200, the White Book, para 1209.

14 Paying money into court: county court

1 Defendant posts to county court (or attends in person);
(*a*) solicitor's cheque or draft, in favour of HMPG;

(*b*) letter (quoting plaint number, etc) requesting that money be paid into court in satisfaction of plaintiff's claim;

(*c*) stamped addressed envelope.

2 Court will:

(*a*) make note in court record;

(*b*) send receipt to defendant;

(*c*) send Notice of Payment In to all parties.

3 The court will place the money on a basic account earning interest (currently 8 per cent) if it is not accepted within 21 days.

15 Acceptance of money paid into court: county court

(a) Within 21 days of payment in

(i) Plaintiff sends Notice of Acceptance to all defendants (and copy to court) within 21 days of receipt of Notice of Payment In. No prescribed form; letter will often be accepted, but it is preferable to type out a notice as though it was a pleading (ie with heading of action, etc stating it is 'notice of acceptance' and reading 'take notice that the plaintiff hereby accepts the sum of £ paid into court by the defendant on the day of 199 in full satisfaction of the claim herein. And further take notice that the plaintiff requires costs to be taxed. Dated

(ii) Court will arrange payment out of money.

(b) More than 21 days after payment in

If the money is accepted more than 21 days later (or if plaintiff is minor; if several defendants and claim against other is not abandoned), then court consent is needed.

(i) Plaintiff prepares Notice of Application (Form N244). For wording, see Precedents 22 and 32.

(ii) Send Notice of Application to court (copy for court, plus copy for each defendant). Court may agree to make consent order (through post) if other side's consent is endorsed, and if application relates to acceptance out of time. They will not do this if it is infant approval.

(iii) Parties attend before district judge who makes order.

(iv) Court pays money to plaintiff's solicitor.

16 Originating Application or Summons

(a) County Court Originating Application

This procedural table sets out the steps to be taken for an Ordinary Originating Application (eg to get discovery of medical records before proceedings are commenced). There is a different procedure in an Infant Approval Originating Application (refer to Procedural Table 17 below).

(i) *Plaintiff prepares a request for Originating Application*
There is no official form provided but Form N203 could be used amended as appropriate. It is also helpful to complete an Originating Application (Form N393) and insert the appropriate wording of the application. In medical negligence (for disclosure of records) see precedent.

(ii) File with the court the following:
Documents
(*a*) Request.

(*b*) Originating Application with as many copies as there are respondents.

(*c*) Fee made payable to Her Majesty's Paymaster General.

(*d*) Request for Applicant's Service if required.

(*e*) Addressed reply envelope (where issuing through post).

(iii) The court will issue the Originating Application and fix a return day. It will serve a copy of the application together with notice of the return day on each respondent and deliver a plaint note to the applicant.

(iv) The plaintiff swears an Affidavit in Support (if necessary). This would be needed for instance with an Application for Disclosure of Medical Notes and Records in a medical negligence case. This affidavit should be filed with the court and a copy served on the defendant at least two days before the return date. However it is better to serve it much earlier since serving an affidavit without giving the respondent a chance to reply is likely to lead to an adjournment of the entire action.

(v) The parties will attend before the district judge on the return date. The district judge will listen to the arguments of both parties, and make the order.

(vi) The court will draw up the order in the normal way and serve it on all parties.

(*b*) *High Court*

This procedural table sets out the steps to be taken for an ordinary Originating Summons (eg to get discovery of medical records before proceedings are commenced). There is a different procedure in an Infant Approval Originating Summons (refer to Procedural Table 17, below).

(i) Plaintiff prepares Originating Summons. Use Oyez Form S35, or type out the specimen printed below. Insert the appropriate wording of the summons. In medical negligence (for disclosure of records) see precedent. Alternatively use Oyez Form S35.

(ii) Plaintiff issues Originating Summons. This can be by post or personally. Procedure is same as for issuing a writ—see Procedural Table 10 below. Fee is £70.

(iii) Originating Summons is served on the defendant who files an Acknowledgment of Service within 14 days.

(iv) Plaintiff swears affidavit in support (if necessary). This would be needed, for instance, with an application for disclosure of medical notes and records in a medical negligence case. The affidavit must be filed with the court and copy served on defendant within 14 days of Acknowledgment of Service. Defendant then has 28 days to file an affidavit (if it wants to).

(v) Plaintiff prepares Notice of Appointment (Oyez Form B67).

(vi) Plaintiff posts (or attends Summons and Order Department) with:

(*a*) original Originating Summons

(*b*) Acknowledgment of Service;

(*c*) Notice of Appointment (if hearing is likely to last more than ten minutes, then return date and time will be inserted by the master for a private hearing in his room. Otherwise, court officer will insert date in Notice of Appointment and return it to plaintiff.)

(vii) Plaintiff serves copy Notice of Appointment on defendant at least four clear days before return date.

(viii) If any party wishes to be represented by counsel that party should apply to the master for an order transferring the appointment to counsel's list, or produce the consent of all parties.

(ix) Parties attend before the master on return date. Plaintiff hands Originating Summons (and any affidavit) to master, who having listened to the arguments, indorses the order on the Originating Summons.

(x) Order is drawn up in the usual way (see Procedural Table 1, steps (vii)-(xi)).

17 Originating Summons—minor approval

(a) County court

In the county court minor approval is by way of ordinary summons. See Precedent 1 and Precedent 22A for specimen particulars of claim.

(b) High Court

(i) Plaintiff prepares Originating Summons. Refer to Precedents 21–23 for the different forms of Originating Summons to be used. Refer to Precedent 23 if it is a fatal case.

(ii) Plaintiff issues Originating Summons. This can be by post or personally. Procedure is same as for issuing a writ—see Procedural Table 10. The fee is £70. Plaintiff should lodge Consent of Next Friend, and Solicitor's Certificate (refer to Precedent 19).

(iii) Attend before Queen's Bench Master who has been assigned to the case, for appointment. The date and time of the appointment will be inserted in the Originating Summons.

(iv) Plaintiff serves Originating Summons on the defendant (at least four clear days before the return date). There is no need for the defendant to file an Acknowledgment of Service.

(v) Parties attend before the master on return date. Plaintiff hands Originating Summons to master who, having listened to the arguments, indorses the order on the Originating Summons.

(vi) Order is drawn up in the usual way (see Procedural Table 1, steps (vii)-(xi)).

18 Provisional damages

(a) Following trial

1 The judgment will have specified the deterioration (or disease) that is to be covered by the provisional damages order, and the time period during which application for further damages can be made. The associate's certificate, and the judgment will have wording to the effect 'the judge awarded to the plaintiff by way of immediate damages (. . . *set out general and special damages in usual way* . . .) upon the assumption that the plaintiff would not at a future date as a result of the act or remission giving rise to the cause of action suffer deterioration in his physical, or mental, condition of the following type . . . *specify* . . . (*or* develop the following disease, namely . . .) AND the judge further orders that if the plaintiff at a future date did so suffer such deterioration (or did so develop such disease) s/he should be entitled to apply for further damages.' The specified period within which a claim for further damages can be made will be set out

in the associate's certificate and the judgment.

2 The judge will also direct what documents are to be lodged and preserved for the case file. Normally, this will include:
- copy chief clerk's or associate's certificate
- copy judgment
- pleadings
- transcript of judge's oral judgment
- all medical reports that were before the court
- transcript of such parts of the plaintiff's own evidence as to his/her physical condition, and of the medical evidence, as the judge may think necessary.

It is for the chief clerk or associate to prepare the case file (the contents of the file are attached, as a schedule, to the certificate and the judgment). If a transcript, or other documents, are needed, then the chief clerk or associate will ask the plaintiff's solicitor to get them. Note that the judgment in a provisional damages case must always be drawn up, so that a copy can be placed in the case file.

3 The associate then forwards the case file to the court office. In the High Court a copy of the judgment goes to the Officer in Charge, Filing Department, Central Office, Royal Courts of Justice, Strand, London WC2. On the copy judgment is written 'Case File lodged in . . . (date)'.

4 There are no specific guidelines on what the plaintiff's solicitor should do to protect a client's position for the future. It is suggested that:
- the plaintiff be specifically warned of the importance of the specified time period (ie the client must apply for an extension of time within that period, or apply for further damages within that time).
- the client should be told that the solicitor will not write again with a reminder of that time period.
- the solicitor should extract from the file those parts that seem relevant to the provisional damages award (eg letters, statements, etc relating to the medical condition, and possible effect on earning capacity, etc). It would probably be advisable to put those in a separate sub-file which is marked: 'Not to be destroyed until the specified date.' It is also suggested that a lengthy covering note is put inside the file, which will simplify matters should an application be made for time to be extended, or for further damages to be awarded.
- consider diarising the case prior to the expiry of the specified time period, so that a reminder letter can be sent to the client.

(b) Provisional damages by way of consent order (not trial)

Similar procedures have to be followed if the provisional damages are agreed, by consent order, without the case going to trial.

1 Issue an application or summons (this can be by consent—unless a person under disability). Refer to Precedent 3, for specimen wording of the order, which will have to be amended to include a reference to the specified deterioration (or disease), and the specified time period—adapt the wording in the judge's order (above). Include a separate paragraph detailing the contents of the case file. This will normally be:
- copy order
- copy judgment
- copy pleadings
- an agreed statement of the fact

- agreed medical reports.

2 The plaintiff's solicitor must:

(*a*) prepare and bind the case file.

(*b*) draw up the order, and then the judgment. Copies of each must then be placed in the case file.

(*c*) the case file must then be lodged in the court office.

(*d*) a copy of the judgment should be lodged with the chief clerk in the county court, or in the High Court with the Officer in Charge, Filing Department, Central Office, Royal Courts of Justice, Strand, London WC2. On the judgment must be written 'Case file lodged in . . . (date)'.

(c) Action settled prior to commencement of proceedings

If proceedings have not been begun, it will be necessary to commence proceedings so that the provisional damage rules can apply. It is suggested that this be done by way of Originating Application or Summons. Once those proceedings have been commenced, a consent order can be sought—following the procedures set out above.

19 Fixing a date for trial or setting down for trial

(a) County court

Fixing a trial date

(i) The plaintiff should write to the defendant(s) with an estimate of the length of the trial and the number of the witnesses to be called by the plaintiff and request that the defendant agrees with such estimate and states the number of the defendant's witnesses.

(ii) Write to the chief clerk of the county court asking them to fix a date for the hearing and filing a note (if possible as agreed with the defendant) giving an estimate of the length of the trial and the number of the witnesses to be called. It is sensible also to state any dates which you wish to avoid. The plaintiff should make this request within six months of close of pleadings. If it is not made within 15 months of close of pleadings the case will automatically be struck out.

(iii) The court will fix a date for the hearing and notify all parties, giving them not less than 21 days' notice (but usually considerably more).

(iv) Within 14 days before the hearing the defendant should inform the plaintiff of documents to be included in the court bundle.

(v) Within seven days before the hearing the plaintiff should file a paginated and indexed bundle of relevant documents together with two copies of the particulars, pleadings (and request), interrogatories, witness statements (if exchanged), experts' reports and legal aid certificates. It is sensible to make separate indexed bundles for each category of documents.

(b) High Court

Setting down for trial

It is the plaintiff who sets the case down for trial. To do this you must prepare two bundles of pleadings. The full requirements are listed below but note that these must be copy documents (ie not originals). Both bundles must be in the correct order, both should be bound in the margin, with green tape or secure plastic binding and printed on A4 paper with an index. Larger bundles must be paginated.

The following documents are not required:

(i) Individual backsheets.
(ii) Legal aid certificates.
(iii) Original documents.
(iv) Notice of Intention to Set Down.
(v) Acknowledgment of Service of Writ.
(vi) Affidavits.
(vii) Letters.
(viii) Summonses.

The bundle

Note that the documents are not set out in chronological order but are bundled in the following order:

(i) Notice of Legal Aid Certificate (this may be either the first or the last document).
(ii) Writ. (with the £30 fee on setting down endorsed on the right hand side).
(iii) Statement of Claim.
(iv) Any Further and Better Particulars of a Statement of Claim. If a request has not been answered the request must be included; any interrogatories and the plaintiff's answers.
(v) The defence (if none then the reason why).
(vi) Further and Better Particulars of Defence and interrogatories as in (iv) above. If there is more than one defendant the relevant Further and Better Particulars and interrogatories should follow the defence referred to.
(vii) Reply (if any).
(viii) All Interlocutory Orders except those relating only to time, in chronological order.
(ix) Third Party Notice and Contribution Notices.
(x) Orders for Third Party Notices.
(xi) Defences to Third Party Notices.
(xii) Replies to Third Party Defences.
(xiii) A Statement of Value of the Action (in the following form: 'this action includes a claim for personal injury but may be commenced in the High Court because the value of the action for the purposes of Art 5 of the High Court and County Courts Jurisdiction Order 1991 exceeds £50,000').
(xiv) A note or, failing agreement, notes from each party of the estimated length of the trial and of the list in which the action is to be included.
(xv) The bundle should have a backsheet facing outwards on which is printed the full title of the action with the parties' solicitors' names and addresses with their telephone, fax and document exchange numbers and full reference. This is sometimes also referred to as a Statement of Parties. These documents should be lodged with the Clerk of the Lists, Room 545 for Queen's Bench actions. You should first pay the fee of £30 in Room 84-HMPG.

The master will consider the matter within seven days of setting down. The master may either order that the proceedings shall remain in the High Court for trial or direct the court to give notice in Form No PF200 or PF202 to transfer the matter to the county court.

20 Trial bundles

(a) County court

(i) Within 14 days before the hearing the defendant should inform the plaintiff of documents to be included in the court bundle.
(ii) Within seven days before the hearing the plaintiff should file a paginated and indexed bundle of relevant documents together with two copies of the particulars, pleadings (and requests), interrogatories, witness statements (if exchanged), experts' reports and legal aid certificates. It is sensible to make separate indexed bundles for each category of documents.

(b) High Court

There are now two sets of papers which may become known confusingly as 'the court bundle' that are required on setting down (see 19 above) and that are required under RSC Ord 34, r 10 which is actually given the title court bundle and is required to be lodged with the court a few days before the trial to enable the trial judge to read in advance the witness statements, experts' reports and a summary of the issues and authorities. The rules for that bundle are as follows:

(i) At least 14 days before the date fixed for the trial or, in the case of an action entered in any running list, within three weeks of the defendant receiving notice of such entry, the defendant should write to the plaintiff identifying those documents which it wishes to have included in the bundle. Normally the plaintiff would in fact write to the defendant asking whether there are any documents that they would like included.
(ii) At least two clear days before the date fixed for the hearing the plaintiff must lodge with the clerk of the list two bundles consisting of one copy of each of the following documents:
(*a*) Witness statements which have been exchanged and experts' reports which have been disclosed together with an indication of whether the contents of such documents are agreed.
(*b*) Those documents which the defendant wishes to have included in the bundle.
(*c*) Those documents which the plaintiff wishes to have included in the bundle.
(*d*) (if directed) A note by each party setting out a summary of the issues involved (unusual in personal injury cases).

Appendix E

Actuarial Tables

In 1984 HMSO published 'Actuarial tables with explanatory notes for use in personal injury and fatal accident cases'. These notes were the result of a working party comprised of actuaries and lawyers. As yet, they have no legal status in the sense that the courts are obliged to take note of them, but it does seem that the courts do have power to take note of such tables—if the judge wishes. What follows is an abbreviated version of the explanatory notes, together with the tables. In summary, the tables should be used as follows:

1 Choose the right table. There are different tables for men and women, and for:

- losses for the rest of the plaintiff's life, beyond retirement age (Tables 1 and 2);
- losses to normal retirement age (Tables 3 and 4);
- loss of pension rights from retirement age (Tables 5 and 6).

2 Choose the rate of interest. If some or all of the award will bear interest then reduce the rate of interest accordingly.

3 Use the appropriate table to find the appropriate multiplier (based on age at trial—unless fatal case, in which case it is age at death). Multiply that by the net annual loss.

4 In Tables 1 and 2 the loss or expense is assumed to begin immediately and to continue for the whole of the rest of the plaintiff's life allowing for the possibility of early death or prolonged life. ('The plaintiff' here includes the deceased in fatal accident cases.)

In Tables 3 and 4 the loss or expense is assumed to begin immediately but to continue only until the plaintiff's retirement or earlier death. The age of retirement is assumed to be 65 for men and 60 for women.

In Tables 5 and 6 it is assumed that the annual loss or annual expense will not begin until the plaintiff reaches retirement (at 65 in the case of men and 60 for women) but will then continue for the whole of the rest of his or her life. The tables make due allowance for the chance that the plaintiff may never live to reach the age of retirement.

5 To find the appropriate figure for the present value of a particular loss or expense you must first choose that table which relates to the period of loss or expense for which the individual plaintiff is to be compensated *and* to the sex of the plaintiff.

6 If for some reason the facts in a particular case do not correspond with the assumptions on which one of the tables is based (if, for instance, it is known that the plaintiff will have a different retiring age from that assumed in the table) then the tables can only be used by making an appropriate allowance for this difference; possibly with the assistance of an actuary.

7 The basis of the multipliers set out in the tables is that the lump sum will be invested and yield income (but that over the period in question the plaintiff will gradually reduce the capital sum so that at the end of the period it is exhausted). Accordingly, an essential factor in arriving at the right figure is to choose the appropriate rate of interest. The tables set out multipliers based on rates of interest ranging from 1.5 per cent to five per cent.

8 The purpose of setting out figures based upon a range of rates of interest is to enable the user to choose a rate which reflects the 'real rate of interest' that can be obtained upon the capital sum. In times of inflation high rates of interest can be obtained; these rates compensate the investor in part for the fall in the value of his capital and of the dividends he receives due to inflation. The real rate of interest may be defined as that part of the actual rate which excludes this element. It has been held that in times of stable currency, when there is little or no inflation, a return on capital of four per cent or five per cent has been usual (see *Lim* v *Camden* [1980] AC 174 and cases cited therein). However, there are now available Index-Linked Government Stocks and it is accordingly no longer necessary to speculate about either the future rates of inflation or the real rate of return obtainable on an investment. The redemption value and dividends of these stocks are adjusted from time to time so as to maintain the real value of the stock in the face of inflation. The current rates of interest on such stocks are published daily in *The Financial Times* and hitherto have fallen into the range of about 2.5 per cent to 3.5 per cent (gross). It may be thought that the return on such Index-Linked stocks is the most accurate reflection of the real rate of interest available to plaintiffs seeking the prudent investment of awards of damages. In any event, when using the tables it will be necessary to use the real rate of interest which is deemed the most appropriate.

9 In order to arrive at a true present capital value of the plaintiff's future loss or expense it will be necessary to consider whether he will have to pay a significant amount of tax on the income from his compensation. If he will pay little or no tax no adjustment of rate of interest will be required. If he will have to pay a significant percentage of that income in tax, then the rate of interest chosen to determine the present capital value of his loss or of his expense should be reduced accordingly.

10 Thus, if it is decided that the rate of interest to be used to value the loss, without allowing for tax, is (say) 3.5 per cent and the plaintiff will pay no tax, the figure of present value is to be found by using the multiplier in the column headed 3.5 per cent. If, however, he will pay 30 per cent on the income from his compensation, so that the net income he receives will be at the rate of only 70 per cent of 3.5 per cent, that is at 2.45 per cent, then the best figure is to be found in the column headed 2.5 per cent. (In some cases it may be appropriate to take a figure lying between that given in two adjoining columns; if, for instance, the net return is 2.25 per cent.) However, it should be borne in mind that as the capital is gradually exhausted the total income obtainable from the interest upon it will fall; and the rate of tax payable may therefore also fall. This may mean that the deduction to be made for tax should be a smaller percentage than the rate of tax apparently applicable at the outset.

Table 1 Multipliers for pecuniary loss for life (males)

Age at date of trial	Multiplier calculated with allowance for population mortality and rate of interest of 1.5%	2%	2.5%	3%	3.5%	4%	4.5%	5%
16	36.9	32.8	29.4	26.5	24.1	22.0	20.2	18.7
17	36.5	32.5	29.2	26.3	24.0	21.9	20.1	18.6
18	36.0	32.2	28.9	26.2	23.8	21.8	20.0	18.5
19	35.6	31.8	28.7	25.9	23.6	21.7	19.9	18.4
20	35.2	31.5	28.4	25.7	23.5	21.5	19.8	18.4
21	34.7	31.1	28.1	25.5	23.3	21.4	19.7	18.3
22	34.3	30.8	27.8	25.3	23.1	21.2	19.6	18.2
23	33.8	30.4	27.5	25.1	22.9	21.1	19.5	18.1
24	33.3	30.1	27.2	24.8	22.7	20.9	19.4	18.0
25	32.9	29.7	26.9	24.6	22.5	20.8	19.2	17.9
26	32.4	29.3	26.6	24.3	22.3	20.6	19.1	17.8
27	31.9	28.9	26.3	24.1	22.1	20.4	18.9	17.6
28	31.4	28.5	26.0	23.8	21.9	20.2	18.8	17.5
29	30.9	28.1	25.6	23.5	21.7	20.1	18.6	17.4
30	30.4	27.6	25.3	23.2	21.4	19.9	18.5	17.2
31	29.8	27.2	24.9	22.9	21.2	19.6	18.3	17.1
32	29.3	26.8	24.6	22.6	20.9	19.4	18.1	16.9
33	28.8	26.3	24.2	22.3	20.7	19.2	17.9	16.8
34	28.2	25.9	23.8	22.0	20.4	19.0	17.7	16.6
35	27.7	25.4	23.4	21.7	20.1	18.7	17.5	16.4
36	27.1	24.9	23.0	21.3	19.8	18.5	17.3	16.2
37	26.6	24.5	22.6	21.0	19.5	18.2	17.1	16.1
38	26.0	24.0	22.2	20.6	19.2	18.0	16.9	15.9
39	25.4	23.5	21.8	20.3	18.9	17.7	16.6	15.7
40	24.9	23.0	21.4	19.9	18.6	17.4	16.4	15.5
41	24.3	22.5	20.9	19.5	18.3	17.2	16.1	15.2
42	23.7	22.0	20.5	19.2	18.0	16.9	15.9	15.0
43	23.1	21.5	20.1	18.8	17.6	16.6	15.6	14.8
44	22.5	21.0	19.6	18.4	17.3	16.3	15.4	14.5
45	21.9	20.5	19.2	18.0	16.9	16.0	15.1	14.3
46	21.4	20.0	18.7	17.6	16.6	15.7	14.8	14.0
47	20.8	19.4	18.3	17.2	16.2	15.3	14.5	13.8
48	20.2	18.9	17.8	16.8	15.9	15.0	14.2	13.5
49	19.6	18.4	17.3	16.4	15.5	14.7	13.9	13.3
50	19.0	17.9	16.9	16.0	15.1	14.3	13.6	13.0
51	18.4	17.4	16.4	15.5	14.7	14.0	13.3	12.7
52	17.8	16.9	15.9	15.1	14.4	13.7	13.0	12.4
53	17.3	16.3	15.5	14.7	14.0	13.3	12.7	12.1
54	16.7	15.8	15.0	14.3	13.6	13.0	12.4	11.9
55	16.1	15.3	14.5	13.8	13.2	12.6	12.1	11.6
56	15.6	14.8	14.1	13.4	12.8	12.3	11.7	11.3
57	15.0	14.3	13.6	13.0	12.4	11.9	11.4	11.0
58	14.4	13.8	13.1	12.6	12.0	11.5	11.1	10.6
59	13.9	13.3	12.7	12.1	11.6	11.2	10.7	10.3
60	13.4	12.8	12.2	11.7	11.3	10.8	10.4	10.0
61	12.8	12.3	11.8	11.3	10.9	10.5	10.1	9.7
62	12.3	11.8	11.3	10.9	10.5	10.1	9.7	9.4
63	11.8	11.3	10.9	10.5	10.1	9.7	9.4	9.1
64	11.3	10.9	10.5	10.1	9.7	9.4	9.1	8.8
65	10.8	10.4	10.0	9.7	9.4	9.0	8.8	8.5
66	10.3	10.0	9.6	9.3	9.0	8.7	8.4	8.2
67	9.9	9.5	9.2	8.9	8.6	8.4	8.1	7.9
68	9.4	9.1	8.8	8.6	8.3	8.0	7.8	7.6
69	9.0	8.7	8.5	8.2	8.0	7.7	7.5	7.3
70	8.6	8.3	8.1	7.9	7.6	7.4	7.2	7.0

Table 2 Multipliers for pecuniary loss for life (females)

Age at date of trial	Multiplier calculated with allowance for population mortality and rate of interest of							
	1.5%	2%	2.5%	3%	3.5%	4%	4.5%	5%
16	39.4	34.8	30.9	27.7	25.0	22.7	20.8	19.1
17	39.0	34.5	30.7	27.5	24.9	22.6	20.7	19.1
18	38.6	34.2	30.5	27.4	24.8	22.5	20.6	19.0
19	38.2	33.9	30.2	27.2	24.6	22.4	20.6	18.9
20	37.8	33.5	30.0	27.0	24.5	22.3	20.5	18.9
21	37.4	33.2	29.7	26.8	24.3	22.2	20.4	18.8
22	37.0	32.9	29.5	26.6	24.2	22.1	20.3	18.7
23	36.5	32.6	29.2	26.4	24.0	22.0	20.2	18.6
24	36.1	32.2	29.0	26.2	23.8	21.8	20.1	18.6
25	35.6	31.9	28.7	26.0	23.7	21.7	20.0	18.5
26	35.2	31.5	28.4	25.8	23.5	21.5	19.8	18.4
27	34.7	31.1	28.1	25.5	23.3	21.4	19.7	18.3
28	34.2	30.8	27.8	25.3	23.1	21.2	19.6	18.2
29	33.8	30.4	27.5	25.0	22.9	21.1	19.5	18.1
30	33.3	30.0	27.2	24.8	22.7	20.9	19.3	18.0
31	32.8	29.6	26.9	24.5	22.5	20.7	19.2	17.8
32	32.3	29.2	26.6	24.3	22.3	20.6	19.0	17.7
33	31.8	28.8	26.2	24.0	22.1	20.4	18.9	17.6
34	31.3	28.4	25.9	23.7	21.8	20.2	18.7	17.5
35	30.8	28.0	25.6	23.4	21.6	20.0	18.6	17.3
36	30.3	27.6	25.2	23.2	21.4	19.8	18.4	17.2
37	29.7	27.1	24.8	22.9	21.1	19.6	18.2	17.0
38	29.2	26.7	24.5	22.6	20.9	19.4	18.1	16.9
39	28.7	26.2	24.1	22.3	20.6	19.2	17.9	16.7
40	28.1	25.8	23.7	21.9	20.3	18.9	17.7	16.6
41	27.6	25.3	23.4	21.6	20.1	18.7	17.5	16.4
42	27.1	24.9	23.0	21.3	19.8	18.5	17.3	16.2
43	26.5	24.4	22.6	21.0	19.5	18.2	17.1	16.0
44	26.0	24.0	22.2	20.6	19.2	18.0	16.8	15.8
45	25.4	23.5	21.8	20.3	18.9	17.7	16.6	15.6
46	24.9	23.0	21.4	19.9	18.6	17.4	16.4	15.4
47	24.3	22.5	21.0	19.6	18.3	17.2	16.2	15.2
48	23.7	22.1	20.6	19.2	18.0	16.9	15.9	15.0
49	23.2	21.6	20.1	18.8	17.7	16.6	15.7	14.8
50	22.6	21.1	19.7	18.5	17.4	16.3	15.4	14.6
51	22.0	20.6	19.3	18.1	17.0	16.1	15.2	14.4
52	21.5	20.1	18.8	17.7	16.7	15.8	14.9	14.1
53	20.9	19.6	18.4	17.3	16.3	15.4	14.6	13.9
54	20.3	19.1	17.9	16.9	16.0	15.1	14.4	13.6
55	19.8	18.6	17.5	16.5	15.6	14.8	14.1	13.4
56	19.2	18.1	17.0	16.1	15.3	14.5	13.8	13.1
57	18.6	17.5	16.6	15.7	14.9	14.2	13.5	12.9
58	18.0	17.0	16.1	15.3	14.5	13.8	13.2	12.6
59	17.4	16.5	15.6	14.9	14.1	13.5	12.9	12.3
60	16.8	16.0	15.2	14.4	13.7	13.1	12.5	12.0
61	16.3	15.4	14.7	14.0	13.4	12.8	12.2	11.7
62	15.7	14.9	14.2	13.6	13.0	12.4	11.9	11.4
63	15.1	14.4	13.7	13.1	12.6	12.0	11.5	11.1
64	14.5	13.9	13.2	12.7	12.1	11.7	11.2	10.8
65	13.9	13.3	12.8	12.2	11.7	11.3	10.8	10.4
66	13.4	12.8	12.3	11.8	11.3	10.9	10.5	10.1
67	12.8	12.3	11.8	11.3	10.9	10.5	10.1	9.8
68	12.3	11.8	11.3	10.9	10.5	10.1	9.8	9.4
69	11.7	11.3	10.8	10.4	10.1	9.7	9.4	9.1
70	11.2	10.8	10.4	10.0	9.7	9.3	9.0	8.8

Table 3 Multipliers for loss of earnings to pension age 65 (males)

Age at date of trial	Multiplier calculated with allowance for population mortality and rate of interest of							
	1.5%	2%	2.5%	3%	3.5%	4%	4.5%	5%
16	33.1	30.0	27.2	24.9	22.9	21.1	19.5	18.1
17	32.6	29.6	26.9	24.6	22.7	20.9	19.4	18.0
18	32.1	29.2	26.6	24.4	22.5	20.7	19.2	17.9
19	31.6	28.8	26.3	24.1	22.2	20.6	19.1	17.8
20	31.1	28.4	26.0	23.9	22.0	20.4	19.0	17.7
21	30.6	28.0	25.6	23.6	21.8	20.2	18.8	17.6
22	30.1	27.6	25.3	23.3	21.6	20.0	18.6	17.4
23	29.6	27.1	24.9	23.0	21.3	19.8	18.5	17.3
24	29.1	26.7	24.6	22.7	21.1	19.6	18.3	17.1
25	28.5	26.2	24.2	22.4	20.8	19.4	18.1	17.0
26	28.0	25.8	23.8	22.1	20.6	19.2	17.9	16.8
27	27.4	25.3	23.4	21.8	20.3	18.9	17.7	16.7
28	26.8	24.8	23.0	21.4	20.0	18.7	17.5	16.5
29	26.2	24.3	22.6	21.1	19.7	18.4	17.3	16.3
30	25.7	23.8	22.2	20.7	19.4	18.2	17.1	16.1
31	25.1	23.3	21.7	20.3	19.1	17.9	16.8	15.9
32	24.4	22.8	21.3	19.9	18.7	17.6	16.6	15.7
33	23.8	22.3	20.8	19.5	18.4	17.3	16.3	15.5
34	23.2	21.7	20.4	19.1	18.0	17.0	16.1	15.2
35	22.6	21.2	19.9	18.7	17.7	16.7	15.8	15.0
36	21.9	20.6	19.4	18.3	17.3	16.4	15.5	14.7
37	21.3	20.0	18.9	17.9	16.9	16.0	15.2	14.5
38	20.6	19.5	18.4	17.4	16.5	15.7	14.9	14.2
39	20.0	18.9	17.9	16.9	16.1	15.3	14.6	13.9
40	19.3	18.3	17.3	16.5	15.7	14.9	14.2	13.6
41	18.6	17.7	16.8	16.0	15.2	14.5	13.9	13.3
42	18.0	17.1	16.3	15.5	14.8	14.1	13.5	12.9
43	17.3	16.5	15.7	15.0	14.3	13.7	13.1	12.6
44	16.6	15.8	15.1	14.5	13.9	13.3	12.8	12.3
45	15.9	15.2	14.5	13.9	13.4	12.9	12.4	11.9
46	15.2	14.5	14.0	13.4	12.9	12.4	11.9	11.5
47	14.5	13.9	13.4	12.9	12.4	11.9	11.5	11.1
48	13.8	13.2	12.8	12.3	11.9	11.5	11.1	10.7
49	13.0	12.6	12.1	11.7	11.3	11.0	10.6	10.3
50	12.3	11.9	11.5	11.1	10.8	10.5	10.1	9.8
51	11.6	11.2	10.9	10.5	10.2	9.9	9.6	9.4
52	10.8	10.5	10.2	9.9	9.6	9.4	9.1	8.9
53	10.1	9.8	9.5	9.3	9.1	8.8	8.6	8.4
54	9.3	9.1	8.9	8.7	8.4	8.2	8.1	7.9
55	8.6	8.4	8.2	8.0	7.8	7.7	7.5	7.3
56	7.8	7.6	7.5	7.3	7.2	7.0	6.9	6.8
57	7.0	6.9	6.7	6.6	6.5	6.4	6.3	6.2
58	6.2	6.1	6.0	5.9	5.8	5.7	5.6	5.5
59	5.4	5.3	5.2	5.2	5.1	5.0	5.0	4.9
60	4.5	4.5	4.4	4.4	4.3	4.3	4.2	4.2
61	3.7	3.7	3.6	3.6	3.6	3.5	3.5	3.5
62	2.8	2.8	2.8	2.8	2.7	2.7	2.7	2.7
63	1.9	1.9	1.9	1.9	1.9	1.9	1.9	1.9
64	1.0	1.0	1.0	1.0	1.0	1.0	1.0	1.0

Table 4 Multipliers of loss of earnings to pension age 60 (females)

Age at date of trial	Multiplier calculated with allowance for population mortality and rate of interest of							
	1.5%	2%	2.5%	3%	3.5%	4%	4.5%	5%
16	31.6	28.8	26.3	24.2	22.3	20.7	19.2	17.9
17	31.1	28.4	26.0	23.9	22.1	20.5	19.0	17.7
18	30.6	27.9	25.7	23.6	21.9	20.3	18.9	17.6
19	30.0	27.5	25.3	23.3	21.6	20.1	18.7	17.5
20	29.5	27.1	24.9	23.0	21.4	19.9	18.5	17.3
21	28.9	26.6	24.5	22.7	21.1	19.6	18.4	17.2
22	28.4	26.1	24.2	22.4	20.8	19.4	18.2	17.0
23	27.8	25.7	23.8	22.1	20.5	19.2	18.0	16.9
24	27.2	25.2	23.4	21.7	20.3	18.9	17.8	16.7
25	26.6	24.7	22.9	21.4	20.0	18.7	17.5	16.5
26	26.0	24.2	22.5	21.0	19.6	18.4	17.3	16.3
27	25.4	23.7	22.1	20.6	19.3	18.2	17.1	16.1
28	24.8	23.1	21.6	20.2	19.0	17.9	16.8	15.9
29	24.2	22.6	21.2	19.8	18.7	17.6	16.6	15.7
30	23.6	22.1	20.7	19.4	18.3	17.3	16.3	15.5
31	22.9	21.5	20.2	19.0	17.9	16.9	16.0	15.2
32	22.3	20.9	19.7	18.6	17.6	16.6	15.8	15.0
33	21.6	20.4	19.2	18.1	17.2	16.3	15.4	14.7
34	21.0	19.8	18.7	17.7	16.8	15.9	15.1	14.4
35	20.3	19.2	18.2	17.2	16.3	15.5	14.8	14.1
36	19.6	18.6	17.6	16.7	15.9	15.2	14.5	13.8
37	18.9	17.9	17.1	16.2	15.5	14.8	14.1	13.5
38	18.2	17.3	16.5	15.7	15.0	14.4	13.7	13.2
39	17.5	16.7	15.9	15.2	14.5	13.9	13.3	12.8
40	16.8	16.0	15.3	14.7	14.1	13.5	12.9	12.4
41	16.0	15.4	14.7	14.1	13.6	13.0	12.5	12.1
42	15.3	14.7	14.1	13.5	13.0	12.5	12.1	11.7
43	14.5	14.0	13.5	13.0	12.5	12.1	11.6	11.2
44	13.8	13.3	12.8	12.4	11.9	11.5	11.2	10.8
45	13.0	12.6	12.2	11.8	11.4	11.0	10.7	10.3
46	12.2	11.9	11.5	11.1	10.8	10.5	10.2	9.9
47	11.5	11.1	10.8	10.5	10.2	9.9	9.6	9.4
48	10.7	10.4	10.1	9.8	9.6	9.3	9.1	8.8
49	9.9	9.6	9.4	9.1	8.9	8.7	8.5	8.3
50	9.0	8.8	8.6	8.4	8.2	8.1	7.9	7.7
51	8.2	8.0	7.9	7.7	7.5	7.4	7.2	7.1
52	7.4	7.2	7.1	7.0	6.8	6.7	6.6	6.5
53	6.5	6.4	6.3	6.2	6.1	6.0	5.9	5.8
54	5.6	5.5	5.5	5.4	5.3	5.2	5.2	5.1
55	4.7	4.7	4.6	4.6	4.5	4.5	4.4	4.4
56	3.8	3.8	3.8	3.7	3.7	3.6	3.6	3.6
57	2.9	2.9	2.9	2.8	2.8	2.8	2.8	2.8
58	2.0	1.9	1.9	1.9	1.9	1.9	1.9	1.9
59	1.0	1.0	1.0	1.0	1.0	1.0	1.0	1.0

Table 5 Multipliers for loss of pension commencing age 65 (males)

Age at date of trial	Multiplier calculated with allowance for population mortality and rate of interest of							
	1.5%	2%	2.5%	3%	3.5%	4%	4.5%	5%
16	3.8	2.9	2.2	1.6	1.3	1.0	.7	.6
17	3.8	2.9	2.2	1.7	1.3	1.0	.8	.6
18	3.9	3.0	2.3	1.8	1.3	1.0	.8	.6
19	4.0	3.0	2.3	1.8	1.4	1.1	.8	.7
20	4.0	3.1	2.4	1.9	1.4	1.1	.9	.7
21	4.1	3.2	2.5	1.9	1.5	1.2	.9	.7
22	4.2	3.2	2.5	2.0	1.6	1.2	1.0	.8
23	4.2	3.3	2.6	2.0	1.6	1.3	1.0	.8
24	4.3	3.4	2.7	2.1	1.7	1.3	1.1	.8
25	4.4	3.4	2.7	2.2	1.7	1.4	1.1	.9
26	4.4	3.5	2.8	2.2	1.8	1.4	1.1	.9
27	4.5	3.6	2.9	2.3	1.9	1.5	1.2	1.0
28	4.6	3.7	2.9	2.4	1.9	1.6	1.3	1.0
29	4.6	3.7	3.0	2.4	2.0	1.6	1.3	1.1
30	4.7	3.8	3.1	2.5	2.1	1.7	1.4	1.1
31	4.8	3.9	3.2	2.6	2.1	1.8	1.4	1.2
32	4.9	4.0	3.3	2.7	2.2	1.8	1.5	1.2
33	4.9	4.1	3.4	2.8	2.3	1.9	1.6	1.3
34	5.0	4.2	3.4	2.9	2.4	2.0	1.6	1.4
35	5.1	4.2	3.5	2.9	2.5	2.1	1.7	1.4
36	5.2	4.3	3.6	3.0	2.5	2.1	1.8	1.5
37	5.3	4.4	3.7	3.1	2.6	2.2	1.9	1.6
38	5.4	4.5	3.8	3.2	2.7	2.3	2.0	1.7
39	5.4	4.6	3.9	3.3	2.8	2.4	2.1	1.8
40	5.5	4.7	4.0	3.4	2.9	2.5	2.2	1.9
41	5.6	4.8	4.1	3.6	3.1	2.6	2.3	2.0
42	5.7	4.9	4.3	3.7	3.2	2.7	2.4	2.1
43	5.8	5.0	4.4	3.8	3.3	2.9	2.5	2.2
44	5.9	5.2	4.5	3.9	3.4	3.0	2.6	2.3
45	6.1	5.3	4.6	4.0	3.5	3.1	2.7	2.4
46	6.2	5.4	4.8	4.2	3.7	3.3	2.9	2.5
47	6.3	5.6	4.9	4.3	3.8	3.4	3.0	2.7
48	6.4	5.7	5.0	4.5	4.0	3.6	3.2	2.8
49	6.6	5.8	5.2	4.6	4.2	3.7	3.3	3.0
50	6.7	6.0	5.4	4.8	4.3	3.9	3.5	3.2
51	6.9	6.2	5.5	5.0	4.5	4.1	3.7	3.3
52	7.0	6.3	5.7	5.2	4.7	4.3	3.9	3.5
53	7.2	6.5	5.9	5.4	4.9	4.5	4.1	3.8
54	7.4	6.7	6.1	5.6	5.1	4.7	4.3	4.0
55	7.6	6.9	6.4	5.9	5.4	5.0	4.6	4.2
56	7.8	7.2	6.6	6.1	5.6	5.2	4.8	4.5
57	8.0	7.4	6.9	6.4	5.9	5.5	5.1	4.8
58	8.2	7.7	7.2	6.7	6.2	5.8	5.4	5.1
59	8.5	8.0	7.5	7.0	6.6	6.2	5.8	5.4
60	8.8	8.3	7.8	7.3	6.9	6.5	6.2	5.8
61	9.1	8.6	8.2	7.7	7.3	6.9	6.6	6.3
62	9.5	9.0	8.6	8.1	7.7	7.4	7.0	6.7
63	9.9	9.4	9.0	8.6	8.2	7.9	7.5	7.2
64	10.3	9.9	9.5	9.1	8.8	8.4	8.1	7.8
65	10.8	10.4	10.0	9.7	9.4	9.0	8.8	8.5

Table 6 Multipliers for loss of pension commencing age 60 (females)

Age at date of trial	Multiplier calculated with allowance for population mortality and rate of interest of 1.5%	2%	2.5%	3%	3.5%	4%	4.5%	5%
16	7.8	6.0	4.6	3.5	2.7	2.1	1.6	1.3
17	8.0	6.1	4.7	3.6	2.8	2.2	1.7	1.3
18	8.1	6.2	4.8	3.7	2.9	2.3	1.8	1.4
19	8.2	6.4	4.9	3.9	3.0	2.4	1.8	1.5
20	8.3	6.5	5.1	4.0	3.1	2.5	1.9	1.5
21	8.5	6.6	5.2	4.1	3.2	2.6	2.0	1.6
22	8.6	6.8	5.3	4.2	3.3	2.7	2.1	1.7
23	8.7	6.9	5.5	4.3	3.5	2.8	2.2	1.8
24	8.9	7.0	5.6	4.5	3.6	2.9	2.3	1.9
25	9.0	7.2	5.7	4.6	3.7	3.0	2.4	2.0
26	9.1	7.3	5.9	4.8	3.8	3.1	2.5	2.1
27	9.3	7.5	6.0	4.9	4.0	3.2	2.6	2.2
28	9.4	7.6	6.2	5.0	4.1	3.4	2.8	2.3
29	9.6	7.8	6.4	5.2	4.3	3.5	2.9	2.4
30	9.7	7.9	6.5	5.4	4.4	3.6	3.0	2.5
31	9.9	8.1	6.7	5.5	4.6	3.8	3.2	2.6
32	10.0	8.3	6.9	5.7	4.7	3.9	3.3	2.8
33	10.2	8.5	7.0	5.9	4.9	4.1	3.5	2.9
34	10.3	8.6	7.2	6.0	5.1	4.3	3.6	3.1
35	10.5	8.8	7.4	6.2	5.3	4.5	3.8	3.2
36	10.7	9.0	7.6	6.4	5.5	4.6	3.9	3.4
37	10.8	9.2	7.8	6.6	5.6	4.8	4.1	3.5
38	11.0	9.4	8.0	6.8	5.9	5.0	4.3	3.7
39	11.2	9.6	8.2	7.0	6.1	5.2	4.5	3.9
40	11.4	9.8	8.4	7.3	6.3	5.4	4.7	4.1
41	11.6	10.0	8.6	7.5	6.5	5.7	5.0	4.3
42	11.8	10.2	8.9	7.7	6.8	5.9	5.2	4.6
43	12.0	10.4	9.1	8.0	7.0	6.2	5.4	4.8
44	12.2	10.7	9.4	8.2	7.3	6.4	5.7	5.0
45	12.4	10.9	9.6	8.5	7.5	6.7	6.0	5.3
46	12.6	11.2	9.9	8.8	7.8	7.0	6.2	5.6
47	12.8	11.4	10.2	9.1	8.1	7.3	6.5	5.9
48	13.1	11.7	10.5	9.4	8.4	7.6	6.9	6.2
49	13.3	12.0	10.8	9.7	8.8	7.9	7.2	6.5
50	13.6	12.3	11.1	10.0	9.1	8.3	7.6	6.9
51	13.8	12.6	11.4	10.4	9.5	8.7	7.9	7.3
52	14.1	12.9	11.8	10.8	9.9	9.1	8.3	7.7
53	14.4	13.2	12.1	11.1	10.3	9.5	8.7	8.1
54	14.7	13.5	12.5	11.5	10.7	9.9	9.2	8.5
55	15.0	13.9	12.9	12.0	11.1	10.4	9.7	9.0
56	15.3	14.3	13.3	12.4	11.6	10.8	10.2	9.5
57	15.7	14.7	13.7	12.9	12.1	11.4	10.7	10.1
58	16.1	15.1	14.2	13.4	12.6	11.9	11.3	10.7
59	16.4	15.5	14.7	13.9	13.2	12.5	11.9	11.3
60	16.8	16.0	15.2	14.4	13.7	13.1	12.5	12.0

11 In paragraph 6 of these notes reference was made to the problem that will arise where the plaintiff's retiring age is different from that assumed in the tables. Such a problem may arise in valuing a loss or expense beginning immediately but ending at retirement; or in valuing a loss or expense which will not begin until the plaintiff reaches retirement but will then continue until death. In the former case, that is where the loss or expense to be valued covers the period up to retirement, the following procedure will be found to be satisfactory in most cases. Where the plaintiff's actual retiring age would have been earlier than that assumed in the tables he is treated as though he were correspondingly older than his true age. Thus a man of 42, who would have retired at 60, is treated as though he were 47. The appropriate multiplier is then obtained from the table (Table 3). A further correction should then be made, because the plaintiff's chances of survival are greater at 42 than if he were in fact 47. There should therefore be added a half per cent to the multiplier for each year (here five years) by which the plaintiff's personal retiring age is earlier than 65. In the case of a woman the correction required would only be one quarter per cent for each such year. This is because, on average, women live longer than men.

12 Where the plaintiff would have retired later than the age assumed in the table the procedure is reversed. Thus a woman of 42, who would have retired at 65, is treated as though she were 37. The appropriate multiplier is then obtained from the table (in this case Table 4) and the further correction required is made by reducing the multiplier by one quarter per cent for each year by which the retiring age of the plaintiff exceeds the retiring age assumed in the table. In the case of a man the reduction would, of course, be by one half per cent for each year.

13 When the loss or expense to be valued is that from the date of retirement to death, and the plaintiff's date of retirement differs from that assumed in the tables, a different approach is necessary. The first step is to assume that there is a present loss which will continue for the rest of the plaintiff's life and from Table 1 or 2 establish the value of that loss or expense over the whole period from the date of assessment until the plaintiff's death. The second step is to establish the value of such loss or expense over the period from the date of assessment until the plaintiff's expected date of retirement following the procedure explained in paragraphs 11 and 12 above. The third step is to subtract the second figure from the first. The balance remaining represents the present value of the plaintiff's loss or expense between retirement and death.

14 The tables have been calculated to take into account the chances that the plaintiff will die young (or live to be very old) based on population mortality. They do not take account of the other risks and vicissitudes of life, such as the possibility that the plaintiff would for periods have ceased to earn due to ill-health or loss of employment. Similarly, they take no account of the fact that many women cease work for substantial periods to have and care for children.

15 The tables do not provide an immediate answer when the loss or expense to be valued is not assumed to be stable; where, for instance, the plaintiff's lost earnings were on a sliding scale or he was expected to achieve promotion. It may be possible to use the tables to deal with such situations by increasing the basic figure of annual loss or expenses; or by choosing a lower rate of interest and so a higher multiplier than would otherwise have been chosen.

Appendix F

The Motor Insurers' Bureau Agreements

Contents

1 Compensation of victims of uninsured drivers
2 Compensation of victims of untraced drivers—principal agreement
3 Compensation of victims of untraced drivers—supplemental agreement

* * *

1 Compensation of victims of uninsured drivers

MEMORANDUM OF AGREEMENT made the 21st day of December 1988 between the Secretary of State for Transport and the Motor Insurers' Bureau, whose registered office is at New Garden House, 78 Hatton Garden, London EC1N 8JQ (hereinafter referred to as 'MIB') SUPPLEMENTAL to an Agreement (hereinafter called 'the Principal Agreement') made the 31st Day of December 1945 between the Minister of War Transport and the insurers transacting compulsory motor insurance business in Great Britain by or on behalf of whom the said Agreement was signed and in pursuance of paragraph 1 of which MIB was incorporated.

IT IS HEREBY AGREED AS FOLLOWS—

DEFINITIONS

1. In this Agreement—
'contract of insurance' means a policy of insurance or a security;
'insurer' includes the giver of a security;
'relevant liability' means a liability in respect of which a policy of insurance must insure a person in order to comply with Part VI of the Road Traffic Act 1972,

and references to the Road Traffic Act 1972 are references to that Act as amended by the Motor Vehicles (Compulsory Insurance) Regulations 1987 (No 2171).

SATISFACTION OF CLAIMS BY MIB

Basic obligation of MIB

2. (1) If judgment in respect of any relevant liability is obtained against any person or persons in any Court in Great Britain whether or not such a person or persons be in fact covered by a contract of insurance and any such judgment is not satisfied in full within seven days from the date upon which the person or persons in whose favour the judgment was given became entitled to enforce it then MIB will, subject to the provisions of paragraphs (2), (3) and (4) below and to Clauses 4, 5 and 6 hereof, pay or satisfy or cause to be paid or satisfied to or to the satisfaction of the person or persons in whose favour the judgment was given any sum payable or remaining payable thereunder in respect of the relevant liability including any sum awarded by the Court in respect of interest on that sum and any taxed costs or any costs awarded by the Court without taxation (or such proportion thereof as is attributable to the relevant liability) whatever may be the cause of the failure of the judgment debtor to satisfy the judgment.

(2) Subject to paragraphs (3) and (4) below and to Clauses 4, 5 and 6 hereof, MIB shall incur liability under paragraph (1) above in respect of any sum awarded under such a judgment in respect of property damage not exceeding £250,000 or in respect of the first £250,000 of any sum so awarded exceeding that amount.

Compensation from other sources

(3) Where a person in whose favour a judgment in respect of a relevant liability which includes liability in respect of damage to property has been given, has received or is entitled to receive in consequence of a claim he has made, compensation from any source in respect of that damage, MIB may deduct from the sum payable or remaining payable under paragraph (1) above an amount equal to the amount of that compensation in addition to the deduction of £175 by virtue of paragraph (4) below. The reference to compensation includes compensation under insurance arrangements.

(4) MIB shall not incur liability under paragraph (1) above in respect of any amount payable or remaining payable under the judgment in respect of property damage liability where the total of amounts so payable or remaining payable is £175 or less, or, where the total of such amounts is more than £175, in respect of the first £175 of such total.

PERIOD OF AGREEMENT

3. This Agreement shall be determinable by the Secretary of State at any time or by MIB on twelve months' notice without prejudice to the continued operation of the Agreement in respect of accidents occurring before the date of termination.

RECOVERIES

4. Nothing in this Agreement shall prevent insurers from providing by conditions in their contracts of insurance that all sums paid by them or by MIB by virtue of the Principal Agreement or this Agreement in or towards the discharge of

the liability of their insured shall be recoverable by them or by MIB from the insured or from any other person.

CONDITIONS PRECEDENT TO MIB's LIABILITY

5. (1) MIB shall not incur any liability under Clause 2 of this Agreement unless—

Written notice of proceedings

(*a*) notice in writing of the bringing of the proceedings is given within seven days after the commencement of the proceedings—
  (i) to MIB in the case of proceedings in respect of a relevant liability which is either not covered by a contract of insurance or covered by a contract of insurance with an insurer whose identity cannot be ascertained, or
  (ii) to the insurer in the case of proceedings in respect of a relevant liability which is covered by a contract of insurance with an insurer whose identity can be ascertained;

Such notice shall be accompanied by a copy of the writ, summons or other document initiating the proceedings;

Supply of information by claimant

(*b*) the person bringing the proceedings furnishes to MIB—
  (i) such information (in such form as MIB may specify) in relation thereto as MIB may reasonably require; and
  (ii) such information (in such form as MIB may specify) as to any insurance covering any damage to property to which the claim or proceedings relate and any claim made in respect of that damage under the insurance or otherwise and any report which may have been made or notification which may have been given to any person in respect of that damage or the use of the vehicle giving rise thereto, as MIB may reasonably require;

Obtaining insurance details from person claimed against

(*c*) the person bringing the proceedings has demanded the information and, where appropriate, the particulars specified in section 151 of the Road Traffic Act 1972 in accordance with that section or, if so required by MIB, has authorised MIB to do so on his behalf;

Judgment against all persons liable

(*d*) if so required by MIB and subject to full indemnity from MIB as to costs the person bringing the proceedings has taken all reasonable steps to obtain judgment against all the persons liable in respect of the injury or death or damage to property and, in the event of any such person being a servant or agent, against his principal; and

Assignment of Judgment

(*e*) the judgment referred to in Clause 2 of this Agreement and any judgment referred to in paragraph (*d*) of this Clause which has been obtained (whether or not either judgment includes an amount in respect of a liability other than a relevant liability) and any order for costs are assigned to MIB or their nominee.

(2) In the event of any dispute as to the reasonableness of a requirement by MIB for the supply of information or that any particular step should be taken to obtain judgment against other persons it may be referred to the Secretary of State whose decision shall be final.

(3) Where a judgment which includes an amount in respect of a liability other than a relevant liability has been assigned to MIB or their nominee in pursuance of paragraph (1)(*e*) of this Clause MIB shall apportion any monies received in pursuance of the judgment according to the proportion which the damages in respect of the relevant liability bear to the damages in respect of the other liabilities and shall account to the person in whose favour the judgment was given in respect of such monies received properly apportionable to the other liabilities. Where an order for costs in respect of such a judgment has been so assigned monies received pursuant to the order shall be dealt with in the same manner.

EXCEPTIONS

Exceptions to claims against MIB Crown vehicles

6. (1) MIB shall not incur any liability under Clause 2 of this Agreement in a case where—

(*a*) the claim arises out of the use of a vehicle owned by or in the possession of the Crown, except where any other person has undertaken responsibility for the existence of a contract of insurance under Part VI of the Road Traffic Act 1972 (whether or not the person or persons liable be in fact covered by a contract of insurance) or where the liability is in fact covered by a contract of insurance;

Vehicles exempted from insurance

(*b*) the claim arises out of the use of a vehicle the use of which is not required to be covered by a contract of insurance by virtue of section 144 of the Road Traffic Act 1972, unless the use is in fact covered by such a contract;

Exclusion of subrogation claims

(*c*) the claim is in respect of a judgment or any part thereof which has been obtained by virtue of the exercise of a right of subrogation by any person.

Claimant failing to insure as RTA requires

(*d*) the claim is in respect of damage to property which consists of damage to a motor vehicle or losses arising therefrom if at the time of the use giving rise to the damage to the motor vehicle there was not in force in relation to the use of that vehicle when the damage to it was sustained such a policy of insurance as is required by Part VI of the Road Traffic Act 1972 and the person or persons claiming in respect of the loss or damage either knew or ought to have known that that was the case;

(*e*) at the time of the use which gave rise to the liability the person suffering death or bodily injury or damage to property was allowing himself to be carried in or upon the vehicle and either before the commencement of his journey in the vehicle or after such commencement if he could reasonably be expected to have alighted from the vehicle he—

Stolen vehicle–knowledge by passenger

(i) knew or ought to have known that the vehicle had been stolen or unlawfully taken, or

Uninsured vehicle–knowledge by passenger

(ii) knew or ought to have known that the vehicle was being used without there being in force in relation to its use such a contract of insurance as would comply with Part VI of the Road Traffic Act 1972.

(2) The exception specified in sub-paragraph (1)(*e*) of this Clause shall apply only in a case where the judgment in respect of which the claim against MIB is made was obtained in respect of a relevant liability incurred by the owner or a person using the vehicle in which the person who suffered death or bodily injury or sustained damage to property was being carried.

(3) For the purposes of these exceptions—

(*a*) a vehicle which has been unlawfully removed from the possession of the Crown shall be taken to continue in that possession whilst it is kept so removed;

(*b*) references to a person being carried in a vehicle include references to his being carried in or upon or entering or getting on to or alighting from the vehicle; and

(*c*) 'owner' in relation to a vehicle which is the subject of a hiring agreement or a hire-purchase agreement, means the person in possession of the vehicle under the agreement.

AGENTS

7. Nothing in this Agreement shall prevent MIB performing their obligations under this Agreement by Agents.

OPERATION

8. This Agreement shall come into operation on 31 December 1988 in relation to accidents occurring on or after that date. The Agreement made on 22 November 1972 between the Secretary of State and MIB shall cease and determine except in relation to claims arising out of accidents occurring before 31 December 1988.

IN WITNESS whereof the Secretary of State has caused his Corporate Seal to be hereto affixed and the Motor Insurers' Bureau have caused their Common Seal to be hereto affixed the day and year first above written.

Notes

The following notes are for the guidance of those who may have a claim on the Motor Insurers' Bureau under the Agreement, and of their legal advisers, but they must not be taken as rendering unnecessary a careful study of the Agreement itself. Communications on any matter connected with the Agreement should be addressed to the Motor Insurers' Bureau whose address is New Garden House, 78 Hatton Garden, London EC1N 8JQ.

On the date of coming into force of the Road Traffic Act 1988 references to the provisions of the Road Traffic Act 1972 are by virtue of section 2(4) of the Road Traffic (Consequential Provisions) Act 1988 to be read as references to the corresponding provisions of the Road Traffic Act 1988.

1. The Agreement, which operates from 31 December 1988, supersedes earlier Agreements made on 17 June 1946 (which was operative from 1 July 1946) and on 1 February 1971 (which was operative from 1 March 1971), and on 22 November 1972 (which was operative from 1 December 1972) in relation to claims arising out of accidents occurring on or after 1 December 1988.

2. If damages are awarded by a Court in respect of death or personal injury or damage to property arising out of the use of a motor vehicle on a road in circumstances where the liability is one which was, at the time the accident occurred, required to be covered by insurance and such damages, or any part of them, remain unpaid seven days after the judgment becomes enforceable, the Bureau will, subject to the limit specified in Clause 2(2) which corresponds with the limited insurance requirement in section 145(4)(*b*) of the Road Traffic Act 1972, and the exceptions in paragraphs (3) and (4) of Clause 2 and Clause 6 of the Agreement, pay the unrecovered amount (including any interest awarded by the Court and costs) to the person in whose favour the judgment has been given against an assignment of the judgment debt. This applies whether the judgment debtor is a British resident or a foreign visitor.

3. Clause 1 defines 'relevant liability' as a liability in respect of which a policy of insurance must insure a person in order to comply with Part VI of the Road Traffic Act 1972, which includes liability in respect of property damage caused by, or arising out of, the use of a motor vehicle on a road in Great Britain. This provision gives effect to Article 1.1 of Council Directive (84/5/EEC) of 30 December 1983 on the approximation of the laws of Member States relating to insurance against civil liability in respect of the use of motor vehicles (OJ No L8, 11.1.84, p17). In the context of the Directive 'damage to property' means damage to material property. Accordingly in this Agreement the reference to damage to property is understood in that sense. With regard to liability in respect of such damage which is covered by the Agreement, MIB would expect to meet the consequential loss elements of a claim flowing from damage to the claimant's material property which a Court would allow. It must be emphasised that MIB's obligation does not extend to those liabilities not required to be covered by the policy under section 145(4) of the Road Traffic Act 1972.

4. Nothing in the Agreement affects the position at law of the parties to an action for damages arising out of the driving of a motor vehicle. The Bureau's liability under the Agreement can only arise when the plaintiff has successfully established his case against the person or persons liable in the usual manner and judgment has been given in his favour. There is, of course, nothing to exclude the acceptance of compensation by the plaintiff under a settlement negotiated between the plaintiff and the alleged person liable or the Bureau.

5. The purpose of Clause 2(3) is to oblige any claimant in respect of property damage to give credit for compensation which he may have received or be entitled to receive under a claim he has made on another source or sources relative to that damage. The most common instances will involve compensation recovered under comprehensive motor or household policies. Policyholders with these covers cannot be forced to claim under them but will normally wish to do so for their convenience. Furthermore legal liability for the accident will not affect that claim and the MIB excess of £175 (Clause 2(4)) will not apply. Where such a claim has been made successfully MIB will only be concerned with the claimant's uninsured losses eg any excess he may have under his own policy, or loss of use of his vehicle subject to legal liability and the MIB excess of £175.

6. WHERE THERE IS A POLICY. In cases where it is ascertained that there is in existence a policy issued in compliance with the Road Traffic Act 1972, the insurer concerned will act as the agent of the Bureau even if entitled to repudiate liability under the policy and, subject to notice being given as provided for in Clause 5(1)(*a*)(ii), will handle claims within the terms of the Agreement.

In many cases, particularly where the vehicle was being used without the policyholder's authority, the provisions of the Road Traffic Act preclude repudiation by the insurer of a victim's claim. Victims and those acting on their behalf are expressly reminded of the requirements as to the giving of notice to the insurer if the protection afforded to third parties by section 149 of the Road Traffic Act 1972 is sought.

It must be stressed that the above arrangements are without prejudice to any rights insurers may have against their policy holders and, to avoid any possible misunderstanding, it is emphasised that there is nothing in this Agreement affecting any obligations imposed on a policyholder by his policy. Policyholders are not released from their contractual obligations to their insurers, although the Road Traffic Act and MIB protect THIRD PARTY VICTIMS from the consequences of failure to observe them. For example, if a policyholder fails to notify claims to his insurers as required by his policy or permits an unauthorised person to drive, he may be liable to his insurers.

WHERE THERE IS NO POLICY OR THE IDENTITY OF THE INSURER CANNOT BE ASCERTAINED. In cases where there is no policy, or for any reason the existence of a policy is in doubt or where there is a policy but the identity of the insurer cannot be ascertained, the victim or those acting on his behalf must notify the Bureau, and in practice it is desirable to inform the Bureau in all cases where the name of the insurer is not speedily forthcoming. It is a condition of the Bureau's liability that they should be given notification in writing (with relevant documents) within 7 days after the commencement of proceedings against the alleged person liable. It should always be remembered that the requirement for notice of issue of proceedings under Clause 5(1)(*a*)(i) and (ii) must be complied with strictly. Notice should be given immediately on issue of the proceedings, and such notice must be accompanied by copies of the writ or summons.

7. Claims arising out of the use of uninsured vehicles owned by or in the possession of the Crown will in the majority of cases be outside the scope of the Bureau's liability (see Clause 6 of the Agreement—Exceptions). In such cases the approach should be made to the responsible authority in the usual way. The same benefits in respect of compensation will normally be afforded by the Crown to the victims in such cases as they would receive were the accident caused by a private vehicle, except where the victim is a serviceman or service woman whose death or injury gives rise to an entitlement to a pension or other compensation from public funds.

8. The purpose of Clause 6(1)(*c*) is to relieve MIB of liability to meet judgments in respect of damage to property obtained by persons who have compensated the victim such as the victim's own insurers. Such insurers have the right to attempt to recoup their outlay by requiring an insured to lend his name to proceedings against the person responsible, but MIB will not meet such claims as the victim has already been compensated.

9. Claims for damage to a vehicle or for losses arising therefrom for which a policy of insurance issued in compliance with Part VI of the Road Traffic Act 1972 is required, are excluded from the Agreement if the vehicle was not insured and the claimant knew or ought to have known that it was not. See Clause 6(1)(*d*). The claim may also be excluded under Clause 6(1)(*e*).

10. It should be noted that the monetary limit applicable to property damage claims by virtue of Clause 2(2) corresponding with the insurance limit in section 145(4)(*b*) of the Road Traffic Act 1972, and the excess prescribed by Clauses 2(3) and (4) of this Agreement will be subject to review from time to time.

11. The Bureau have no liability UNDER THIS AGREEMENT to pay compensation in respect of any person who may suffer bodily injury or death or may sustain damage to property resulting from the use on a road of a vehicle, the owner or driver of which cannot be traced. A separate Agreement between the Secretary of State for Transport and the Bureau for the Compensation of Victims of Untraced Drivers in respect of bodily injury and death applies, but this Agreement does not embrace damage to property.

2 Compensation of victims of untraced drivers—principal agreement

IT IS HEREBY AGREED as follows:

1. (1) Subject to paragraph (2) of this Clause, this Agreement applies to any case in which an application is made to MIB for a payment in respect of the death of or bodily injury to any person caused by or arising out of the use of a motor vehicle on a road in Great Britain and the case is one in which following conditions are fulfilled, that is to say—

(*a*) the event giving rise to the death or injury occurred on or after 1 December 1972;

(*b*) the applicant for the payment either—

(i) is unable to trace any person responsible for the death or injury, or

(ii) in a case which Clause 5 hereof applies where more than one person was so responsible, is unable to trace one of those persons.

(Any person so untraced is hereinafter referred to as 'the untraced person');

(*c*) the death or injury was caused in such circumstances that on the balance of probabilities the untraced person would be liable to pay damages to the applicant in respect of the death or injury;

(*d*) the liability of the untraced person to pay damages to the applicant is one which is required to be covered by insurance or security under Part VI of the Road Traffic Act 1972, it being assumed for this purpose, in the absence of evidence to the contrary, that the vehicle was being used in circumstances in which the user was required by the said Part VI to be insured or secured against third party risks;

(*e*) the death or injury was not caused by the use of the vehicle by the untraced person as a weapon, that is to say, in a deliberate attempt to run the deceased or injured person down;

(*f*) the application is made in writing within three years from the date of the event giving rise to the death or injury.

(2) This Agreement does not apply to a case in which—

(*a*) the death or bodily injury in respect of which any such application is made was caused by or arose out of the use of a motor vehicle which at the time of the event giving rise to the death or bodily injury was owned by or in the possession of the Crown, unless the case is one in which some other person has undertaken responsibility for the existence of a contract of insurance under Part VI of the Road Traffic Act 1972;

(*b*) at the time of the accident the person suffering death or bodily injury in respect of which the application is made was allowing himself to be carried in a vehicle and—

(i) knew or had reason to believe that the vehicle had been taken without the consent of the owner or other lawful authority, except in a case where—
   (A) he believed or had reason to believe that he had lawful authority to be carried or that he would have had the owner's consent if the owner had known of his being carried and the circumstances of his carriage; or
   (B) he had learned of the circumstances of the taking of the vehicle since the commencement of the journey and it would be unreasonable to expect him to have alighted from the vehicle; or

(ii) being the owner of or being a person using the vehicle he was using or causing or permitting the vehicle to be used without there being in force in relation to such use a policy of insurance or such security as would comply with Part VI of the Road Traffic Act 1972, knowing or having reason to believe that no such policy or security was in force.

(3) The exemption from the application of this Agreement specified in subparagraph (2)(*b*) of this Clause shall apply only in a case where the application is made to MIB in respect of a liability arising out of the use of the vehicle in which the person who suffered death or bodily injury was being carried.

(4) For the purpose of paragraph (2) of this Clause—

(*a*) a vehicle which has been unlawfully removed from the possession of the Crown shall be taken to continue in that possession whilst it is kept so removed;

(*b*) references to a person being carried in a vehicle include references to his being carried in or upon, or entering or getting on to or alighting from the vehicle;

(*c*) 'owner' in relation to a vehicle which is the subject of a hiring agreement or a hire purchase agreement means the person in possession of the vehicle under that agreement.

2. (1) An application to MIB for a payment in respect of the death of or bodily injury to any person may be made either by the person for whose benefit that payment is to be made (hereinafter called 'the applicant') or by any solicitor acting for the applicant or by any other person whom MIB may be prepared to accept as acting for the applicant.

(2) Any decision, award or payment given or made or other thing done in accordance with this Agreement to or by a person acting as aforesaid on behalf of the applicant, or in relation to an application made by such a person, shall, whatever may be the age, or the circumstances affecting the capacity, of the applicant, be treated as having the same effect as it had been done to or by, or in relation to an application made by, an applicant of full age and capacity.

3. Subject to the following provisions of this Agreement, MIB shall, on any application made to them in a case to which this Agreement applies, award to the applicant in respect of the death or injury in respect of which the application is made a payment of an amount which shall be assessed in like manner as a court, applying English law in a case where the event giving rise to the death or injury occurred in England or Wales or applying the law of Scotland in a case where that event occurred in Scotland, would assess the damages which

the applicant would have been entitled to recover from the untraced person in respect of that death or injury if proceedings to enforce a claim for damages in respect thereof were successfully brought by the applicant against the untraced person.

4. In making an award in accordance with Clause 3 hereof—

(*a*) MIB shall not be required to include in the payment awarded any amount in respect of any damages for loss of expectation of life or for pain or suffering which the applicant might have had a right to claim under the Law Reform (Miscellaneous Provisions) Act 1934, or, as the case may be, under any corresponding rule of law in force in Scotland nor, in a case where the application is made in respect of a death, shall MIB be required to include in the payment awarded any amount in respect of solatium for the grief of any relative of the deceased which the applicant might have had a right to claim under any enactment or rule of law in force in Scotland; and

(*b*) in assessing the amount to which the applicant is entitled in respect of loss of earnings if the applicant has received his wages or salary in full or in part from his employer, whether or not upon an undertaking given by the applicant to reimburse his employer if he recovers damages, he shall not to the extent of the amount so received be regarded as having sustained a loss of earnings.

5. (1) This Clause applies to any case to which this Agreement applies where the death or bodily injury in respect of which an application had been made to MIB under this Agreement (hereinafter in this Clause referred to as 'the relevant death or injury') was caused partly by the untraced person and partly either by an identified person, or by identified persons, or by some other untraced person or persons whose master or principal can be identified and was so caused in circumstances making the identified person or persons or any such master or principal as aforesaid liable to the applicant in respect of the relevant death or injury.

(2) If in a case to which this Clause applies one or other of the conditions specified in the next following paragraph is satisfied, the amount to be awarded by MIB to the applicant in respect of the relevant death or injury shall be determined in accordance with the provisions of paragraph (4) of this Clause and their liability to the applicant shall be subject also to the provisions of paragraph (7) of this Clause and to Clause 6 hereof.

(3) The conditions referred to in the last foregoing paragraph are—

(a) that the applicant has obtained a judgment in respect of the relevant death or injury against the identified person or against one or more of the identified persons or against any person liable as their master or principal or the master or principal of any other person which has not been satisfied in full within three months from the date on which the applicant became entitled to enforce it; or

(*b*) that the applicant—

(i) has not obtained and has not been required by MIB to obtain a judgment in respect of the relevant death or injury against the identified person or persons or against any person liable as the master or principal of any such identified person or persons or as the master or principal of any other person, and

(ii) has not received any payment by way of compensation from any such person or persons.

(4) The amount to be awarded by MIB to the applicant in a case to which this Clause applies shall be determined as follows:

(*a*) if the condition specified in paragraph (3)(*a*) of this Clause is satisfied and the judgment mentioned in that paragraph is wholly unsatisfied within the period of three months therein referred to, the amount to be awarded shall be an amount equal to the untraced person's contribution to a full award;

(*a*) if the condition specified in paragraph (3)(*a*) of this Clause is satisfied and the judgment mentioned in that paragraph is wholly unsatisfied within the period of three months therein referred to, the amount to be awarded shall be an amount equal to the untraced person's contribution to a full award;

(*b*) if the condition specified in paragraph (3)(*a*) of this Clause is satisfied but the judgment mentioned in that paragraph is satisfied in part only within the period of three months therein referred to, the amount to be awarded—

(i) if the unsatisfied part of the said judgment is less than the untraced person's contribution to a full award, shall be an amount equal to that unsatisfied part, or

(ii) if the unsatisfied part of the said judgment is equal to or greater than the amount of the untraced person's contribution to a full award, shall be an amount equal to the untraced person's said contribution;

(*c*) if the condition specified in paragraph (3)(*b*) of this Clause is satisfied, the amount to be awarded shall be an amount equal to the untraced person's contribution to a full award.

(5) The following provisions of this paragraph shall have effect in any case in which an appeal from or any proceeding to set aside any such judgment as is specified in paragraph (3)(*a*) of this Clause (hereinafter in this Clause referred to as 'the original judgment') is commenced within a period of three months beginning on the date on which the applicant became entitled to enforce the original judgment:

(*a*) until the said appeal or proceeding is disposed of the foregoing provisions of this Clause shall have effect as if for the period of three months referred to in the said paragraph (3)(*a*) there were substituted a period expiring on the date when the said appeal or proceeding is disposed of;

(*b*) if as a result of the said appeal or proceeding the applicant ceases to be entitled to receive any payment in respect of the relevant death or injury from any of the person or persons against whom he has obtained any such judgment as is specified in the said paragraph (3)(*a*), the foregoing provisions of this Clause shall have effect as if he had neither obtained nor been required by MIB to obtain a judgment against any person or persons;

(*c*) if as a result of the said appeal or proceeding, the applicant becomes entitled to recover an amount which differs from that which he was entitled to recover under the original judgment, the foregoing provisions of this Clause shall have effect as if for the reference in the said paragraph (3)(*a*) to the original judgment there were substituted a reference to the judgment under which the applicant became entitled to the said different amount;

(*d*) if as a result of the said appeal or proceeding the applicant remains entitled to enforce the original judgment the foregoing provisions of this Clause shall have effect as if for the period of three months referred to in the said paragraph (3)(*a*) there were substituted a period of three months beginning on the date on which the appeal or other proceeding was disposed of.

The foregoing provisions of this paragraph shall apply also in any case where any judgment given upon any such appeal or proceeding is itself the subject of a further appeal or similar proceeding and shall apply in such a case in relation to that further appeal or proceeding in the same manner as they apply in relation to the first mentioned appeal or proceeding.

(6) In this Clause—

(*a*) 'full award' means the amount which would have fallen to be awarded to the applicant under Clause 3 hereof in respect of the relevant death or injury if the untraced person had been wholly responsible for that death or injury; and

(*b*) 'untraced person's contribution' means that proportion of a full award which on the balance of probabilities would have been apportioned by a court as the share to be borne by the untraced person in the responsibility for the event giving rise to the relevant death or injury if proceedings to recover damages in respect of that death or injury had been brought by the applicant against the untraced person and all other persons having a share in that responsibility.

(7) MIB shall not be under any liability in respect of the relevant death or injury if the applicant is entitled to receive compensation from MIB in respect of that death or injury under the Agreement providing for the compensation of victims of uninsured drivers entered into between the Secretary of State and MIB on 22 November 1972.

6. (1) The following shall be conditions precedent to any liability falling upon MIB upon an application made to them under this Agreement in respect of any death or injury, that is to say—

(*a*) the applicant shall give all such assistance as may reasonably be required by or on behalf of MIB to enable any investigation to be carried out under this Agreement, including, in particular, the furnishing of statements and information either in writing, or, if so required, orally at an interview or interviews between the applicant and any person acting on behalf of MIB;

(*b*) if so required by MIB at any time before MIB have communicated their decision upon the application to the applicant, the applicant shall, subject to the following provisions of this Clause, take all such steps as in the circumstances it is reasonable to require the applicant to take to obtain judgment against any person or persons in respect of their liability to the applicant in respect of the death or injury as having caused or contributed to that death or injury or as being the master or principal of any person who has caused or contributed to that injury; and

(*c*) if so required by MIB the applicant shall assign to MIB or to their nominee any judgment obtained by him (whether or not obtained in pursuance of a requirement under sub-paragraph (*b*) of this paragraph) in respect of the death or injury to which his application to MIB relates upon such terms as will secure that MIB or their nominee shall be accountable to the applicant for any amount by which the aggregate of all sums recovered by MIB or their nominee under the said judgment (after deducting all reasonable expenses incurred in effecting such recovery) exceeds the amount payable by MIB to the applicant under this agreement in respect of that death or injury.

(2) If MIB require the applicant to bring proceedings against any specified person or persons:

(*a*) MIB shall indemnify the applicant against all costs reasonably incurred by the applicant in complying with that requirement unless the result of those proceedings materially contributes to establish that the untraced person did not cause or contribute to the relevant death or injury; and

(*b*) the applicant shall, if so required by MIB and at their expense, furnish MIB with a transcript of any official shorthand note taken in those proceedings of any evidence given or judgment delivered therein.

(3) In the event of a dispute arising between the applicant and MIB as to the reasonableness of any requirement by MIB under paragraph (1)(*b*) of this Clause, or as to whether any such costs as are referred to in paragraph (2)(*a*) of this Clause were reasonably incurred, that dispute shall be referred to the Secretary of State whose decision thereon shall be final.

Provided that any dispute arising between the applicant and MIB as to whether MIB are required to indemnify the applicant under paragraph (2)(*a*) of this Clause shall, in so far as it depends on the question whether the result of any procccdings which MIB have required the applicant to bring against any specified person or persons have or have not materially contributed to establish that the untraced person did not cause or contribute to the relevant death or injury, be referred to the arbitrator in accordance with the following provisions of this Agreement, whose decision on that question shall be final.

7. MIB shall cause any application made to them for a payment under this Agreement to be investigated and, unless MIB decide that the application should be rejected because a preliminary investigation has disclosed that the case is not one to which this Agreement applies, they shall cause a report to be made on the application and on the basis of that report MIB shall decide whether to make an award and, if so, the amount of the award which shall be calculated in accordance with the foregoing provisions of this Agreement.

8. MIB may before coming to a decision on any application made to them under this Agreement request the applicant to furnish them with a statutory declaration to be made by the applicant, setting out to the best of his knowledge, information and belief the facts and circumstances upon which his claim to an award under this Agreement is based, or such of those facts and circumstances as may be specified by MIB.

9. (1) MIB shall notify their decision to the applicant and when so doing shall—

(*a*) if the application is rejected because a preliminary investigation has disclosed that it is not one made in a case to which this Agreement applies, give their reasons for the rejection; or

(*b*) if the application has been fully investigated furnish him with a statement setting out—

(i) the circumstances in which the death or injury occurred and the evidence bearing thereon,

(ii) the circumstances relevant to the assessment of the amount to be awarded to the applicant under this Agreement and the evidence bearing thereon, and

(iii) if they refuse to make an award, their reasons for that refusal; and

(*c*) in a case to which Clause 5 of this Agreement applies specify the way in which the amount of that award has been computed and its relation to those provisions of Clause 5 which are relevant to its computation.

(2) Where MIB have decided that they will not indemnify the applicant against the costs of any proceedings which they have under Clause 6(1)(*b*) hereof required the applicant to bring against any specified person or persons on the ground that those proceedings have materially contributed to establish that the untraced person did not cause or contribute to the relevant death or injury, they shall give notice to the applicant of that decision and when doing so they shall give their reasons for it and furnish the applicant with a copy of any such transcript of any evidence given or judgment delivered in those proceedings as is mentioned in Clause 6(2)(*b*) thereof which they regard as relevant to that decision.

10. Subject to provisions of this Agreement MIB shall—

(*a*) on being notified by the applicant that MIB's award is accepted; or

(*b*) if at the expiration of the period during which the applicant may give notice of an appeal under Clause 11 hereof there has not been given to MIB either any such notification as aforesaid of the acceptance of MIB's award or a notice of an appeal under the said Clause 11,

pay the applicant the amount of that award, and such payment shall discharge MIB from all liability under this Agreement in respect of the death or injury in respect of which that award has been made.

11. The applicant shall have a right of appeal to an arbitrator against any decision notified to him under Clause 9 hereof on any of the following grounds, that is to say—

(*a*) that the case is one to which this Agreement applies and that his application should be fully investigated by MIB with a view to their deciding whether to make an award to the applicant and, if so, the amount of that award; or

(*b*) where the application has been fully investigated—

(i) that MIB were wrong in refusing to make an award, or

(ii) that the amount they have awarded to the applicant is insufficient; or

(*c*) in a case where a decision not to indemnify the applicant against the costs of any proceedings has been notified under Clause 9(2) hereof, that the decision was wrong,

if, within six weeks from the date when notice of the decision against which he wishes to appeal was given to him, the applicant, not having previously notified MIB that their decision is accepted, give notice to MIB that he wishes to appeal against their decision.

12. A notice of appeal under Clause 11 hereof shall state the grounds of the appeal and shall be accompanied by an undertaking to be given by the applicant or by the person acting on his behalf as provided in Clause 2 hereof, that—

(*a*) the applicant will accept the decision of the arbitrator; and

(*b*) the arbitrator's fee shall be paid to MIB by the applicant or by the person giving the said undertaking in any case where MIB are entitled to reimbursement of that fee under the provisions of Clause 22 hereof.

13. The applicant may, when giving notice of his appeal or at any time before doing so, make comments to MIB on their decision and may supply them with such particulars as the applicant may think fit of any other evidence not contained in the written statement supplied to the applicant by MIB which he considers is relevant to the application and MIB may, before submitting the applicant's appeal to the arbitrator, cause an investigation to be made into this further evidence and shall report to the applicant the result of that investigation and of any change in their decision which may result from it. The applicant may, within six weeks from the date on which this report was sent to him, unless he withdraws his appeal, make such comments thereon as he may desire to have submitted to the arbitrator.

14. (1) In a case where MIB receive from the applicant a notice of appeal in which the only ground of appeal which is stated is that the amount awarded to the applicant is insufficient MIB may before submitting that appeal to the arbitrator give notice to the applicant that if the appeal proceeds they will request the arbitrator to decide whether the case is one in which MIB should make an award at all and if they do so they shall at the same time furnish the applicant with a statement setting out such comments as they may consider relevant to the decision which the arbitrator should come to on that question.

(2) Where MIB give a notice under paragraph (1) of this Clause, the applicant may within six weeks from the date on which that notice is given make such comments to MIB and supply them with such particulars of other evidence not contained in any written statement furnished to him by MIB as he may consider relevant to the question which the arbitrator is by that notice requested to decide, and Clause 13 hereof shall apply in relation to any comments made or particulars supplied by the applicant under this paragraph as it applies in relation to any comments made or particulars supplied under the said Clause 13.

15. MIB shall, where they receive notice of an appeal from the applicant under the foregoing provisions of this Agreement, unless the appeal is previously withdrawn, submit that appeal (but in a case where they cause such an investigation to be made as is mentioned in Clause 13 hereof, not until the expiration of six weeks from the date on which they sent the applicant a report as to the result of that investigation and, in a case where they gave such a notice to the applicant as is mentioned in Clause 14(1) hereof, not until the expiration of six weeks from the date on which they gave that notice and, if they have caused an investigation to be made into any evidence supplied under Clause 14(2) hereof, not until the expiration of six weeks from the date on which they sent the applicant a report as to the result of that investigation) to an arbitrator for a decision, sending to the arbitrator for that purpose the application made by the applicant, a copy of their decision thereon as notified to the applicant and of all statements, declarations, notices, undertakings, comments, transcripts, particulars of reports furnished, given or sent under this Agreement either by the applicant or any person acting for him to MIB or by MIB to the applicant or a person so acting.

16. On any such appeal—

(*a*) if the appeal is against a decision by MIB rejecting an application because a preliminary investigation has disclosed that the case is not one to which this Agreement applies, the arbitrator shall decide whether the case is or is not one to which this Agreement applies and, if he decides that it is such a case, shall remit the application to MIB for full investigation and for a decision by MIB in accordance with the foregoing provisions of this Agreement;

(*b*) if the appeal is against a decision by MIB given after an application has been fully investigated by MIB (whether before the appeal or in consequence of its being remitted for such investigation under paragraph (a) of this Clause), the arbitrator shall decide, as may be appropriate, having regard to the grounds stated in the notice of appeal and to any notice given by MIB to the applicant under Clause 14 hereof, whether MIB should make an award under this Agreement to the applicant and, if so, the amount which MIB should award to the applicant under the foregoing provisions of this Agreement;

(*c*) if the appeal related to a dispute which has arisen between the applicant and MIB which is required by the proviso to Clause 6(3) hereof to be referred to the arbitrator, the arbitrator shall also give his decision on that dispute.

17. The arbitrator shall decide the appeal on the documents submitted to him as set out in Clause 15 hereof and no further evidence shall be produced to him:

Provided that—

(*a*) the arbitrator shall be entitled to ask MIB to make any further investigation which he considers desirable and to submit a written report of their findings to him for his consideration; and

(*b*) MIB shall send a copy of any such report to the applicant who shall be entitled to submit written comments on it to MIB within four weeks of the date on which that copy is sent to him; and

(*c*) MIB shall transmit those comments to the arbitrator for his consideration.

18. The arbitrator by whom any such appeal as aforesaid shall be decided shall be an arbitrator to be selected by the Secretary of State from two panels of Queen's Counsel appointed respectively by the Lord Chancellor and the Lord Advocate for the purpose of determining appeals under this Agreement, the arbitrator to be selected from the panel appointed by the Lord Chancellor in cases where the event giving rise to the death or injury occurred in England or Wales and from the panel appointed by the Lord Advocate where that event occurred in Scotland.

19. The arbitrator shall notify his decision on any appeal under this Agreement to MIB and MIB shall forthwith send a copy of the arbitrator's decision to the applicant.

20. Subject to the provisions of this Agreement, MIB shall pay the applicant any amount which the arbitrator has decided shall be awarded to the applicant, and such payment shall discharge MIB from all liability under this Agreement in respect of the death or injury in respect of which that decision has been given.

21. Each party to the appeal will bear his own costs.

22. MIB shall pay the arbitrator a fee approved by the Lord Chancellor or the Lord Advocate, as the case may be, after consultation with MIB:

Provided that the arbitrator may in his discretion, in any case where it appears to him that there were no reasonable grounds for the appeal, decide that his fee ought to be paid by the applicant and, where the arbitrator so decides, the person giving the undertaking required by Clause 12 hereof shall be liable to reimburse MIB the amount of the fee paid by them to the arbitrator except in so far as that amount is deducted by MIB from any amount which they are liable to pay to the applicant in consequence of the decision of the arbitrator.

23. If in any case it appears to MIB that by reason of the applicant being under the age of majority or of any other circumstances affecting his capacity to manage his affairs it would be in the interest of the applicant that all or some part of the amount which would otherwise be payable to him under an award made under this Agreement should be administered for him by the Family Welfare Association or by some other body or person under a trust MIB may establish for that purpose a trust of the whole or part of the said amount to take effect for such period and subject to such provisions as may appear to MIB appropriate in the circumstances of the case.

24. This Agreement may be determined at any time by the Secretary of State or by MIB by either of them giving to the other not less than twelve months previous notice in writing:

Provided that this Agreement shall continue to have effect in respect of any case where the event giving rise to the death or injury occurred before the date on which this Agreement terminates in accordance with any notice so given.

25. This Agreement shall come into operation on 1 December 1972 in relation to accidents occurring on or after that date, and the Agreement made on 21 April 1969 between the Secretary of State and MIB shall cease and determine except in relation to applications arising out of accidents which occurred on or after 1 May 1969 and before the said 1 December 1972.

Notes

The following Notes are for the guidance of those who may wish to make application to the Motor Insurers' Bureau for payment under the Agreement, and for the guidance of their legal advisers, but they must not be taken as rendering unnecessary a careful study of the Agreement itself. Communications connected with the Agreement should be addressed to the Motor Insurers' Bureau whose address is Aldermary House, Queen Street, London EC4 1TR. [*Author's note*: Now incorrect—52 Silbury Boulevard, Central Milton Keynes, MK9 1NB]

1. This Agreement replaces a previous one dated 21 April 1969 which put on a formal basis the arrangements which have existed since 1946 under which the Bureau have made ex gratia payments in respect of death or personal injury resulting from the use on a road of a motor vehicle the owner or driver of which cannot be traced. Provision is made for an appeal against the Bureau's decision in such cases.

2. The Agreement dated 21 April 1969 applies to a death or bodily injury arising out of an accident occurring on a road in Great Britain on or after 1 May 1969, and before 1 December 1972. This Agreement applies in relation to accidents occurring on or after 1 December 1972.

3. Subject to the terms of the Agreement, the Bureau will accept applications for a payment in respect of the death of, or bodily injury to, any person resulting

from the use of a motor vehicle on a road in Great Britain in any case in which—

(*a*) the applicant for the payment cannot trace any person responsible for the death or injury (or, in certain circumstances, a person partly responsible) (Clause 1(1)(*b*)); and

(*b*) the death or injury was caused in such circumstances that the untraced person would be liable to pay damages to the applicant in respect of the death or injury (Clause 1(1)(*c*)); and

(*c*) the untraced person's liability to the applicant is one which at the time the accident occurred, was required to be covered by insurance or security (Clause 1(1)(*d*)).

The Bureau will not, however, deal with deliberate 'running down' cases (Clause 1(1)(*e*)) nor with certain other cases relating to Crown vehicles and certain categories of 'voluntary' passenger (Clause 1(2)–(4)).

4. Applications for a payment under the Agreement must be made in writing to the Bureau within 3 years of the date of the accident giving rise to the death or injury (Clause 1(1)(*f*)).

5. Under Clause 3, the amount which the Bureau will award will (except for the exclusion of those elements of damages mentioned in Clause 4) be assessed in the same way as a Court would have assessed the amount of damages payable by the untraced person had the applicant been able to bring a successful claim for damages against him.

6. Clause 5 relates to cases where an untraced person and an unidentified person are each partly responsible for a death or injury, and defines the conditions under which the Bureau will in such cases make a contribution in respect of the responsibility of the untraced person.

7. Under Clause 6(1)(*b*), the Bureau may require the applicant to bring proceedings against any identified person who may be responsible for the death or injury, subject to indemnifying the applicant as to his costs as provided in Clause 6(2) and (3).

8. On receipt of an application, the Bureau will, if satisfied that the application comes within the terms of the Agreement, investigate the circumstances and, when this has been done, decide whether to make a payment and, if so, how much (Clause 7).

9. The Bureau may request the applicant to make a statutory declaration setting out all, or some, of the facts on which his application is based (Clause 8).

10. The Bureau will notify the applicant of their decision, setting out the circumstances of the case and the evidence on which they base their decision and, if they refuse to make payment, the reasons for that refusal (Clause 9).

11. If the applicant does not exercise his right to appeal against the Bureau's decision, the Bureau's decision will be final and the applicant will be entitled to be paid the amount awarded by the Bureau (Clause 10).

12. If the applicant wishes to appeal against the decision on the grounds specified in Clause 11, he must notify the Bureau within six weeks of being notified of the decision, and give the undertakings set out in Clause 12.

13. The Bureau may, as a result of comments made by the applicant on their decision, investigate the application further, and if so they will communicate with the applicant again. In such a case, the applicant will have six weeks from the date of that further communication in which to decide whether or not to go on with his appeal (Clause 13).

14. Where the applicant appeals only on the grounds that the amount awarded to him is low, the Bureau may give him notice that if the matter proceeds to

appeal, they will ask the arbitrator to decide also the issue of the Bureau's liability to make any payment. The applicant will have six weeks from the date of any such notice in which to comment to the Bureau on this intention (Clause 14).
15. Appeals will be decided by an arbitrator who will be a Queen's Counsel selected by the Secretary of State for the Environment from one of two panels to be appointed by the Lord Chancellor and the Lord Advocate respectively (Clause 18).
16. All appeals will be decided by the arbitrator on the basis of the relevant documents (as set out in Clause 15) which will be sent to him by the Bureau. If the arbitrator asks the Bureau to make a further investigation, the applicant will have an opportunity to comment on the result of that investigation (Clause 17).
17. The arbitrator may, at his discretion, award the cost of his fee against the applicant if he considers the appeal unreasonable; otherwise, each party to the appeal will bear their own costs, the Bureau paying the arbitrator's fee (Clauses 21 and 22).
18. In certain circumstances, the Bureau may establish a trust for the benefit of an applicant on the whole or part of any award (Clause 23).

3 Compensation of victims of untraced drivers supplemental agreement

IT IS HEREBY AGREED as follows:

1. (1) In any case in which an application has been made to MIB in pursuance of clause 2(1) of the principal agreement on or after 3 January 1978 and in which a preliminary investigation in pursuance of clause 7 thereof has disclosed that the case is one to which that agreement, but not clause 5 thereof, applies MIB may, instead of causing a report to be made on the application as provided by the said clause 7, make, or cause to be made, to the applicant an offer to settle his application in a specified sum, assessed in accordance with clause 3 of the principal agreement.

(2) Where an offer is made in pursuance of paragraph (1) above, there shall be furnished to the applicant (at the same time) in writing particulars of (i) the circumstances in which the death or injury occurred and the evidence bearing thereon, and (ii) the circumstances relevant to the assessment of the amount to be awarded to the applicant and the evidence bearing thereon.

2. On receipt by MIB or its agent of an acceptance of the offer referred to in the foregoing clause, in the form specified in the Schedule hereto and duly completed by the applicant:

(*a*) the principal agreement shall have effect in relation to the application as if in clause 7 the words 'and unless MIB decide' to the end of that clause, and clauses 9 to 22 inclusive were omitted, and

(*b*) MIB shall pay to the applicant the amount specified in the offer, and such payment shall discharge MIB from all liability under this and the principal agreement in respect of the death or injury in relation to which the payment has been made.

3. In clause 4(*a*) of the principal agreement after the words 'solatium for the grief of any relative of the deceased' there shall be inserted the words 'or a loss of society award to a member of the immediate family of the deceased under section 1(4) of the Damages (Scotland) Act 1976'.

4. In clause 16 of the principal agreement there shall be added at the end the following proviso:—'Provided that where the arbitrator has dealt with an appeal under paragraph (*a*) of this clause all the foregoing provisions of this agreement shall apply as if the case were an application to which this agreement applies upon which MIB had not communicated a decision'.

5. This agreement shall be construed as one with the principal agreement and, without prejudice to the operation of clause 6 thereof, shall cease to have effect on the date that that agreement terminates in accordance with clause 24 thereof, and subject to the proviso there mentioned.

6. Clauses 1 and 2 of this agreement may be determined at any time by the Secretary of State or by MIB, by either of them giving to the other not less than 12 months previous notice in writing; Provided that the said clauses shall continue to have effect in respect of any case where the event giving rise to the death or injury occurred before the date on which those clauses terminate in accordance with any notice so given.

SCHEDULE (referred to in clause 2)
Form of Acceptance (under Supplemental Agreement dated 7 December 1977)

I, [*full name of applicant*] of [*address*] HEREBY ACCEPT the sum of £
offered, in pursuance of clause 1 of an agreement made between the Secretary of State for Transport and the Motor Insurers' Bureau (hereinafter called 'MIB') and dated 7 December 1977, by or on behalf of MIB in settlement of the application made by me or on my behalf on [*date*] to MIB in pursuance of clause 2(1) of an agreement made between the Secretary of State for the Environment and MIB and dated 22 November 1972 relating to compensation of victims of untraced drivers in respect of:—[*particulars of, and circumstances giving rise to, injuries*] AND UNDERSTAND that payment of that sum will discharge MIB from all liability under the aforementioned agreements, and that I shall have no further rights under those agreements (in particular any right of appeal to an arbitrator under clause 11 of the agreement of 22 November 1972).

Name and address and description of witness:

Signature of applicant:
Date:

IN WITNESS etc.

Notes

1. This agreement supplements the agreement dated 22 November 1972 concerning compensation for personal injuries suffered by victims of untraced drivers.
2. The following notes are for guidance only and must not be taken as rendering unnecessary a careful study of this supplemental agreement itself together with the main agreement to which it relates. Communications concerning these agreements should be addressed to the Motor Insurers' Bureau, whose address is Aldermary House, Queen Street, London EC4N 1TR. [*Author's note*: now incorrect—52 Silbury Boulevard, Central Milton Keynes, MK9 1NB]

3. Clause 1 of the supplemental agreement provides for the use of a shorter form of procedure than that stipulated in the main agreement with the object of securing speedier disposal of certain applications to the Bureau. Except in a case where both an untraced person and an identified person may each partly be responsible for the injuries giving rise to an application, the Bureau may, at its discretion, make an offer of an award in a specified sum furnishing the applicant at the time with particulars of the circumstances of the case and of the evidence on which the offer is based. If the applicant is prepared to accept the offer and undertake, on payment by the Bureau, to discharge them from all liability and forgo any right of appeal to an arbitrator the Bureau will pay the sum offered forthwith. If the offer is not acceptable the application will thereafter be dealt with in accordance with the full procedure as set out in the main agreement.

4. The purpose of clause 4 of the supplemental agreement is to make clear that the Bureau remain entitled to require any applicant to take proceedings against a known person in accordance with clause 6(1)(*b*) of the main agreement, notwithstanding that the applicant had successfully appealed against a decision by the Bureau to reject the application after a preliminary investigation.

Appendix G

Specimen Pleadings

Contents

County court documents

C1 Request for issue of Default Summons.
C2 Default Summons.
C3 Particulars of Claim.
C4 Schedule of Special Damage.
C5 Defence.
C6 Request for Further and Better Particulars of defence.
C7 Notice of Application.
C8 Court order.
C9 Further and Better Particulars of the defence.
C10 List of documents.
C11 Judgment after trial before judge without jury.

High Court

H1 Writ endorsed with Statement of Claim.
H2 Acknowledgment of Service of writ.
H3 Statement of Claim.
H4 Defence.
H5 Request for Further and Better Particulars of the defence.
H6 Master's Summons.
H7 Master's Orders.
H8 Further and Better Particulars of the defence.
H9 Judgment after trial before judge without jury.
H10 Originating Summons.

C1 Request for Issue of Default Summons

Request for Issue of Default Summons

For court use Case number	
Summons in form:	N1 ☐
	N2 ☐
Service by:	Post ☐
	Plaintiff('s Solr) ☐

- Please read the notes over the page before filling in this form.

1 Plaintiff's full name address.

NICOLA SOLOMON
3 Pritchard's Terrace
Golders Green
London NW11

2 Name and address for service and payment *(if different from above)* **Ref/Tel No.**

Messrs. FIGHT & BITEM
2 Aggressive Road
London W3
NB/321 071 - 404 2000

3 Defendant's name address.

PRITCHARD LTD
78 Poynines Place
Portsmouth Hants
NB Please serve on Solicitors
Messrs GREED AND VICE
2 Pleasant Road
Portsmouth Hants

- Please be careful when filling in the request form. Do not write outside the boxes.
- Type or write in BLOCK CAPITALS using **black ink**.
- If the details of the claim are on a separate sheet you must also give the court a copy for each Defendant.
- You can get help to complete this form and information about court procedures at any county court office or citizens' advice bureau.

4 What the claim is for

Give brief description of the type of claim.

Personal Injury

5 Particulars of the Plaintiff's claim

See attached

7 Signed
Plaintiff('s solicitor)
(or see enclosed "Particulars of claim")

6

	£	p
Plaintiff's claim	unliquidated	
Court fee	43	00
Solicitor's costs	38	00
Total Amount	81	00
For court use **Issued on**		

8 Arbitration (small claims procedure)

Any defended claim for £1,000 or less will be automatically dealt with by arbitration. If you do not want the claim to be dealt with by arbitration you will have to apply to the court. The court office can give you more details.

If the claim is for more than £1,000 and you would like it to be dealt with by arbitration, please tick this box ☐

N.201 Request for Default Summons (Order 3, rule 3(1))

Notes

1 Plaintiff *(the person making the claim)*
Fill in the Plaintiff's full name and address or place of business. If the Plaintiff is:

- **a company registered under the Companies Act, 1985,** give the address of the registered office and describe it as such.
- **a person trading in a name other than his own,** give his own name followed by the words, "trading as" and the name under which he trades.
- **two or more co-partners suing in the name of their firm,** add "A Firm".
- **an assignee,** say so and give the name, address and occupation of the assignor.
- **a minor required to sue by next friend,** state this, and give the full names, address or place of business, and occupation of next friend. You will also need to complete and send in Form N 235 (which you can get from the court office).
- **suing in a representative capacity,** say in what capacity.

2 Address for service and payment
If this request is completed by a solicitor or by your legal department, the name, address and reference of the solicitor or legal department should be in Box 2. The court will use this address for sending documents to you (service). (If the address is the same as shown at Box 1, please write "as above" in Box 2).

- **A plaintiff who is not represented by a solicitor or legal department must not use Box 2** except for an address to which payment may be made. In this case you must delete the word 'service in the title to Box (2).

3 Defendant *(the person against whom the claim is made)*
Fill in the Defendant's surname, and (where known) his or her initials or names in full. **It is essential that the Defendant should be identified as fully and as accurately as possible.** Also give the Defendant's address or place of business (if the owner of a business). Say whether Defendant is male or female and, if under 18, state "minor". If the Defendant is:

- **a company registered under the Companies Act, 1985,** the address given can be the registered office of the company (you must describe it as such), or its place of business. If the summons is not sent to the registered office, there is a risk that it will not come to the notice of an appropriate person in the company. As a result, the court may be asked to set aside any judgment or order that has been made. **For fixed amount cases only** – Bear in mind that if the company you are suing defends the case, the case will automatically be transferred to his local court. If the registered office and place of business are not in the same court area, you may decide to choose the address which is most convenient to you.
- **a person trading in a name other than his own** who is sued under that name, add "A Trading Name".
- **two or more co-partners** sued in the name of their firm, add "A Firm".
- **sued in a representative capacity,** say in what capacity.

To be completed by the court

Served on:	
By posting on:	
Officer:	

4 What the claim is for
Put a brief description of your claim in the box (e.g. price of goods sold and delivered, work done, money due under an agreement).

5 Particulars of your claim
Give a brief statement of the facts of your claim and the amount for which you are suing. Include any relevant dates and sufficient details so that the Defendant understands what your claim is for. He is entitled to ask for further details. If there is not enough space or the details of your claim are too complicated, you should enclose a separate sheet for the court and a copy for each Defendant. The court can help you in setting out your particulars of claim.

6 Amount claimed
Fill in the total amount you are claiming. The court fee and solicitor's costs are based on this and you should enter these too. A leaflet setting out the current fees is available from the court.

7 Signature
The person filling in the form should sign and date it unless enclosing separate details of claim (in which case the enclosed sheets should be signed).

8 Arbitration (small claims procedure)
Any defended claim for £1.000 or less will be automatically dealt with by arbitration (small claims procedure). If the claim is for more than £1,000 and you would like it to be dealt with by arbitration, you may include such a request in your particulars of claim. (Solicitor's costs and the grounds for setting aside an arbitrator's award are strictly limited).

9 Personal injury claims
In these cases you must include a medical report for the court and for each Defendant. If you are also claiming special damages (eg loss of income, medical expenses etc). an up to date statement, to include details of loss of any future expenses or losses, must also be included for the court and for each Defendant. If you cannot provide these you should apply to the court for directions.

10 Unliquidated claims for more than £5,000
If your claim is not for a fixed amount and you expect to recover more than £5,000 (excluding interest and costs), you must state this in your particulars of claim.

11 Where to send the summoms

- **If the summons is for a fixed amount,**
you can ask any county court in England and Wales to issue the summons but you will usually choose your local court or the court for the area where the Defendant lives or carries on business. Bear in mind that if the person you are suing defends the case, the case will automatically be transferred to the Defendant's local court.
- **For a personal injury or other unliquidated claim,**
you may prefer to choose the court where the cause of action arose. The case will not be automatically transferred if a defence is filed.

Further information on how to issue a default summons and what happens after issue can be obtained from any county court office.

OYEZ The Solicitors' Law Stationery Society Ltd., Oyez House, 7 Spa Road, London SE16 3QQ 1991 Edition 5.91 F19926
5039082

County Court N201

C2 Default Summons

County Court Summons

Case Number *Always quote this.*	9210560
In the ANYTOWN **County Court**	

The court office is open from 10am to 4pm Monday to Friday

Telephone:

Seal

This summons is only valid if sealed by the court.
If it is not sealed it should be sent to the court.

Plaintiff's full name address.	NICOLA SOLOMON 3 Pritchard's Terrace Golders Green London NW11
Plaintiff's Solicitor's address. **Ref./Tel. No.**	Messrs. FIGHT AND BITEM 2 Aggressive Road London W3 NB1321 071 404 2000
Defendant's name address.	PRITCHARD LTD 78 Poynines Place Portsmouth Hants

What the Plaintiff claims from you

Give brief description of type of claim: Personal injury

Particulars of the Plaintiff's claim against you

See attached

Signed
Plaintiff('s solicitor)
(or see enclosed "Particulars of claim")

Amount claimed	see particulars	
Court fee	43	00
Solicitor's costs	38	00
Total Amount	81	00
Summons issued on	1st September 1992	

What you should do

Within 14 days from the date of service (which is explained overleaf under the heading **General Information**), you should either

- **defend the claim** by filling in the back of the enclosed form and **sending it to the court; or**
- **admit the claim** and make an offer of payment, by filling in the front of the enclosed reply form and **sending it to the court.**

If you do nothing judgment may be entered against you.

For more information on what to do next, please read the back of the form.

N2 Default summons (amount not fixed) (Order 3, rule 3(2)(b))

Please read this page: it will help you deal with the summons

If you dispute all or part of the claim

You may be entitled to help with your legal costs. Ask about the legal aid scheme at any county court office, citizens' advice bureau, legal advice centre or firm of solicitors displaying the legal aid sign.

- Say how much you dispute in the part of the enclosed form for defending the claim and return it to the court. The court will tell you what to do next.
- If you dispute only part of the claim, you should also fill in the part of the form for admitting the claim and pay the amount admitted into court.
- If the court named on the summons is not your local county court, you may write to the court named asking for the case to be transferred to your local county court and explaining your reasons. However, if the case is transferred and you later lose the case, you may have to pay more in costs.
- A claim for £1,000 or less will normally be dealt with by arbitration under the small claims procedure.

If you want to make a claim against the Plaintiff

This is known as a counterclaim

Fill in the part of the enclosed form headed 'Counterclaim'. If your claim is for more than the Plaintiff's claim you may have to pay a fee - the court will let you know. Unless the Plaintiff admits your counterclaim there will be a hearing. The court will tell you what to do next.

If you admit the claim or any part of it

- **You may pay an appropriate amount into court** to compensate the Plaintiff (see **Payments into Court** box on this page), accompanied by a notice (or letter) that the payment is in satisfaction of the claim. If the Plaintiff accepts the amount paid he is also entitled to apply for his costs.
- **If you need time to pay,** complete the enclosed form of admission and give details of how you propose to pay the Plaintiff. If your offer is accepted, the court will send an order telling you how to pay. If it is not accepted, the court will fix a rate of payment based on the details given in your form of admission and the Plaintiff's comments. Judgment will be entered and you will be sent an order telling you how and when to pay.
- **If the Plaintiff does not accept the amount paid or offered,** the court will fix a hearing to decide how much you must pay to compensate the Plaintiff. The court will tell you when the hearing, which you should attend, will take place.

To be completed on the court copy only

Served on:

By posting on:

Officer:

This summons was returned by the Post Office marked 'Gone Away' on:

General information

- If you received this summons through the post the date of service will be 7 days (for a limited company at its registered office, the second working day) after the date of posting as shown by the postmark.
- You can get help to complete the enclosed form and information about court procedures at any county court office or citizens' advice bureau. The address and telephone number of your local court is listed under 'Courts' in the phone book.
- Please address forms or letters to the Chief Clerk.
- Always quote the whole of the case number which appears at the top right corner of the front of this form; the court is unable to trace your case without it.

Registration of judgments

If the summons results in a judgment against you, your name and address may be entered in the Register of County Court Judgments. **This may make it difficult for you to get credit.** A leaflet giving further information can be obtained from the court.

Interest on judgments

If judgment is entered against you and is for more than £5,000, the Plaintiff may be entitled to interest on the total amount.

Payments into Court

You can pay the court by calling at the court office which is open 10 am to 4 pm Monday to Friday.

You may only pay by:

- cash,
- banker's or giro draft,
- cheque supported by a cheque card,
- cheque (unsupported cheques may be accepted, subject to clearance, if the Chief Clerk agrees).

Cheques and drafts must be made payable to HM Paymaster General and crossed.

Please bring this form with you.

By post

You may only pay by:

- postal order,
- banker's or giro draft,
- cheque (cheques may be accepted, subject to clearance, if the Chief Clerk agrees).

The payment must be made out to HM Paymaster General and crossed.

This method of payment is at your own risk

And you must:

- pay the postage,
- enclose this form,
- enclose a self addressed envelope so that the court can return this form with a receipt.

The court **cannot** *accept stamps or payments by bank and giro credit transfers.*

Note: You should carefully check any future forms from the court to see if payments should be made directly to the Plaintiff.

OYEZ The Solicitors' Law Stationery Society Ltd., Oyez House, 7 Spa Road, London SE16 3QQ 1991 Edition 5.91 F19867

5039650

C3 Statement of Claim

IN THE ANYTOWN COUNTY COURT **Case No. 9210560**
BETWEEN

NICOLA SOLOMON

Plaintiff

and

PRITCHARD LTD

Defendant

PARTICULARS OF CLAIM

---

1. The Plaintiff was born on 1st May 1960.
At all material times the Plaintiff was employed as a technician by the defendant at its factory at 78 Poynines Place, Portsmouth, Hants.

2. On or about 1st May 1992 the plaintiff was instructed to attend the plant room and check the tension of the drive belts. The plaintiff attended the plant room as instructed. The plaintiff was not given any formal instructions on how to carry out the particular job and she placed a ladder against the cabinet with the lower feet of the ladder against the cabinet with the lower feet of the ladder flat on the floor. In order to check the tension of the drive belt she placed her left hand through the gap between the top of the cabinet and the ceiling at the rear of guard. She then changed position and checked the tension of the right hand drive belt with her right hand. Suddenly the ladder slipped on the floor and the plaintiff caught her right forearm on the corner of the steel angle at the top of the cabinet sustaining serious personal injuries.

3. The matters complained of were caused by the negligence and/or breach of statutory duty of the defendant.

PARTICULARS OF NEGLIGENCE

1. Failing to provide a safe system of work.
2. Providing a ladder with metal feet which was liable to slip on the metal floor.
3. Allowing the metal floor of the room to become wet with rain water.
4. Failing to ensure that the ladder was properly footed or secured.
5. Failing to provide an additional employee to foot or secure the ladder.
6. Failing to adequately instruct the plaintiff with specific instructions on how to safely carry out the job.
7. Failing to provide competent supervision for the Plaintiff.
8. Allowing the guard to be inadequately constructed.

PARTICULARS OF BREACH OF STATUTORY DUTY

The plant room was a factory within the meaning of the Factories Act 1961 and the matters complained of constituted breaches of Section 29 of that Act.

4. By reason of the matters aforesaid the plaintiff sustained personal injuries and has thereby suffered pain, injury, loss and damage.

PARTICULARS OF INJURIES

The plaintiff sustained a severe injury to her right forearm when it caught upon the sharp metal edge of the guard. The plaintiff required admission to hospital for one month with her arm elevated immobilised in a dorsal slab of plaster. Subsequently she required physiotherapy and rehabilitation. She will be permanently scarred. Full details of her injuries and the prognosis are disclosed in the medical report of Mr. Bodger FRCS dated 17th July 1992 and served herewith.

PARTICULARS OF SPECIAL DAMAGE

These are disclosed in a Schedule and served herewith.

5. The plaintiff claims interest at such rate and for such period on both general and special damages as may to the Court seem just pursuant to section 69 of the County Court Act 1984.

The Plaintiff claims:

1. Damages.
2. Interest thereon pursuant to section 69 of the County Courts Act 1984.
3. Costs.

....

Messrs. Fight and Bitem

Served this 13th day of August 1992
To the Court
and to the Defendant.

C4 Schedule of Special Damage

IN THE ANYTOWN
COUNTY COURT **Case No. 9210560**
BETWEEN

NICOLA SOLOMON

Plaintiff

and

PRITCHARD LTD

Defendant

SCHEDULE OF SPECIAL DAMAGE

1.	*Loss of Earnings* 1st May 1992 – 1st September 1992 three months at £1,000.00 per month		£3,000.00
2.	*Value of Clothing*		
	Overalls	£13.00	
	T-shirt	£ 4.00	
	Ring—cut off and repaired	£10.00	
	Total		£27.00
3.	*Travelling expenses* Physiotherapist and to see Solicitors—13 journeys at £2.00 per journey		£26.00
4.	Three days taken as holiday		£90.00
5.	Two visits to Solicitors at £41.94 net per day		£125.82
6.	Osteopathic fees		£125.00
			£3393.82

Dated this 13th day of August 1992

SIGNED ....
Messrs. Fight and Bitem

C5 Defence

IN THE ANYTOWN COUNTY COURT BETWEEN **Case No. 9210560**

NICOLA SOLOMON

Plaintiff

and

PRITCHARD LTD

Defendant

DEFENCE

---

1. The defendant admits paragraph 1 of the Particulars of Claim.

2. The defendant denies that the plaintiff was instructed to attend at the plant room as alleged or at all.

3. The defendant admits that the plaintiff was injured by catching her right forearm on the corner of a steel angle at the top of the cabinet but denies this was caused by the negligence or breach of statutory duty of the defendant or at all.

4. The accident was solely caused or alternatively contributed to by the negligence of the plaintiff.

PARTICULARS OF NEGLIGENCE

1. Did not carry out her work in a safe manner.

2. Placed a ladder with metal feet which was liable to slip on the metal floor without checking whether an alternative was available.

3. Failed to request an additional employee to foot or secure the ladder.

4. Carried on work without authority from the defendant.

5. Failed to follow the defendant's safety instructions.

6. The defendant does not admit that the plaintiff suffered personal injuries loss and damage as alleged in paragraph 4 of the Particulars of Claim or at all.

7. Save as set out above the defendant denies each and every allegation in the Particulars of Claim as if the same were herein set out and traversed seriatim.

. . . .
Messrs. Greed and Vice

SERVED this 10th day of October 1992
by Messrs. Greed and Vice, 2 Pleasant Road, Portsmouth,
Hampshire, Solicitors for the defendant.

To the Court and to the Plaintiff

C6 Request for Further and Better Particulars of the Defence

IN THE ANYTOWN
COUNTY COURT **Case No. 9210560**
BETWEEN

NICOLA SOLOMON

Plaintiff

and

PRITCHARD LTD

Defendant

REQUEST FOR FURTHER AND BETTER PARTICULARS OF THE DEFENCE

Of Paragraph 4(5) of the defence 'Failed to follow the defendant's safety instructions'. Set out precisely which safety instructions of the defendant were not followed with reference to a document if any.

SIGNED ....
Messrs. Fight and Bitem

Served the day of January 1993
by Messrs. Fight and Bitem of 2 Aggressive Road, London W3
Solicitor for the Plaintiff

To the Court and the Defendant

C7 Notice of Application

IN THE ANYTOWN **COUNTY COURT**

CASE No. 9210560

Between NICOLA SOLOMON

Plaintiff

AND

PRITCHARD LTD.

Defendant

(1) State nature and grounds of application.

I wish to apply for (1) an Order that the Defendant do within fourteen days serve the Further and Better Particulars of the Defence requested in the attached document and in default of doing so be debarred from further defending.

Dated 3rd February 1993

(*Signed*) Messrs. FIGHT AND BITEM

Plaintiff/~~Defendant~~

Address for service 2 Aggressive Road, London W3

THIS SECTION TO BE COMPLETED BY THE COURT

To the Plaintiff/Defendant

TAKE NOTICE that this application will be heard by the Registrar [Judge]

at

on at o'clock

IF YOU DO NOT ATTEND THE COURT WILL MAKE SUCH ORDER AS IT THINKS FIT.

Address all communications to the Chief Clerk AND QUOTE THE ABOVE CASE NUMBER

THE COURT OFFICE AT

is open from 10 am to 4 pm Monday to Friday.

N.244 Notice of application O.13, r.1(2)

OYEZ The Solicitors' Law Stationery Society Ltd., Oyez House, 7 Spa Road, London SE16 3QQ

County Court N244

7.91 F20347

5039197

C8 Order on application

IN THE ANYTOWN COUNTY COURT
BETWEEN

Case No. 9210560

NICOLA SOLOMON

Plaintiff

and

PRITCHARD LTD

Defendant

UPON HEARING Solicitors for the Parties

IT IS ORDERED THAT the defendant do within fourteen days serve on the Plaintiff Further and Better Particulars of the defence as initialled by the district judge and that the costs of this application be the plaintiff's in any event.

DATED the 5th day of April 1993

C9 Further and Better Particulars of Defence

IN THE ANYTOWN COUNTY COURT **Case No. 9210560**
BETWEEN

NICOLA SOLOMON

Plaintiff

and

PRITCHARD LTD

Defendant

FURTHER AND BETTER PARTICULARS OF THE DEFENCE

REQUEST

Of Paragraph 4(5) of the defence 'Failed to follow the defendant's safety instructions'. Set out precisely which safety instructions of the defendant were not followed with reference to a document if any.

REPLY

The plaintiff failed to follow s6(3) and 9(4) of the defendant's safety manual which states

'6(3) An employee should not use a ladder without another employee being present.'

'9(4) An employee should not carry out any work unless adequately supervised.'

Served this 16th day of April 1993 by
Messrs. Greed & Vice of 2 Pleasant Road, Portsmouth, Hants
Solicitors for the Defendant

To the Court
And to the Defendant

C10 List of Documents

List of Documents

In the Anytown County Court	
Case Number (Always quote this)	9210560

Plaintiff

Defendant

(1) Delete words in brackets if list is sent in response to automatic directions (O17 r11).
(2) Insert date.

The following is a list of documents which contain information about matters in dispute in this case which are or have been in my possession(1). [~~They are sent in response to your request dated~~(2) 19 .]

Schedule 1 PART I

(3) List and number here in a convenient order the documents (or bundles of documents if of the same nature, eg: invoices) in your possession which you do not object to being inspected. Give a short description of each document or bundle so that it can be identified and say if it is kept elsewhere i.e bank, solicitor.

I have in my possession the documents numbered and listed here. I do not object to you inspecting them(3).

1. Contract of Employment dated 13th June 1982.
2. Receipt for new overall.
3. Copy of record in accident book.
4. Correspondence between Solicitors (dates various)
5. Pleadings orders and all other documents in the action.

N.265 List of documents
O. 14, r. 1(5)

[P.T.O.

Schedule 1 PART II

(4) List and number here, as above, the documents in your possession which you object to being inspected.

I have in my possession the documents numbered and listed here but I object to you inspecting them(4).

Correspondence between me and my Solicitor and the Legal Aid Board
Correspondence between my Solicitors and witnesses
Instructions to Counsel
Notes, documents and other inter-office memoranda and other documents brought into possession for the purposes of the action

(5) Say what your objections are

I object to you inspecting these documents because(5): —
they are by their nature privileged

Schedule 2

(6) List and number here, the documents you once had in your possession but which you no longer have when this list is served. For each document listed say when it was last in your possession and where it is now.

I have had the documents numbered and listed below, but they are no longer in my possession(6).

Those documents referred to as copies in Schedule 1 Part 1

All the documents which are or have been in my possession and which contain information about the matters in dispute in this case are listed in Schedules 1 and 2.

(7) "Plaintiff" or "Defendant".

(8) Insert date.

Signed(7): Messrs. FIGHT AND BITEM Dated(8): 16th March 1993

In the **County Court**

Dated the *day of* *19 .*

v.

List of Documents

Solicitors

Solicitor's Reference:

OYEZ The Solicitors' Law Stationery Society Ltd., Oyez House, 27 Crimscott Street, London SE1 5TS 10.90 F18207
5039202
County Court N265 * * *

C11 Judgment after trial before judge without a jury

IN THE ANYTOWN COUNTY COURT **Case No. 9210560**
BETWEEN

NICOLA SOLOMON

Plaintiff

and

(Seal)

PRITCHARD LTD

Defendant

JUDGMENT AFTER TRIAL BEFORE JUDGE WITHOUT A JURY

ON HEARING Solicitors for the Parties

IT IS ADJUDGED that the Plaintiff do recover against the defendant the sum of £12,321.00 damages and her costs of the action to be taxed on the higher scale and that there be taxation of the Plaintiff's costs pursuant to the Legal Aid Act 1988.

DATED 1st June 1993

H1 Writ indorsed with statement of claim

COURT FEES ONLY

Writ indorsed with Statement of Claim [Unliquidated Demand] (O.6,r.1)

IN THE HIGH COURT OF JUSTICE 1992.— F.—No. 0269

Queen's Bench Division

[~~District Registry~~]

Between

MARY MARGARET FREEMAN Plaintiff

AND

JOHN MICHAEL PRITCHARD Defendant

(1) Insert name.

To the Defendant (1) JOHN MICHAEL PRITCHARD

(2) Insert address.

of (2) 78 Poynings Place Portsmouth in the County of Hampshire

This Writ of Summons has been issued against you by the above-named Plaintiff in respect of the claim set out on the back.

Within 14 days after the service of this Writ on you, counting the day of service, you must either satisfy the claim or return to the Court Office mentioned below the accompanying **Acknowledgment of Service** stating therein whether you intend to contest these proceedings.

If you fail to satisfy the claim, or to return the Acknowledgment within the time stated, or if you return the Acknowledgment without stating therein an intention to contest the proceedings the Plaintiff may proceed with the action and judgment may be entered against you forthwith and without further notice.

(3) Complete and delete as necessary.

Issued from the (3) [Central Office] [~~District Registry~~]
of the High Court this 17th day of February 1992.

NOTE:—This Writ may not be served later than 4 calendar months beginning with that date unless renewed by order of the Court.

IMPORTANT

Directions for Acknowledgment of Service are given with the accompanying form.

H1 contd

Statement of Claim

The Plaintiffs claim is for damages for personal injury sustained losses and expenses incurred (together with interest thereon pursuant to section 35A Supreme Court Act 1981) as a result of an accident which occurred on or about the 25th April 1991 at Banley Road junction with Stoke Green Coventry in the West Midlands through the negligent driving management and or control of a motor vehicle owned and driven by the Defendant.

This Writ includes a claim for personal injury but may be commenced in the High Court because the value of the action for the purposes of Article 5 of the High Court and County Courts jurisdiction order 1991 exceeds £50,000.

(Signed)

(1) If this Writ was issued out of a District Registry, this indorsement as to place where the cause of action arose should be completed.

(2) Delete as necessary.

(3) Insert name of place.

(4) For phraseology of this indorsement where the Plaintiff sues in person, see *Supreme Court Practice*, Vol 2, para 1

(1) [(2) [The cause (one of the causes) of action in respect of which the Plaintiff claims relief in this action arose wholly or in part at (3) in the district of the District Registry named overleaf]

(4) **This Writ** was issued by Messrs Jones & Co

of 110 Morrison Place, London W1

[Agent for

of

Solicitor for the said Plaintiff whose address (2) [is] [are]

91 Clifton Road, London W9

H2 Acknowledgment of service of writ

Acknowledgment of Service of Writ of Summons (Queen's Bench)

IN THE HIGH COURT OF JUSTICE
Queen's Bench Division

1992.– .–**No.**

The adjacent heading should be completed by the Plaintiff

Between

MARY MARGARET FREEMAN — Plaintiff

AND

JOHN MICHAEL PRITCHARD — Defendant

If you intend to instruct a Solicitor to act for you, give him this form IMMEDIATELY. Please complete in black ink.

IMPORTANT. Read the accompanying directions and notes for guidance carefully before completing this form. If any information required is omitted or given wrongly, THIS FORM MAY HAVE TO BE RETURNED. Delay may result in judgment being entered against a Defendant whereby he or his solicitor may have to pay the costs of applying to set it aside.

See Notes 1, 3, 4 and 5

1 State the full name of the Defendant by whom or on whose behalf the service of the Writ is being acknowledged. John Michael Pritchard

---

2 State whether the Defendant intends to contest the proceedings (*tick appropriate box*) ☒ yes ☐ no

---

See Direction 3

3 If the claim against the Defendant is for a debt or liquidated demand, AND he does not intend to contest the proceedings, state if the Defendant intends to apply for a stay of execution against any judgment entered by the Plaintiff (*tick box*) ☐ yes

---

See Direction 4

4 If the Writ of Summons was issued out of a District Registry and

(*a*) the Defendant's residence, place of business or registered office (if a limited company) is NOT within the district of that District Registry AND

(*b*) there is no indorsement on the Writ that the Plaintiff's cause of action arose wholly or in part within that district,

state if the Defendant applies for the transfer of the action (*tick box*) ☐ yes

If YES, state— (*tick appropriate box*)
☐ to the Royal Courts of Justice, London:
OR
☐ to the* District Registry

**State which Registry*

Service of the Writ is acknowledged accordingly

(*Signed*) Messrs Evans & Co

†[Solicitor] [~~Agent for~~]

Address for service **(*See notes overleaf*)**

Messrs Evans & Co., 2 Springsteen Road, London W2

† Where words appear between square brackets delete if inapplicable. Insert "Defendant in Person" if appropriate

---

Please complete overleaf

H2 contd

Indorsement by Plaintiff's solicitor (or by Plaintiff if suing in person) of his name address and reference, if any, in the box below.

Messrs Jones & Co 110 Morrison Place London W1

Notes as to Address for Service

Solicitor. Where the Defendant is represented by a Solicitor, state the Solicitor's place of business in England or Wales. If the Solicitor is the Agent of another Solicitor, state the name and the place of business of the Solicitor for whom he is acting.

Defendant in person. Where the Defendant is acting in person, he must give his residence OR, if he does not reside in England or Wales, he must give an address in England or Wales where communications for him should be sent. In the case of a limited company, "residence" means its registered or principal office.

Indorsement by Defendant's solicitor (or by Defendant if acting in person) of his name address and reference, if any, in the box below.

Messrs Evans & Co 2 Springsteen Road London W2

oyez The Solicitors' Law Stationery Society plc, Oyez House, 237 Long Lane, London SE1 4PU

F4933 4-85

High Court E22 (PR)

* * * * *

H3 Statement of claim

IN THE HIGH COURT OF JUSTICE 1992 F No 0269

QUEEN'S BENCH DIVISION

Writ issued the 17th Day of February 1992

B E T W E E N :

MARY MARGARET FREEMAN **Plaintiff**

-and-

JOHN MICHAEL PRITCHARD **Defendant**

STATEMENT OF CLAIM

1 On or about the 25th day of April 1991 the Plaintiff was riding her Honda motor cycle registered number TPL 979 F in a westerly direction along Banley Road, Coventry in the West Midlands, when the Defendant so drove an Austin motor car registered number TLN 79 M out of a side turning namely Stock Green as to collide with the Plaintiff's said motor cycle.

2 The said collision caused by the negligence of the Defendant in that he:

(a) Failed to keep any or any proper lookout.

(b) Failed so to stop, steer, slow down, or otherwise manage the said motor car so as to avoid the said collision.

(c) Failed to observe or heed the presence of the Plaintiff.

(d) Failed to accord precedence to the Plaintiff.

(e) Drove out of a minor road into a major road when it was not safe to do so.

(f) Failed to observe or heed the 'Give Way' sign and/or the give way lines at the mouth of Stoke Green.

(g) Drove out into Banley Road before ensuring that the said road was clear.

(h) Drove across the path of the Plaintiff.

3 In the circumstances, the Plaintiff suffered personal injuries, loss and damage.

H3 contd

PARTICULARS OF PERSONAL INJURIES

The Plaintiff sustained a compound fracture of the lower third of the left tibia and fibula with displacement. There was a small puncture wound over the fracture site.

The Plaintiff was treated as a hospital in-patient for one month.

Under general anaesthetic surgical toilet of the wound was carried out and stitches were inserted. The fracture was manipulated and immobilised in a thigh length plaster.

The fracture was unstable and a subsequent plaster had to be wedged on one or two further occasions, under anaesthetic, to maintain the alignment.

The plaster was removed at the end of three months and the Plaintiff attended hospital as an out-patient for exercise to mobilise the knee and strengthen the leg. There is some stiffness in the ankle and toes and the Plaintiff limps somewhat.

There is thickening and swelling around the ankle joint. The Plaintiff has regained a useful range of movement but there is still 25 per cent loss of normal movement. There is some stiffness of the toes.

The Plaintiff is unable to carry out her former work and resigned on 1st January 1992. She is unlikely to be able to work again.

PARTICULARS OF SPECIAL DAMAGE

Loss of earnings from 25.4.91 - 01.01.92 23½ weeks @ £359.70 per week	£8,453.00
Loss of earnings from 1st January 1992 to date 8 weeks at £359.70 per week	£2,877.60
Husband's travelling expenses to hospital from 25.4.85 to 24.5.85	£ 5.60
Ambulance fee on 25.4.91	£ 1.25
Cost of freighting motor cycle to Plaintiff's home following the accident	£ 50.00
Loss of holiday deposit	£ 60.00
Loss of 1 pair of shoes & tights	£ 14.00
Loss of 1 motor cycle coat	£ 21.00
	£11,512.45

The Plaintiff will suffer continuing loss of earnings at the rate of £359.70 per week or £18,704.40 per annum.

AND the Plaintiff claims DAMAGES and INTEREST thereon pursuant to section 35A Supreme Court Act 1981.

BARRY STER

SERVED the 25th day of February 1992 by Messrs Jones & Co of 110 Morrison Place London W1

Solicitor for the Plaintiff.

H4 Defence

IN THE HIGH COURT OF JUSTICE 1992-F-No 0269

QUEEN'S BENCH DIVISION

B E T W E E N:

MARY MARGARET FREEMAN **Plaintiff**

-and-

JOHN MICHAEL PRITCHARD **Defendant**

D E F E N C E

1 The Defendant admits that on 25th April 1991 a collision occurred between the Plaintiff who was riding a Honda Motor cycle and an Austin motor car driven by the Defendant in Banley Road, Coventry, West Midlands. Save as aforesaid paragraph 1 of the Statement of Claim is not admitted.

2 The Defendant denies that the said collision was caused by his negligence as alleged in paragraph 2 of the Statement of Claim or at all. The Defendant denies that he was guilty of negligence as alleged or at all.

3 The said collision was solely caused or alternatively contributed to by the negligence of the Plaintiff.

PARTICULARS OF NEGLIGENCE

The Plaintiff was negligent in that she:-

(a) drove too fast;

(b) failed to keep a proper lookout;

(c) overtook a line of traffic when it was unsafe so to do;

(d) failed to observe the Defendant's said motor car stationary in the centre of the road waiting to turn to its right;

(e) drove on the wrong side of the road;

(f) drove onto and across white diagonal stripes on the road contrary to Rule 54 of the Highway Code;

(g) ran into the front of the defendant's said motor car;

(h) failed to slow down, stop, swerve or take such other action as was necessary to avoid the said collision.

H4 contd

4 The Defendant does not admit that the Plaintiff suffered personal injuries loss and damage as alleged in paragraph 3 of the Statement of Claim or at all.

5 Save as aforesaid the Defendant denies each and every allegation in the Statement of Claim as if the same were here set forth and traversed seriatim.

<u>A COUNSEL</u>

SERVED THIS 1st day of April 1992 by Messrs Evans & Co,
of 2 Springsteen Road London W2

Solicitors for the defendant.

H5 Request for further and better particulars of the defence

IN THE HIGH COURT OF JUSTICE 1992 F No 0269

QUEEN'S BENCH DIVISION

B E T W E E N:

MARY MARGARET FREEMAN Plaintiff

-and-

JOHN MICHAEL PRITCHARD **Defendant**

REQUEST FOR FURTHER AND BETTER PARTICULARS OF THE DEFENCE

Under Paragraph 3

of (d)

By reference to a plan or other suitable means showing the precise position of the Defendant's motor car when it was so stationary as alleged.

Of (g)

By reference to a plan or other suitable means showing the precise position of the Defendant's motor car at the time of the said collision and stating whether it be alleged that the Defendant's motor car was stationary at the time of collision.

BARRY STER

SERVED the 24th day of June 1992 by Messrs Jones & Co,
of 110 Morrison Place London W1

Solicitor for the Plaintiff.

Master's Summons (General Form) (O. 32)

IN THE HIGH COURT OF JUSTICE
Queen's Bench Division

19 92 F **.—No.** 0269

* If action assigned

*Master

Between MARY MARGARET FREEMAN

Plaintiff

AND

JOHN MICHAEL PRITCHARD

Defendant

Let all parties concerned attend the Master in Chambers, in Room No. Central Office, Royal Courts of Justice, Strand, London, on day, the day of 19 , at o'clock in the noon, on the hearing of an application on the part of the (1) Plaintiff for an order that the Defendant do within fourteen days serve on the Plaintiff the Further and Better Particulars of the Defence and initialled by the Master and in default they be debarred from defending the matter and

(1) Plaintiff *or* Defendant *or* as the case may require.

that the costs of the said application be paid by the (1) Plaintiffs in any event.
~~to the~~(1)

Dated the 15th day of August 19 92.

To The Defendant

Solicitor or Agent for

This Summons was taken ~~out~~ served by
~~Agents for~~ Messrs. Evans & Co.
of 2 Springsteen Road
London W2
Solicitor for the Defendant

H7 Master's order

Master's Order (General Form) (O 32)

IN THE HIGH COURT OF JUSTICE 1992 .— F .—No. 0269

Queen's Bench Division

*Insert name of Master

Master* BETA Master in Chambers.

Between

MARY MARGARET FREEMAN Plaintiff

AND

JOHN MICHAEL PRITCHARD Defendant

Upon hearing

Solicitors for the parties

~~and upon reading the affidavit~~ of

~~filed herein~~,

IT IS ORDERED that the Defendant do within 14 days serve on the Plaintiff the Further and Better Particulars of the Defence as initialled by the Master.

and that the costs of this application be costs in the cause

Dated the 17th day of November 1992

H8 Further and better particulars of the defence

IN THE HIGH COURT OF JUSTICE 1992 F No 0269

QUEEN'S BENCH DIVISION

B E T W E E N :

Mary Margaret Freeman Plaintiff

-and-

John Michael Pritchard Defendant

FURTHER AND BETTER PARTICULARS OF THE DEFENCE

Under Paragraph 3: of (d)

By reference to a plan or other suitable means showing the precise position of the Defendant's motor car when it was so stationary as alleged

Annexed to these Particulars is a plan showing the position of the Defendant's motor vheicle when it was so stationary as alleged.

Under paragraph 3: of (c)

By reference to a plan or other suitable means showing the precise position of the Defendant's motor car at the time of the said collision and stating whether it be alleged that the Defendant's motor car was stationary at the time of the collision

The Defendant's motor vehicle was stationary in the position as indicated on the plan referred to above at the time of the collision.

SERVED this 29th day of November 1992 by Messrs Evans & Co. of 2 Springsteen Road London W2

Solicitors for the Defendant

H9 Judgment after trial before judge without jury

Judgment after Trial before Judge without Jury (O. 42, r. 1)

IN THE HIGH COURT OF JUSTICE 19 92 .— .—**No.** 0269

Queen's Bench Division

Between

MARY MARGARET FREEMAN **Plaintiff**

AND

JOHN MICHAEL PRITCHARD **Defendant**

Dated and entered the 6th day of March 19 94 .

(1) "the Royal Courts of Justice" *or as may be.*

(2) "Plaintiff" *or* "Defendant"

THIS ACTION having been tried before the Honourable Mr. Justice XYZ without a jury, at(1) BIRMINGHAM , and the said Mr. Justice XYZ having on the 6th day of March 19 94 , ordered that judgment as hereinafter provided be entered for the(2) Plaintiff ~~[and directed that execution be stayed for the period and on the terms hereinafter provided]~~

(3) "the Defendant do pay the Plaintiff £ and his costs of action to be taxed" *or* "the Plaintiff do pay the Defendant his costs of defence to be taxed" *or as may be according to the judge's order.*

IT IS ADJUDGED that(3) the Defendant do pay to the Plaintiff the sum of £53,753 and her costs of the action to be taxed.

(4) *or as may be according to the judge's discretion.*

~~[It is further adjudged that execution be stayed for days and if within that time the (2) gives notice of appeal and sets down the appeal, execution be further stayed until the determination of the appeal.(4)]~~

The above costs have been taxed and allowed at £ as appears by a taxing officer's certificate dated the day of 19 .

Messrs Jones & Co,
Solicitor

H10 Originating summons

COURT FEES ONLY

Originating Summons—Expedited Form (O. 7, r. 2)

IN THE HIGH COURT OF JUSTICE **19 .— .—No.**

Division

[Group]

District Registry

[In the matter of]

Between

Plaintiff

AND

Defendant

(1) Insert name of Defendant.

Let (1)

(2) Insert address of Defendant.

of (2)

attend before Mr District Registrar in chambers at

[on day, the day of 19 , at o'clock] [(3) on a day to be fixed] on the hearing of an application by the Plaintiff that

(3) Or, if no application has yet been made for a day to be fixed

H10 contd

(1) 14, or the number of days fixed by the order of the Court for service out of the jurisdiction. Delete if inapplicable.

And let the defendant within (1) days after service of this summons on h counting the day of service, return the accompanying Acknowledgment of Service to the appropriate Court Office.

Dated the day of 19

(2) Or if the Plaintiff is applying for a new tenancy under section 24 of the Landlord and Tenant Act 1954, two calendar months.

NOTE:—This Summons may not be served later than 12(2) calendar months beginning with the above date unless renewed by order of the court.

(3) **This Summons** was taken out by

of

(3) For phraseology of this indorsement where the Plaintiff sues in person, see *Supreme Court Practice*, Vol. 2, para 12.

[Agent for

of

]

Solicitor for the said Plaintiff whose address is

NOTE:—If a Defendant does not attend personally or by his Counsel or Solicitor at the time and place above-mentioned, such order will be made as the court may think just and expedient.

In the case of an application under section 1 of the Inheritance (Provision for Family and Dependants) Act 1975. A defendant who is a personal representative must, within 21 days after service of this summons on him, inclusive of the day of service, lodge with the court an affidavit in answer, stating the particulars required by Order 99, rule 5, of the Rules of the Supreme Court.

IMPORTANT

Directions for the Acknowledgment of Service are given with the accompanying form.

Appendix H

The Human Body: Bones and Muscles

Contents

1 Human skeleton, front view
2 Human skeleton, side view
3 Muscles of human body, superficial layer, front view
4 Muscles of human body, superficial layer, back view
5 Bones of hand, arm and shoulder
6 Muscles of hand
7 Bones of foot, leg and hip
8 Muscles of foot

*   *   *

1 Human skeleton, front view

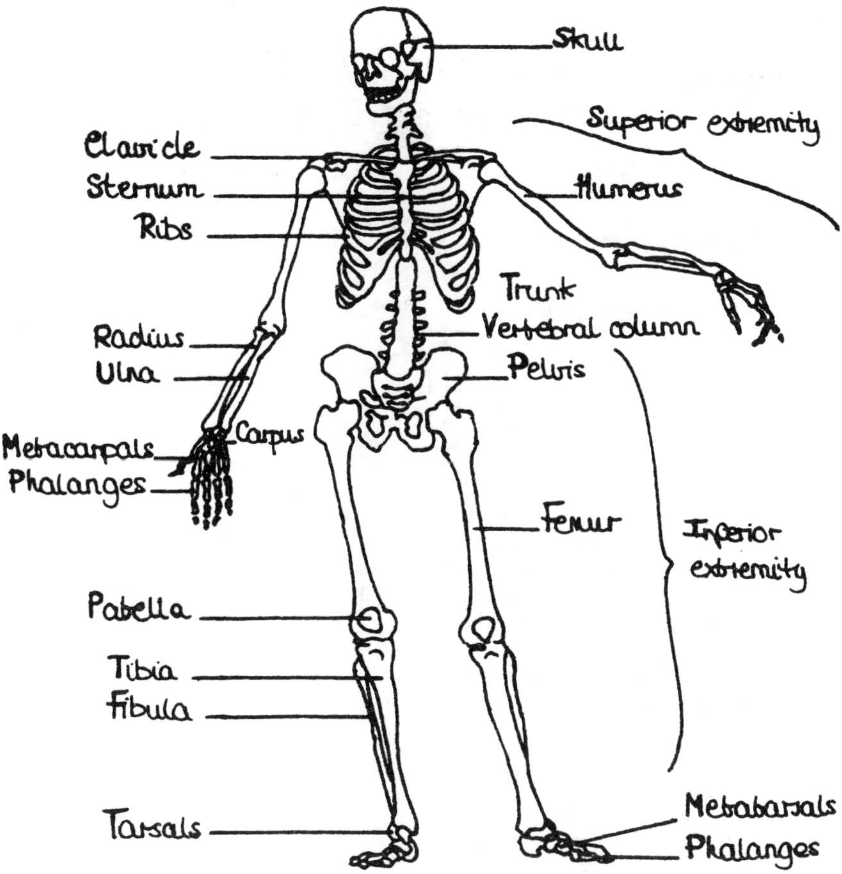

2 Human skeleton, side view

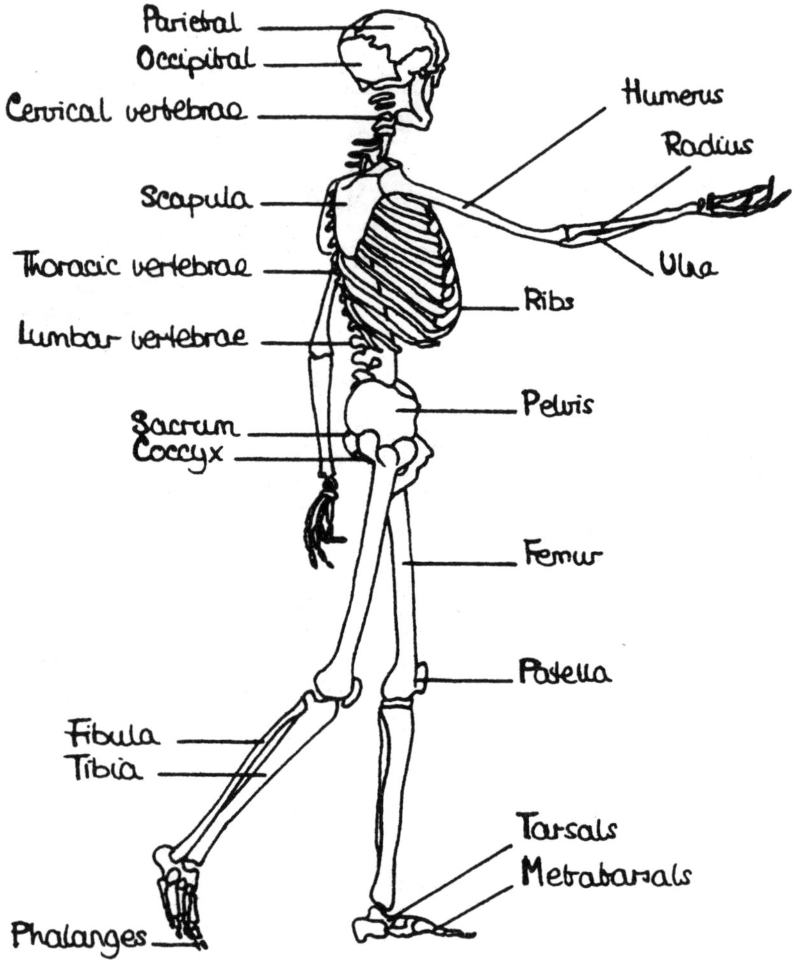

3 Muscles of human body, superficial layer, front view

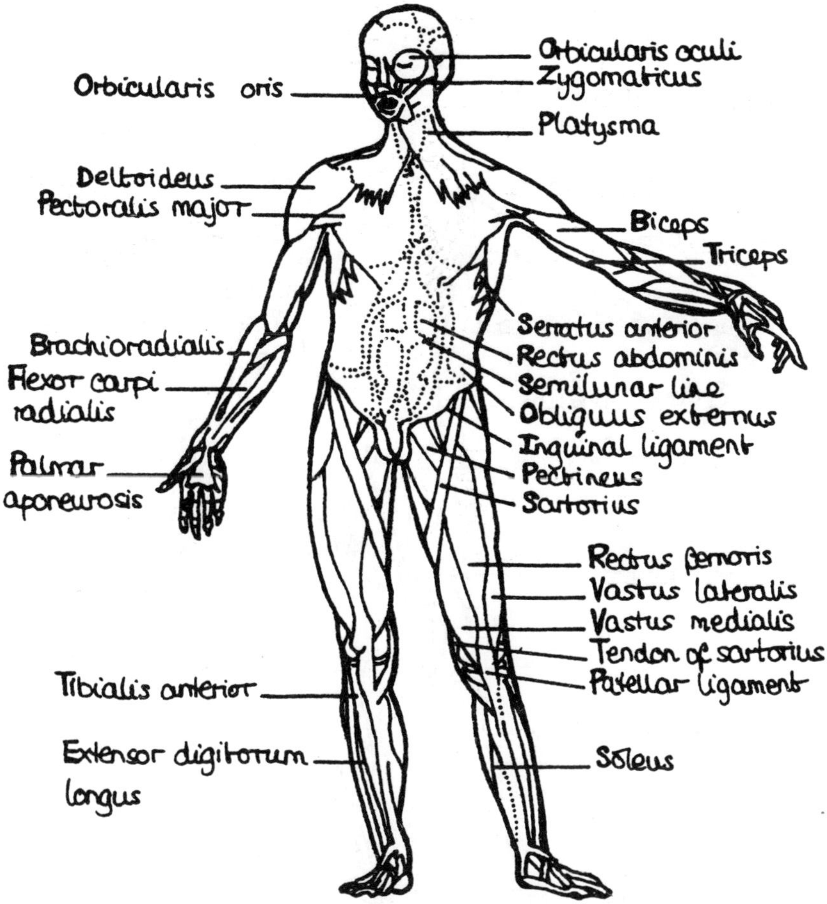

4 Muscles of human body, superficial layer, back view

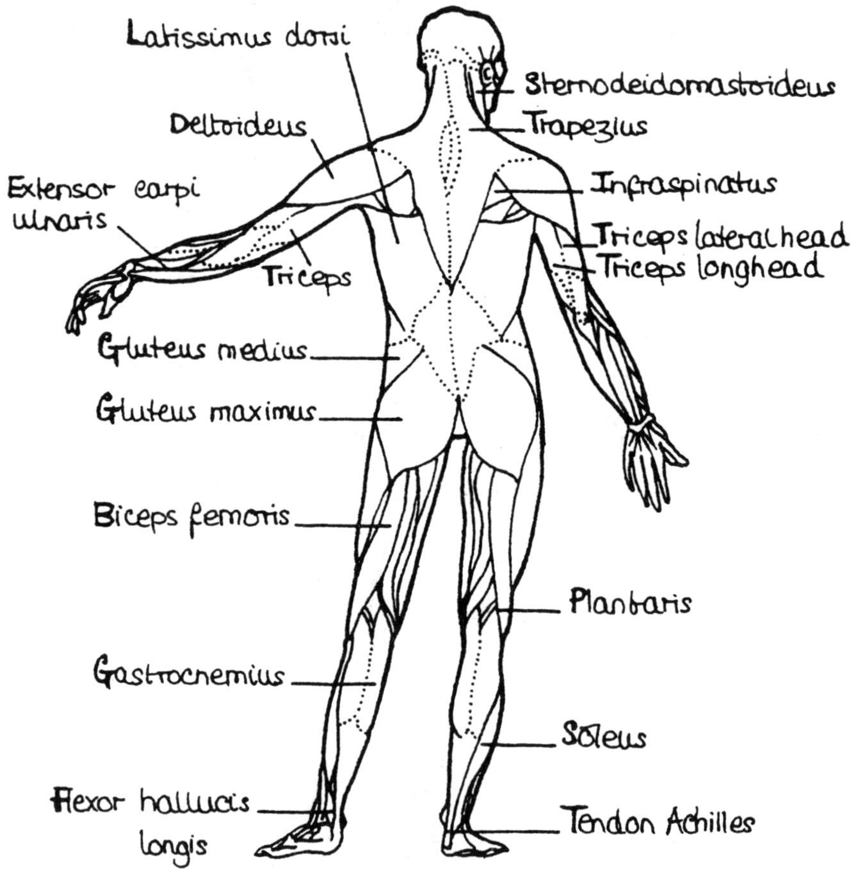

5 Bones of hand, arm and shoulder

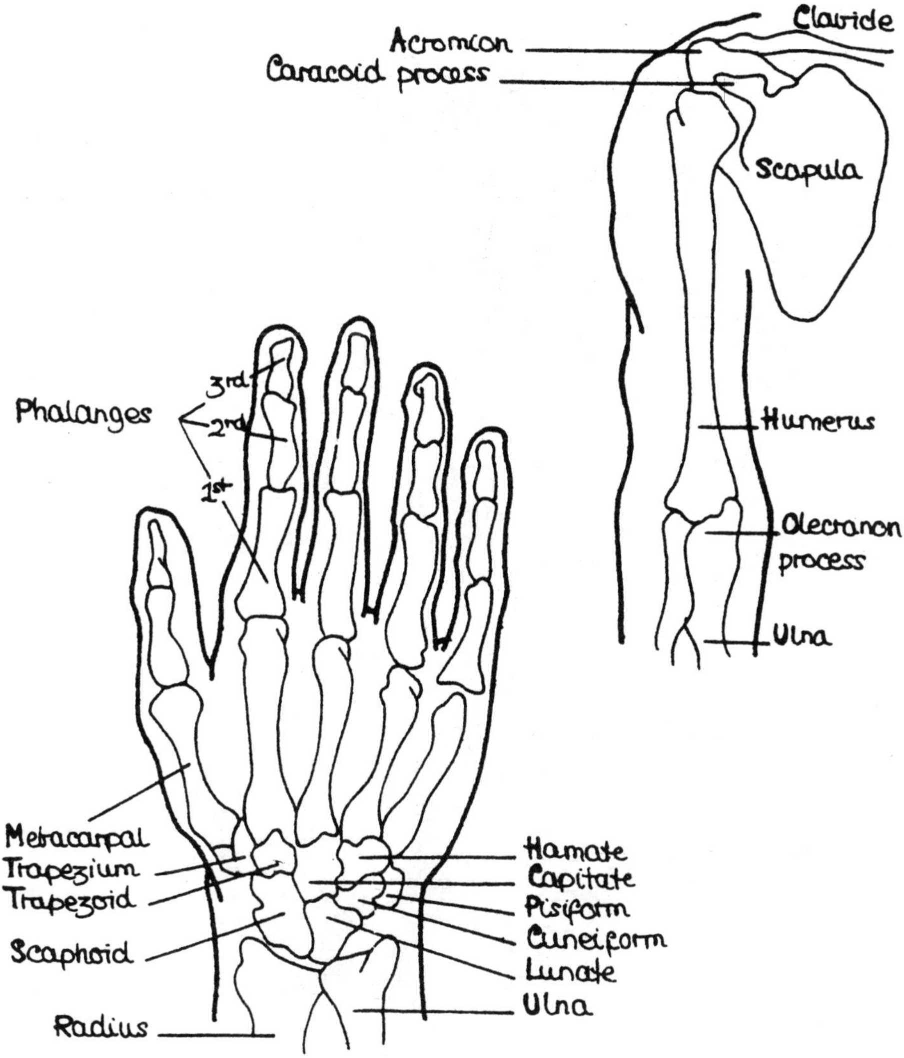

6 Muscles of hand

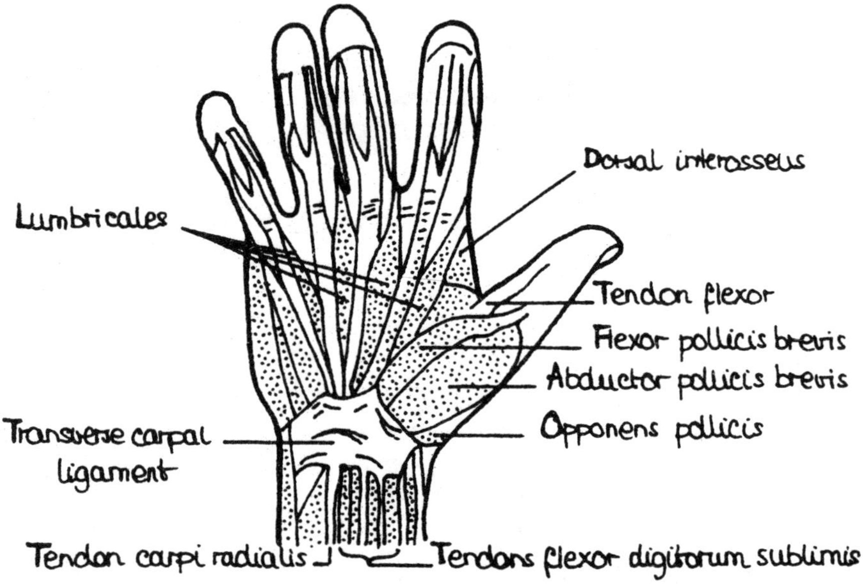

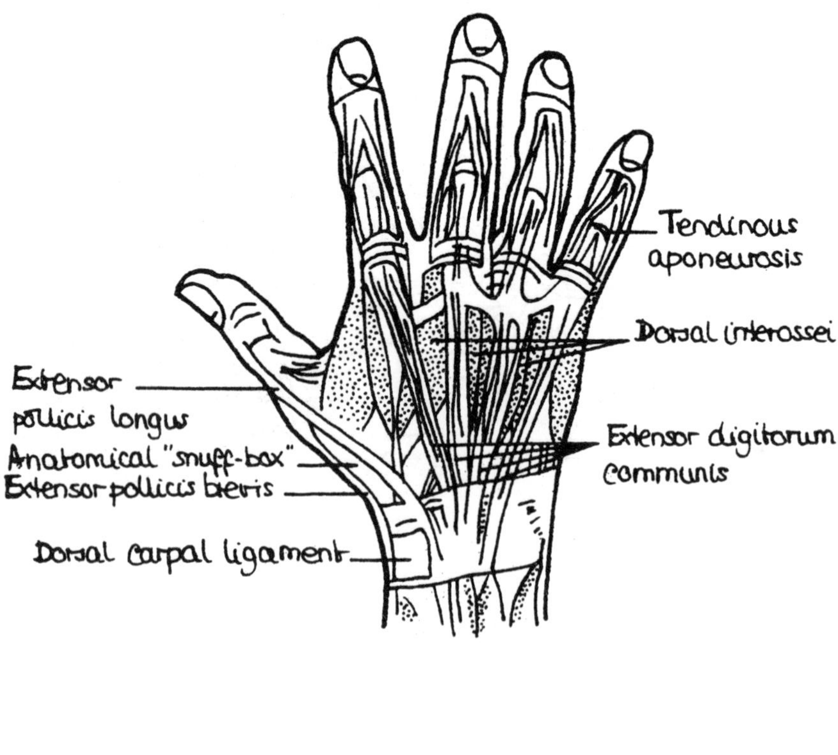

7 Bones of foot, leg and hip

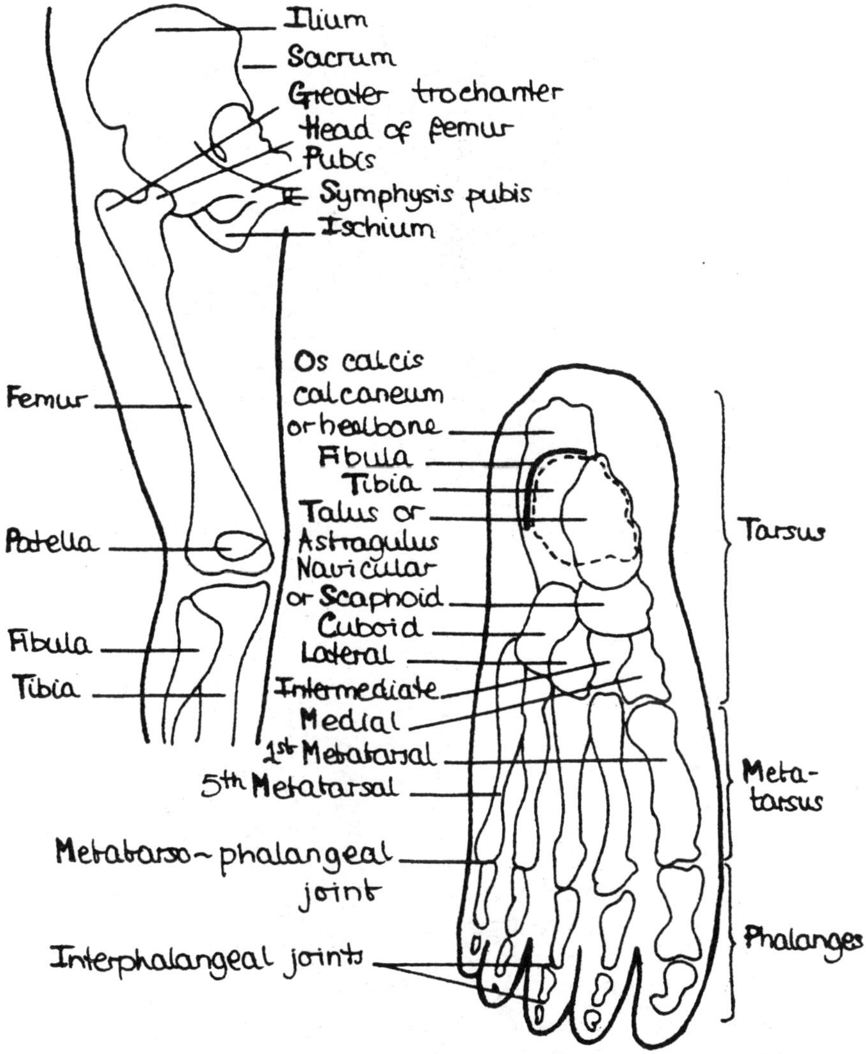

8 Muscles of foot

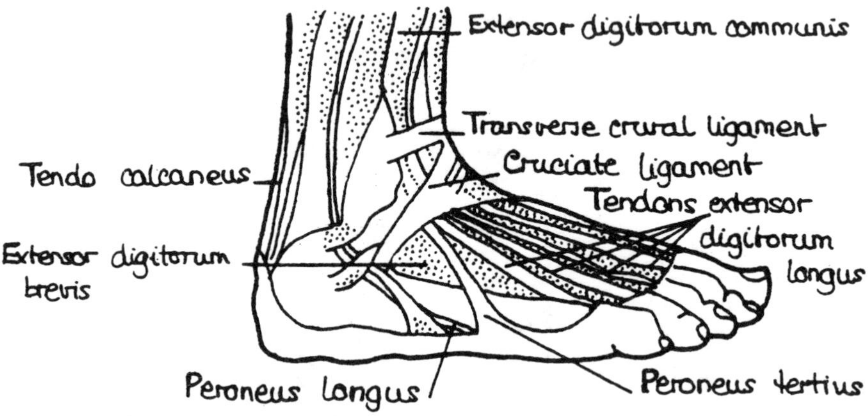

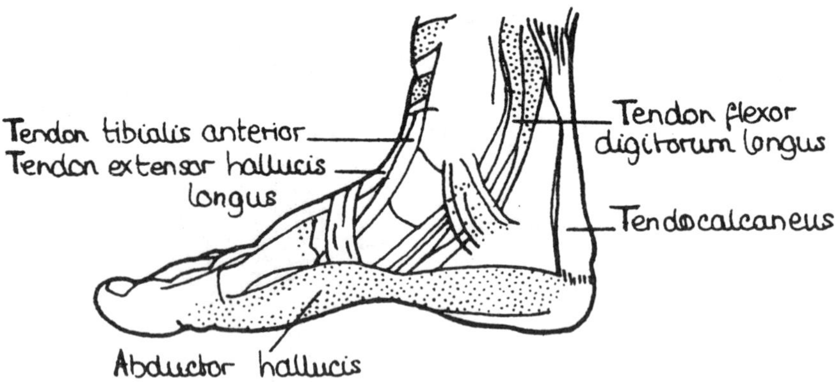

Index

Accident questionnaire, 11, 18–21
  multi-party cases, 20–21
Acknowledgment of service
  defendant failing to file, 236–237
Accountants
  special damage, and, 46–47
Action
  stock letters, 226–233
Actuarial tables, 284–292
  multipliers for loss of earnings to pension age, 288, 289
  multipliers for loss of pension, 290, 291
  multipliers for pecuniary loss for life, 286, 287
Actuary
  actuarial evidence without calling, 47
  special damage, and, 46–47
Adoption
  notice of, 251
Affidavit
  preparing, 274
Agreed evidence, 125–126
Amendment of pleadings, 106–109
  adding parties, 108
  colouring, 108
  county court, 107–108
    after pleadings closed, 108
    before pre-trial review, 107–108
    before service of particulars of claim, 107
  disallowing, 108
  High Court, 109
  precedents, 246–247
Appeal
  judge in chambers, to, 270–271
    notice of, 256
Assessment of damages
  after judgment, 272–273
Automatic directions, 95–97
  discovery, 95
  estimated length, 96
  expert evidence, 95
Automatic directions,—*contd*
  experts' reports, 96–97
    medical, 96–97
    non-medical, 96–97
  inspection, 95
  medical reports, and, 122
  photographs, 96
  plans, 96
  setting down, 96
  trial, 96
  venue, 96

Bones of hand, arm and shoulder, 355
Brief to counsel, 145–148
  contents, 146–148
  delivery, 148
  dictating, 146–148
  return of, 146

Calderbank letter, 80–82
Civil Evidence Act
  notices, 143–145
Close of pleadings, 106
Commencing proceedings, 54–68
  county court, 59–61. *See also* County court
  government departments, 55
  High Court or county court, 55
  hospitals, 56
  limited company, 55
  local authority, 56
  partnership, 55
  police, 56
  sole trader, 55
  state schools, 56
  vicarious liability, 56
  who to sue, 55–56
Compromise
  precedent, 258–259
Consent to action being stood out of list
  form, 258
Consolidation
  precedent, 249

Contributory negligence
  defence, and, 72–73
Costs, 156–157
  cases settled for less than £1,000, 35
  infant cases, 171–172
  legal aid, and. *See* Legal aid
Counsel
  brief to. *See* Brief to counsel
  choice of, 57–58
  fee, 57
    legal aid, 189–190
  instructing to settle claim, 56–59
  instructions to, 57
Counsel's advice, 127–129
  action on receipt, 128
  dictating instructions, 127–128
  legal aid, and, 129
  preparing for trial, 131
Counterclaim, 75–76
  road accident cases, 76
County court, 59–61
  address for service, 60
  amendment of pleadings. *See* Amendment of pleadings
  arbitration, 60
  default summons, 59–60
  High Court compared, 55
  issuing proceedings in, 59–61, 261–262
  jurisdiction, 4
  legal aid cases, 60–61
  notifying other side, 61
  renewing proceedings, 61
  request to issue proceedings, 228
  serving proceedings, 62–63
    defendant's solicitors, on, 63
    firm, on, 62
    individual, on, 62
    limited company, on, 62
    substituted, 63
  solicitors costs, 60
  steps in action, 7
  transfer of proceedings from High Court, 259–260
  witness summons, 149
Criminal Compensation Order, 22
Criminal Injuries Compensation Board, 22

Damages
  fatal accidents. *See* Fatal accidents
  provisional. *See* Provisional damages
Default summons
  request for issue, 315, 316
  specimen, 317, 318
Defence, 69-76
  allegations against third persons, 73–75
    ignoring, 73–74
    issue of separate proceedings, and, 74
    joinder, and, 74
Defence,—*contd*
  allegations against third persons,—*contd*
    legal aid, and, 74
    third party proceedings, 75
  contributory negligence, and, 72–73
    further and better particulars, 73
  counterclaim, and, 75–76
  county court
    specimen, 322, 323,
  defendant failing to file, 236–237
  form, 70–71
  further and better particulars of
    specimen, 327
  High Court
    specimen, 339
  none except as quantum, 237–238
  responding to, 71–76
  significant dates, 70–71
  time for filing, 69–70
Defendant
  meaning, 4
Delay, 126–127
  county court, 126–127
  High Court, 127
Diary, 9–10
Discovery of documents, 98–106
  affidavit verifying list, 105
  before commencement of proceedings, 25–26
  compulsory exchange of witness statement, 103–104, 105
  High Court, 109
  liability admitted, where, 98
  list of documents, 99–104
    documents to be particularly looked for, 100–102
    prescribed form, 99
  no list served, where, 104
  not complete, when, 104–105
  precedents, 239–243
  privilege, and, 102–103
  road accident claim, 98
  specific, 105
  third person, from, 105–106
Dismissal for failure to fix date, 202
Dismissal for want of prosecution, 200–202
  affidavit, 201
Dismissal of action, 161
Draft letters
  use of, 11–13

Engineer's report, 123–124
  importance of, 123
  inspection, 124
  meeting of experts, 124

Experts' reports, 96–97
  legal aid, and, 190
Extension of time
  precedent, 238

Fatal accidents, 175–182
  apportioning settlement monies, 181–182
  assessment of damages, 177–181
    actuarial evidence, 180
    dependency figures, 177–178
    funeral expenses, 180–181
    multiplicand, 177
    multiplier, 179–180
    O'Connor's approach, 179
  bereavement, 175–176
  choice of court, 177
  date of death, 177
  dependant, who is, 176
  Fatal Accidents claim, 175–176
  inquest, 176–177
  inquest notes, 176–177
  interest, 48
  Law Reform claim, 175
  limitation period, 177, 199
  supplementary questionnaire, 19–20
  taking instructions, 176–177
  two causes of action, 175
Filing system
  standardised, 13–14
Foot, leg and hip
  bones of, 355
Foot, muscles of, 356
Forms, 12–13
Further and better particulars, 111–113
  answering request, 112
  contributory negligence, of, 73
  making request, 113
  precedent, 246
  request for
    specimen, 324
  special damage, 113
Further and better particulars of defence
  High Court, 344
  request for
    High court, 341–342
Future loss of earnings
  interest, 48

General damages
  interest, 47–48
Government departments
  name, 55
Green form, 186

Hand, muscles of, 354
Heads of damages, 32–34
Hearsay evidence
  precedents, 256–257
High Court
  county court compared, 55
  interest, 49
  request to issue writ, 229
  special damage, 49
  transfer of proceedings to county court, 259–260
  writ, 63–66. *See also* Writ
Hospitals
  name, 56
Human body
  bones and muscles, 348–356
Human skeleton
  front view, 349
  side view, 350

Income tax, 43
  rates, 52
  costs, 171–172
  legal aid, and, 171–172
  next friend, 167–168
  settlement, 168–171
    accepting payment into court, 171
    applications for sums to be paid out, 173–174
    approval by court, 169
    case not issued, where, 168–170
    investment of settlement money, 172–174
    issued case, 170–171
    order, 174
    paying-out of settlement money, 172–174
Inspection
  after commencement of proceedings
    precedent, 244–245
  prior to commencement of proceedings
    precedent, 243–244
Interest, 47–51
  calculation, 49–51
  claiming, 47
  fatal accidents, 48
  future loss of earnings, 48
  general damages, 47–48
  High Court, 49
  payment into court, and, 81
  provisional damages, and, 37
  rates, 47–48
  special damages, 48
  working out, 48–49
Interim payment, 82–86
  application for, 83–84
  legally aided plaintiff, 84, 86
  obtaining
    precedent, 247–248
  payment in, 85

Interlocutory orders, 131
Interloctutory proceedings, 87–94
  application, 87–92
    adjourning, 92
    amending, 92
    blank notices, 88
    consent orders, 89–90
    counsel, 90–91
    ex parte, 89
    hearing — county court, 91
    hearing — High Court, 91–92
    issuing, 88
    other side not attending, 92
    special appointment, 91
  disadvantages, 85–86
  judgment with damages to be assessed, 94
  order, 92–94
    appealing, 94
    county court, 92
    High Court, 92–93
    wording, 93–94
Interrogatories, 115–116
  precedent, 246
Investigating accident
  stock letters, 219–222
Investigating circumstances of accident, 21–28
  initial letter of claim, 21–22
Investigating claim, 17–37
Issuing proceedings in county court, 261–262

Judge in chambers
  appeal to, 270–271
Judgment, 154–155
  after trial by judge, 273–274
  costs, 154
  county court
    specimen, 332
  enforcement, 157–158
  form, 156
  High Court, 345
  interest, 154–155
  payment of money into court, 154
  payment out of money in court, 154
  pursuant to order, 271–272
  stay of execution, 155
  when no defence, 272

Legal aid, 17, 183–194
  application, 183
  certificate, 184–185
    advising client, 185
    discharge, 191–192
    filing with court, 186
    limited, 184–185
    notice of issue, 186, 260
Legal aid,—*contd*
  certificate—*contd*
    notice of issue and revocation, 260
    revocation, 191–192
  costs, and, 192–194
    assessment by Area Director, 192–193
    client's liability for, 193–194
  counsel, 189–190
  counsel's advice, and, 129
  counsel's fees, 189–190
    conferences, 189
    interlocutory applications, 190
    opinions, 189
    settling, 189–190
    summonses, 190
  county court, and, 60–61
  disbursements, 188–191
    recovering cost of, 191
  duty to Legal Aid Fund, 187–188
    obtain costs, 187
    recoupment of money, 187
    report by defendant, 188
    report to area office, 187–188
  experts' reports, 190
  green form, 185
  infant cases, and, 171–172
  interim payment, and, 84, 86
  letter to Area Committee for approval of costs, 233
  medical negligence claims, and, 204
  notifying court and other parties, 185–186
  obtaining client's authority, 190
  payment into court, and, 191
  settling case, and, 194
Limitation period, 195–202
  discretion of court to extend three-year period, 197–199
    adding new defendant out of time, 198–199
    matters to be considered, 197–198
  fatal cases, 199
  'knowledge', acquisition of, 196–197
  procedure, 199–200
  when three year period starts to run, 195–197
Limited company
  name, 55
  service on, 62, 229
List of documents
  county court
    specimen, 328–331
Listing
  High Court, 136–137
Local authority
  name, 56

Master
form of application for special appointment, 239
Master's order
High Court, 343
Medical evidence
preparing for trial, and, 139–141
Medical matters
stock letters, 222–225
Medical negligence claims, 203–211
choice of expert, 207–209
commencing proceedings, 209–211
choice of court, 209
discovery, 209–210
exchange of witness statements, 210–211
medical report, 209
order for directions, 210
difficulties, 203
disclosure of medical notes and records, 206–207
originating application or summons, 206–207
exchange of witness statements, 207
legal aid, and, 204
letter of claim, 205–206
taking instructions, 204
Medical reports, 26–28, 58–59, 120–123
agreed, 139
agreed, lodging, 140
agreeing, 122–123
allowing other side to examine plaintiff, 120–121
automatic directions, 122
disclosing notes and records, 121–122
exchanging, 122–123
meetings of experts, 123
own, 120
payment for, 28
psychiatrists, 27
several, 120
specialists, 27
without prejudice meeting of experts, 140
Mental Health Act patients, 174
Minor
notice of adoptions, 251
Minor approval
originating summons, 279
Minor approval: county court precedents, 251, 252
Minor approval: fatal claim precedents, 255–256
Minor approval: High Court precedents, 252–254
Minor cases, 167–174
Motor Insurers' Bureau, 212–214
hit and run cases, 213–214
uninsured defendant, 212–213
untraced motorist, 213–214
Motor Insurers' Bureau Agreements, 293–313
compensation of victims of uninsured drivers, 293–300
compensation of victims of untraced drivers, 300–313
Multi-party cases
accident questionnaire, 20–21
Multipliers for loss of earnings to pension age, 288, 289
Multipliers for loss of pension, 290, 291
Multipliers for pecuniary loss for life, 286, 287
Muscles of human body
superficial layer
back view, 352
front view, 351

National Insurance, 43
rates, 52
Negotiating with insurers, 29–35
conduct of negotiations, 29–31
contributing negligence, and, 30
costs, and, 31
Negotiations
preparing for trial, and 141–142
Next friend
precedents, 250–251
Non-pecuniary losses, 33–34
Notes
importance of, 14
Notice of application
county court
specimen, 325
Notice of discontinuance, 160, 258
Notice of intention to defend
defendant failing to file, 236–237
Notice to admit documents, 114–115
Notice to admit facts, 114
precedent, 245–246
Notice to be served after one year's delay
precedent, 256
Notices
Civil Evidence Act, 143–145

Obtaining an order, 263–270
application or summons, by, 263–265
consent application or summons, by, 265–268
ex parte application, 269–270
Order on application
county court
specimen, 326

Originating application
  county court, 277–278
  High Court, 278–279
Originating summons
  High Court, 346, 347
  minor approval, 279

Particulars of claim
  drafting, 56–59
  medical reports, 58
  special damage, 58, 59
Partnership
  name, 55
  service of proceedings on, 62
Payment into court, 77–82
  acceptance, 275–276, 277
  acceptance out of time, 79–80
  acceptance within 21 days, 78–79
  advising client to accept, 229
  advising client to reject, 229
  Calderbank letter, 80–82
  county court, 276–277
  High Court, 274–275
  interest, 81
  legal aid, and, 191
  more than one defendant, 80–81
  provisional damages, 82
  rejection, 80–82
Pecuniary losses, 32–33
Photographs, 125
  preparation for trial, 141
Persons under a disability. *See* Minor
Plaintiff
  change of name, 249
  meaning, 4
Plans, 125
  preparation for trial, 141
Pleadings, 6–8
  amendment. *See* Amendment of pleadings
  close of, 106
  form of, 67–68
  layout, 67–68
Police
  name, 56
Pre-action inspection, 24–25
Precedents, 234–260
  use of, 11–13
Preparing for trial, 130
  adjournment, 152
  counsel's advice, 131
  medical evidence, 139–141
  negotiations, 141–142
  notice after one year's delay, 132
  photographs, 141
  plans, 141
  special damages, 138–139
Private health insurance, 43
Privilege
  discovery of documents, and, 102–103
Procedural tables, 261–283
Proof of evidence, 116–118
  heading, 117
  time spent drafting and dictating, 118
Provisional damages, 35–37, 279–281
  action settled prior to commencement of proceedings, 281
  applying for further damages, 36
  consent order, by way of, 280–281
  following trial, 279–280
  High Court, 37
  interest, 37
  order for, 36
  payment into court, and, 82
  settlement, and, 162–163

Questionnaires, 215–218
  fatal accident, 217–218
  road accident, 215–217
  workplace accident, 217

Renewing proceedings
  precedent, 236
Reply, 73
Road accident
  counterclaims, 76
Road accident police report, 22–23
Road accident questionnaire, 18–19

Settling down for trial, 132–138
  county court, 132–133
    adjournment, 133
    automatic striking out, 132
    fixing date, 132–133
    transfer to High Court, 133
    which court, 132
  High Court, 133–138
    adjournments, 137–138
    compulsory transfer to county court, 135–136
    consent to set down, 133
    listing of case, 136–137
    non-compulsory transfer to county court, 136
    notifying other side, 135
    procedure on setting down, 134–135
    which court, 133–134
Settlement, 34–35
  precedent, 258–259
Settling the case, 159–163
  after proceedings begun, 159–160
    case not set down, 160
    case set down, 160
  alternative ways of ending case, 160–161
  before proceedings commenced, 159

Settling the case,—*contd*
drawing up order, 161–162
money in court, where, 162
infant cases, 159, 168–171. *See also* Infant cases
legal aid, and, 194
order, need for, 160
provisional damages, 162–168
Simple accident claim, 6–8
Sole trader
name, 55
Solicitor
change of, 259
Special damage, 38–47
accountants, 46–47
actuarial evidence without calling actuary, 47
actuaries, 46–47
calculating figures, 44–47
High Court, 49
income tax, 43
interest, 48
meaning, 38
National Insurance, 43
rates, 52
particulars, 113
particulars of claim, in 58, 59
preparing for trial, and, 138–139
private health insurance, 43
questionnaire, 38–40
schedule
specimen, 321
specimen calculation, 53
state benefits, 42–43
statutory sick pay, 41–42
stock letters, 226
tax rates, 52
wage losses, 40–41
working out, 38–43
Specimen pleadings, 314
Split trial, 126
application to obtain, 249–250
State benefits, 42–43
State schools
name, 56
Statement of claim
drafting, 56–59
High Court
specimen, 337–338
specimen, 319–320
Statistics, 5
Statutory sick pay, 41–42
Stay of proceedings, 161
Stock letters, 219–233
action, 226–233
investigating accident, 219–222

Stock letters,—*contd*
medical matters, 222–225
special damage, 226
Structured settlements, 142–143
Subpoenas, 149–150
ad testificandum, 149
duces tecum, 149
High Court, 149–150
service, 150
System of working, 9–14

Taking instructions, 17
Textbooks, 5
Time calculation, 68
Time limits, 9–10
Trade unions, 17
Trial, 153–156
associate's certificate, 155–156
fixing date for, 281–282
general conduct, 153–154
judgement, 154–155. *See also* Judgment
preparing for, 130
setting down for, 281–282
Trial bundles, 283
Trial documents
county court, 151
High Court, 151–152

Vicarious liability, 56

Wage losses, 40–41
Warned List, 152
Witness statements, 118–119
compulsory exchange, 103–104, 105
effect, 119
exchanging, 118–119
facts, containing, 119
Witness summons
county court, 149
precedent, 257–258
Workplace accident engineer's report, 23–25
Workplace accident questionnaire, 19
Writ, 63–66
acknowledgment of service, 66–67
High Court, 335–336
amendment, 65
District Registry cases, 64–65
general indorsement, 64
indorsed with statement of claim, 333–334
issuing, 63–65, 262–263
serving, 65–66
transfer to another District Registry, 67
Writ indorsement (High Court), 235–236